INTERORGANIZATIONAL
COLLABORATION

INTERORGANIZATIONAL COLLABORATION

Complexity, Ethics, and Communication

Renee Guarriello Heath
University of New Hampshire

Matthew G. Isbell
Boise State University

WAVELAND PRESS, INC.

Long Grove, Illinois

For information about this book, contact:
  Waveland Press, Inc.
  4180 IL Route 83, Suite 101
  Long Grove, IL 60047-9580
  (847) 634-0081
  info@waveland.com
  www.waveland.com

Credits:
Chapter 1, p. 7. Daryl Cagle. Reprinted with permission from PoliticalCartoons.com
Chapter 5, p. 98. Chris Wildt. Reprinted with permission from CartoonStock.com
Figure 12.1, p. 279 reprinted with permission from Sam Bradd. Visit his website
(http://drawingchange.com/about/) to learn more about visual thinking and
drawing change.

Contents

PART I
The Complexity of Collaboration   1

3   Stakeholders   43

PART II
A Collaborative Ethic   67

4   Ethical Contexts   71

5   Diversity   95

PART III
Language of Collaborative Praxis 171

Preface

This book outlines the questions and answers we have found throughout our combined four decades of research and professional experience with interorganizational collaborations. The organization centers around three key assertions: (1) interorganizational collaboration is complex and warrants study as a specific type of leadership and communication; (2) successful collaborative relationships are grounded in a principled ethic of democratic and egalitarian participation; and (3) interorganizational collaboration requires a specific communication language of practice. Whether the idea of interorganizational collaboration is new to you or you are a seasoned stakeholder, we hope the book fosters the thinking and skills readers need to execute interorganizational collaboration in this increasingly complex and diverse world. From the ethics of decisions to the talk associated with navigating differences, this book develops cornerstone assumptions and principled practices that stakeholders will need to address problems.

The book moves from the macro to the micro in considering the difficulties inherent when diverse stakeholders tackle problem solving. It is organized into four major parts. Part I focuses on the complexity of interorganizational collaboration. Part II highlights the ethics of interorganizational collaboration as participants make influential decisions and share power while including diverse perspectives. Part III introduces the notion of praxis and develops a language of collaboration as participants move from understanding one another to identifying solutions together. Part IV puts collaboration into action by examining how practitioners across various fields have operationalized collaboration amidst wicked problems.

Each chapter begins with a vignette, most of which are grounded in our own research and practice. We use these exemplars to orient the reader to the goals of the chapter and to aid in the application of abstract concepts as they are introduced in the text. Our approach is to build on the classic and contemporary scholarship available on interorganizational collaboration and the communication practices and structures with which it is most associated. To these ends our chapters connect collaboration theory with some of today's most influential writers and thinkers in this area.

Chapters 2 through 12 include spotlight scholar boxes in which a scholar discusses her or his research and thoughts regarding collaborative practice. We are excited to include the contributions from scholar/practitioners—what Gregg Walker calls "pracademics"—pioneer thinkers such as J. Kevin Barge, Stanley Deetz, Sheila McNamee, Gregg Walker, and Diana Whitney. You will also read about the contributions to collaboration research by scholars JoAnn Keyton, Matthew Koschmann, and Laurie Lewis. Researchers Lynn Cooper, Elizabeth Eger, and Natalie Nelson-Marsh present exciting new cases. We encourage readers of advanced courses to seek out the research of our spotlight scholars.

The reader will also find stories of interpersonal communication throughout the text because sometimes it is easier to understand a complex communication concept when first applying it to a communication situation between two persons. We then magnify the complexity of that same concept as it plays out among several collaborative group members. Because one of the goals of our text is to develop collaborative pedagogy, we pause throughout the chapters to engage the reader in questions and consideration of how the concepts we are teaching can be applied. Each chapter ends with a bulleted summary of the primary take-aways from the discussion.

Acknowledgments

We want to acknowledge the many believers, readers, and participants of this project. First, thank you to our publishers Carol and Neil Rowe who offered early support and inspiration for writing this book. We are also grateful to Steve McCornack and George Cheney who provided helpful feedback on our book proposal. The development of the text is indebted to reviewers Natalie Nelson-Marsh and John McClellan. We cannot thank you enough for taking time from your busy academic schedules, and busy young families, to provide detailed responses to the text. It is no doubt stronger due to your attention to meaning and organization. Other readers who provided valuable and thoughtful insights include Elizabeth Eger, whose expertise in diversity helped us attend to respectful language, and Sheila McNamee, who managed to squeeze time from her insane schedule to ensure we did justice to dialogue.

In addition, we would like to thank the collaboration scholars featured in our spotlight boxes whose work we both admire and we believe is especially important to developing our understanding of communication and collaboration, in the pages that come. Thank you J. Kevin Barge, Natalie Nelson-Marsh, Lynn Cooper, Elizabeth Eger, Stanley Deetz, JoAnn Keyton, Sheila McNamee, Matthew Koschmann, Gregg Walker, Laurie Lewis, and Diana Whitney. Your influence on collaboration research undeniably advances our thinking regarding this phenomenon. We would also be remiss if we did not acknowledge the foundational influence of Barbara Gray's contributions to collaboration theory. Additionally, we would like to acknowledge the support of our departments and universities, the University of New Hampshire, Merrimack College, Boise State University, and our many colleagues and friends in the field who encouraged us to write this book. Finally together, we want to remain humble in our knowledge that this book would not be possible without the vulnerability and openness of the people who are part of the communities and cases mentioned in our book. Our insights are largely informed by your hard work.

Separately, I would like to thank my supportive friends and patient family, especially Madeline, Kennedy, Cullen, and Julianne. Of course, Chris and I have been partners in life and marriage for twenty years. You have been down this road with me before; thank you, as always, Chris, for giving me the space and time to think and write. We are the most successful collaboration that I know. But that's a different book. To close I would like to wax on a bit about my coauthor Matthew Isbell. I met Matt almost ten years ago at a conference; we were drawn together by our shared research interests. Matt was the perfect partner in this project—not only because he studied collaboration but also because he works passionately to apply collaborative lessons in his work outside of academia as a consultant on multiple health projects. He is as committed to teaching and practicing collaborative concepts as he is to studying them. Matt has to be one of the easiest persons with whom I have ever worked, matching my intensity and passion with his laid-back yet thoughtful and insightful contributions. I am so very grateful to have shared this journey with you. We made a good team. Thank you.

Renee Heath
Newburyport, MA
June 14, 2016

I called Renee on a whim several years ago to see if she wanted to work on a project. I had no real idea what the project would be, but knew that I wanted to work with her on something. In that very phone call, Renee said, "I want to write a book on collaboration. Let's do it together." It was her drive that propelled us, and I can honestly say, I have never worked with a more passionate person. It was and remains a truly wonderful and rewarding experience. I never would have guessed that from that one phone call would emerge this book. I am humbled to share this byline with Renee. During my time writing, I spent longer writing retreats in three places that became very dear to me: Stowe, Vermont; Lincoln, New Hampshire; and Rangeley, Maine. My time with this book project would not have been the same without my time in the "mountains" to read, write, and retreat. Finally, I would like to thank my partner at those retreats and in life, Kelly. There were many nights where I needed to go for a walk to talk through this book, and you listened to me every time offering insight, encouragement, support, and love.

Matt Isbell
Boise, ID
June 27, 2016

About the Authors

In 1991 Renee was invited to participate in a collaboration composed of stakeholders from multiple organizations in Skagit County, Washington. Sixteen organizations representing the county, school districts, nonprofits, and private citizens joined forces to prevent at-risk children from dropping out of school and entering the juvenile justice system. At that time, Renee was a coordinator with the Private Industry Council, a federally supported, nonprofit job-training and placement program for qualifying teens. This introduction to, and participation in, interorganizational collaboration had a profound effect. It seeded the curiosity that drove an academic career and eventually a PhD (University of Colorado, Boulder) focused on communication and collaborating.

Renee's first role was as a nonprofit stakeholder and founding partner of the **Best SELF** (Summer Education and Learning Fun) Program. The program won two national awards in the five years Renee worked with it and continued as an interorganizational partnership for more than a decade. It significantly influenced Renee's thinking about interorganizational collaboration. Her experiences there are woven through many of the vignettes that open our chapters.

Renee's experience with four additional multi-year academic case studies illustrate concepts throughout the text. Two collaborative partnerships (referenced in the text as **Metro Collaboration** and **West Collaboration**) were part of a state-wide initiative focused on developing and strengthening early care and education. Names and places associated with these partnerships have been altered to provide confidentiality to those who participated in these studies. The third study was a prevention-oriented collaboration based in the northwest, and the fourth, **Shaping America's Youth**, was a national collaboration aimed at diminishing childhood obesity.

Today, Renee is a scholar and teacher of shared decision making in organizations, especially those collaborating across sectors to accomplish community-oriented goals. She was nominated for the Carnegie Professor of the Year in 2012 and won the most prestigious teaching award as a tenured professor at the University of Portland, Oregon (2011). Her first book was an edited volume of studies, *Understanding Occupy from Wall Street to Portland: Applied Studies in Communication Theory*. The studies examined the democratic processes and philosophies of the movement from the standpoint of communication and influenced her understandings of consensus decision-processes. Renee teaches in the Department of Communication at the University of New Hampshire. She trains and consults in areas related to organizational communication.

In 2002, Matt began working with interorganizational collaborations. Propelled by an interest in health issues at a community level, he worked in a collaboration in Missoula to bring a more comprehensive voice to safe-sex education in a conservative region. While living in Austin, Texas, Matt worked with and studied several different partnerships, including emergency crisis management collaborations during the Katrina/Rita Hurricanes, a homeless service collaboration, and a broad based study of collaborative experiences by stakeholders from across several different sectors. His dissertation research site was in East Austin at **OCEAN** (the Organization of Central East Austin Neighborhoods), a collaboration of neighborhoods working together to protect residents' interests and to prevent unethical regentrification proposals. More recently, Matt has continued his work with the Women, Infants and Children (**WIC**) program, both in Texas and New Hampshire, on health and nutrition education programing. WIC is a government run organization that works in conjunction with many local area doctors, nutrition organizations, and low-income families.

An applied scholar with research interests in collaboration, nonprofit organizations, and health program implementation, Matt works with many at-risk populations around the topics of nutrition and infant development. His work has been published in many top journals, including *Communication Monographs*, *Management Communication Quarterly*, and the *American Journal of Public Health*. Matt teaches classes on nonprofit organizations, interorganizational collaboration, and organizational communication. He is an outdoor enthusiast, hiker, and runner. Born and raised in Detroit, he joined Boise State University in 2016. Prior to joining the faculty at Boise State, Matt was an associate professor at Merrimack College. He received his Bachelor's Degree from Michigan State University, a Master's Degree from the University of Montana, and a PhD from the University of Texas at Austin.

PART I

The Complexity
of Collaboration

The three chapters in part I highlight the complexity of interorganizational collaboration.

The first chapter, "Introducing Complexity," sets the context for why interorganizational collaboration is such an important construct. The problems of the world are increasingly interconnected, and the necessity of communicating across groups influences the meaning of organization. The skills to organize and communicate in bureaucratic organizations are not the same skills required to facilitate working across organizational sectors.

Chapter 2 introduces key terminology and definitions associated with collaboration. It distinguishes collaboration from similar types of interorganizational behavior such as cooperation and coordination. "Interorganizational Collaboration" reviews three conceptual frames: collaborative forms and structures, collaborative processes, and collaborative outcomes. The reader will gain an understanding of when collaborative versus adversarial tactics may or may not be effective in community problem solving. The chapter scrutinizes the notion of collaboration and introduces the concepts of interdependence and shared power. It also deals with the question looming in the shadows, what exactly is successful collaboration anyway?

"Stakeholders" concludes the first section and reminds us that interorganizational collaboration approaches problem solving from a different starting point. Rather than asking what is the problem, it asks who should be a part of defining and solving the problem. The essential task of inviting stakeholders to collaborate shapes and influences the definition of the problem and the potential for the solutions. Chapter 3 traces the development of stakeholder theory and introduces the tensions and paradoxes that plague stakeholders in collaboration. It develops the concepts of singular and collective stakeholder identity and how they work to influence interdependence and group behavior. The vocabulary and themes introduced in part I of this book will be carried throughout the text.

1

Introducing Complexity

Interconnected Problems

Death by overdose attributed to heroin use and prescription drug abuse has quadrupled between the years of 1999 and 2013. After four consecutive untimely deaths, police in Gloucester, Massachusetts, collaborated with the health department, the city council, and the mayor's office to come up with "out of the box" ideas that might help solve the problem. The result was a radical shift in police thinking; addiction was viewed as a disease as opposed to a crime. The altered approach encouraged scores of people suffering to get help, with the police as the first point of contact. The program has garnered national attention and has led to further collaboration among the police, pharmaceutical companies, and legislators as they continue to identify methods for stemming the problem at its source.[1]

In what many have called a cost-cutting measure gone horribly awry, over one hundred thousand people from mostly economically disadvantaged populations found their drinking water contaminated with lead. In Flint, Michigan, lead levels were over 800 times higher than allowed by law; residents were forced to drink bottled water and were restricted from using the tap water in their homes for months. Government agencies, nonprofit organizations, and local community members scrambled to work together to restore a safe water supply for Flint residents. Agencies such as the Environmental Protection Agency, The US Department of Agriculture, The Michigan Department of Education, the Centers for Disease Control, and the Department of Health and Human Services (just to name a few) were all involved in various aspects of this crisis. But was there a coordinating body? How did all of these organizations work together on this issue? Who talked to whom? In a crisis, these can be important questions, and answers are unclear in the case of Flint.[2]

Since 2011, drought has been a mainstay in the summer news headlines. Water scarcity and its effects on our entire national ecosystem have touched all our lives. In California, two major collaborations worked to address the drought while breaking down the traditional governmental barriers to water management. The Western Governors' Drought Forum brought local, state, and national government agencies together on water resource management—a topic with little traditional interagency cooperation. The forum released a unified operation plan and enabled communication between agencies to allow leaders to cultivate collaborative strategies.[3] In a similar collaborative effort, the California Roundtable on Agriculture and the Environment (CRAE) brought together diverse stakeholders in a forum for dialogue to "adopt a fresh perspective" on water management. In creating this dialogic space, the members of the forum identified three key areas of discourse not present in previous discussions of drought: (1) Blame is not a productive response; (2) We are all part of an interdependent system, experiencing this problem together; and (3) to move toward solutions, we must talk with—not—at each other and be willing to work collaboratively. Identifying these absent discourses around drought and water management, CRAE can focus "on how we might work together rather than who's to blame, we can all come to the table and find solutions for better stewarding our water supply."[4]

Millions of Syrians are fleeing their homeland during the ISIS occupation. Countries all over Europe, Asia, and the Americas are trying to address how to handle this influx of displaced people. One small piece of this large international crisis is how to connect displaced persons with the services they need and with concerned family members. Organizations like NetHope are bringing together cross-sector innovators who can collaborate on ways to develop programs and mitigate risk through information communication technologies.[5] Collaborations partner technology companies like Google and Microsoft with international nonprofits like WWF International, Relief International and Catholic Relief Services. They facilitate the efforts of diverse stakeholder groups in tackling this humanitarian crisis in new ways.

Many people are aware of the spread of disease when it poses a threat internationally, as with the Zika and Ebola viruses. But what about other diseases that we don't hear about—the ones that don't have a lot of government funding for research or the possibility of lucrative drug sales to encourage research and development? These "neglected diseases" are seeing new funding avenues thanks to product development partnerships (PDPs) that create self-governing, private nonprofit organizations. PDPs emerged to address public health challenges that don't receive a national spotlight. PDPs can coordinate the efforts of numerous research groups, share industry knowledge, and set goals for everyone involved in the research program in order to create efficiencies in research and design while working to prevent one of these neglected diseases from becoming the next Zika outbreak.[6]

Why Interorganizational Collaboration?

Interorganizational collaboration is an essential concept to understand in our contemporary world and is related to at least three phenomena that challenge traditional conceptions of top-down organizing.

First, the nature of large-scale problems has spurred increased interconnectedness among diverse people and places. Consider how the Zika or the Ebola virus mobilized the medical community, the pharmaceutical industry, and governments and industry to counteract the spread of the virus throughout the world. Reflect on the politics and ethics associated with solving such a problem—issues such as a lack of resources, infrastructure, and the presence of sustained poverty intersect with the ability to administer to the sick, invent vaccines, and stifle the spread of a flourishing virus.

Second, interorganizational collaboration influences what it means to organize. The jurisdiction of solving what are often described as wicked problems[7] falls to many organizations and types of organizational structures, including the government, communities, corporations, nonprofits, as well as interested private citizens. Imagine how different the organizational structures and leadership practices are among the stakeholders of the heroin/drug collaboration in Gloucester. Organizational leaders and members learn to work outside their usual customs and expectations. For example, a police officer may be familiar with direct orders, chains of command, and bureaucratic procedures that are essential to police work. Those practices could slow, stall, or—worse yet, disrupt—the progress of interorganizational collaboration that functions by sharing decision-making duties.

Finally, younger workers and the influence of technology are changing expectations and the way we communicate in the workforce. A growing cohort of millennials are entering boundary-spanning positions where they will work within and across their organizations to address problems. They bring new skill sets and values to the workforce.

We are only beginning to acknowledge that the assumptions we have about working and the skills needed to run, organize, and communicate in traditional, bureaucratic organizations are *not* the same skills needed to run, organize, and communicate when working across groups, organizations, industries, and communities.[8] In interorganizational collaboration, power is shared; partners do not work for each other; and they likely have collateral positions and responsibilities in other organizations and teams. Incentives are not bound by pay and promotion, and work is not governed by policies and procedures but by the relationships stakeholders have to each other and the problems they are trying to resolve. Previously learned communication skills, such as persuasion and debate, are grounded in different values and assumptions. They are not sufficient for solving the contemporary problems posed by our diverse yet interconnected society. Persuasion and debate are important when we need to rally support and resources around good solutions, but they work counter to innovation and problem solving when we don't have the answers and need to be open to new ideas.

Communication skills associated with collaboration need to be taught to today's workers. Refocusing our university curriculum to emphasize skills such as dialogue, critical listening, principled negotiation, consensus decision making, and appreciative inquiry will strengthen our ability to function within the collaborative environment. We believe students and workers seeking success in today's workplace should be as familiar with collaborative communication practices as they are with almost any other communication principle covered in college courses. The purpose of this book is to help the reader understand the complex phenomena of interorganizational collaboration and the ethics required to work within a world of diverse perspectives and experiences. After establishing that foundation, the text turns to the communication practices and skills needed to innovate and identify solutions to the problems that plague our communities and planet.

Global Problems Interconnect Us

Droughts in the west, epidemic viruses in developing countries, water contamination in an urban poor community, displaced people in a war torn country—what do they all have in common? Each of these wicked problems affect all of us. As comforting as it might be to bury our heads in the sand and act as though we are not affected, each one of the issues highlighted at the beginning of the chapter hits as close to home as the cost of gasoline. This interconnectedness of our global world means the local is intertwined with the national and the international. Wicked problems abound and need to be addressed. These twenty-first century problems are key features of our society—and demand interorganizational collaboration.

Wicked Problems.   So what are wicked problems? We spend time in this chapter and throughout the book talking about collaboration being key to working on wicked problems. The term first came into common usage in the mid-70s as a way to better understand societal problems.[9] As opposed to problems in the sciences that deal with natural phenomena, societal problems are created by humans. The issues can be ill-defined, have multiple causes, involve stakeholders with different values and priorities; the problems are constantly changing and may never be "solved." Every wicked problem is unique and yet interconnected with other problems.[10] There is no obvious solution to a wicked problem. There is usually no means of testing a solution before implementing one, and there may be unintended consequences that create another problem. Solutions are judged as good or bad rather than verifiably right or wrong. In short, wicked problems are complex interconnected problems that need complex and interconnected stakeholder participation to generate solutions.

It is expensive to develop solutions to complex problems, as highlighted in the opening synopsis about the lack of funding for research and development on neglected diseases. Collaborating allows for efficiency of processes and also expands the network of perspectives to increase the potential for creative solutions. Compare collaborative organizing to the

DARYL CAGLE POLITICALCARTOONS.COM

disparate practices of government agencies and organizations in the Flint water crisis. Numerous organizations, state agencies, and independent stakeholders worked, usually autonomously, toward solving the problem. While this approach is common during a crisis, the replication of efforts and issues over accountability are not optimal or efficient in the long run.

Beyond the exigency for optimal and efficient solutions, wicked problems present a quagmire of ethical issues that complicate an already complex process. We focus on wicked problems not only as examples of the need for collaboration but also as illustrations of the need for ethical approaches. The western US drought highlights how a wicked problem can sometimes force interdependency (i.e. shared water rights) and bring strange bedfellows (i.e., farmers and conservationists) to the table to collaborate on solutions that would be beyond the scope of individuals or individual entities. When addressing the drought in California, the resolution is not just to conserve water. The issues involve: who can use water; who "owns" the water; what should be prioritized—the good of the individual or the common good? Does one farmer get to use water while another does not? Worse yet, does one farmer conserve water while another does not and becomes more profitable or better situated economically? These questions are just the tip of the iceberg when it comes to drought issues and water management. We can't think of a wicked problem that does not invoke similar types of ethical questions around rights and responsibilities.

The Collaboration Economy. Solutions to wicked problems involve multiple levels and types of stakeholders. The resulting orientation toward the interconnectedness of all levels of stakeholders underpins the notion of what Eric Lowitt called a "collaboration economy."[11] In a collaboration economy, the strategies of stakeholders reflect the interconnected world in which we live. The problems that this interconnection generates are larger than any one person or organization can tackle. In the collaboration economy leaders from private, public, and civil sectors—deemed the "Golden Triangle"—come together, contributing multiple tools and skills for creative solutions.[12] The move from a waste economy to a collaboration economy is imperative to addressing wicked problems and their inherent complexity.[13] In the Gloucester case opening this chapter, we can see how influence at the local level and stakeholders in the community spur progress at the state and federal legislative levels. The voices from diverse groups and the solutions they generated together did not cure the heroin epidemic, but they had an impact on how to handle a crisis, illustrating a collaboration economy in action.

In order for a collaboration economy to thrive, cross-sectoral partnerships need to be encouraged and supported. By definition, cross-sector partnerships are voluntary collaborative efforts of numerous stakeholder groups from two or more economic sectors in an attempt to solve problems of mutual societal concern.[14] In practice, cross-sector partnerships are difficult. There are power inequities between larger and smaller organizations; issues of resource dependency can dictate action in the collaborative dialogue.[15] This book was written with these issues in mind. In each of the vignettes at the beginning of this chapter, there is a need for cross-sector partnerships to create a collaboration economy. Deeper analysis reveals issues of ethics, participation, power, diversity, and interdependency in each one of the issues. In this complex and interconnected world, getting the appropriate stakeholders to the table to address wicked problems is just the first hurdle of many to fostering a collaborative environment for cooperative solutions.

Organizational Shifts Demand Collaboration

In a recent study scholars argued, "In today's global economy, knowledge is overturning the old rules of strategy. Global competition as the foundation of industrialized economies has shifted from natural resources to intellectual assets in such a way that the current era is titled the knowledge era."[16] The most successful knowledge-creation organizations today foster a culture of collaboration, trust, and learning and promote decentralized and less formal structures and procedures.[17] These trends are linked to spontaneity and creativity. The implications are profound for organizational design requiring loose, informal structures, where employees have the authority to make decisions. Employees in the most successful organizations are encouraged to work together both formally on teams and informally across all sectors of organizing. In this era of knowledge organizations, managers need to be skilled at cultivating trust. Distrust leads to hoarding and holding of information and knowledge that runs counter to innovation.[18] Learning environments must be created to encourage employees to ask questions and to challenge one another.[19] Hence organizational structures and practices today require distinct knowledge and skills associated with collaborating.

Leadership Is Needed. In a review of studies and articles regarding the future of the workplace, it was found that 84 percent of global business and human resource executives are scrambling to develop leaders "as traditional leadership models are not keeping pace with today's rapidly changing business and work environment."[20] With the proliferation of collaboration as a mechanism for solving problems, it makes sense that organizational leadership needs are changing. Lowitt argued that the leadership necessary to sustain business and to solve the most pressing problems in our world (such as shortages of water and food, and the destruction of natural resources on which businesses rely) must come from all sectors of society. He predicted organizations will increasingly rely on a partnership of private businesses, the public sector, and the civil society (nonprofits and social organizations) to remain viable. Organizations will adopt a "collaborative mind-set," and they will "want to hire and develop leaders who are adept at building relationships with a range of stakeholders."[21] Whether you work in the nonprofit or for-profit organizational world, you are likely to find your organization involved in social and environmental problem solving. Hence, the changing leadership needs of organizations are not limited to a particular sector of society. Collaborative leadership skills are essential in today's workforce.

The era of collaboration holds leaders accountable to their employees, communities, and distant stakeholders. Consider the issues at the beginning of this chapter. All of the organizations involved have missions that are *related* to but are not the same as the mission of the collaborative endeavor. The people organizing the collaborative program are paid by the organizations they represent. So how do they get anything done? What motivates them to make decisions with other people? Why do they stay involved? How do they make those decisions? Who is ultimately accountable? These are some of the questions associated with understanding and participating in collaboration. The process requires rethinking how communication and participation work in cross-sectoral collaboration.

The focus on training workers in the collaborative mind-set is evident with the emergence of several new institutes and professional resources. For example, the Intersector Project states it is a nonprofit organization that:

> seeks to empower practitioners in the business, government, and nonprofit sectors to collaborate to solve problems that cannot be solved by one sector alone. We conduct research in inter-sector collaboration and convey our findings to leaders in every sector to help them design and implement their own effective collaborative initiatives.[22]

This project has created a number of free online tools and resources. *The Stanford Social Innovation Review, Informing and Inspiring Leaders of Social*

Change (SSIR) has been highly influential for collaborative organizations in its development of "collective impact."[23] SSIR offers ongoing training, webinars, and resources for cross-sectoral leadership. Organizations partner with leading universities such as Harvard and Stanford to prepare individuals to work within a collaborative environment.

The Workforce Is Changing

Coinciding with complex world and community problems and organization and leadership shifts toward collaboration is the burgeoning influence of the millennial generation—those persons born after 1980.[24] In the year 2020, some research polls have predicted that millennials will comprise 75 percent of the workforce,[25] and this percentage has organizations scrambling to understand how to attract, train, manage, and retain this sector of employees. The good news is that the millennial generation is predisposed to collaborate. Generational cohort theory argues that each generation is grounded in powerful values that influence choices about how to work and live and what to buy.[26] Significant and value-forming events operate as "signposts."[27] Generational cohorts are not defined only by age but also by the social and historical events they experience.[28] For millennials, these signposts include having been: raised by "helicopter parents;" born into technology with a well-developed affinity for social groups and social networking; and educated with an emphasis on volunteerism and community service.[29]

Some have stated that the millennial generation is the most wanted generation of children ever born thanks to social and medical advances affecting working women, fertility, and access to birth control.[30] This has resulted in close relationships with parents who, in some cases, have been said to treat "their offspring as worldly equals."[31] Communicatively, and indeed often to their employer's chagrin, millennials are the generation least likely to honor or even recognize hierarchy in the workplace.[32] This generation already communicates horizontally with most of their significant relationships. Accordingly, millennials are likely to eschew the typical chains of command and hierarchical lines of communication that frequently get in the way interorganizational collaboration.

Technological adroitness adds to the millennial collaborative skill set. Digital natives grew up with digital devices; they easily integrate technology into their lives. Organizations increasingly depend on younger, less senior employees to lead technological advances in the workplace.[33] Millennials' skills with technology and social media enrich collaborative efforts. The desire to stay constantly connected through social media has contributed to a generation that seeks connection.[34] Millennials enjoy working with others, making them ideal partners for collaboration.

Finally, a prolific signpost of the millennial generation, and one relevant to collaboration, has been their volunteerism.[35] Having been raised by educated (and in some cases, activist) parents[36] coupled with the fact that many millennials have been volunteering and providing community service since their grade-school days, they are a generation known for their social conscience.[37] College students today may be the most prepared generation for collaboration in the workforce. These values bode well for interorganizational and cross-sectoral collaboration aimed at solving social and environmental problems. The millennial generation cares deeply about making a difference in the world in which they live. Accordingly, they are a segment of the workforce highly motivated toward collaborative problem solving.

Changing Organizational Curricula with the Times

Our curricula are playing catch up with the interconnected world, organizations, and millennials. With 70 percent of graduates a decade from now ending up in jobs not yet invented, it is imperative that we develop in students the collaboration skills needed to attack problems not yet identified.[38] This book answers a call to help students learn different perspectives, empathy toward others, and respect—characteristics needed in the new workplace.[39] We address the need to introduce students to interorganizational collaboration and its accompanying complexity, ethical dilemmas, and communication practices. Our goals for the reader include greater access to collaborative pedagogy that assists students (and practitioners) in developing a collaborative ethic that seeds their collaborative praxis.

Interorganizational collaboration is a fairly new phenomenon that gained the attention of scholars through the work of management scholar, Barbara Gray and her colleagues.[40] Thanks to Gray and many more studies across disciplines in education, public management, health care, environmental studies, and communication, we now have more than thirty-five years of scholarship to draw from to prepare future leaders and participants. The confluence of social and ethical factors, changing organizational demands, and the changing face of the workforce create a momentum toward interorganizational collaboration never before experienced. Simply put, we have not done a very good job of training students for this new interorganizational world.

Much of what we teach about organizations, especially at the undergraduate level, is still grounded in hierarchical or bureaucratic models. Our assumptions about what motivates workers are tied to traditional work structures. Our communication tactics, such as persuasive speech, assume strong, directive leadership. Students have been taught that they will experience upward communication and appropriate strategies for speaking to supervisors.[41] We have taught our students to negotiate competitively and to run meetings with Roberts Rules of Order.

Our students also bring assumptions about workplace communication. In a leadership course Renee taught, students collectively admitted that they expected their bosses to speak to them aggressively or even abusively. These lessons and assumptions about how communication happens in the workplace are relevant to bureaucratic organizations that have clear hierarchies and formal streams and channels of communication. These practices and patterns of communication do not, however, address all the communication practices in today's interorganizational structures.

We are not suggesting that organizations are no longer hierarchical and competitive, or that communication does not move vertically from subordinates to superiors and vice versa, or even that abusive communication does not happen. But this book operates from a very different set of assumptions about organizations, power, and communication that constitute an opportunity to strengthen organizational communication pedagogy. Simply put, workplace communication practices and models need to keep up with changing and flattening work structures that are increasingly part of our organizations and the social world in which they are embedded. In particular, we believe specific communication skills are associated with collaborating and these skills are not taught with the same rigor or understanding as other related concepts in organizational and communication curricula.

We join a growing list of scholars and teachers who believe that collaboration requires a unique set of structures, practices, and skills. Our present emphasis on debate, argumentation, public speaking, and persuasion are just part of the skill set needed by collaborative stakeholders and leaders. These participants *also* need to be skilled at: recognizing and validating the needs of their fellow stakeholders; separating people's positions from their underlying interests; listening for things that are never quite said; identifying overlapping commonalities; building trust while respecting difference; and constructively navigating conflict. The communication field does teach these values and skills dispersed in interpersonal courses or in classes focused on dialogue. This book is our attempt to present the communicative practices vital to interorganizational participation.

The first assumption we hold is that the reader of this text is somewhat unfamiliar with interorganizational collaboration. Knowledge about collaboration has grown so much that many disciplines offer specific texts, frequently for master or PhD level students. Having taught upper division and graduate-level college courses for more than a decade, we have found most of these books assume that the reader has some prior familiarity with the concept. Although many popular books and practitioner materials exist on the subject of collaboration, we do not believe that many books or texts have focused on introducing the concepts of interorganizational collaboration to a novice audience.

The treatment of communication in collaboration has been somewhat underdeveloped. The complexities of communicating and making decisions in the context of power, identity, and navigating multiple interests simultaneously are undertheorized. In this text, our focus is communication—specifically the communication of collaboration from a social constructionist stance, which emphasizes the communicative ways in which we create our world.[42] Communication constitutes our collaborative experiences, successes, and failures. Other books may tell you concepts like identity and dialogue are important to collaboration. In our text, you will learn how we communicatively generate and foster identity. We detail the assumptions behind dialogue and offer suggestions for how to achieve dialogue in conflict situations. As such, a primary goal of this text is to coalesce existing communication scholarship in the effort to develop a particular collaboration pedagogy.

A second assumption we bring to this text is that collaboration is a principled process.[43] We talk a lot about assumptions throughout this text because they explain and frame our actions; our assumptions about collaboration matter. We view collaboration as something that is beyond an exchange of resources and knowledge. Our text is a departure from group and organizational texts that approach collaboration from a functional or strategic perspective. We do not take a transactional view of collaboration. Micropractices of communication are fundamental not only to collaborating across organizations but also to fostering just and trusting relationships. This book anchors collaboration in the assumption that democratic and principled communication will foster both creative and accountable outcomes for those practicing collaborative problem solving. Thus, a second goal of this book is to articulate a collaborative ethic that will aid the reader in communicative contexts.

A third influential assumption we hold is that the act of collaborating is contingent—how and what we do in our practice of collaboration depends on the situation. Rather than providing the reader with prescriptions of how to accomplish collaboration, this book will focus on building collaborative *praxis,* which is based on the assumption of contingency.[44] Praxis entails *phronesis*—good judgment that is grounded in knowledge and moral obligation.[45] You will experience collaboration in a multitude of different contexts; each of those unique contexts will demand that you proceed with wisdom that is grounded in moral obligation and unique to the context in which you find yourself.

In a role-play designed to teach facilitation skills, one of our students questioned the decision of the facilitator (who was also a stakeholder) to introduce her own background before asking others in the group to discuss their backgrounds. The student questioning the facilitator was operating on the *prescription* that facilitators should be careful not to influence communication by speaking on topics first, before others in the group have had an opportunity to speak. Praxis draws our attention to the contingent nature of the process and to making good decisions based on moral obligation. In this case, the facilitator *modeled* the communication she sought from others in the group by speaking first. If, however, the group was at the point of making a decision, it would be unethical for the facilitator who is also a stakeholder to lead with her opinion on the subject, as it might unduly sway others given her power in running the meetings. Prescription tells you what you *should* do. Praxis cultivates your knowledge and ethical understanding of the situation so that you can make the best decision about what to do based on the specific circumstances. With ethical knowledge being every bit as important as applied knowledge, a third aim of the text is to develop the reader's collaborative praxis.

CONCLUSION

Interorganizational collaboration is influenced by our increased interconnectedness, shifting organizational needs, and changing workforce. Collaboration invokes ethical questions and ethical responsibilities that must be considered in our communication practices and structures.

CHAPTER TAKE-AWAYS

▶ Understand key influences in the momentum toward interorganizational collaboration

▶ Recognize features of wicked problems and their relationship to cross-sectoral solutions

▶ Distinguish ethical questions embedded in interorganizational problems

▶ Appreciate the changing needs of organizations and changing talents of the workforce

ENDNOTES

[1] Julie Beck, "'Any Addict Who Asks for Help Will NOT Be Charged,'" *The Atlantic*, May 11, 2015, http://www.theatlantic.com/health/archive/2015/05/gloucester-massachusetts-police-department-helping-not-arresting-drug-addicts/392873/

[2] Roberto Acosta, "DHHS Provides List of Steps Being Taken in Flint Water Crisis," *MLive.com*, February 1, 2016, http://www.mlive.com/news/flint/index.ssf/2016/01/dhhs_provides_list_of_steps_be.html

[3] Western Governors' Association, "Cross-Agency Collaboration in Addressing Record Drought in California," http://westgov.org/drought-forum/case-studies/327-water-supply/857-case-study-drought-forum-3

[4] Lucas Patzek, "California's Drought: We're All in This Together," http://www.aginnovations.org/post/2015-12-29/california-s-drought-we-re-all-in-this-together

[5] NetHope, "Emergency Response: Syrian Refugee Crisis," http://nethope.org/project/emergency-response-syrian-refugee-crisis/

[6] V. Muñoz et al., "Can Medical Products Be Developed on a Non-Profit Basis? Exploring Product Development Partnerships for Neglected Diseases," *Science and Public Policy* 42, no. 3 (June 1, 2015): 315–38, doi:10.1093/scipol/scu049.

[7] Horst W. J. Rittel and Melvin M. Webber, "Dilemmas in a General Theory of Planning," *Policy Sciences* 4, no. 2 (June 1973): 155–69, doi:10.1007/BF01405730.

[8] Kevin Barge, "Enlarging the Meaning of Group Deliberation: From Discussion to Dialogue," in *New Directions in Group Communication*, ed. Lawrence R. Frey (Thousand Oaks, CA: Sage, 2002), 159–78.

[9] Rittel and Webber, "Dilemmas in a General Theory of Planning."

[10] Ibid.

[11] Eric Lowitt, *The Collaboration Economy: How to Meet Business, Social, and Environmental Needs and Gain Competitive Advantage* (Hoboken, NJ: Wiley, 2013).

[12] Ibid.

[13] Ibid.

[14] Sandra A. Waddock, "A Typology of Social Partnership Organizations," *Administration & Society* 22, no. 4 (February 1, 1991): 480–515, doi:10.1177/009539979102200405.

[15] John W. Selsky and Barbara Parker, "Cross-Sector Partnerships to Address Social Issues: Challenges to Theory and Practice," *Journal of Management* 31, no. 6 (December 1, 2005): 849–73, doi:10.1177/0149206305279601.

[16] Majid Nejatian, Meran Nejati, Mohammad Hossein Zarei, and Somaye Soltani, 2013. "Critical Enabler for Knowledge Creation Process: Synthesizing the Literature." *Global Business and Management Research: An International Journal* 5, nos. 2 &3: 106.

[17] Ibid.

[18] Ibid.

[19] Ibid., p. 110.

[20] Art Currier, "12 Significant Workplace Considerations," *Newburyport Education Foundation: Business Coalition*, Spring 2015.

[21] Lowitt, *The Collaboration Economy*, p. 35.

[22] The Intersector Project, "The Intersector Project," *The Intersector Project*, 2016, http://intersector.com/about/the-intersector-project/

[23] John Kania and Mark Kramer, "Collective Impact," *Stanford Social Innovation Review*, Winter 2011.

[24] Pew Research Center, "Millennials: Confident. Connected. Open to Change," February 24, 2010, http://www.pewsocialtrends.org/2010/02/24/millennials-confident-connected-open-to-change/

[25] Richard Eisenberg, "Generational Training: What's in It for Boomers?" *Forbes*, http://www.forbes.com/sites/nextavenue/2013/10/18/generational-training-whats-in-it-for-boomers/

[26] Ronald Inglehart, *The Silent Revolution: Changing Values and Political Styles Among Western Publics* (Princeton, NJ: Princeton University Press, 1977).

[27] Meagan Johnson and Larry Johnson, *Generations, Inc.: From Boomers to Linksters—Managing the Friction Between Generations at Work* (New York: AMACOM, 2010).

[28] Andrew S. Fullerton and Jeffrey C. Dixon, "Generational Conflict or Methodological Artifact? Reconsidering the Relationship between Age and Policy Attitudes in the U.S., 1984–2008," *Public Opinion Quarterly* 74, no. 4 (December 21, 2010): 643–73, doi:10.1093/poq/nfq043.

[29] Johnson and Johnson, *Generations, Inc.*

[30] Lauren Stiller Rikleen, *You Raised Us—Now Work with Us: Millennials, Career Success, and Building Strong Workplace Teams* (Chicago: American Bar Association, 2014).

[31] Stephanie Rosenbloom, "Mommy and Daddy's Little Life Coach," *The New York Times*, April 5, 2007, http://www.nytimes.com/2007/04/05/fashion/05advice.html

[32] Rikleen, *You Raised Us—Now Work with Us.*

[33] Ibid.

[34] Johnson and Johnson, *Generations, Inc.*

[35] Ibid.

[36] Rikleen, *You Raised Us—Now Work with Us.*

[37] Johnson and Johnson, *Generations, Inc.*

[38] Jonathan Lash, "Lifelong Learners in a Rapidly Changing World," *The Huffington Post*, April 15, 2015, http://www.huffingtonpost.com/jonathan-lash/lifelong-learners-in-a-rapidly-changing-world_b_7069552.html

[39] Lowitt, *The Collaboration Economy.*

[40] Barbara Gray, *Collaborating: Finding Common Ground for Multiparty Problems* (San Francisco: Jossey-Bass, 1989).

[41] Jeffrey W. Kassing, "Speaking Up: Identifying Employees' Upward Dissent Strategies," *Management Communication Quarterly* 16, no. 2 (November 1, 2002): 187–209, doi:10.1177/089331802237234.

[42] Peter L. Berger and Thomas Luckmann, *The Social Construction of Reality: A Treatise in the Sociology of Knowledge* (New York: Anchor, 1967); Kenneth J. Gergen, *Realities and Relationships: Soundings in Social Construction*, Revised ed. (Cambridge: Harvard University Press, 1997).

[43] David Straus and Thomas C. Layton, *How to Make Collaboration Work: Powerful Ways to Build Consensus, Solve Problems, and Make Decisions* (San Francisco: Berrett-Koehler Publishers, 2002).

[44] W. Barnett Pearce, *Interpersonal Communication: Making Social Worlds* (New York: HarperCollins, 1994).

[45] Aristotle, *Nicomachean Ethics*, trans. Terence Irwin, 2nd ed. (Indianapolis, IN: Hackett Publishing Company, Inc., 1999).

2

Interorganizational Collaboration

The Case of Best SELF

The chief financial officer of Skagit County, Washington, figured out the county had a problem. Mike was crunching the numbers on juvenile crime and learned that every time a youth was arrested, it cost the county tens of thousands of dollars. That money covered only the immediate expenses of youth crime such as the criminal defender, the probation officer, temporary incarceration, the judge, food, and transportation. Should the child end up in long-term incarceration, the county would be footing a much larger bill. He wondered what if we intervened in children's lives before they got off track? He believed the money was better spent preventing juvenile incarceration than paying for it. He was not alone. Mike partnered with a local nonprofit grant writer, Kate, and the assistant superintendent of a local school district, Maggie. Together they learned that school was often the most stable environment for children at risk of committing crimes. School provided caring, adult supervision and offered children who could not afford to eat at home a guaranteed lunch, and often a breakfast, under the Federal Free and Reduced Lunch Program Act. School offered a safe atmosphere for children who might be at risk of domestic violence in their home situations. All of these factors contributed to youth crime. Together they envisioned, "What if we recreated that stable environment that children have during the school year during their most vulnerable time—and high activity time for juvenile crime—the summer?"

This was the impetus for the innovative Best Summer Education Learning Fun (SELF) program. This award-winning program was a collaboration of more than a dozen organizations and individuals including the county and several departments, nonprofit organizations such as the federally funded Private Industry Council, the local community college, and eventually seven school districts. Thousands of children throughout those districts grew up with a Best SELF program where the schools provided an all-day facility and managed the federal lunch program. The school district provided bussing once a week for every class to take a field trip and to participate in service-learning projects that ultimately created a connection between children and their

17

community. Board-certified teachers supervised the classrooms and were hired and paid by the county. Every class was limited to twenty-five students; two college students and two high school students assisted the teacher, providing a 1 to 5 adult to student ratio. Teachers were encouraged to push the boundaries of creativity and to teach by using the community and the environment around them. No packets or tests were allowed; one of the guiding values of the program was to make learning fun for children who traditionally fell behind in school. The program was so attractive to local families that it was offered on a sliding-fee scale to any family who wanted to participate. It grew from a few hundred children the first year to more than a thousand children, representing all socioeconomic levels, in less than five years.

No single organization, not even the county, could afford to do this program alone. While the county could support a modest payroll as an investment toward decreasing juvenile crime, the schools provided the facilities, and the employees were paid through colleges and the Private Industry Council. Funding came from more than a dozen public and private organizations. I was a training coordinator for the Private Industry Council when Mike called and asked me to participate. I managed a budget that I could use to place high school students in on-the-job training positions; Mike thought my high school students could work in the program. The Private Industry Council was dedicated to helping people learn job skills and training them to be successful in life, so its mission aligned with the mission of Best SELF. We had a stake in helping at-risk youth succeed. It was beneficial for our organization to get to know county and school officials better. My high school students were also an at-risk population (potential detrimental behaviors included dropping out of school or early pregnancy); they shaped Best SELF in unexpected ways. The program became committed to helping at-risk teenagers find self-worth by helping younger children.

No single entity could have sustained Best SELF. No single entity could have provided the organizations and people necessary. Each stakeholder cared about children from a different point of view. The county was worried about crime. Schools were worried about drop-outs. Colleges wanted to prepare future teachers. I wanted to give my high school workers a sense of pride and worth through work. None of us worked for the other. We all worked for different organizations—organizations that felt they had something to gain by being involved. All of us had other full-time jobs. We had responsibilities in our home organizations that did not overlap with our work with Best SELF. As a recent college graduate with a communication degree, I was amazed by the processes associated with the organizing of Best SELF. There was no "boss" because representatives of the organizations volunteered their time. We made decisions together. There was no top down leadership. How did we achieve so much?

—Renee, reflecting on her introduction to collaboration

When we ask our students or clients what they think collaboration means, most often they will tell us that it means to "work together." To be sure, collaboration requires working together. However, collaboration is also saturated with complexities that become more apparent as we dig deeper into the meaning of the concept. Working from a shared framework of collaboration is important because it provides a common vocabulary among other collaborating partners and allows you to identify areas of strength and weakness in your collaborative processes. That said, our goal in this chapter is to build a scaffolding in which to create this shared framework of collaboration rather than providing a concrete definition of collaboration. Definitions are often debatable and are usually contextually and culturally driven. We build a theoretical scaffolding of the defining characteristics of collaboration by examining and deconstructing multiple definitions. We begin this chapter by distinguishing collaboration from two related concepts: cooperation and coordination. Next we introduce classic definitions of collaboration. We elaborate on the structural elements of collaboration and its systemic qualities. We then consider collaboration as a process and problem-solving method before attending to collaboration as composed of ideal characteristics. We conclude the chapter with consideration of how we might measure success in this complex phenomenon.

Cooperation, Coordination, and Collaboration

For those new to collaboration, it can be difficult to parse out the difference between words like collaboration, cooperation, and coordination. Often we use them interchangeably, yet all three words have different meanings and implications. While collaboration requires cooperation and coordination, the mere presence of either of those behaviors does not necessarily indicate interorganizational collaboration.

Cooperation is often associated with reciprocity.[1] However, cooperating stakeholders do not have to share the same vision. Relationships and agreements tend to be informal. The parties may simply be agreeing to do something for one another, such as referring clients. For example, a school teacher may promise the director of the local Boys and Girls Club to refer teenagers she suspects are being recruited into gangs to the after school program. Cooperation should be considered the simplest, least formal interorganizational relationship. Stakeholders may cooperate because organizational partners are friends or acquaintances, not necessarily because formal agreements have been set up between their respective organizations. If cooperation is neither required nor contracted, it may be the most vulnerable interorganizational relationship in terms of long-term sustainability.

Coordination implies increased formalization in the structures and processes associated with the organizational relationship.[2] Coordinating organizations may have interorganizational agreements that define specific methods and detailed procedures for referring clients, sometimes referred to as memoranda of understanding (MOU). For example, the school, rather than the teacher, may have a formalized policy to refer students to the Boys and Girls Club. The school might also share resources such as money or equipment with the Boys and Girls Club and may agree to bus children to the Club. Coordination is a relatively stable interorganizational structure because processes among organizations have been formalized in agreements. It is less fragile than cooperation in that coordinating organizations may not easily back out of agreements that have been codified and ritualized. However, coordinating organizations may be troubled when partners are not cooperative—not willing to reciprocate. In other words, the presence of a formal agreement between organizations does not guarantee that those carrying out the agreement are eager to do so. Sometimes coordinating partnerships are determined at one level (i.e., superintendent of schools) and implemented at another level, leaving service providers (i.e., teachers) frustrated with the extra work. Coordinating interorganizational structures are complex. Think of coordinating organizations as stable and static organizational relationships among partners.[3] Coordination refers to executing activities that are *already in place,* such as, agreements, ongoing procedures, arrangements, and practices.

Interorganizational collaboration is not necessarily stable and is definitely not static. Instead, collaboration is "indeterminate."[4] Agreements, procedures, arrangements, and practices are *not yet in place*; collaborative partners will make decisions regarding these things. The differences among organizational partners make it very difficult to reach agreement. Because collaboration requires decision making, interorganizational partners often formalize their partnerships by crafting governance structure agreements that outline and codify partner responsibilities, decision-making processes, and other accountabilities. The whole point of collaboration is to capitalize on stakeholder differences, to come up with creative and innovative ideas and solutions. However, the indeterminate nature of collaboration, and the ambiguous quality of what those agreements and procedures look like, will vary depending on the positions and interests of the individuals and organizations involved. Cooperation will definitely help collaborating partners arrive at joint decisions, and coordination will be required to implement those decisions. Therefore, collaboration requires both cooperation and coordination, but its quality of uncertainty forges fragile interorganizational relationships that are vulnerable to all of the same breakdowns as cooperation and coordination.

The Wilder Research Center developed tools and resources for those practicing collaboration. They distinguish cooperation, coordination, and collaboration and address four areas: (1) vision and relationships, (2) structure and responsibilities (3) authority and accountability, and (4) resources and rewards.[5] Table 2.1 summarizes these elements. As organizations move from cooperating and coordinating to collaborating, participating members experience increased complexity in deciding on a mission;

Table 2.1 The elements of cooperation, coordination, and collaboration[6]

Essential Elements	Cooperation	Coordination	Collaboration
Vision and Relationships	• Basis for cooperation is usually between individuals but may be mandated by a third party • Organizational missions and goals are not taken into account • Interaction is on an as needed basis, may last indefinitely	• Individual relationships are supported by the organizations they represent • Missions and goals of the individual organizations are reviewed for compatibility • Interaction is usually around one specific project or task of definable length	• Commitment of the organizations and their leaders is fully behind their representatives • Common, new mission and goals are created • One or more projects are undertaken for longer term results
Structure, Responsibilities, and Communication	• Relationships are informal; each organization functions separately • No joint planning is required • Information is conveyed as needed	• Organizations involved take on needed roles, but function relatively independently of each other • Some project-specific planning is required • Communication roles are established and definite channels are created for interaction	• New organizational structure and/or clearly defined and interrelated roles that constitute a formal division of labor are created • More comprehensive planning is required that includes developing joint strategies and measuring success in terms of impact on the needs of those served • Beyond communication roles and channels for interaction, many "levels" of communication are created as clear information is a keystone of success

(continued)

Essential Elements	Cooperation	Coordination	Collaboration
Authority and Accountability	• Authority rests solely with individual organizations • Leadership is unilateral and control is central • All authority and accountability rests with the individual organizations that act independently	• Authority rests with the individual organizations but there is coordination among participants • Some sharing of leadership and control • There is some shared risk, but most of the authority and accountability falls to the individual organization	• Authority is determined by the collaboration to balance ownership by the individual organizations with expediency to accomplish purpose • Leadership is dispersed, and control is shared and mutual • Equal risk is shared by all organizations in the collaboration
Resources and Rewards	• Resources (staff, time, dollars and capabilities) are separate, serving the individual organizations' needs	• Resources are acknowledged and can be made available to others for a specific project • Rewards are mutually acknowledged	• Resources are pooled or jointly secured for a longer-term effort that is managed by the collaborative structure • Organizations share in the products; more is accomplished jointly than could have been individually

their structures, responsibilities and communication; the ways in which authority and accountability work; and the expectations regarding how resources and rewards are shared.

 APPLICATION: Interview a leader in your community involved in interorganizational partnerships. Determine the type of activities in which they are involved. Based on the Wilder chart are they collaborating?

Building a Collaborative Scaffold

Three common ways to identify collaboration are: (1) as a particular type of structure; (2) as composed of particular types of processes; and (3) as the idealized principles and outcomes associated with particular structures and/or process.[7] Understanding just what it means to collaborate can be confusing because collaboration is frequently talked about in all three of these ways, sometimes simultaneously. One definition of collaboration influential across fields of business, public management, education, health care and many others was proposed by management professor Barbara Gray: "a process through which parties can constructively explore their differences and search for solutions that go beyond their own limited vision of what is possible."[8] She elaborated on the definition:

> Collaboration involves a process of joint decision making among key stakeholders of a problem domain about the future of that domain. Five features are critical to the process: (1) the stakeholders are interdependent, (2) solutions emerge by dealing constructively with differences, (3) joint ownership of decisions is involved, (4) stakeholders assume collective responsibility for the future direction of the domain, and (5) collaboration is an emergent process.[9]

Parts of Gray's definition refer to the structural elements of collaboration—its form and its membership. Other parts explain how the processes of collaboration are conducted. Yet other elements of the definition reference an ideal or value-based characteristic of collaboration. To develop a sophisticated conception of collaboration, we unpack these definitional features throughout this chapter, beginning with structure.

Collaboration as a Particular Type of Structure

One of the most complex aspects of interorganizational collaboration is its structural composition. We begin our analysis of the components of structure by discussing the interdependent motives that bring stakeholders together and the horizontal relationships. We then shift our focus to variants in collaborative structures such as their temporality (long-term versus temporary) and whether they are mandated or voluntary partnerships. Finally, we identify the associated structures that must be taken into account when we view collaboration from a system perspective, such as the organizations who participate and the communities in which collaboration takes place.

Interdependent Motives for Collaboration. According to Gray's five critical features of collaboration, stakeholders are interdependent. They most likely do not work in the same organization but are instead collaborating within a very fluid structure. Interdependence is a primary reason collaboration is tricky to navigate and implies "the ways in which the stakeholders' are intertwined and the reasons they need each other to solve the problem."[10] Their actions, or the outcomes of their actions, can affect one another neutrally, positively, or negatively. In the case of collaboration, stakeholders are linked to each other through their generalized goal or overarching vision; they are dependent on one another for the success or failure of achieving that vision. For example, in Renee's reflection at the beginning of this chapter, all of the stakeholders were interested in preventing children from participating in risky behaviors and activities that would lead to dropping out and possibly incarceration. The structural composition of the group was complex because of the varied and different organizations that participated. However, all of these organizations and groups shared the vision of at-risk prevention. This overarching vision is referred to as a problem domain.[11] Scholars argue that the impetus for collaboration is to either *advance a vision* or solve a conflict within their respective problem domain.[12] Improving the problem domain is one of the drivers of stakeholders' interdependence.

The motives for collaboration typically are to capitalize on opportunity or to find resolution (albeit temporary) for conflict. For example, collaborations motivated by the opportunity to advance a vision may gather to learn more specifically about one another in the context of the vision (appreciative planning) and/or may create strategies for collective problem solving for achieving that vision. Collaborations motivated by conflict may participate in dialogues designed to increase understanding across conflicting parties or may work to design governance strategies to help parties proceed through conflict.[13]

Organizations form collaborative relationships when they are dependent on one another for access to necessary resources.[14] Resource dependence was visible in the Best SELF collaboration. The Private Industry Council participated in the collaboration because they wanted to advance the vision of preventing drops-outs and juvenile incarceration *and* to build relationships with local public officials and the superintendents of schools. The federal law at that time required that the Private Industry Council place their youth clients in on-the-job trainings with *public* and *private-nonprofit* organizations. It was in their best interest to strengthen relationships with powerful public entities in their community. Both of these goals—one shared and one specific to an individual organization—contributed to interdependence within the structure.

Horizontal Relationship Structures. Organizational relationships in interorganizational collaboration differ from the types of relationships structured in traditional organizations. Most notably, relationships are arranged in a horizontal hierarchy. As you may have guessed, this adds considerably to the complexity of collaboration. Stakeholders generally are not paid to participate; however, they do anticipate gaining something from their involvement (as in our example of the Private Industry Council). Therefore, informal governance structures are closely tied to relationships. The quality of their relationships will likely determine the level of stakeholder participation. These complex membership structures are unlike most organizational structures where a supervisor has ultimate authority over the work. The collaboration provides fertile learning ground for understanding leadership in horizontal organizations. Thus, sometimes collaboration is considered to be present simply because of the way stakeholder relationships are structured. Much more will be said about how horizontal structures influence collaboration throughout this book.

Mandated vs. Grassroots. Another structural influence that contributes to the complexity of collaboration is the manner in which collaboration is convened—whether mandated from the top down or initiated at a grassroots level by volunteer stakeholders. Collaboration usually is initiated in the following three ways: (1) internal catalysts—collaboration begins within the community, (2) external catalysts—an external funder encourages collaboration, or (3) policy catalysts—collaboration is mandated by law.[15] Internal catalysts—grassroots collaborations—tend to be the most successful in achieving macrolevel outcomes, perhaps because they are not tied to federal funding and are free to pursue outcomes in creative ways. Although externally catalyzed groups often have a very powerful funder, their funding frequently comes with restrictions as to what types of activities the collaborative group can conduct. Finally policy-catalyzed groups, born primarily from government mandates, are best positioned to affect long-term sustainable change, but "group momentum may not be as strong as with internally and externally catalyzed groups, given there may not be a strong sense of ownership since the process began as a mandate."[16]

Mandated collaboration can be problematic for other reasons. When collaboration is required for funding, typically by foundations and government-funded grants, most applicants can easily identify existing and potential partners and obtain letters of support. However, in the later stages, when collaborations implement their work plans, it can be a challenge to develop a planning process that is inclusive and able to facilitate goal achievement.[17] In mandated collaborations, many organizations do not have the capacity (i.e., resources, time, and infrastructure support) to participate in collaborative efforts.[18]

Temporary or Stable Structures. Collaborative structures are also difficult to understand because they may or may not be long-term organizational structures. There has been significant debate regarding whether collaboration is a stable or temporary structure. For example, some researchers have noted that collaboration can become embedded in communities and last as long as, or longer than, traditional organizational structures.[19] This was true for the Best SELF collaboration. It continued for 15 years, well beyond the typical life of the average business (estimated to be just 12.5 years).[20] The long-term stability of collaborative structures, called institutionalization,[21] can foster a political environment where collaborating becomes the norm for solving problems in a given community.[22] Yet, collaborations can also be temporary structures, referred to as Negotiated Temporary Structures (NTS).[23] For example, an ad hoc collaboration was formed in Oregon to solve the issue of what to do with a new commercial business that would be shining its lights on a drive-in theater. This temporary collaboration disbanded when a resolution to the problem was reached.

Collaborations can be more or less temporary in nature, or they may begin as a temporary structure only to become institutionalized over time. Some interesting differences surface between long-term collaboration and NTS. For example, NTS collaborations can be highly volatile and have less routine relationships. Some scholars found that these collaborative networks changed frequently depending on their needs for resources and their ability to accomplish their tasks.[24] Temporary collaborations also develop trust differently than longer term collaborations. Rather than building trust through "traditional sources [such as] shared experience, reciprocity, disclosure, and familiarity of past commitments,"[25] the building of trust in NTS groups is tied to their needs for task development as opposed to relationship development.[26] Accordingly, collaboration can take place with temporary or stable structures, and those structures will influence and be influenced by the communication that takes place within them. The length of time a collaboration has been established does not necessarily affect its ability to accomplish change.[27] However, how a collaboration operates, its dynamism, and its mechanisms for building trust and attaining accomplishments will be influenced by the permanence or lack thereof in its structures.

QUESTION: How do traditional, top down organizational structures look different from collaborative structures? How will communication be handled in each structure? How are employees motivated versus how stakeholder members are motivated to participate in collaboration?

APPLICATION: Make a list of problems in your community for which a collaboration would be useful. Which types of problems are likely to call for temporary structures? Which type of problems will demand a longer-term commitment?

Collaboration as a System.   Table 2.2 on pp. 27–29 uses a systems lens to understand collaboration and its many structural components. It looks at the considerations for participating in collaboration before it takes place (antecedents), while it takes place (throughputs) and as a result of it taking place (outputs).[28] Systems theory applied to group behavior assumes "*communication* is the observable phenomenon binding together constituent components of systemic entities. . . . Thus, group members (or sets of groups) are joined together as a social system through their communication."[29] Renee and Lawrence Frey identified four structural levels that need to be considered when trying to understand collaboration: (1) the individual person who collaborates, (2) the stakeholder organization they represent, (3) the group of stakeholders who collaborate, and 4) the community in which collaboration takes place.[30] From all perspectives— individual, organizational, collaborative group, and community—thought must be given to collaborative processes and outcomes.

Table 2.2 Four structural levels that need to be considered when trying to understand collaboration[31]

Structural level	Antecedents of ideal collaboration	Processes of ideal collaboration	Outcomes of ideal collaboration
	Traits: Cognitive complexity (ability to integrate complex goals of collaboration) and self-monitoring; predisposition to engage in collaborative conflict management	Understands and takes part in participative processes	Increased self-efficacy
	Collaborative competence/ethic, including ability to trust others; values processes such as consensus, flat hierarchy, and shared power—things that are not easily trainable	Enacts dialogic processes	Greater appreciation of participative processes
	Power to make decisions	Attentive to/willingness to spend time on communication processes and structures (time spent talking about)	Greater collaborative communication competence
	Committed to long-term engagement with the collaborative group	Manages ongoing dialectic tensions (e.g., organizational versus collaborative group's goals)	Identification with group goals and processes—culture of group
Individual Representative		Displays organizational agendas	Greater understanding of complexities/boundaries of other organizations
		Participates in informal networking and communication processes outside of formal settings	Increased knowledge/better informed about partners, partners' organizations, and community
			Greater trust of other individuals and organizations
			Increased political power
			Satisfaction with group processes and outcomes

(continued)

Structural level	Antecedents of ideal collaboration	Processes of ideal collaboration	Outcomes of ideal collaboration
Collaborative Group	Flat hierarchy	Communication focuses on group mission	Accomplish group goals (e.g., fiscal and/or philanthropic)
	Nonhierarchical convener or facilitator	Group legitimizes conversation about organizational vision	Consensus decision making
	Ability to meet face-to-face occasionally	Culture fosters dialogue and direction	Increased creativity and innovation
	Physical structures reflecting egalitarian environment (e.g., round table seating)	Narrative helps to socialize changing representatives	Increased political power as a collaboration
		Communication processes reflect egalitarian values (e.g., uses rotating structures for responsibilities)	Increased recognition or legitimacy by communities
		Limits use of hierarchical structures (e.g., executive committees)	
		Communication processes are designed to represent various constituencies (e.g., open to new members or visitors)	
		Communication enhanced by media technologies	
Stakeholder Organizations	Organizational need (e.g., fiscal or public relations) and/or organizational desire (e.g., philanthropic related to goal)	Organizational leaders display commitment to process of collaborating in their community (e.g., commitment to display organizational agenda and respect for dialectics)	Stronger links with other organizations
	Organizational leaders' ability to entrust decision-making power	Culture allows for arenas of accessibility	Organizational leaders' greater understanding of other organizations' processes and boundaries

Structural level	Antecedents of ideal collaboration	Processes of ideal collaboration	Outcomes of ideal collaboration
Stakeholder Organizations (continued)	Organizational leaders' ability to share a common goal	Organizational leaders share ongoing information and resources with their individual collaboration representatives	Decreased competitiveness of organizations with potential partners
	Organizational leaders' ability to commit resources		Increased political power of organization
	Organizational leaders' ability to be flexible to radical structural changes		Organizational leaders' increased collaborative communication competence
	Organizational leadership fosters a question-legitimizing culture		Organizational leaders' increased willingness to participate in other collaborations
Collaborating Community	Embraces nontraditional public policy	Experiences and celebrates small successes with the collaboration	New community leaders
	Provides a neutral legitimizing entity for the collaboration	Facilitates the sharing of information between the collaboration and the greater community	New institutions
	Interdependent need transcends stakeholders' needs and is rooted in a larger community need	Ratifies the consensus of the collaboration through legislative action	New civic culture, including norms, heuristics, and discourses
	Provides boundary spanners, leaders, and conveners	Oversees the implementation of decisions and projects brought forth by the collaboration	Ability to mobilize new collaborations
	Boundary spanners, leaders, and conveners initiate the communicative groundwork for collaboration		Community

As we have noted, the structure of collaborations is complex. For example, do individuals have the power to make decisions when meeting with collaborating partners or must they first obtain authorization from the leaders of their individual organizations? Environmental collaboration scholar Jonathon Lange refers to this particular dilemma in the context of "constituency communication." Individual stakeholders need to be sure they are keeping their own organization's leaders (their constituents) apprised of the collaborative and decision-making process.[32] Lange metaphorically refers to the collaborative group as the "first table" and the constituent organization who is being represented in the collaboration as the "second table"—one that may have ultimate authority over the decisions made at the first table.

Group expert JoAnn Keyton and colleagues argued that interorganizational collaboration is best understood from a mesotheory lens, which draws our attention to the interplay between collaborative structural elements and how collaboration works at multiple structural levels—individual representative, organizational, collaboration, and public.[33] This interplay between levels becomes apparent when we view collaboration as a system, and it is key to developing a thorough understanding of collaborative processes. These processes move between levels. Examples of questions that incorporate thinking of collaboration on multiple levels include: Is the collaborative group composed of the appropriate stakeholders (individual level)? Who can accomplish the goal of the collaboration (collaboration level)? Does the community (public level) support collaborative outcomes (collaboration level)? The systems perspective of collaboration highlights the moving parts—the dynamic and contingent nature of collaboration.

Collaboration as Process

The critical features of collaboration in many definitions also include specific references to *how* collaboration is accomplished, thus defining it in part by its processes and procedures. Gray's definition describes collaboration as a process in which, "joint ownership of decisions is involved; stakeholders assume collective responsibility for the future direction of the domain, and collaboration is an emergent process."[34] Communication scholars have been particularly interested in articulating how these processes unfold; communication is a central process in their conceptions of collaboration. For example, Virginia Stallworth asserted that four elements were essential to collaborative success: (1) a shared goal, (2) interdependence, (3) equal input of participants, and (4) shared decision making.[35] Two of these elements are process-oriented or communicative in nature—equal input and shared decision making. Similarly, Thomas Lawrence, Cynthia Hardy and Nelson Phillips defined collaboration as "a cooperative, interorganizational relationship that is negotiated in an ongoing communicative process."[36] Their definition illuminates how difficult it is to conceive of collaboration outside of the communication process. In the remainder of this section we point out key considerations when conceiving of collaboration as process, juxtaposing it with adversarial problem solving.

Collaboration as Problem Solving.   Understanding collaboration as a process draws our attention to the role it plays as an alternative problem-solving method. To understand collaboration as a problem-solving method, we first distinguish problem solving from decision making. While problem solving often includes making a decision, decision making does not always include solving a problem.[37] Decision making is the act of choosing among possible solutions, such as taking a vote or making a unilateral decision.[38] Often the problem or issue is not easily defined, making it nearly impossible to choose—let alone agree on—solutions.

For example, the *problem domain* of gang violence involves numerous stakeholders, including the police, schools, and local nonprofit organizations. Each of the potential stakeholders views the *problem* very differently and often defines the problem narrowly, frequently as an absence of their preferred solution.[39] For example, the police officer might define the gang violence problem as having a lack of law enforcement to deal with gang members. The officer would like the collaboration to decide on more funding for the police department. However, the school administrator is likely to view the problem of gang violence as a lack of education and resources to help children stay in school. She would like the collaboration to focus on after-school programs. Because each stakeholder's narrow view of the problem illuminates only a sliver of the issue, voting on their preferred solutions would not do much to solve the gang violence problem.

Discussion, dialogue, joint fact-finding, and deliberation—all elements in effective problem solving—help stakeholders integrate their disparate definitions of the problem.[40] Stakeholders seeking to make improvements around the problem-domain of gang violence would not be ready to make decisions without comprehensive problem solving that cultivates each stakeholder's understanding of the issue to make sure any decision making takes into account multiple perspectives.

Juxtaposed with collaborative problem solving is adversarial problem solving depicted in table 2.3. The most obvious prototype for the adversarial process is the legal system. In most cases conflicts are brought before a third party—a judge, jury, or arbitrator—to determine the outcome of a particular conflict. The stakeholders are opponents who try to convince the third party that their position is correct. This process discourages face-to-face interaction between the conflicting parties, literally seating opponents at opposite tables, a notable distinction from collaborative problem-solving. Parties using an adversarial process attempt to prove the worthiness of their evidence to an impartial third party. In collaborative problem solving, stakeholders may have conflicts over what counts as "facts" or "evidence," but they work together to solve a problem that has consequences for everyone involved. In very complex situations, collaborative

Table 2.3   Comparing the collaborative process to the adversarial process[41]

Adversarial	Collaborative
Rules position parties as adversaries	Parties positioned as joint problem solvers
Third parties intervene before issues are mature	Issues can be identified before positions crystallize
Characterized by positional bargaining	Characterized by interest-based bargaining
Facts used to buttress positions	Joint search used to determine facts
Seeks winning arguments	Seeks workable options
Yields all or nothing resolution of issues	Yields resolution by integrating interests
Narrows options quickly	Broadens field of options
Authority for decisions rests with judge	Authority for decisions rests with parties
Characterized by suspicion and high emotion	Characterized by respect and use of reason
Parties often dissatisfied with outcome	Outcome must be satisfactory to all parties
Often fosters bitterness and long-term mistrust	Promotes trust and positive relationships

problem solving may be preferred because the problem is so elaborate it warrants solving by the people who understand it best. This is often the case with wicked problems.

If you or a loved one have experienced a harrowing court case (for example, a custody battle over children or property), you are probably familiar with the devastating effect the adversarial process can have on relationships. Attorneys are bound by law to advocate on behalf of their clients; the functionality of the relationship between conflicting parties is too often a casualty of the win-lose process. Some couples never recover from the battle wounds of their divorce, yet they have joint responsibility for raising their children despite a rancorous severed relationship.

In cases where you are likely to be making decisions with people for years to come, collaborative problem solving is a wise choice. Indeed, the legal field has made great strides in recent decades in recognizing the collateral damage of bitter legal battles and has developed legal mediation as an alternative. In some states, mediation (a process that can resemble collaboration) is mandatory before couples are allowed to proceed to divorce court. Given the drawn out and costly process of the adversarial court system, collaboration, despite its own lengthy commitment, can be a reasonable problem-solving option.

Sometimes problem solving cannot occur among stakeholders because of disparities in power. Stakeholders with less power will fear that their perspective will be dismissed when considering approaches to the problem. Collaborative problem-solving should not be attempted if participating stakeholders are not willing to share and distribute power to others. Some adversarial processes can set the stage for collaboration. For example, a public relations campaign could draw attention to a particular stakeholder's business decisions that do not meet public expectations. The campaign might be enough to "level the playing field" and to convince the stakeholder to pay attention to a less powerful stakeholder. This was the case with the decommissioning of an oil platform called the Brent Spar.[42] The British government had approved the sinking of the rig (owned by Shell UK) off the coast of Scotland in 1995. Greenpeace, an environmental organization, launched a very successful adversarial campaign to illuminate the potential environmental damage from sinking an oil rig. Until the adversarial campaign, the British government and Shell ignored the concerns of Greenpeace. The negative press attention prompted the oil company to include public opinion in its decision-making process about disposing of Brent Spar.

While adversarial processes such as negative press and public protests have a place in a democratic society (and often serve a useful purpose regarding public education), they entail risks if the end goal is to win a spot at the decision-making table. Greenpeace remained distrusted throughout the participative processes. That said, collaboration, while best grounded in an ethical and transparent process, may involve adversarial processes to motivate more powerful stakeholders to invite others to the table.

 APPLICATION: Read the local newspaper or peruse the Internet and identify problems that are being adjudicated in the court system. Do you see potential for collaboration in any of these cases? Why or why not?

Other Collaborative Processes. A substantial body of research focuses in-depth on the communication process of consensus decision making associated with collaborating.[43] Collaboration requires greater space for dialogue, a process by which stakeholders can begin to understand each other's unique differences and perspectives.[44] Collaborations sometimes use innovative procedures such as rotating the chairperson of a meeting among stakeholder organizations to create a safe space for dialogue.[45] Recent scholarship also introduces the idea of how collaboration stakeholders are able to create "authoritative texts."[46] Authoritative texts are the shared discourses members use to talk about their work and to align their values and mission. For example, Renee and her colleague Patricia Sias found collaboration members spent a lot of time talking about their mission and used testimony from success cases to help reinforce that mission.[47] These studies, many of which we return to in greater length in subsequent chapters of this book, describe *how* stakeholders come to assume collective responsibility and how collaboration emerges as a process.[48] Part III of this text is devoted to understanding how communication and other processes work in collaboration. As a part of this understanding we posit that collaboration demands a particular language in order to foster the results it seeks.

The research of our spotlight scholar J. Kevin Barge spans collaboration, conflict, and appreciative inquiry. His work illuminates the process of collaboration as communicative and generative of the worlds we in which we live, play, and work. Kevin describes the social construction perspective of communication, a perspective we introduced in the last chapter that pervades our thinking in this text.

SCHOLAR SPOTLIGHT

One Take On Collaboration
J. Kevin Barge

My interest in collaboration stems from a long-held interest in finding ways to foster better conversations among people in order to accomplish desirable goals and outcomes. From my perspective, how we coordinate our messages in everyday conversation is crucial for creating collaboration that leads to tangible results. I am inspired by social constructionist theorists such as Barnett Pearce and others who believe that communication does much more than simply transmit information. For social constructionists, communication builds our social worlds—our personal and professional identities, relationships, groups, organizations, cultures, and institutions. The way we talk shapes our understanding of situations, how we see our role and the role of others, what purpose a particular conversation serves, and how we act.

We cannot not collaborate with each other, as conversation is inherently a collaborative process that is reflected in the joint activity of people when they talk. What gets made in conversation is not determined by the actions of one person alone; it is also determined by the responses others make to earlier turns in the conversation as well as what turns follow. John Shotter has a lovely line where he says that when asked what we mean by an utterance we make, the appropriate response should be that we won't know until the conversation is completed. His point is that what an individual turn means in a conversation is not determined solely by the person making the utterance. Rather, the meaning of the turn depends, in part, on how others respond to it. This suggests that we build our social worlds through the sequence of unfolding turns in conversation, and each turn represents a choice point by people regarding what kind of conversation they wish to create.

Take for example how people create power differences in relationships when they talk. Power differences are made when the conversation reflects a pattern of talk where one person makes a one-up move asserting power and the other makes a one-down move accepting it. If this pattern of conversation persists over time, a strong story is created by the people in the relationship that one person is clearly in charge and has power, and the other does not. However, what happens when people jointly produce patterns of conversation where a person makes a one-up move asserting power and the other responds by also making a one-up move, a move that asserts power and that simultaneously resists the power attempt by the other? In this pattern of conversation, who has power is contested as both parties resist the power attempt by the other. Whether people create relationships where power is centralized in one person or contested depends on the choices they make turn-by-turn and the patterns of communication they jointly create with each other over time.

If all conversations are collaborative and varied forms of conversations create different identities, relationships, and cultures, then people need to be mindful of the choices they make in conversations about what they want to create with the other person, how it fits with the aims and purposes of the other person, and the consequences of the jointly produced conversation. In the field of dialogical organizational development, an often-used phrase is, "If you want to change the organization, change the conversation." The idea is that patterns of conversations create mental models about how we interpret events and how we act. Therefore, if you want people to act differently and respond differently to each other and to situations, you need to create new kinds of conversations. So an important question for people wishing to facilitate collaboration is, "What kind of conversation needs to happen at this particular moment to help move forward and accomplish desirable goals?"

My research attempts to answer this question in two ways. First, I am interested in exploring the ways that conversation enhances collaboration by focusing attention on the kinds of communication skills that people need to develop to manage conversations and to make interventions.[49] I have been fascinated with developing practices that help people become mindful of the consequences of their communication and helping them develop their critical awareness regarding how to frame conversations, how the patterning and temporal flow of conversation invites certain social worlds and not others, how appreciative and dialogical forms of conversation enhance collaboration, and at identifying possible intervention points in the flow of communication to make positive differences.

For me, generative conversations are ones that enhance our ability to play off each other's responses in ways that foster learning, creativity, and innovation. Such conversations are marked by managing the tension between: (1) supporting what other people are saying, recognizing the value and worth of people's identity, ideas, and interests, and (2) challenging what they say by introducing different perspectives, interests, and viewpoints into the conversation. One of my favorite phrases that I like to use when talking about generative forms of talk, is "creating a difference that connects." What I mean is that persons have to find ways of talking to one another that affirm the value and worth of the other while simultaneously introducing differences in the conversation that challenge the other and enable learning and possibilities for new understanding and actions to emerge. Supportive forms of communication without challenge inhibits learning, and developing new perspectives while challenging forms of communication without support can make people defensive and undermine the development of common ground that can serve as the basis for subsequent organizing.

(continued)

Second, and more recently, I have become interested in how we design communication forums and meetings to enable better conversations.[50] My feeling is that there are a number of methods and procedures we can use to design our conversations with others in order to address important issues and challenges. For example, one of my recent research projects explores how we can create meeting designs that facilitate multistakeholder dialogues to grow the number of the members of underrepresented groups in the science, technology, engineering, and math (STEM) disciplines. Such conversations are always challenging. Some stakeholders may not be aware of or know each other; others may be in conflict with each other; and yet others are disheartened because they don't see a way of changing their relationships and coordinating their work to achieve their goals. There are a variety of communication design technologies (including small group procedures such as brainstorming and Devil's Advocacy as well as large group interventions such as Open Space and Appreciative Inquiry) that can be used to design meetings. There is a lot work to do in this area, as we need to have a better understanding of how various meeting techniques generate particular outcomes such as enhanced collaboration, innovation, and learning.

This is the challenge for communication scholars and professionals committed to developing collaboration—to find creative ways to build the capacity of individuals and to design meetings and events that enable people to talk to each other in rich ways and to develop creative, innovative responses to the dilemmas and challenges they face. Collaboration is built and made through conversation, which requires people to make wise choices regarding how they talk in order to create the social worlds they desire.

Collaboration as an Ideal

A third defining and complicating aspect of understanding collaboration are the values and/or principles with which it is aligned. As seen in the second critical feature of Gray's definition, "solutions emerge by dealing constructively with differences."[51] Collaboration is often associated with an *ideal* ethic for interaction. Gray emphasizes that collaboration deals *constructively* with differences. Other scholars have used similar valuative terminology. Dee Appley and Alvin Winder, two of the earliest organizational psychologists to define collaboration, characterized it by "justice and fairness" and "a caring concern for the other."[52] Public management scholars Mark Haskins, Jeanne Liedtka, and John Rosenblum claimed, "At the core of . . . collaboration is a set of moral values and principles that are rooted in a desire to serve and manage."[53]

In many ways table 2.3 reflects collaborative problem solving in its most ideal state. The point is that historical and contemporary conceptions of collaboration incorporate ideals that are not often typical or associated with other types of organizing. However, not all scholarship has adopted this narrower ideal of collaboration. Some argue, "it can be legitimate to use a degree of manipulative and political behavior in collaboration" referred to as "collaborative thuggery."[54] Yet, most scholars who accept a broader, perhaps more neutral definition of collaboration, still identify principles such as trust and democracy as essential parts of the collaborative process.

Viewing collaboration as emergent also idealizes our understanding of it. Nonprofit expert Laurie Lewis described collaborative interaction as "creating something completely new," "win-win" conflict resolution, and learning together.[55] Lewis summarized collaboration research as converging around the idea that "while formal collaborations may exist in name, collaborative interaction, by this definition, is not truly present until a specific type of relationship between participants develops." In other words, "collaboration cannot be formally convened, but rather, it emerges when the participants choose to engage one another in a certain way or manner."[56] The emphasis on emergent reinforces the notion that processes and solutions are not predetermined but evolve over time with the influence of stakeholders. This raises the question of whether groups can be considered collaborating if they are not generating something new (emergent). Taken together, collaboration strictly understood as ideal processes and outcomes leaves us to ask, are we collaborating if we are not acting principled and achieving innovative solutions?

Consider how these idealistic conceptions of collaboration complicate how we might execute it. Some scholars have warned about the bias inherent in thinking of collaboration as idealized. Lewis argued that the "problem of describing collaboration (or its variants) in terms of the idealized version obfuscates readers' abilities to disguise what is merely desirable from what is basic to this phenomenon."[57] Keyton and colleagues solve the ideal dilemma with their neutral definition:

> interorganizational collaboration is the set of communicative processes in which individuals representing multiple organizations or stakeholders engage when working interdependently to address problems outside the spheres of individuals or organizations working in isolation. The outcomes of these processes have the potential to benefit or harm the parties to the collaboration, as well as others.[58]

Their definition facilitates conceptualizing collaboration that may or may not be carried out in a principled manner, that may or may not result in win-win, innovative solutions for all parties involved.

In this book, we ground our arguments in the assumption that successful collaboration—collaboration that achieves synergistic outcomes *while preserving relationships*—does require a different ethic of communication. Although we do think that members of collaboration who seek winning solutions and strong relationships strive toward ideal processes and outcomes, we reject the idea that groups that do not achieve a particular process or outcome are not collaborating. We marry collaboration to an ethical framework not to idealize the process but because of the political and social consequences collaborative decisions have for communities and publics.[59] This ethic is embedded in principles of democracy and shared decision making and will be explored in part II of this book. We believe that in order to solve some of the wicked problems that plague our planet—problems that require working across public, for-profit, and nonprofit sectors—we will need to approach communication and decision making in a just manner.

Measuring Success

We intimated that successful collaboration is that which achieves synergistic outcomes while preserving relationships. But whose outcomes, what relationships? Indeed, measuring collaborative success is tricky business and has long been a subject of debate both in and out of academia. It makes sense that collaboration measurements have also taken into account the complexity of its structures, processes, and principles. Early work contributed by scholars include instruments such as "Working Together: A Profile of Collaboration," which measures collaboration on five dimensions.[60] The first is the context for the collaborative group, determining the timing and the critical need for collaboration. The second dimension measures the structure of the collaboration, examining such things as membership dominance and expertise. The third dimension measures collaboration among members with items such as, "members are willing to let go of an idea for one that appears to have more merit."[61] The fourth dimension examines processes such as decision making, and the final and fifth dimension examines "concrete and measurable goals."[62]

More recently, the Stanford Social Innovation Review has discussed interorganizational collaboration in terms of collective impact—the commitment of a group of important actors from different sectors to a common agenda for solving a specific social problem. "Collective impact initiatives involve a centralized infrastructure, a dedicated staff, and a structured purpose that leads to a common agenda, shared measurement, continuous communication and mutually reinforcing activities among all participants."[63] Shared measurement is essential to collective impact. Without agreement about how to monitor performance, track progress toward goals, and learn what is or is not working, agreement on a common agenda is illusory. Shared measurement allows participants to learn from each other's successes and failures and to hold each other accountable.

Language from environmental collaboration research identifies elements for measuring collaborative success—social capital, outputs, and outcomes.[64] *Social capital* refers to the relational dimension of collaboration such as trust and reciprocity among collaborating stakeholders. *Outputs* are "intermediary causal mechanisms between collaboration processes and collaborative outcomes."[65] Examples of outputs would include the creation of shared standards and the articulation of plans and agreements. Outputs indicate process-level successes achieved by collaborative groups. Beyond outputs, *outcomes* refer to the measurable changes affecting the particular problem domain. For example, in environmental collaboration, outcomes would be changes in water quality or ecological habitat. Social outcomes are important and include things like changes in behavior, attitudes, and ethics of the constituencies on whose behalf collaboration members work.[66] Because the wicked problems that interorganizational collaboration seeks to affect are ongoing and evidenced-based changes can take a long time, measuring success by improvements in social capital and process outcomes can be important indicators of progress in a particular domain.

 QUESTION: How might a collaboration measure its social capital? What behaviors and practices might indicate high levels of trust and cooperation?

CONCLUSION

Collaboration challenges some of our taken-for-granted knowledge about how organizations work. This chapter develops a conceptual understanding of collaboration by acknowledging it operates as a particular type of horizontal structure and a set of communicative processes and principles. Collaborative stakeholders will have to consider the impacts of collaborative actions at multiple levels—individual, group, organizational, and community/public—and recognize its systemic properties. Levels of collaboration interact continuously to affect social capital, collaborative outputs, and outcomes.

CHAPTER TAKE-AWAYS

▶ Differentiate among cooperation, coordination, and collaboration

▶ Distinguish a problem vs. problem domain

▶ Understand collaboration as a structure, process, and principled ideal

▶ Recognize the differences between adversarial and collaborative problem-solving models

▶ Identify the various ways collaborative success can be measured

ENDNOTES

[1] Barbara Gray, *Collaborating: Finding Common Ground for Multiparty Problems* (San Francisco: Jossey-Bass, 1989).

[2] Ibid.

[3] Ibid.

[4] Renee Guarriello Heath, "Rethinking Community Collaboration through a Dialogic Lens: Creativity, Democracy, and Diversity in Community Organizing," *Management Communication Quarterly* 21, no. 2 (November 1, 2007): 145–71, doi:10.1177/0893318907306032.

[5] Paul W. Mattessich, Marta Murray-Close, and Barbara R. Monsey, *Collaboration: What Makes It Work: A Review of Research Literature on Factors Influencing Successful Collaboration*, 2nd ed. (Saint Paul, MN: Amherst H. Wilder Foundation, 2001).

⁶ Ibid. Reprinted with permission.
⁷ Joann Keyton, Debra J. Ford, and Faye l. Smith, "A Mesolevel Communicative Model of Collaboration," *Communication Theory* 18, no. 3 (August 1, 2008): 376–406, doi:10.1111/j.1468-2885.2008.00327.x.
⁸ Gray, *Collaborating*, p. 5.
⁹ Ibid., p. 11.
¹⁰ Ibid., p. 11.
¹¹ Ibid.
¹² Ibid.
¹³ Barbara Gray and Jill Purdy, "Conflict in Cross-Sector Partnerships," in *Social Partnerships and Responsible Business: A Research Handbook*, ed. M. May Seitanidi and Andrew Crane (Abingdon-on-Thames, UK/New York: Routledge, 2014), 205–26.
¹⁴ Jeffrey Pfeffer and Gerald R. Salancik, *The External Control of Organizations: A Resource Dependence Perspective* (Redwood City, CA: Stanford University Press, 1978).
¹⁵ Jeanelle J. Sugimoto-Matsuda and Kathryn L. Braun, "The Role of Collaboration in Facilitating Policy Change in Youth Violence Prevention: A Review of the Literature," *Prevention Science* 15, no. 2 (2014): 194–204.
¹⁶ Ibid., p. 201.
¹⁷ Jan Ivery, "Policy Mandated Collaboration," *Journal of Sociology & Social Welfare* 35, no. 4 (December 2008): 53–70.
¹⁸ Ibid.
¹⁹ David D. Chrislip and Carl E. Larson, *Collaborative Leadership: How Citizens and Civic Leaders Can Make a Difference* (San Francisco: Jossey-Bass, 1994).
²⁰ Arie de Geus, *The Living Company* (Brighton, MA/New York: Harvard Business Review Press, 2002).
²¹ Thomas B. Lawrence, Cynthia Hardy, and Nelson Phillips, "Institutional Effects of Interorganizational Collaboration: The Emergence of Proto-Institutions," *The Academy of Management Journal* 45, no. 1 (February 1, 2002): 281–90, doi:10.2307/3069297.
²² Chrislip and Larson, *Collaborative Leadership*.
²³ Kasey L. Walker and Cynthia Stohl, "Communicating in a Collaborating Group: A Longitudinal Network Analysis," *Communication Monographs* 79, no. 4 (December 1, 2012): 448–74, doi:10.1080/03637751.2012.723810.
²⁴ Ibid.
²⁵ Ibid., p. 468.
²⁶ Ibid.
²⁷ Sugimoto-Matsuda and Braun, "The Role of Collaboration in Facilitating Policy Change in Youth Violence Prevention," *Prevention Science* 15, no. 2 (April, 2014): 194–204, doi:10.1007/s11121-013-0369-7.
²⁸ Edward Mabry, "The Systems Metaphor in Group Communication," in *The Handbook of Group Communication Theory and Research*, ed. Lawrence R. Frey, Dennis Gouran, and Marshall Scott Poole (Thousand Oaks, CA: Sage, 1999), 71–91.
²⁹ Ibid., p. 72.
³⁰ Renee Heath and Lawrence Frey, "Ideal Collaboration: A Conceptual Framework of Community Collaboration," in *Communication Yearbook 28*, ed. Pamela Kalbfleisch (Mahwah, NJ: Lawrence Erlbaum, 2004), 189–231.
³¹ Adapted and reprinted with permission from Renee Heath and Lawrence Frey, "Ideal Collaboration: A Conceptual Framework of Community Collaboration," *Annals of the International Communication Association* 28, Iss. 1, 189–231, doi:10.1080/23808985.2004.11679836.
³² Jonathan Lange, "Environmental Collaboration and Constituency Communication," in *Group Communication in Context: Studies of Bona Fide Groups*, ed. Larry R. Frey (Mahwah, NJ: Lawrence Erlbaum, 2003), 209–34.
³³ Joann Keyton and Virginia Stallworth, "On the Verge of Collaboration: Interaction Processes versus Group Outcomes," in *Group Communication in Context: Studies of Bona Fide Groups*, ed. Larry R. Frey (Mahwah, NJ: Lawrence Erlbaum, 2003), 235–60.

[34] Gray, *Collaborating*, p. 11.

[35] V. Stallworth, "Building a Model of Interorganizational Nonprofit Collaboration" (Memphis, TN: University of Memphis, 1998).

[36] Lawrence, Hardy, and Phillips, "Institutional Effects of Interorganizational Collaboration," p. 282.

[37] Kevin Barge, "Enlarging the Meaning of Group Deliberation: From Discussion to Dialogue," in *New Directions in Group Communication*, ed. Lawrence R. Frey (Thousand Oaks: Sage, 2002), 159–78.

[38] Karen Tracy and Christina Standerfer, "Selecting a School Superintendent: Sensitivities in Group Deliberation," in *Group Communication in Context: Studies of Bona Fide Groups*, ed. Larry R. Frey, 2nd ed. (Mahwah, NJ: Psychology Press, 2002), 109–36.

[39] Roger Fisher, William L. Ury, and Bruce M. Patton, *Getting to Yes: Negotiating Agreement Without Giving In*, 2nd ed. (Boston: Houghton Mifflin Harcourt, 1992).

[40] Barge, "Enlarging the Meaning of Group Deliberation"; Gray, *Collaborating*.

[41] Reprinted with permission from Barbara Gray and the Center for Policy Negotiation, Inc., 1985.

[42] Tony Rice and Paula Owen, *Decommissioning the Brent Spar* (Boca Raton, FL: CRC Press, 2003).

[43] Judith E. Innes and David E. Booher, "Consensus Building and Complex Adaptive Systems: A Framework for Evaluating Collaborative Planning," *Journal of the American Planning Association* 65, no. 4 (September 1999): 412–27; Matthew J. McKinney, "What Do We Mean by Consensus? Some Defining Principles," in *Across the Great Divide: Explorations in Collaborative Conservation and the American West*, ed. Philip Brick, Donald Snow, and Sarah van de Wetering (Washington DC: Island Press, 2001), 33–40; Steven Daniels and Gregg Walker, *Working through Environmental Conflict: The Collaborative Learning Approach* (Westport, CT: Praeger Publishers, 2001).

[44] Renee Guarriello Heath, "Rethinking Community Collaboration through a Dialogic Lens"; Heather M. Zoller, "'A Place You Haven't Visited Before': Creating the Conditions for Community Dialogue," *Southern Communication Journal* 65, no. 2–3 (March 1, 2000): 191–207, doi:10.1080/10417940009373167.

[45] Renee Guarriello Heath and Patricia M. Sias, "Communicating Spirit in a Collaborative Alliance," *Journal of Applied Communication Research* 27, no. 4 (November 1, 1999): 356–76, doi:10.1080/00909889909365545; Keyton and Stallworth, "On the Verge of Collaboration."

[46] Matthew A. Koschmann, Timothy R. Kuhn, and Michael D. Pfarrer, "A Communicative Framework of Value in Cross-Sector Partnerships," *Academy of Management Review* 37, no. 3 (July 2012): 332–54.

[47] Heath and Sias, "Communicating Spirit in a Collaborative Alliance."

[48] Gray, *Collaborating*.

[49] J. Kevin Barge, "Systemic Constructionist Leadership and Working from within the Present Moment," in *Advancing Relational Leadership Theory: A Conversation among Perspectives*, ed. S. Ospina and M. Uhl-Bien (Charlotte, NC: Information Age Publishing, 2012), 107–42; J. Kevin Barge, "Pivotal Leadership and the Art of Conversation," *Leadership* 10 (2014): 56–78.

[50] J. Kevin Barge, "Consulting as Collaborative Co-Inquiry," in *Dialogic Organizational Development: Theory and Practice*, ed. G. Bushe and R. Marshak (San Francisco, CA: Berrett-Koehler Publishers, 2015), 177–96; J. Kevin Barge and D. Andreas, "Communication, Conflict, and the Design of Dialogic Conversations," in *The Sage Handbook of Conflict Management*, ed. Oetzel, John G. and Stella Ting-Toomey, 2nd ed. (Thousand Oaks, CA: Sage, 2013), 609–34.

[51] Gray, *Collaborating*.

[52] Dee G. Appley and Alvin E. Winder, "An Evolving Definition of Collaboration and Some Implications for the World of Work," *The Journal of Applied Behavioral Science* 13, no. 3 (July 1, 1977): 279–91, doi:10.1177/002188637701300304, p. 281.

53 Mark E. Haskins, Jeanne Liedtka, and John Rosenblum, "Beyond Teams: Toward an Ethic of Collaboration," *Organizational Dynamics* 26, no. 4 (March 22, 1998): 34–51, p. 34.

54 Chris Huxham and Siv Vangen, *Managing to Collaborate: The Theory and Practice of Collaborative Advantage* (Abingdon-on-Thames, UK/New York: Routledge, 2005).

55 Laurie Lewis, "Collaborative Interaction: Review of Communication Scholarship and a Research Agenda," in *Communication Yearbook 30*, ed. C. Beck (Thousand Oaks, CA: Sage, 2006), 197–247.

56 Ibid., p. 209.

57 Ibid., p. 223.

58 Keyton, Ford, and Smith, "A Mesolevel Communicative Model of Collaboration," p. 381.

59 Jessica MacDonald Milam and Renee Guarriello Heath, "Participative Democracy and Voice: Rethinking Community Collaboration Beyond Neutral Structures," *Journal of Applied Communication Research* 42, no. 4 (October 2, 2014): 366–86, doi:10.1080/00909882.2014.911944.

60 Chrislip and Larson, *Collaborative Leadership*.

61 Ibid., p. 180.

62 Ibid., p. 182.

63 John Kania and Mark Kramer, "Collective Impact," *Stanford Social Innovation Review*, Winter 2011.

64 John Charles Morris et al., *The Case for Grassroots Collaboration: Social Capital and Ecosystem Restoration at the Local Level* (Lanham, MD: Lexington Books, 2013).

65 Tomas M. Koontz and Craig W. Thomas, "What Do We Know and Need to Know about the Environmental Outcomes of Collaborative Management?" *Public Administration Review* 66 (December 1, 2006): 111–21, doi:10.1111/j.1540-6210.2006.00671.x., p. 115.

66 Morris et al., *The Case for Grassroots Collaboration*.

3

Stakeholders

An OCEAN of Issues

East Austin is one of the last traditionally African American historic districts in Austin. There is a long history here and one that many "heritage" neighbors (those that have been residents for multiple generations) are proud to claim. If I had a dollar for every time someone reminded to me that Stevie Ray learned to play the Blues here, I could easily pay my mortgage every month. The problem that became the impetus for OCEAN (the Organization for Central East Austin Neighborhoods) was the "regentrification" effort to move heritage neighbors out of the area in order to construct large condominium complexes. Some of the stories I heard made me sick. One woman got behind on her tax bill, and her land was taken. Several people complained that the builders predetermine how much to pay current owners and then profit by hundreds of thousands of dollars when they sell the new properties.

When OCEAN first formed, we wanted to create a space for all Central East Austin stakeholders to have a voice in development and also to cultivate a larger voting block of people that could be represented at city council. Any neighborhood member could attend meetings, as could city officials, small business owners, and land developers who owned land in Central East. What started as a collaboration to find a common voice quickly became one where discord dominated communication. In any given meeting, a developer might try to derail the agenda or a neighborhood member would invoke NIMBY (not in my back yard) about a particular issue. OCEAN was a great space for everyone to talk, and it was a safe space to hash things out versus the public forum typical of city council meetings. The downside was the inability to determine if people who attended any given monthly meeting were there to help advance the goals of OCEAN (which were vague and primarily oriented toward protecting the status quo and preventing new development), or if they attended solely to derail the meeting and to obstruct working toward a common voice. The darkest period occurred after one of the developers convinced people to attend the annual election meeting and to vote him in as OCEAN chair. For several months, all the meetings were cancelled, and a major development project was approved by the city council without OCEAN making a statement. The chair was "impeached" soon after that vote. OCEAN then settled into a nice routine—meeting monthly, discussing projects, planning our collective opinion, and representing all six neighborhoods at city council meetings. The city council president honored OCEAN as a model collaboration and an exemplar of how public, private, and state interests can all work together to come up with a plan that suits everyone's needs.

That was all before the E5 condo proposal was submitted for approval with the city development commission. I knew it was going to get messy as soon as I read about the land purchase in the local paper. The E5 condo was to be built on land that had major historical significance surrounding the slave trade. The land had been scheduled to be preserved as part of a memorial; at the last minute, it was sold to a developer and the E5 condos were proposed. The plans called for about 300 expensive units, but there was very little parking and no plans for how to adjust traffic flow to accommodate the new residents. After several months of contentious meetings, the E5 condo plan was scheduled for a vote at the next monthly meeting. OCEAN used Robert's Rules of Order and majority voting, and I heard groups of people talking about "stuffing" the vote and bringing in any neighborhood member they could find to vote against the proposal. The next monthly meeting was setting up to be a barn burner.

When the boardroom was half full in the East Austin Library where we held our meetings, the atmosphere was already tense. People were talking about the injustice of the proposal. Several people were wearing pins stating their opposition to E5, and the room was becoming increasingly segregated by the different neighborhoods and stakeholder groups. I arrived 15 minutes early for the meeting and saw all the regulars—plus more people than I had ever seen at any meeting. I had no idea who they were or what/who they were representing. Were they contractors, people from the city, area small business owners? I kind of chuckled to myself as I thought, "Wow, nice of you to only care once there is a big issue to vote on."

—Matt reflecting on his experiencing working
with the East Austin Housing Program

"Who gets to define the problem?" may be a more important question than "what is the problem?" for interorganizational collaboration. Depending on the stakeholder, the problem can be conceived of in different ways. "Stakeholder" can be a challenging term to define. Indeed, much research has been conducted on the boundaries and limitations of what it means to be a stakeholder. Put in the most simplistic terms, stakeholders are any constituency that can affect or be affected by an organization (or in our case a collaboration).[1] What is more relevant to collaboration is *considering* how each stakeholder sees the problem and what their unique perspective can add to innovation regarding the issue. Therefore, articulating who stakeholders are and what motivates them to participate is essential to understanding interorganizational collaboration.

The composition and motives of its membership are vital components in collaboration, as are structures, processes, and principles. We begin this chapter by unpacking the definition of stakeholder, pointing out the origin of the construct as a linguistic approach to think more ethically about the effects of organizing practices. We also introduce tensions inherent to stakeholder-organizational relationships. In the next major section, we examine stakeholder identity as a complicating element of stakeholder participation. We discuss how identity is both drawn from—and influences—interaction and collaborative problem solving. Finally, we return to the construct of interdependence as key to motivating stakeholder involvement. Interdependence is sometimes located at the intersection of our individual and collective identities. Together these concepts articulate what is meant by stakeholder in the context of interorganizational collaboration.

The Ethical Turn to "Who?"

Stakeholder theory first emerged as a counterpoint to popular managerial and economic theories of organizations. Managerial texts approach organizing through ideas like transaction cost, (i.e., what is the cost of collaborating with others in terms of time and other resources versus what we will gain?)[2] and resource dependency (i.e., what and whose resources do we need to accomplish our vision?).[3] These economic-driven organizing concepts are rooted in the idea that the boundaries of an organizational entity limit the scope or range of what the organization can effect. Consequently, the focus of study, prior to the introduction of stakeholder theory, was the organization and the people who owned the organization (shareholders in publicly traded companies).[4] Stakeholder theory added to organizational theory by highlighting the business-society relationship in organizational forms. By making a greater connection between a company and society, stakeholder theory makes explicit the needed link between "business" decisions and "ethical" decisions.[5]

Illuminating ethics in business, stakeholder theory became a balance to more internally focused economic theories and also reconceptualized several managerial questions such as how does value creation affect the larger public, what are the ethics of capitalism, and what are the inherent problems with solely adopting a managerial mind-set to outcomes?[6] Much of the current work on stakeholder theory focuses on business ethics and corporate-social responsibility.[7] Over time, stakeholder theory has evolved to become a way of thinking (a perspective or a framework) that focuses on the stakeholder—both the effects on and actions taken.[8] As pioneer thinker R. Edward Freeman once stated about the evolution of stakeholder thinking, it is the principle of who and what really counts.[9]

Stakeholders in Interorganizational Collaboration

Determining who and what counts in wicked problems can be a widening spiral in which everyone potentially has a stake or claim. Consequently, we all can be stakeholders of a particular collaboration. In this text, we use the term stakeholder to not only refer to those who are *affected* by a given problem but also to name the participants who *act* as decision makers within a given interorganizational domain. Drawing from interorganizational research, we agree that stakeholders in a given problem domain must be present or represented with some measure of inclusivity and of equality of voices.[10] Prizing inclusivity in stakeholder identification contributes to having relevant and varied expertise at the table, cocreating a vision everyone buys into, developing an environment where the vision is likely to succeed, and avoiding having unrepresented (or overrepresented) voices eventually derail or undermine the work of the collaborative whole.[11] In addition and aligned with the purpose of this book, inclusivity is a vital principle for balancing power in decision making around wicked problems.

Stakeholder Influence

Stakeholder selection influences the direction and outcomes of a collaboration, including its ability to implement a decision and whether or not its work will be deemed credible. Leaving out particular stakeholders can have dramatic effects on how the domain is defined.[12] Stakeholder participation cannot be detangled from power (discussed in detail in chapter 6). For example, Cynthia Hardy and Nelson Phillips conducted a study of the British Refugee Council. They described how the eventual inclusion of a less powerful stakeholder (the Refugee Forum) "embarrass[ed] established agencies, like the 'white-run' British Refugee Council, into sharing power with refugees, engaging in initiatives . . . and employing more refugees."[13] The Refugee Forum "pushed its way in the domain and helped to shape the constitution of that domain."[14] Hardy and Phillips concluded stakeholder participation resides in power that is derived from (a) formal authority—a "recognized, legitimate right to make a decision," (b) control over critical resources including money, expertise, and facilities, and/or (c) discursive legitimacy—the right to speak regarding particular issues.[15] The influence of the Refugee Forum resided in their right to speak on behalf of refugees.

> **QUESTION:** How did stakeholders influence OCEAN, the case that opens this chapter? How might the problem domain be redefined based on the stakeholders who were missing and the stakeholders who participated? Where did the power of stakeholders reside—formal authority, resource control, discursive legitimacy?

Traditional stakeholder research classifies stakeholders based on: (1) power—the ability to influence the collaboration, (2) legitimacy of relationship to the collaboration, and (3) urgency of claim to the problem domain (see figure 3.1). You can begin to parse out a typology of stakeholders depending on how many of these three attributes are present. Stakeholders with all three attributes are *definitive stakeholders* (7). Stakeholders with only two are expectant and can be subcategorized as *dominant stakeholders* (4—powerful and legitimate but not urgent), *dependent stakeholders* (6—legitimate and urgent but not powerful), and *dangerous stakeholders* (5—urgent and powerful but not legitimate). Finally, stakeholders with just one of the three attributes are called latent and can be subcategorized as *dormant stakeholders* (1—powerful but not legitimate or urgent), *discretionary stakeholders* (2—legitimate but not powerful or urgent), and *demanding stakeholders* (3—urgent but not powerful or legitimate).[16]

Consider how these attributes help us understand the stakeholders involved in OCEAN. A member of one of the East Austin neighborhoods may have a *legitimate* reason to participate in OCEAN, but if they don't live near the condo units going up, they may not have an *urgency* to the problem domain or the *power* to do much about it. This person would be a discretionary stakeholder. In contrast, a member of an East Austin neighborhood

Figure 3.1   Classifications of stakeholders[17]

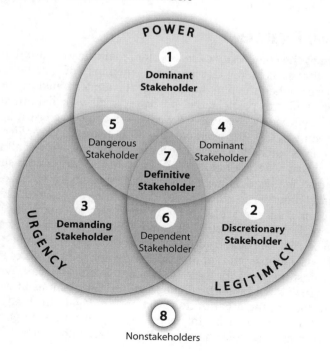

(legitimate) that is directly affected by the condos (urgent) but has no way to influence the group can be seen as a dependent stakeholder—a different level than a discretionary stakeholder but still in need of others to influence the group. Finally, think of a community member in an affected neighborhood who also happened to be a sitting city council person (powerful). This definitive member has all three attributes of a stakeholder.

Typologies like these can assist in identifying stakeholders in a problem domain, but they should not be used solely as a way to prioritize voices that might be missing. There are many possible subjective categorizations; for example, Who gets to determine what is urgent? What is considered a legitimate relationship to the organization? These questions can't be answered in a textbook because of the contingent nature of collaboration. Instead, they will be determined in the interaction of stakeholders in the context of the collaborative problem-solving domain. Think back to the Flint water crisis issue in chapter one. When the decision to switch water sources was originally discussed, who were the stakeholders at the table? Was there a diversity of stakeholder participation? How did cost cutting measurement become the dominant criterion for making the decision to switch water sources? And now that the full effects of that decision are coming to light, how many of the stakeholders now active in the crisis were included in the decision making at the beginning? Identifying stakeholders and fostering inclusivity can be difficult, and we don't always get it right. Unfortunately, not getting it right can be exceedingly costly to communities and individuals.

Stakeholder Paradoxes

Adding to the complexity of stakeholder identification are the ongoing paradoxes that stakeholders encounter as members of a collaboration. A paradox occurs when the pursuit of one goal is undermined by the pursuit of another goal.[18] In participative processes such as collaboration, paradoxes are inevitable.[19] "The web we weave will come to constrain us, often in unforeseen ways."[20] For example, the aptly named *stakeholder paradox* posits that an organization should account for the interests of all its stakeholders, not just the shareholders. Yet, in an organization with shareholders, organizational leaders have a fiduciary responsibility to make a profit for the shareholders. The ethic of considering everyone (stakeholders) versus the responsibility of profit (shareholders) sets up a paradox.[21] Pursuing both goals becomes a logical impossibility (or paradox). It makes ethical sense that an organization has a duty to be accountable to people affected by its actions, but that duty sometimes pits the needs of the stakeholders against the needs of the shareholders. Such is the case when organizations wreak environmental damage in the communities in which they operate. As long as the organization's actions are legal, this bind limits the possible actions that can be taken by the organization. Organizational leaders would have to "put the needs of the shareholders above the other stakeholders and at the same time place the other stakeholders' interests above shareholders."[22] Impossible.

Although stakeholder paradox may not appear fully in collaboration, elements of the paradox can emerge. Instead of the toggle between the shareholders and the stakeholders of a single organization, stakeholders in a collaboration context vacillate between the needs of the organization they represent and the needs of the collaboration. Like stakeholder paradox, participants may find the collaboration difficult when the needs of one constituent conflict with the needs of another.

In exploring environmental collaboration, Jonathan Lange identified five additional paradoxes of collaboration that stakeholders may encounter (summarized in table 3.1). With the *entry paradox*, collaborative participants feel forced to collaborate due to strong social pressures from other parties. In this paradox people who are supposed to be self-selecting into a collaborative process are instead forced to participate. The attendance of the unwilling works against collaborative processes and creates an environment where outcomes may be counter to the hopes or desires that underpinned the initiation of the group.

A second paradox of collaborating is *authority expropriation*. During these first few chapters, and especially here, we are emphasizing the need to carefully select the people who participate in collaboration. Authority expropriation occurs when key decision makers are not at the table. This is a common frustration with collaborative members. The people at the table are identified as being stakeholders with the authority to represent their organizations. Yet, those who attend the meeting do not have the power to make decisions on behalf of their organizations, thus making the collaborative process slow or nothing more than a symbolic effort on the part of its members.

Table 3.1   The paradoxes of collaborative stakeholder participation[23]

Paradox	Definition
Stakeholder	The ethic of considering everyone versus the responsibility of considering one
Entry	Participants feel forced into collaborating rather than self-selecting
Authority Expropriation	The people participating in the collaboration are not the people who can make key decisions
Inclusive	Having a mandate to include everyone can lead to less inclusivity
Constituency	The needs of one stakeholder and their representative constituency can be at odds with another stakeholder and her or his constituency
Mainstreamer	How can everyone be included when some stakeholders and their constituencies are opposed to collaboration

The third paradox is the *inclusive paradox*. This paradox wrangles with how and why some members are invited to collaborate and others are not. Often people are invited to the collaboration by the members who are already at the table, which can lead to less inclusivity—a collaboration that is "preaching to the choir." Matt experienced the inclusivity paradox while working on a safe-sex education collaboration. All of the members of the collaboration ended up coming from a comprehensive sex education approach, and no members representing the abstinence-only approach were encouraged to participate. At one point during the collaboration, the members even acknowledged that there was a very large group of stakeholders not present at these meetings. Yet stakeholders worried that including these members would slow down the process and make collaborative decision making more difficult. Consequently, some stakeholders were never invited to the table.

The *constituency paradox* is the fourth paradox of collaborating. As we discussed earlier, collaborative members have to shift back and forth between the needs of their organization and the needs of the collaboration. One of the driving forces behind the movement back and forth is the accountability individual stakeholders have to the constituencies they represent. One constituency has needs that may influence how a person acts in the collaborative process, and the needs of one collaborative member may then be at odds with the needs of another. This paradox is likely to emerge with particularly contentious collaborative topics. When parties have very different needs or entrenched beliefs about one another, the collaborative process can devolve into an adversarial process between two conflicting parties, each serving to protect their constituencies' interests.

The final paradox of collaborating is called the *mainstreamer paradox*. This paradox is connected to the other four. In the mainstreamer paradox, radicals seat themselves at the table with no intention of following a collaborative ethic. In this situation, their presence (while important as a legitimate stakeholder group) sabotages the process. By definition, a radical would reject a mainstream process; doing so causes a double bind with no logical solution. If the radicals are not invited to the table, the collaboration may experience an inclusive paradox, but if they are represented at the table, the collaboration experiences a constituency paradox. These six paradoxes highlight the array of issues and tensions that create a difficult environment for collaboration.

 QUESTION: If you were convening a collaboration regarding an issue important to you, what criteria would you use to invite stakeholders? What paradoxes are you most likely to encounter regarding your problem domain?

Identity and Stakeholders

Further complicating stakeholder participation is the way in which singular and collective identities collide, intersect, and overlap. Identity involves the central, distinctive and enduring parts of who we are,[24] capturing our beliefs, assumptions, values, attitudes, and habits.[25] Our identity is a messy tangle of different facets of our lives—an amalgam of life experiences, family, relationships, social circles, community, faith, career, and culture (just to name a few). All of these influences and experiences shape and mold us; our beliefs, values, and attributes help us make decisions, mentor, guide, lead, coach, and learn. Thus, identity is an integral concept that explains why communication and decision making in collaboration are so complicated.

Identity intersects with power, dialogue, and stakeholders' interests and positions (covered in future chapters of this book). A thorough grasp of identity also deepens our knowledge regarding why stakeholders encounter paradoxes that constrain and complicate the collaborative environment. After developing the conceptual framework of identity as rooted in social identity theory, we examine the process of identification and some of the consequences of identity as it relates to collaboration. We end this section with a discussion of collective identity as an important development for collaborative groups and an examination of the tensions involved with toggling between individual and collective identities in collaboration.

Social Identity Theory

Stakeholders have numerous affiliations; they must navigate among the associated identities.[26] Think of it this way: people are members of many different groups and organizations. When someone takes part in any one of those memberships, that person is affected by their respective groups and acts accordingly.[27] When at work, people have a "work persona," when attending church, a "church persona," and so on. Each one of these personas is enacted within that group. In collaborations, self-concept (identity) is affected by group affiliations and how those groups interact with other groups.[28] For example, if a collaboration is working on issues of racism and police brutality, members define their identity in relationship to the collaboration and others who are working on this issue. Members also view their own identity in relation to other groups working on this topic and other members of the community who may or may not be actively involved in the issues of racism and police brutality.

A person learns more about who they are based on the groups in which they hold membership. A person also learns who they are not by comparing themselves to other groups.[29] For instance, you may be part of Red Sox Nation, a fan group for the Boston Red Sox. By claiming membership with Red Sox Nation, you can identify and affiliate with others in the group, and that helps you to better understand your own Red Sox "fandom." Being a member of Red Sox Nation also creates boundaries that help to identify who you are not. As a Red Sox fan you always cheer for your team, but when an archrival (an opposing group to compare your membership against) comes to town, you become even more ardent in your cheering, more celebratory in your team's victory, and more distraught over your team's loss. By associating with certain groups, individuals identify themselves as members—and as nonmembers of other groups.[30] Understanding a little about how identities are formed and how they affect actions and behaviors, helps to explain stakeholder interaction.

At the core of our social identity is the belief that people want to (a) create and maintain positive self-esteem and that (b) part of our self-esteem comes from the groups we are a part of, thus (c) positive associations with groups (especially compared to the competing groups) are important for enhancing our own identity.[31] As a result, people create "fuzzy" sets of attributes about what it means to be a member of a certain group based on the similarities and differences of that group to others.[32] In many ways, the construction of attribute sets is analogous to the more common practice of stereotyping. Both processes can be constructive or destructive in the practice of collaboration where diverse groups encounter one another. For example, a collaboration focused on water management in California might include stakeholders who represent farmers, ranchers, environmentalists, state agencies, and federal agencies. All of these groups have different sets of attributes associated with themselves *and* ascribed to the others at the table. This diversity can be an asset to creating solutions that meet the members' needs, but it can also be a powder keg waiting to ignite tensions about water, water rights, and water management. Fostering an ethical collaborative environment involves changing the focus of individual stakeholders (shifting their identity) away from solely identifying with their respective group attributes to focusing on the attributes associated with being a member of the collaboration.

Identification

People do not have a single identity; instead, multiple salient identities become important at certain times and in certain contexts. Parents invoke a parental identity at the dinner table and a coworker identity during a staff meeting, a sports fan identity at a baseball game, and an arts enthusiast identity at a charity gala. Some have likened the complexity of multiple identities to a prism—depending on the situation and context, a person portrays a different part of themselves.[33] Others have conceptualized identities as target areas that move forward and backward in importance depending on the situation.[34]

Accordingly, *identification* (the active process by which individuals link parts of their identity to elements in an organization, social scene, or a collaboration)[35] depends on the extent to which individuals are attached to targets (i.e., work, family, church).[36] The processes of communicating identity affect how stakeholders act.[37] The construction and maintenance of stakeholders' identities are inherently rooted in communicative interactions, where

> [i]ndividual identities are created as people talk particularistically about an individual, constituting her or his reputation. Thus, one acquires an identity through inclusion, by being "on" the collaboration team; for being "a member" of the management committee, for being "important," perhaps by sending out the memos, for deciding where the meetings are held.[38]

While communicating identity is necessary to create collaborative interaction, it may hinder one's willingness to interact collaboratively.[39] For example, a stakeholder may identify more strongly with the goals and values of the collaborative group than with their own organization. Or their identity might be stronger as a professional, such as a doctor who may find that his values and decisions are motivated by his profession, rather than his organization, or by the collaborative group's values. In OCEAN, having stakeholders from each of the neighborhoods was important so that all relevant voices would be included in forming a collaborative identity for the alliance. However, members at times invoked the identity of their neighborhood rather than their identity as an OCEAN member. The NIMBY talk at the meetings was spurred by the salient identity of neighborhood membership. Those most closely affected by the condominiums were more likely to be less OCEAN-oriented and more self- or neighborhood focused.

It may be easier to think of identity as drawing meaning *from* interactions with different groups as distinct discursive *sources* of identity, rather than simply attaching ourselves to certain targets.[40] For example, John McClellan and Stanley Deetz found that stakeholders engaged in collaborative action associated with a change movement at a university discursively arrived at different ways of defining their university—as a place of art, education, community, and business. Their different frames for understanding their organization constituted different ways of understanding themselves in relation to the university (i.e., I am an artist).[41]

Some identity sources are grounded in what we do, but powerful identity sources often come from how we live. A cultural/ethnic identity can be particularly relevant in the context of collaboration. Based on the cultural experiences and backgrounds of the collaborative members, participants *avow* their own identity and/or *ascribe* identity to other members. This communicative process of invoking membership categories in collaborative contexts is called "going categorical."[42] While going categorical can create an inclusivity with members who share the same or similar cultural background, not self-identifying to a particular cultural or ethnic identity category can be just as meaningful. Alexandra Murphy and Maria Dixon, scholars immersed in work on international and intercultural collaboration claim: "We cannot ignore the complex ways in which our social identities intersect, conflict, form and resist power relationships."[43] Indeed, unresolved cultural and identity differences increase the likelihood that an intercultural alliance will dissolve by 70 percent.[44] As Murphy and Dixon advise, "as the world continues to become flatter throughout the use of collaborative relationships across racial, national, and ethnic boundaries, the success of global partnerships depends on the partners' ability to manage their competing identity needs."[45]

 QUESTION: Do you hold a strong cultural, racial, religious, gender, or sexual identity that typically influences the way you think and act? What is important to you about that identity? How has this identity influenced your behavior in groups?

Identity Is Consequential

As collaborative members explore the problem domain, the sources for how they perceive themselves may become more or less important at any given time. Someone may have a confluence of several parts of their identity that create a passionate member (which is the case for many long-term members of nonprofits like Mothers Against Drunk Driving). Or identities may conflict in certain situations causing a person to privilege one identity over another.

Stakeholders interpret the identities of others and can view them in tension with their own.[46] For example, in a study of a waste-management collaboration, stakeholders identified strongly in one of four professional identities: scientist, regulator, engineer, or project manager. Each identity invoked different purposes for the collaboration—creating knowledge for discovery (scientist), checking knowledge against policy and regulation (regulator), applying knowledge to solve problems (engineer), and scheduling knowledge (project manager). As a result, much of the group's conflict swirled around finding agreement within those competing identities. Participants in collaborations must negotiate and navigate how they perceive themselves as well as others and the effects of those perceptions on their mission.[47] Table 3.2 illuminates some of the potential sources of identity that may become important during a collaborative process.

Navigating individual identity needs is thus a primary challenge for collaborative stakeholders and a monumental task for collaborative leaders. For example, a study of collaborations focused on human trafficking found that it was not uncommon for victims of human trafficking to be

Table 3.2   Potential sources of identity during a collaborative process

Common Organizational Sources of Identity	Common Individual Sources of Identity
• Group • Organization • Profession	• Cultural//national/ethnic • Racial • Religious • Gender • Sexuality

invited to participate in collaboration, yet rarely were they asked to contribute ideas about policy change.[48] Their identities as victims kept other members from seeing them as having important contributions in the policy context. Instead they were more likely to be asked to share their stories as ways of building knowledge as opposed to offering advice. The contributions of social workers and nonprofit activists were more frequently applied toward policy creation, omitting an important member's perspective from policy formation. Collaborative participants must be careful about ascribing identity in ways that constrain how other members contribute. Members may also have to do additional work to help their partners see them outside of their avowed identities.

> **QUESTION:** How might the identity of a nun representing Catholic Charities influence her interactions and decisions in an international collaboration focused on eliminating AIDS and HIV in poverty stricken cultures? How might her identity sources differ from a doctor working in the same partnership? Where might the values associated with their identities overlap? Where might they collide?

Spotlight scholar Natalie Nelson-Marsh has studied the way identity influences decision making in collaborative partnerships aimed at addressing the wicked problems associated with energy and power. Her work underscores the significant role identity plays in group outcomes.

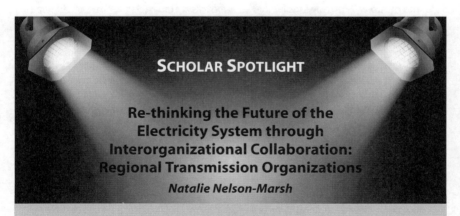

SCHOLAR SPOTLIGHT

Re-thinking the Future of the Electricity System through Interorganizational Collaboration: Regional Transmission Organizations
Natalie Nelson-Marsh

In interorganizational collaboration it quickly becomes clear that stakeholders do not have one, singular identity. What makes interorganizational collaboration complicated is not only which stakeholders at the table are defining the problem but also what identities stakeholders *privilege* that influences how the collaboration unfolds. For example, Regional Transmission Organizations (RTOs) are voluntary, stakeholder-driven organizations with flattened hierarchies tasked with a variety of responsibilities including planning the future of the electricity

(continued)

system and ensuring power system reliability. RTOs are predominantly responsible for the current and future state of the electricity system, including the integration of renewable energy sources such as wind and solar to create a more sustainable energy system for society.

Stakeholders who volunteer to participate in RTOs meet periodically to negotiate, recommend development, make decisions, and develop plans for action. These stakeholders work to rethink how to transform the electricity system so as to reliably "keep the lights on" while reducing our carbon footprint. Diverse stakeholder groups who participate may include transmission owners, alternative energy providers, public interest groups, marketers, etc., who share the responsibility for making decisions and plans to take renewable energy (wind, solar) from the environment and distribute it onto the electricity system in a such a way that ensures the electric system runs reliably and seamlessly even in times of crisis (natural or social disasters). Decisions made by stakeholders in RTOs shape billions of dollars in investments and shape the future of the energy system, impacting society and the environment in critical ways.

What stands out from a qualitative study of RTOs however, is that the same stakeholder will identify differently depending on issues. Participants described how stakeholders from the same group or same company would vote in contradictory ways. Participants described a common scenario in which two stakeholders from the same group are in the room voting on the same issue, but it could not be expected that they would orient to the issue or vote in the same way. As one participant noted, while stakeholders from the same company may be in the room, "one [stakeholder] has his transmission owner hat on. The other has their marketer hat on." In other words, the expectation that stakeholders from the same group will have a singular identity and interact in the same way could not be relied upon. Instead, stakeholders would first pay attention to what "hat" stakeholder's had on in order to know how to negotiate the issues at hand. Thus, decision making and planning in interorganizational collaboration becomes complicated in the sense that stakeholders have more than one salient identity invoked by the situation, the problem, and the other stakeholders in the room.

Interorganizational collaboration around the future of the electricity system then is not simply oriented around the problem that "we have the gift of lots of wind, but . . . how do you get the wind from here to there without it being too expensive for the wrong people." Instead, collaboration is a dynamic process of paying attention to the ways stakeholders identify, recognizing the saliency of multiple identities, negotiating those identities, and managing varying needs as they emerge.

The ability to manage the shifting identifications is important because it allows participants to keep differences affirmative and to preserve spaces of multiplicity. The complexity of identifications is a positive aspect of interorganizational collaboration. It lends to the development of both innovative decisions as well as decisions that, if involving various identifications, benefit all stakeholder groups and their complicated needs. Identities matter in interorganizational collaboration—not as something to overcome but as something to engage. As participants in the study noted "we are 17 years into it. We are making it up as we go."

QUESTION: What kinds of questions could stakeholders ask to engage each other? What can they do to understand different identifications and the value of incorporating those differences when making decisions?

Collective Identity

Successful collaboration is associated with creating a *collective* identity among stakeholders.[49] Collaborative stakeholders find themselves toggling between the two tension points of honoring the salient individual identity of their affiliated group (presumably one of the reasons they were invited) and identification with the collaborative group. Collective identity has been described as "an individual's cognitive, moral, and emotional connection with a broader community, category, practice or institution. It is a perception of shared status or relation."[50]

Our understanding of collective identity is grounded in communication. We agree with scholars who claim collective identity is shared among members, names a group, and gives the group meaning.[51] Collective identity in this view is socially constructed, "a linguistically produced object embodied in talk and other forms of text, rather than as a set of beliefs held in members' minds."[52] Collective identity can also become an informal mechanism for governing the group. Members feel the importance of the work they are doing and do not want to violate the norms of the group by doing something counter to the collaborative goals.[53]

Collective identity is constituted in myriad ways. For example, research emphasizes how our conversations and more formal communication texts contribute to stakeholders' forming a collective identity. Members develop ties to one another and the group by engaging in both assertive talk (talk that emphasizes stakeholders' individual views and positions) and cooperative talk (talk that emphasizes stakeholders' "similarity, mutual affiliations, and shared interests)."[54] Particularized membership ties are those that connect stakeholders to each other while generalized membership ties connect stakeholders to the larger problem domain. Both particularized and generalized membership ties foster collective identity.[55] Matt and his colleagues identified other tensions that exist when stakeholders hold individual and collective identities simultaneously.[56] Specifically, they named the overarching tension as "we versus me" (see the text box on pp. 58–60). The authors argued we cannot eliminate the tensions, but stakeholders can be skilled at navigating them.

Thinking about communication from a "we" stance rather than a "me" stance addresses some of the difficulty of constructing and navigating a collective identity. Part III of this book will elaborate on specific communication language and practices that foster a collective identity for stakeholders.

 QUESTION: What are some strategies the collaborative leaders of OCEAN could use to move members away from their respective neighborhood identities and to foster a collective identity as OCEAN members?

**Me versus We:
Changing the Way We Communicate in Collaborations**

Matthew Isbell, Laurie Lewis, and Matt Koschmann

Collaborations are increasingly commonplace in organizations across sectors and throughout the world. Businesses, nonprofits, governments, and citizen groups often find that collaboration is a necessary tool for involving many stakeholders in important problem solving. A key determinant in the success or failure of collaborations is communication. Collaboration can be a minefield of relational tension and individual needs for everyone involved. Collaborative participants must simultaneously communicate the needs of the organizations they are representing while considering the needs of others "at the table" and the goals of the collaboration overall. This balancing act can feel like an "unnatural act between unwilling participants." After talking to forty nonprofit professionals who have extensive interorganizational collaboration experience, we found that communicating a "me" versus "we" attitude can be a detriment to the collaborative endeavor.

It Is All About Me

For many, it is easier to take a me-orientation toward collaboration. This smash-and-grab type of communication highlights the needs of the individual and what each person can get out of the collaboration. When your individual organization is struggling, it is hard to share resources with others. "When you get down to the nitty gritty, it's 'what am I going to give up and what are you going to get'? My turf, and you don't get to touch that."

In the me-orientation members can ignore others and focus on steering the group toward the goals of one organization. In these instances, collaboration members may ignore the communal relationships created and bully others into a specific agenda. As one professional stated, "Instead of using communication to talk about [expectations] the nonprofit was just going to do it their way anyway."

A second key to me-oriented communication has to do with claiming credit. If a structure is not communicated early on among collaborative members about how successes and failures are credited, there is a greater potential for me-oriented members to control the communication about certain events. One participant discussed her experience this way, "One nonprofit basically took over the collaboration. They hired the staff to take over and they got credit for it."

So how do me-oriented members attempt to cope with issues that are not of personal interest or not in line with their own organization's perspective? Many use silence. While silence implies the absence of communication, it is not powerless. Communicative silence can be seen as powerful in several important ways. First, silence can be used to express dissent in the collaboration. Since one of the primary objectives of a collaboration is decision making, abstaining from a vote and denying consensus can derail the other members' efforts.

Obfuscation is a second form of silence. Some organizations send participants to the collaboration who have little knowledge and even less decision-making power. The goal of this tactic is to send a person to gather information and relay it to the home organization. Both dissent and obfuscation can delay or derail the accomplishment of goals.

Finally, me-oriented collaborative participants may just dissociate themselves from the collaboration if they don't get what they want. They evaluate what the demands are versus the outcomes and decide whether it is easier to dissociate than to work together. This lack of participative permanence can be problematic for both the organization withdrawing and those left in the collaboration. The withdrawing organization will not get a voice in a collaboration that may be addressing issues important to that organization. Dissociation strips unique voices and views that could enrich decision making from the collaboration.

We the People

To create the potential for success, participants can take a we-orientation to their collaborative communication. This orientation attempts to balance the stakes of all members and organizations and to create an environment with more equally distributed participation and power. From a we-orientation, the collaborative process is a group accomplishment wherein all members have equal stakes in the larger endeavor and take pride in achieving consensus.

For a we-orientation to be instilled in the collaboration, several relational and structural components need to be in place. Building a solid foundation of trust is essential. "You bring people together to talk about communication, collabora-tion, and talk about knowing each other, eventually this leads to a culture of trust." With high trust, collaborations can maintain a positive environment and work toward goal accomplishment.

A second component necessary for a we-orientation is buy in. Collaborations should focus on the types of people at the table and what their roles should be. Part of this challenge is deciding when to stop inviting additional participants or whether to close the boundaries of membership at all. Collaborations that are hesitant to draw firm lines around their membership or to define membership sometimes become a revolving door of attendance; each meeting becomes a completely new mix of people at the table. "We have got some of our agencies who send a different person to every meeting. If you get a lot of that, you start over at every meeting"

Structurally, we-oriented collaborations need to think about leadership and mission. The leader needs to guide the group while monitoring members' per-sonal interests so that they do not conflict with or supersede the collaboration's mission. "Issues of power need to be addressed. They need to be said out loud. Often times they are not." The leader needs to address how influence and power are acted upon in the collaboration to help bring everyone together. Likewise, by limiting the power of leaders and trying to attain neutral leadership, collabora-tive members can avoid potential accountability and leadership tensions.

Some collaborations use mission statements as a communicative tool to help manage individual accountability. By creating a statement to which all partici-pants pledge their support, the members have a document to justify their partic-ipation in the collaboration and a means of evaluating their work. The mission statement allows members to "share a vision" and to create a space in which members can operate as collaborative partners as well as representatives of out-side organizations.

By creating an organizational form that allows participants to accomplish goals greater than the scope of their individual organizations, the collaboration can become more than just a decision making body. It becomes a network of

(continued)

friends on whom to rely. The we-orientation communicates a collaborative process that forms alternative uses beyond the mission of the group. People realize that they are not alone and can draw on the support of others:

> "If I am collaborating with someone who already has an expertise and it is one I need, I don't need to go out and learn that expertise if I can join with her . . . . It is being able to appreciate other people's expertise and not having to recreate the world."[57]

Interdependence and Need

Whether collaboration is rooted in opportunity or in conflict, the people involved are interconnected.[58] Interdependence, as we defined in the last chapter, describes the ways in which stakeholders perceive they need each other and the group. Stakeholders "are more dependent [on one another] to the extent that they cannot unilaterally guarantee themselves good outcomes."[59] Rooted in systems thinking, interdependence highlights how all systems and subsystems in an environment affect and are affected by each other either indirectly or directly.[60] Interdependence is the nexus where threats and allies are forged and understood. Wicked problems thrust us into situations in which we are interdependently linked with others to work toward a reasonable solution.

In the collaborative context, stakeholders are interdependent for various reasons and perceive benefits (and/or needs) at multiple levels of involvement. Table 3.3 provides some examples from our research of how stakeholders may be connected to one another at the individual, professional, organizational, environmental, or societal (community) level.

Stakeholders are often linked together for more than one reason. If directly affected by the actions of the collaboration, some are motivated to protect their individual interests. Others may participate more reluctantly, as did the police chief Renee interviewed in a northwest collaboration focused on at-risk prevention. Although he was reticent to join the group, he eventually chose to participate to forge stronger partnerships with the college (particularized membership ties). Others might be interdependently linked to the collaboration via their professional goals—it benefits them professionally and politically to join the group. Of course, most stakeholders are linked more or less directly to the overarching vision or problem domain of the collaboration by caring about the outcomes for their environment or community (generalized membership ties).

> **QUESTION:** How does the level of involvement through which stakeholders become linked to one another and the problem domain influence their reasons for participating in a collaboration? How would you persuade the police chief in table 3.3 to join the collaboration? How might your pitch change if you were talking to the businessman?

Table 3.3   Interdependence and how stakeholders create advantage at different levels of involvement

Stakeholder	Reason for interdependence	Level of involvement in which they are linked together
Citizen from neighborhood affected by increased traffic in proposed development plan	Pollution from traffic will affect health and quality of life	Individual protection, community protection
Police chief of a small town participating in youth prevention collaboration	Going to collaborative meetings has improved relationship with the vice president of the community college	Organizational advantage
Local politician participates in youth education program	Aligning with the popular program will increase likelihood of reelection	Professional advantage
Audubon Society joins development task force associated with local wild lands	Being present at the meetings will keep the Audubon Society in the know and may give them the opportunity to stop harmful action	Environmental protection, organizational and legal advantage
Businessman funds and participates in projects on youth prevention	Businessman envisions youth as his future employees; wants his community to have lower unemployment and dropout rates	Indirect or long-term organizational advantage; more attractive community advantage

When interdependence is not mutually perceived, some relevant stakeholders may potentially be left out or marginalized in the collaboration process. For example, during the historic hurricane season of 2005, many cities created emergency management collaborations in the affected areas around New Orleans. In the city of Austin, collaborations were convened to gather parties involved in disaster management to create a consistent system of care. The more recognized organizational representatives (e.g., the American Red Cross, FEMA, United Way) dominated the collaborations, while some of the smaller churches and grassroots organizations struggled to get their voices heard and to be represented in the discussion. In many cases churches and grassroots organizations felt that they needed to be a part of the collaborative space because they believed their organizations were important components of aid delivery in the Austin area. They identified themselves as service providers—part of the process that would assist other organizations in service delivery in ways that exceeded the limits of any one organization's capabilities to serve. However, the level of participation and influence granted these groups was tied to whether or not *other* organizations recognized and acknowledged their interdependence within the problem domain.

The lesson we glean from this particular case is that interdependence is not always mutually agreed upon or understood. Some stakeholders, although they may perceive themselves as integral to the process, may have to make the case for why their collaborative peers need their involvement. Other stakeholders may be convinced to participate in collaborative processes because they have perceived needs tied to dyadic relationships between particular stakeholders. In other words, interdependence is a doubled-edged sword. On the one hand stakeholders are motivated to participate because they perceive a particular need, dependence, or advantage at the individual, professional, group, organizational, or societal level. On the other hand, those in the position to convene and invite stakeholders to the table must perceive a need, dependence, or advantage that the collaboration will gain by including the respective stakeholder. Indeed, this complex relationship is described as "inter-" dependent precisely because the relationship stakeholders have to the collaborative group dances in the space between.

 QUESTION: How is interdependence visible in OCEAN case? What would be some of the more important particularized and generalized interdependent relationships going into this meeting?

CONCLUSION

We began this chapter by claiming that *who* defines the problem may be more important than *what* the problem is. Stakeholder selection influences the ways in which the problem domain is understood and defined. It is essential to consider not only who is a stakeholder but also how they will influence collaborative interaction. Stakeholder identities play a particular role in determining the issues that are salient to collaborative members. Identity dictates how we act and how we interpret certain topics. Successful collaboration builds a collective identity that will foster commonality among stakeholders. The concept of interdependence addresses how our identities intersect with the problem domain and with fellow stakeholders to influence our motivations for participating. All of these constructs—stakeholders, identity, and interdependence—affect collaboration membership and interaction.

By describing some of the complexities of collaboration, we have provided the vocabulary and context that is needed to tackle the concepts discussed later in this book. Part II addresses the ethics of collaboration. It will return to the topic of identity when exploring the concepts of marginalization, diversity, power, and leadership.

CHAPTER TAKE-AWAYS

▶ Understand what is meant by stakeholder and the possibilities and limitations regarding criteria for considering stakeholder participation

▶ Recognize paradoxes that stakeholders must navigate

▶ Comprehend identity, its influence on collaboration, and how it is rooted in communication

▶ Identify various salient identities for stakeholders

▶ Understand collective identity and its role in collaboration

▶ Distinguish how interdependence connects stakeholders at various need and involvement levels

ENDNOTES

[1] R. Edward Freeman, *Strategic Management: A Stakeholder Approach* (Cambridge, UK/New York: Cambridge University Press, 2010).

[2] Donna J. Wood and Barbara Gray, "Toward a Comprehensive Theory of Collaboration," *The Journal of Applied Behavioral Science* 27, no. 2 (June 1, 1991): 139–62, doi:10.1177/0021886391272001.

[3] Ibid.

[4] R. Edward Freeman et al., *Stakeholder Theory: The State of the Art* (Cambridge, UK/New York: Cambridge University Press, 2010).

[5] R. Edward Freeman, "The Politics of Stakeholder Theory: Some Future Directions," *Business Ethics Quarterly* 4, no. 04 (October 1994): 409–21, doi:10.2307/3857340.

[6] Freeman et al., *Stakeholder Theory*.

[7] Matthew A. Koschmann and Jared Kopczynski, "Stakeholder Theory," in *International Encyclopedia of Organizational Communication*, ed. Craig Scott and Laurie Lewis (Hoboken, NJ: Wiley, 2017).

[8] Bidhan L. Parmar et al., "Stakeholder Theory: The State of the Art," *The Academy of Management Annals* 4, no. 1 (January 1, 2010): 403–45, doi:10.1080/19416520.2010.495581.

[9] Freeman, "The Politics of Stakeholder Theory."

[10] Barbara Gray, *Collaborating: Finding Common Ground for Multiparty Problems* (San Francisco: Jossey-Bass, 1989).

[11] Jonathan Lange, "Environmental Collaboration and Constituency Communication," in *Group Communication in Context: Studies of Bona Fide Groups*, ed. Larry R. Frey (Mahwah, NJ: Lawrence Erlbaum, 2003), 209–34, p. 218.

[12] Cynthia Hardy and Nelson Phillips, "Strategies of Engagement: Lessons from the Critical Examination of Collaboration and Conflict in an Interorganizational Domain," *Organization Science* 9, no. 2 (April 1, 1998): 217–30, doi:10.1287/orsc.9.2, p. 217.

[13] Ibid., p. 225.

[14] Ibid., p. 225.

[15] Ibid., p. 218.

[16] Koschmann and Kopczynski, "Stakeholder Theory."

[17] Adapted from Ronald K. Mitchell, Bradley R. Agle, and Donna J. Wood, "Toward a Theory of Stakeholder Identification and Salience: Defining the Principle of Who and What Really Counts," *Academy of Management Review* 22, no. 4 (October 1, 1997): 853–86, doi:10.5465/AMR.1997.9711022105.

[18] Cynthia Stohl and George Cheney, "Participatory Processes/Paradoxical Practices: Communication and the Dilemmas of Organizational Democracy," *Management Communication Quarterly* 14, no. 3 (February 1, 2001): 349–407, doi:10.1177/0893318901143001.

[19] Kenwyn K. Smith and David N. Berg, *Paradoxes of Group Life: Understanding Conflict, Paralysis, and Movement in Group Dynamics* (San Francisco: Jossey-Bass, 1997).

[20] Stohl and Cheney, "Participatory Processes/Paradoxical Practices," p. 352.

[21] Kenneth E. Goodpaster, "Business Ethics and Stakeholder Analysis," *Business Ethics Quarterly* 1, no. 1 (January 1991): 53–73, doi:10.2307/3857592.

[22] Daniel E. Palmer, Ed., *Handbook of Research on Business Ethics and Corporate Responsibilities* (Hershey, PA: IGI Global, 2015).

[23] Adapted from Jonathan Lange, "Exploring Paradox in Environmental Collaborations," in *Across the Great Divide: Explorations in Collaborative Conservation and the American West*, 2nd ed., ed. Philip Brick, Donald Snow, and Sarah F. Bates (Washington, DC: Island Press, 2000), 200–209.

[24] Barbera Czarniawska-Joerges, "Narratives of Individual and Organizational Identity," in *Communication Yearbook 17*, ed. Stanley Deetz (Thousand Oaks, CA: Sage, 1994), 193–221.

[25] Craig R. Scott, Steven R. Corman, and George Cheney, "Development of a Structurational Model of Identification in the Organization," *Communication Theory* 8, no. 3 (August 1, 1998): 298–336, doi:10.1111/j.1468-2885.1998.tb00223.x.

[26] Kasey L. Walker and Cynthia Stohl, "Communicating in a Collaborating Group: A Longitudinal Network Analysis," *Communication Monographs* 79, no. 4 (December 1, 2012): 448–74, doi:10.1080/03637751.2012.723810.

[27] Henri Tajfel, Ed., *Social Identity and Intergroup Relations*, Reissue ed. (Cambridge, UK/New York: Cambridge University Press, 2010); Michael A. Hogg and Scott A. Reid, "Social Identity, Self-Categorization, and the Communication of Group Norms," *Communication Theory* 16, no. 1 (February 1, 2006): 7–30, doi:10.1111/j.1468-2885.2006.00003.x.

[28] Henri Tajfel and John Turner, "An Integrative Theory of Intergroup Conflict," in *The Social Psychology of Intergroup Relations*, ed. William Austin and Stephen Worchel (Monterey, CA: Brooks/Cole, 1979), 33–47; Dominic Abrams and Michael A. Hogg, *Social Identifications: A Social Psychology of Intergroup Relations and Group Processes*, Reprint ed. (Abingdon-on-Thames, UK/New York: Routledge, 1990).

[29] Craig R. Scott, "Identification with Multiple Targets in a Geographically Dispersed Organization," *Management Communication Quarterly* 10, no. 4 (May 1, 1997): 491–522, doi:10.1177/0893318997104004; Henri Tajfel and John C. Turner, "The Social Identity Theory of Intergroup Behavior," in *Political Psychology: Key Readings*, ed. J. T. Jost and J. Sidanius, Key Readings in Social Psychology. (New York: Psychology Press, 2004), 276–93.

[30] Michael G. Pratt, "To Be or Not to Be?: Central Questions in Organizational Identification," in *Identity in Organizations: Building Theory Through Conversations*, ed. David Whetten and Paul Godfrey (Thousand Oaks CA: Sage Publications, Inc., 1998), 171–208, http://sk.sagepub.com/books/identity-in-organizations/n6.xml

[31] Rolf Van Dick, "Identification in Organizational Contexts: Linking Theory and Research from Social and Organizational Psychology," *International Journal of Management Reviews* 3, no. 4 (December 1, 2001): 265–83, doi:10.1111/1468-2370.00068.

[32] Michael A. Hogg and Deborah I. Terry, "Social Identity and Self-Categorization Processes in Organizational Contexts," *Academy of Management Review* 25, no. 1 (January 1, 2000): 121–40, doi:10.5465/AMR.2000.2791606.

[33] Sarah J. Tracy and Angela Trethewey, "Fracturing the Real-Self↔Fake-Self Dichotomy: Moving Toward 'Crystallized' Organizational Discourses and Identities," *Communication Theory* 15, no. 2 (May 1, 2005): 168–95, doi:10.1111/j.1468-2885.2005.tb00331.x.

[34] Scott, Corman, and Cheney, "Development of a Structurational Model of Identification in the Organization"; Timothy Kuhn and Natalie Nelson, "Reengineering Identity: A Case Study of Multiplicity and Duality in Organizational Identification," *Management Communication Quarterly* 16, no. 1 (August 1, 2002): 5–38, doi:10.1177/0893318902161001.

[35] George Cheney, "On the Various and Changing Meanings of Organizational Membership: A Field Study of Organizational Identification," *Communication Monographs* 50, no. 4 (December 1, 1983): 342–62, doi:10.1080/03637758309390174.

36 John C. Lammers, Yannick L. Atouba, and Elizabeth J. Carlson, "Which Identities Matter? A Mixed-Method Study of Group, Organizational, and Professional Identities and Their Relationship to Burnout," *Management Communication Quarterly* 27, no. 4 (November 1, 2013): 503–36, doi:10.1177/0893318913498824.

37 Nic Beech and Chris Huxham, "Cycles of Identity Formation in Interorganizational Collaborations," *International Studies of Management & Organization* 33, no. 3 (October 1, 2003): 28–52, doi:10.1080/00208825.2003.11043686.

38 Cynthia Hardy, Thomas B. Lawrence, and Nelson Phillips, "Talking Action: Conversations, Narrative and Action in Interorganizational Collaboration," in *Discourse and Organizations*, ed. David Grant, Tom Keenoy, and Cliff Oswick (London: Sage, 1998), 65–83, p. 72.

39 Laurie Lewis, "Collaborative Interaction: Review of Communication Scholarship and a Research Agenda," in *Communication Yearbook 30*, ed. C. Beck (Thousand Oaks, CA: Sage, 2006), 197–247.

40 Lammers, Atouba, and Carlson, "Which Identities Matter?"; in Jayne M. Morgan et al., "Tales from the Fields: Sources of Employee Identification in Agribusiness," *Management Communication Quarterly* 17, no. 3 (February 1, 2004): 360–95, doi:10.1177/0893318903258169.

41 John McClellan and Stanley Deetz, "A Politically Attentive Discursive Analysis of Collaborative Talk," in *Discourse Perspectives on Organizational Communication*, ed. J. Aritz and R. Walker (Madison, NJ: Fairleigh Dickenson University Press Communication Series, 2012), 33–58.

42 Elizabeth Stokoe, "Gender, Conversation Analysis, and the Anatomy of Membership Categorization Practices," *Social and Personality Psychology Compass* 4, no. 7 (July 1, 2010): 428–38, doi:10.1111/j.1751-9004.2010.00261.x; Alan Hansen and Trudy Milburn, "Enacting Cultural Identities in Conversation: Managing Collaboration in Two Nonprofit Organizations," *Journal of International and Intercultural Communication* 8, no. 3 (July 3, 2015): 224–36, doi:10.1080/17513057.2015.1057906.

43 Alexandra G. Murphy and Maria A. Dixon, "Discourse, Identity, and Power in International Nonprofit Collaborations," *Management Communication Quarterly* 26, no. 1 (February 1, 2012): 166–72, doi:10.1177/0893318911424374, p. 170.

44 Saleema Kauser, "Alliance Relationship Dynamics: Conflict, Structure and Control," *Journal of Euromarketing* 16, no. 3 (June 19, 2007): 5–25, doi:10.1300/J037v16n03_02.

45 Murphy and Dixon, "Discourse, Identity, and Power in International Nonprofit Collaborations," p. 170.

46 Laurie Lewis, Matthew G. Isbell, and Matt Koschmann, "Collaborative Tensions: Practitioners' Experiences of Interorganizational Relationships," *Communication Monographs* 77, no. 4 (December 1, 2010): 460–79, doi:10.1080/03637751.2010.523605; Matthew A. Koschmann, "The Communicative Constitution of Collective Identity in Interorganizational Collaboration," *Management Communication Quarterly* 27, no. 1 (February 1, 2013): 61–89, doi:10.1177/0893318912449314.

47 Joshua B. Barbour and Eric P. James, "Collaboration for Compliance: Identity Tensions in the Interorganizational and Interdisciplinary Regulation of a Toxic Waste Storage Facility," *Journal of Applied Communication Research* 43, no. 4 (October 2, 2015): 363–84, doi:10.1080/00909882.2015.1083601.

48 Kirsten Foot, *Collaborating against Human Trafficking: Cross-Sector Challenges and Practices* (Lanham, NJ: Rowman & Littlefield, 2015).

49 Ibid.

50 Francesca Polletta and James M. Jasper, "Collective Identity and Social Movements," *Annual Review of Sociology* 27 (2001): 283–305. p. 285.

51 Cynthia Hardy, Thomas B. Lawrence, and David Grant, "Discourse and Collaboration: The Role of Conversations and Collective Identity," *Academy of Management Review* 30, no. 1 (January 1, 2005): 58–77, doi:10.5465/AMR.2005.15281426, p. 62.

52 Ibid., p. 62.

53 James R. Barker, "Tightening the Iron Cage: Concertive Control in Self-Managing Teams," *Administrative Science Quarterly* 38, no. 3 (1993): 408–37, doi:10.2307/2393374.

[54] Hardy, Lawrence, and Grant, "Discourse and Collaboration."

[55] Ibid.

[56] Lewis, Isbell, and Koschmann, "Collaborative Tensions."

[57] Adapted with permission from the National Communication Association. All rights reserved.

[58] Barbara Gray and Jill Purdy, "Conflict in Cross-Sector Partnerships," in *Social Partnerships and Responsible Business: A Research Handbook*, ed. M. May Seitanidi and Andrew Crane (Abingdon-on-Thames, UK /New York: Routledge, 2014), 205–26.

[59] Andrea B. Hollingshead, "Cognitive Interdependence and Convergent Expectations in Transactive Memory," *Journal of Personality and Social Psychology* 81, no. 6 (2001): 1080–89, doi:10.1037/0022-3514.81.6, p. 1080.

[60] Edward Mabry, "The Systems Metaphor in Group Communication," in *The Handbook of Group Communication Theory and Research*, ed. Lawrence R. Frey, Dennis Gouran, and Marshall Scott Poole (Thousand Oaks, CA: Sage, 1999), 71–91.

PART II
A Collaborative Ethic

Part II develops the underlying assumptions that guide our approach to communication in collaboration. In particular, we build a collaborative ethic, that takes into account (a) the ethical impact of decisions made in interorganizational collaboration, (b) the integral concept of diversity, (c) a commitment to sharing power, and (d) a principled approach to leading. Together these concepts create the foundation for how we understand collaboration and how we believe communication should proceed in interorganizational collaboration. They comprise the four cornerstones of the collaborative ethic on which the remainder of this book rests.

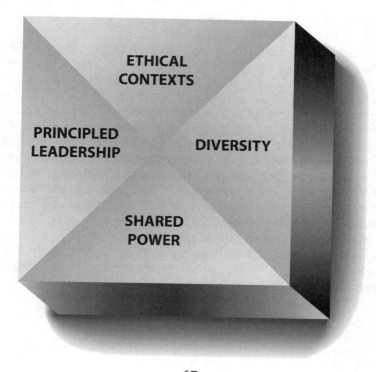

ETHICAL CONTEXTS

PRINCIPLED LEADERSHIP

DIVERSITY

SHARED POWER

A collaborative ethic is the foundation for making decisions on behalf of others. Key to the successful practice of collaboration is the commitment stakeholders must have to principles of sharing power and building a vision by integrating one another's interests. By placing ethics at the foundation of collaborative communication, we illuminate a different set of skills needed to lead and participate as opposed to those grounded in competitive, strategic, and win-lose paradigms.

Chapter 4 acknowledges the political and social contexts in which collaborative decision making often takes place. *Ethical Contexts* is the first cornerstone of the collaborative ethic. In this macrosphere, the discussion and actions of private citizens (collaborating stakeholders) affect the public and have material consequences for participating and nonparticipating stakeholders. Chapter 4 also examines what we call the microsphere—democratic or ethical communication—and develops the link between participative processes and ethical decisions. Acknowledgment of the larger ethical context in which collaboration operates highlights the responsibility inherent in the process. Building on the works of philosopher Jürgen Habermas, we propose that ethical communication in the group decision-making context (microsphere) fosters accountability to stakeholders. By turning our attention to the ethical contexts in which interorganizational collaboration takes place, we are better able to understand the types of communication behaviors and structures we will need to make fair decisions within those contexts.

Diversity is the second cornerstone of the collaborative ethic. Chapter 5 explores what counts as diversity and why it is so essential to generating innovative and just solutions; it challenges the reader to think about diversity as the perspective that is missing from the problem-solving context. Diversity offers many potential benefits for innovation and idea generation in collaborative groups, and it is also key to addressing the needs of marginalized stakeholders. Diversity can create legitimacy in collaborative decision making by including those who typically have little voice when it comes to solving wicked problems. The chapter illuminates the benefits and challenges associated with diversity in interorganizational contexts.

After fleshing out the ways in which power is relational, chapter 6 introduces different mechanisms for accessing power and control in collaborative groups. *(Shared) Power* introduces how ideological power, in the forms of hegemony and systematic distortion, can be embedded in collaborative structures. It distinguishes the concept of equality from parity and warns against the discursive closure strategies that shut down conversations and distort power. Shared power is the third cornerstone of the collaborative ethic, and the chapter identifies some strategies and tactics for fostering egalitarian values.

Chapter 7 grapples with *Principled Leadership*, the fourth cornerstone of the collaborative ethic. It identifies the ways in which egalitarian and transparent practices can cultivate a collaborative culture that both allows for a diversity of values as well as promotes unified values. Principled leadership incorporates all the cornerstone values by maintaining vigilant attention to ethical contexts, seeking diversity in participation, and striving to foster shared power in decision making. Part II sets the cornerstones for the next section, which develops the communication skills and habits of ethical collaboration.

4

Ethical Contexts

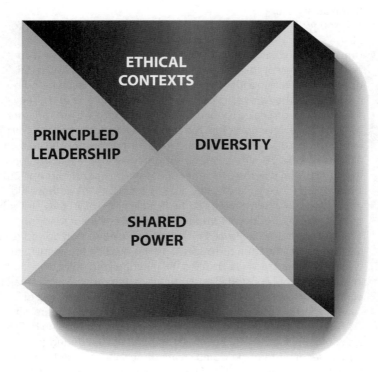

ETHICAL
CONTEXTS

PRINCIPLED
LEADERSHIP

DIVERSITY

SHARED
POWER

From The Darkness

Matt: So I have heard several members talk about the "dark ages" of OCEAN. As the former president, can you tell me a little more about what this time period was all about?

(Russ laughs for a few moments)

Russ: Wow, yeah the dark ages, now that was an interesting era in our history. What can I say? I guess there were a select few of us who came to understand what OCEAN could be well before the entire group came to that same realization.

Matt: What do you mean, "What OCEAN could be"?

Russ: You have to understand that OCEAN was brought about by a city dictate to have neighborhood representation at city council meetings. So all the Austin neighborhoods were grouped into larger bundles, which is how all of the OCEAN neighborhoods came under this collaborative umbrella. The OCEAN neighborhoods were some of the hottest properties for redevelopment. So there was good reason to have representation at city council.

Matt: This sounds like a good thing, so where do the dark ages come into play?

Russ: I am getting to that. See what happened was that OCEAN was supposed to represent the people of these neighborhoods. And it did, does still. But within a lot of our neighborhoods are developers who own land. So they are technically also represented by OCEAN. They "live" here so to speak. So when OCEAN was first being put together, some of these developers realized that if they could control the collaboration, they could control the voice of the entire East Austin area on all sorts of topics, but most importantly on development. Enter John to OCEAN. John was the developer of those ugly apartments on 12th street. Want to see what the dark ages looked like, look at those hideous things. John went to one of the first elections of OCEAN and volunteered to be president. Turnout was low that day. Not many of us even knew what OCEAN was. I mean, come on, how often do you read local announcements in the paper? So John became president, and we entered the dark ages. He filled the meeting with other developers and routinely only posted meeting times to that group. Several major construction projects were "okayed" by OCEAN before the rest of us caught wind of what was going on and started engaging more with OCEAN. Even then, we had to wait for John's term to come up before we could replace him. That is when I stepped up. But during the remainder of his term, he would create these subcommittees and only listen to what they said. And of course you can guess who was on those committees. It was like 99.9% of the neighborhood voice was being controlled by this group of developers who didn't have the interests of the entire group in mind. It still bugs me every time I drive up 12th and see some of those projects OCEAN "approved."

—Adapted from Matt's unpublished interview transcripts

As we strive to find solutions for problems that cross geographic, cultural, religious, political, and economic boundaries, we will have to consider the moral dilemmas inherent in the experience. By foregrounding ethics in collaboration, we direct our attention to the people affected by our decisions. Whose voices are muted or marginalized? Who has power, and how does it influence outcomes? Who will benefit and at what cost? These questions cannot be answered from without; they must be negotiated within—through the interaction of stakeholders. Everything that we propose in the coming chapters of this book is based on the assumption that we engage in *ethical collaboration*. In this chapter, we look at the macro and micro levels of the ethical contexts in which collaboration takes place—the first cornerstone of the ethical foundation on which ethical collaboration is built.

Ethics are defined as the moral standards for a given group.[1] In his article entitled "The Tragedy of the Commons," Garrett Hardin claimed that technical solutions are insufficient to solve [wicked] problems. He used the allegory of a rancher who adds an animal to his herd that grazes on a pasture open to all. The rancher singularly benefits from increasing his herd, yet the costs to overgrazing the grasslands are shared by all who have a claim to the commons. Technical solutions are not suitable for some problems because they are devoid of human values and morality. Yet he also pointed out that in our efforts to "maximize good per person," it would be problematic to determine what is good: "To one person it is wilderness, to another it is ski lodges for thousands. To one it is estuaries to nourish ducks for hunters to shoot; to another it is factory lands."[2] "The Tragedy of the Commons" allegory illuminates inherent tensions of the human experience: individual versus community rights, freedom versus governance, and the accompanying values that constitute our experience such as ownership, responsibility, and human rights. These are by no means insignificant, and collaboration is at the crux of making decisions that impact and are impacted by these tensions and values.

As some scholars have argued, "collaboration is consistent with a broader set of communitarian values."[3] Collaborating at its heart should be an ethical activity because: (a) stakeholders make decisions that have social and political consequences beyond the collaborative group;[4] (b) ethical communication and processes are instrumental in balancing power among stakeholders; and (c) perhaps most significantly, attending to the ethical impact of our interactions and striving to create ethical practices and processes are the best means of cultivating trust from the community and our partners at the table.

This chapter begins with a brief history of social corporate responsibility to review the concept of stakeholders as a part of an ethical response to contemporary organizational practices and impacts on society. We next organize our discussion of ethics by considering the macro context in which collaboration takes place, focusing specifically on political and social accountability. We then move our lens to the micro level of collaboration, examining the structures of the collaborative group and the communication processes and practices that constitute ethical communication. The chapter concludes with a consideration of the functional and instrumental reasons for developing a collaborative ethic—including the integral role of trust.

Collaboration as the Ethical Response to Social Corporate Responsibility

No doubt the significance of what it means to be a stakeholder grew out of and was influenced by Hardin and writers like Rachel Carson, whose damning book *Silent Spring* illuminated the environmental and health crises that resulted from corporate indifference.[5] Stakeholder accountability can be traced to the expansive discourse of corporate social responsibility (CSR), which is defined as organizations that "strive to make a profit, obey the law, be ethical, and be a good corporate citizen."[6] The connection between CSR and stakeholders is well documented. Stakeholder personalizes what is an abstract notion of "social" in the definition of CSR. Stakeholders make employees, suppliers, dealers, local community members, government agencies and any other interested person or group a party to whom organizations have an ethical obligation. Naming stakeholders as relevant signifies an important linguistic turn in CSR that has ethical repercussions.[7] The language highlights the role of significant groups that might not have been included in the past. Additionally, the act of identifying *specific* stakeholders itself is an ethical act—organizations considering to whom they must be accountable. We consider the naming of stakeholders as having particular ethical importance in the macro context of collaboration.

> **QUESTION:** How does using the term "stakeholders" articulate the social in corporate social responsibility? Think back to chapter 3 and how we identify stakeholders. Pick one of your favorite organizations and list their stakeholders. Why did you pick them? Can you think of a stakeholder you missed? If so, think about why you missed that stakeholder and what might be unaccounted for if that stakeholder was also missed by your organization.

The Macro and Micro Contexts of Ethics

Ethical contexts may be conceptualized in different ways. We will focus on two that frame ethics in collaboration—the public sphere and the ideal speech situation.[8] The first frame for thinking about ethics refers to the larger (macro) social and political milieu in which the collaboration takes place. It draws our attention to accountability and the fragile line between public and private. The second frame for conceptualizing ethics describes the specific (micro) communication context, the ideal communication situation that draws our attention to interaction and discursive practices. The two are interrelated, as achieving ethical decisions in the larger social and political milieu depends on how those decisions were achieved in specific communication contexts. Likewise, the larger public sphere influences the specific communication context and the people involved in the ethical process.

Figure 4.1   Ethical contexts

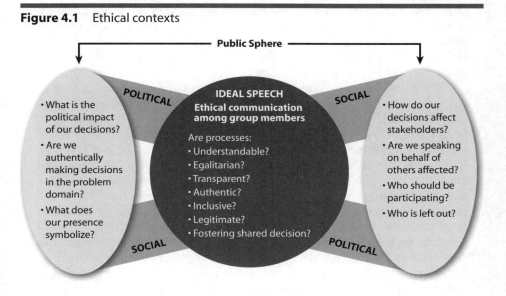

The Macro Ethical Context: Enacting the Public Sphere

In the public sphere, ordinary citizens (as opposed to elected lawmakers) come together to debate policy, law, and other items of interest to society. Critical theorist and philosopher, Jürgen Habermas perhaps best articulated the relationship between the larger milieu and ethical communication. Habermas argued that important societal decisions take place in a public sphere.[9] In this conception, the public sphere is not so much a physical location as it is a *communicative space* that is produced in the act of specific talk and decision making around public issues. Habermas claimed, "a portion of the public sphere comes into being in every conversation in which private individuals assemble to form a public body."[10] When private individuals form a public body that makes decisions, stakeholders have an ethical responsibility to the public body affected by the decisions.

Consider how the public sphere has evolved over the last several decades. The emergence of socially mediated dialogue expands the reach of public debate. The ubiquity of digital connection has despatialized and made asynchronous the traditional notions of the public sphere. Now someone's Twitter post, Facebook group, or Kickstarter campaign can be seen as a creation and promotion of the public sphere if the communication centers around implications regarding the public good. Technology brings forth omnidirectional communication that may have been traditionally harder to enact in in-person public settings. For instance, a town hall meeting may only allow for the arguments of a few people to be heard— those who (a) attend the meeting and (b) are granted the time to make a statement. Compare that to a virtual town hall forum where ideas can be debated and discussed with easier access and less temporal restrictions. Debate in these public spheres can cross space and time, giving voice to more stakeholders in the community.

The public sphere manifests in the organic and emergent nature of collaboration. Decisions made in these forums have an impact at local, state, national, and international levels; issues range from education to health care to housing to the environment to numerous other possibilities. Framing collaborative decision-making as taking place in the public sphere illuminates the accountability private stakeholders have for those who constitute the "publics" affected by their decisions. Questions of accountability are raised when conversations in the public sphere have social and political consequences. From a social perspective, collaborative members must consider: how do decisions affect the publics we represent? Are we speaking on behalf of affected others? Who should be participating in this conversation? Who is left out? From a political perspective, members must consider: what does our presence publicly symbolize? Are we authentically making decisions within the problem domain, or are we a front group to deflect pressure off of other stakeholders? What is the political impact of our decisions? Will they undermine legislation?

The impact of decision making in the public sphere can be seen in the case of the Quincy Library Group.[11] The now legendary collaboration (set in the beautiful Sierra Nevada region of California) began as conversation in the local library among environmental advocates, timber industry representatives, and locals concerned about the economic viability of their dying logging town in the face of strict environmental restrictions on harvesting timber in the 1990s. The participants' conversations eventually led to a comprehensive forest management plan—a keen example of enacting the public sphere through collaborative interaction. Although the plan appeared to be a win-win for *local* stakeholders, it was eventually fought in the court system because the local plan had the potential to unravel years of hard fought *national* forest regulation. The local plan could set a precedent that would enable less benevolent stakeholders in other regions of the US to bypass national forest management laws. Although the outcomes of this case remain tangled in complicated legislative battles, it remains a poignant example of how the public sphere manifests itself in collaborative conversation.

In another case, Renee studied a statewide network of collaborative partnerships dedicated to early childcare and education.[12] In one of the most consequential discussions she observed, stakeholders in a large metropolitan area argued over whether preschool education should be considered a *privilege*—meaning those who could afford it would pay for it—or a *right*—meaning it should be made free to the public. This decision had tremendous consequences for a community and society. The immediate community impact could be economic because preschool education is expensive. Many families who cannot afford it forgo preschool, often delaying parents' return to the workforce.[13] If preschool were offered as a right, families at all income levels would be able to participate. At the societal level, studies have established that children who participate in preschool education show decreased incarceration levels and higher literacy rates.[14] Therefore, a society that offered preschool as an educational right would likely benefit from this investment. In this case, the collaboration composed of voluntary members from private, nonprofit, and government agencies was to advise the district school board on a decision as to whether, and what, to charge for preschool education. The outcomes of collaborative decisions such as this have tremendous ethical consequences in the social and political arena, especially for marginalized populations of families, such as those with low incomes or those for whom English is a second language.

QUESTION: What are some of the ethical issues illuminated in the OCEAN interview that opens this chapter? What are some of the ethical consequences that resulted from the "dark ages?"

Accounting for Marginalized Stakeholders. Marginalized stakeholders are especially at the mercy of decisions made in the public sphere and are part of the macro ethical context that stakeholders must take into account. Marginalization can be conceptualized in various ways. Environmental scholarship describes three types of inequalities that compose a model of injustice: lack of recognition, procedural injustice, and distributive injustice.[15] Recognition is understood as "respect afforded to diverse ways of seeing or knowing."[16] The lack of recognition is evident in biases toward English-only communication and failures to acknowledge the burdens experienced by people of different colors or classes. Procedural injustice refers to an absence of meaningful representation, participation, authority, and funding relative to that afforded to other stakeholders in the decision-making process. Distributive injustice describes the economic, environmental, or political inequality experienced by marginalized stake-holders regarding the distribution of the burdens and benefits of the deci-sion-making process. Exclusion of marginalized stakeholders in decision making (especially when the stakeholders have legitimate reasons for being at the table and potentially urgent claims in the problem domain) can fos-ter distrust in the community.[17]

An example that reinforces the ethical importance of including mar-ginalized stakeholders in collaboration took place in 2012. A coalition developed around the proposed annexation and use of Oregon wild lands on West Hayden Island in Portland, Oregon. The Port of Portland owns and operates the deep-water ports of Portland as well as the international air-port. Stakeholders in this coalition included the Port, the mayor's office, and the Audubon society—who was deeply concerned with the effects development would have on bird life in the region. Other stakeholders included recreational-minded organizations and a neighborhood associa-tion. The involved neighborhood—the largest manufactured-home com-munity in the state of Oregon—described themselves as "elderly and low income, many of whom are in poor health."[18] In ongoing meetings, the Hayden Island Manufactured Home Community protested the annexation and development of West Hayden Island, as the Port of Portland's own documents described a projected increase of daily truck traffic over the next 25 years from 3,823 to 11,715 vehicles.[19] Writing on behalf of the Audubon Society of Portland and the Hayden Island Manufactured Home Community, Bob Sallinger and Donna Murphy claimed trucks would pass the manufactured home community on average every 2.8 minutes. There was significant uncertainty regarding the health effects from diesel pollu-tion caused by the vehicles and the commercial development of the land.[20] In other words, the development of West Hayden Island would dispropor-tionately affect the low-income community of people that lived nearby, potentially exposing them to harmful pollutants and excessive noise. Stakeholders collaborated on this issue for several years before the Port announced its plans to table the project.

It is not uncommon for those with the least resources to be the most negatively affected by social and environmental decisions. Therefore, col-laboration stakeholders must be mindful of the ethical contexts in which they make decisions. Part of this context includes the essential questions of *who gets to participate* and *how do participants gain access to the negotiating table?* Consider what might have been the outcome regarding the develop-ment of Hayden Island if the voices representing Hayden Island residents and the environment were not considered. Even with the seemingly appro-priate stakeholders at the table, collaboration can be misappropriated to rubber stamp decisions that were not arrived at through ethical processes.[21] We will return to the importance of including the perspectives of stakehold-ers who have been typically left out or marginalized in community decision making when we discuss diversity in the next chapter. For now, it is important that we recognize the role marginalized stakeholders play as we consider the moral obligations of collaboration in the public sphere.

 QUESTION: Describe how the citizens living in OCEAN neighborhoods were marginalized by recognition, procedural injustice, and distributive injustice? What were the material consequences of their marginalization?

Be Aware of Collaboration and "Co-operation." Activists are often skeptical of interorganizational collaboration that may be motivated and overtaken by the powerful interests of for-profit stakeholders—afraid that the collaborative process will be co-opted by them, especially since most collaborating stakeholders are not elected to their decision-making positions. The word "co-opt" means to use or take control of something for your own purposes.[22] In such cases, stakeholders arrive at decisions that appear to have been made legitimately through collaborative and cooperative processes. However, there are myriad reasons why imbalances of power occur in the collaborative process, membership, and communication structures. A specific example of this argument is laid out in the text box below. Water activist Maude Barlow and journalist Meera Karunananthan detail their skepticism regarding collaborative partnerships.[23] They claim the standards of sustainability targets for water cannot be trusted because they are primarily generated by multinational organizations that prioritize their own interests.

We Don't Need "Co-operation"—We Need Water Justice[24]

Maude Barlow and Meera Karunananthan

The human right to water has long been a rallying call in our community struggles against the accumulation of wealth through the dispossession of collective rights to water. When thousands took to the streets in Peru in February 2012 in opposition to big foreign mining projects, they did so under the banner of water as a human right in a march dubbed "Gran Marcha Nacional por el Agua" or Great National March for Water. Groups in Europe are calling for an end to EU austerity measures forcing governments to privatize water and sanitation services through a campaign for the implementation of the human right to water. The villagers of Plachimada, India, have also tried to exercise the right to water in their protests of Coca-Cola, alleging that the company is over-exploiting scarce groundwater resources in the area.

Yet over the past few decades, regional development banks, international financial institutions (IFIs), and trade deals have granted corporations the upper hand in these conflicts. In times of financial crisis, IFIs have used loan conditionalities to pry open markets for big multinational corporations demanding massive returns for their investments in basic services. In times of water scarcity, multinational corporations have pushed aggressively for mechanisms that have secured

(continued)

their access to limited water supplies. These strategies have been imposed on governments in the way of Structural Adjustment Programs, investment protection laws, and trade dispute settlement mechanisms that have protected the rights of corporations by giving them the tools to sue governments. They have tied the hands of governments seeking to implement environmentally friendly and socially responsible policies.

In addition, big business has had increasing access to decision making on water issues at the international level through high-level public-private bodies such as the CEO Water Mandate at the UN, the Water Resources Group headed by Nestlé Chair Peter Brabeck, and the World Water Council, which I have long been arguing was created at the behest of multinational water corporations.

Given this context, water justice advocates are naturally suspicious when corporations line up to support "water co-operation" at the United Nations. Especially given the press release issued by Spanish multinational water corporation Agbar, declaring its commitment to the UN Year of Water Co-operation while in the midst of a fierce battle in Barcelona, where it is being accused by nongovernmental organizations, municipalities, and other private sector operators of operating illegally.

For the UN to allow for the inclusion of corporations under the guise of "co-operation" would be a failure to acknowledge the struggles for public control over water that are growing in number around the world. We do not need our policy makers to continue to co-operate with corporations that have generated the global water crisis and cannot put our faith in sustainability targets developed out of a system captured by multinationals. We need democratic and transparent water governance models based on principles of equity and justice.

The potential for interorganizational collaboration to be co-opted poses a real threat to its legitimacy as a problem-solving method. Consultant Eric Lowitt and another well-known environmental activist, Robert Kennedy Jr., argue cross-sectoral partnerships among private, nonprofit, and governmental organizations will be the key to solving wicked problems such as water shortages.[25] Yet as noted in the text box, stakeholders will be motivated to participate for various reasons, and it would be naïve to think they are altruistic[26] or always proceeding ethically—collaborating partners are right to be alert to issues of justice and fairness. We agree with those who call for "democratic and transparent governance models based on principles of equity and justice."[27] The legitimacy of interorganizational collaboration rests on its commitment to these principles. Achieving democracy and transparency is accomplished via ethical communication and decision making.

The Micro Ethical Context: Communication and Decision Making

The ethical communication situation differs from the macro ethical context in that we turn our gaze inward (depicted as the center of figure 4.1). Rather than focusing on the influence collaboration has in the social and political arenas, we now attend to how stakeholders practice collabo-

ration, albeit the two are inextricably related. Consultant and author Sandor Schuman wrote of collaboration, "In democratic systems, the means
are the ends. These are moral issues. The way in which collaboration is
practiced, including the way that process and content are managed and
integrated, is a moral issue, whether or not it is explicitly recognized as
such by the participants."[28] While interorganizational collaboration takes
place within an ethical context that demands attention to the public
sphere and marginalized stakeholders, developing ethical communication
is complicated by the contingent nature of collaborative praxis. In other
words, prescriptions will not fully suffice to guide stakeholders to handle
ethical dilemmas because each dilemma is unique. Many scholars believe
it would be *unethical* to prescribe a moral code because moral codes are
situated, cultural, and contingent.[29]

Habermas wrestled with this paradox and posited we could arrive at
socially just outcomes via an ethical process of communication.[30] The best
we can hope for in ethical decision making in the public sphere is to design
the most ethical communication process possible. If the communication
processes are just and strive to be free of hidden and corrupt power, then
the solutions derived from those processes would be the closest a society
could get to ethical decisions.[31] Many collaboration scholars believe collaboration *at its best* is an ethical process. For example, planning scholars
Judith Inness and David Booher[32] claim a *collaborative rationality* composes
collaborative decision making. Their theory argues the key components of a
collaborative rationality are diversity, interdependence, and authentic dialogue (DIAD). They describe their commitment to diversity as an "ethical"
one and explicate dialogue as a process of being open to the other—calling
forth a moral approach to working with others different than you.

Habermas was chiefly concerned with systematically distorted communication, which is exactly what Barlow and Karunananthan refer to
when they claim water targets cannot be trusted because they were generated by private organizations protecting their own interests. Critical
scholar Stanley Deetz elaborates: "Systematically distorted communication operates like strategic manipulation, but without overt awareness.
The latent prejudice, preconception, predefined personal identity, or object
production precludes open formation. The one-sidedness becomes reproduced rather than opened by conflicting representations."[33] In other
words, our decision-making conversations are often laden with invisible
and insidious influences that can only be made more just and fair with the
opportunity to openly challenge one another in conversation. To rephrase
using the example in the text box, water targets will only be fair and just if
they were reached through a fair and just communication process.

The "ideal speech" situation allows for communicators to discuss
issues and to challenge one another in the context of making decisions in
the public sphere.[34] Deetz explained, "We can claim that each competent,
communicative act represents facts, establishes legitimate social relations,

discloses the speaker's point of view, and is understandable. Any claim that cannot be brought to open disputes serves as the basis for systematically distorted communication."[35] The ideal speech situation constitutes an ethical micro context for communication among collaborative stakeholders. Four conditions—comprehension, truth, sincerity, and legitimacy—nurture an ethical rationality in decision making. The values of symmetry and reciprocity serve as the backdrop for these conditions. Symmetry means that each participant may presuppose equal access to the dialogue and an equally privileged opportunity to influence the decision. Reciprocity orients us toward the inclusive ways in which communicators respond to one another in the communication process, such as turn taking, listening, and acknowledging each stakeholder's contributions to the conversation.[36]

The first condition of the ideal speech situation is that communication must be *comprehensible*—all participants must have the aptitude and ability to communicate on the topic or decision being discussed.[37] Communication should be free of ambiguities and esotericism so that everyone can access the conversation equally. Second, communication must be perceived as *truthful*. What is considered to be true by one person could be seen as contestable by another. Societies privilege different ways of knowing. For example, Western societies value quantitative scientific results over traditional storytelling or oral history. In the ideal speech situation, communicators freely contest knowledge claims that are presented as truth. Third, communication must be *sincere*. Stakeholders "need to be able to express their own authentic interests, needs, and feelings. This would require freedom from various coercive and hegemonic processes by which the individual is unable to form experience openly, to develop and sustain competing identities, and to form expressions presenting them."[38] And finally, each communicator must have *legitimacy* regarding the claims they make. Legitimacy is cocreated within the collaborative group and not preconceived by "nature, or by a privileged, universal value structure." When stakeholders' positions or credentials unduly influence a decision-making direction, the cocreation of legitimacy is threatened.[39]

Consider how this ethic might play out in a collaboration aimed at gang violence. The first condition asks if the subject matter is understandable, comprehensible, and accessible to all of the stakeholders. This might mean that some stakeholders may need to have information interpreted for them—such as complicated statistics or government acronyms. The second condition allows us to question the claims that stakeholders put forth as true. In the case of gang violence, a business owner may claim the business community is suffering in the wake of gang violence. His testimony might serve as evidence of this claim of truth, but it would be open to challenge by others whose experiences differ. The third condition regards the sincerity of stakeholders. Are they authentically representing their organizations? What other motives do they have for participating? Who are they when they speak and negotiate? The final condition considers the legitimacy of stakeholders. This condition gets to the heart of who speaks on behalf of a certain stakeholder group and how engaged that representative is with the issues being discussed. In the gang violence example, we might consider who speaks on behalf of gang members. Can we understand the gang violence problem without engaging a member of that community? Could a former gang member be a legitimate representative of the gang member experience? When participants are free to use the concepts of comprehension, truth, sincerity, and legitimacy to challenge claims made, then communicators have achieved an ethical rationality that facilitates decision making in a context that does not inadvertently favor powerful interests.

The caveat of the ideal speech situation is that it is highly unlikely an "ideal" will be achieved in its purest form. Planning theorist Jean Hillier explains:

> Habermasian-framed consensus-formation processes often fail . . . because Habermasian theorizing is predicated on a metaphysical belief that an ideal communicative situation can create transcendental understanding and agreement for all participants. In reality, actors may see little benefit in behaving 'communicatively rationally' when strategic, instrumental power-plays and manipulation of information could result in more favorable outcomes for themselves.[40]

In response to criticisms of ideal communication processes, Deetz reminds us that the ideal is always the background of communication; lying, manipulation, and strategic communication only work when such acts are presumed to be honest.[41] The point is not that the ideal is achieved in its purest form but that the expectations and culture of communication are grounded in ethics rather than corruption and sanctioned manipulation.

Building on the notion of ideal speech, communication scholars have called for stakeholder processes to incorporate (1) reciprocity for expression, (2) some equality in communication skills, (3) setting aside of authority relations, (4) open investigation of stakeholder positions, (5) open sharing of information and transparency of decision processes, and (6) opening of fact and knowledge claims to contestation in stakeholder settings.[42] We will continue to expand on developing an ethical praxis that is grounded in Habermasian principles throughout this text.

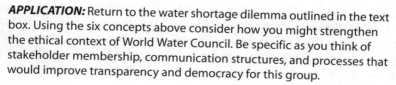

APPLICATION: Return to the water shortage dilemma outlined in the text box. Using the six concepts above consider how you might strengthen the ethical context of World Water Council. Be specific as you think of stakeholder membership, communication structures, and processes that would improve transparency and democracy for this group.

Pragmatic Reasons to Practice Ethical Communication

It would be naïve to expect all stakeholders to adopt a collaborative ethic of communication willingly; however, ethical communication processes have several pragmatic benefits that could motivate participants. Ethical communication builds trust, facilitates shared decision making, stimulates continued participation, cultivates innovation that is lost when decisions are made absent of diverse input, and establishes group legitimacy. These practical benefits may provide the impetus to induce stakeholders to embrace ethical communication principles.

Builds Trust, Sustainability, and Social Capital

A pragmatic reason to embrace a collaborative ethic is that it will build trust, and trust in collaboration is linked to other important outcomes such as social capital and sustainability. Trust in collaboration is loosely defined as associated with ethical interaction that is composed of respect, understanding, listening to others, empathy toward diverse perspectives, commitment to the partnership, predictability, dependability, and transparency.[43] Ann Marie Thomson and James Perry identify norms of trust and reciprocity as the basis for building social capital.[44] Reciprocity can be short term and contingent ("I will if you will") or long term and rooted in a sociological understanding of obligation. Trust is a central component of collaboration and consists of the belief that all participants will be honest, exhibit good-faith efforts to honor commitments, and will refrain from taking advantage. Building trust takes time; collaboration cannot be rushed. Through interaction, participants build reputations for trustworthy behavior. "When personal relationships supplement formal organizational role relationships, psychological contracts substitute for legal contracts, and formal organizational agreements mirror informal understandings and commitments, interorganizational relationships may be sustained over time."[45]

Other scholars confirm that among *established* partnerships,[46] "the driver was trust among stakeholders."[47] Trust and reciprocity also comprise Robert Putnam's influential definition of social capital: "connections among individuals—social networks and the norms of reciprocity and trustworthiness that arise from them."[48] Moreover, scholars develop the link between social capital, trust and reciprocity, and collaboration arguing trust is an antecedent, process value, and output of grassroots collaboration.[49] Trust and reciprocity compose the social capital needed by organizations to participate in collaboration; the concepts are often built into, as well as the result of, collaborative processes. At the group level, cultivating trust through interaction among stakeholders increases a collaboration's capacity by building and strengthening their social capital in the community. At the individual stakeholder level, trust is a potent governing structure of collaborative behavior.

Facilitates Shared Decision Making

Grounding communication processes in ethics facilitates shared decision making. Through the principles of reciprocity and symmetry, stakeholders create methods for participating and decision making that level the playing field. For example, in large-scale democratic decision making practiced in the 21st Century Town Hall Meeting™ designed by the nonprofit *AmericaSpeaks*,[50] participants were prepared for decision-making situations with comprehensive informational packets constructed via nonpartisan committees (which embraces Habermas's principles of comprehensibility and truth). During the meetings, a focus on transparency and the ability to contest information also promoted shared decisions, encouraging access to information and promoting joint fact-finding (embracing principles of sincerity, contestation, and legitimacy). Joint fact-finding acknowledges that one stakeholder's experts and facts may not satisfy the credibility criteria of another stakeholder.[51] Therefore, collaborating stakeholders agree to the experts, the facts, and the processes for obtaining facts together. These ethical practices foster shared-decision making as opposed to endless polarizing debates regarding whose experts are "right"—debates that potentially get resolved in the win-lose of the legal system. When decision-making situations are designed with ethics in mind, stakeholders are more fully prepared to participate and to contribute to deliberations.

Motivates Participation

Ethical communication processes also motivate membership by ensuring all participants have some influence in the process. If collaborating stakeholders believe the collaborative entity is stacked with power players who will ultimately win the day, the less powerful will not continue to participate, believing their time would be wasted and their efforts futile. Processes that set aside authority relations and promote consensus decision making allow participants holding minority perspectives and marginalized stakeholders to influence decision making. The alternative to collaborative processes is generally costly if stakeholders holding the minority viewpoint turn to adversarial processes to procure power and garner public influence. Marginalized stakeholders often turn to the legal system or try to sway public opinion through public resistance and negative publicity campaigns.[52] This was the case with the example of the Brent Spar oil rig discussed in chapter 2.

Fosters Innovation

Collaboration is a process that is grounded in difference and diversity. Implementing ethical communication processes to incorporate less powerful voices gives stakeholders access to more ideas. Research has established the benefits of diversity in the generation of ideas.[53] By prioritizing reciprocity, information sharing, and investigation of stakeholder positions, collaborating groups will more fully access their stakeholders' knowledge capital— increasing the capacity for creativity, innovation, and problem solving. Practically speaking, innovation may be lost in the absence of ethical processes.

Establishes Legitimacy

Finally, stakeholders who do not adopt ethical decision-making processes put the legitimacy of their decisions at risk. Without trust, collaborative decisions and decision making will lack legitimacy. Collaborative processes become suspect when conditions and principles such as transparency and egalitarianism are not practiced. Not only are the decisions that flow from the process suspect but future partnerships are also at risk if constituents do not view the process as a fair one. The power of collaboration to solve wicked problems is thus weakened when stakeholders do not ground their communication in ethics.

Consider the ways the case about the redevelopment of a historical Chicago neighborhood by spotlight scholar Lynn Cooper intersects with the concepts in this chapter.

SCHOLAR SPOTLIGHT

Pullman Park

Lynn Cooper

Building upon the proud history and promise of the neighborhood, Pullman Park has become a success story of how collaboration between diverse partners can positively affect urban poverty and decay.

When George Pullman came to Chicago in 1855, he immediately became involved in improving the welfare of its citizens. Poverty and slums created by waves of immigrants, strikes and riots within the existing workforce, and chaotic governance inspired reformers and entrepreneurs. Pullman's talent for constructing and operating sleeping cars on two Illinois rail lines put him—and Chicago—on the map.

The "Sleeping Car King"

Pullman's prototype took off as President Lincoln's funeral train travelled across the nation. The success of the Pullman Palace Car Company financed his real vision: an ideal urban industrial town that would stand as a utopia of peace and prosperity for workers. In 1880, Pullman established a Disneyesque community south of Chicago that drew thousands of visitors. The town's beautiful design included affordable housing, a library, a theater, a church, and a post office. It featured all the modern amenities of its day: gas streetlights, indoor plumbing, formal landscaping, and public transportation. For many years, it reflected a flourishing, working middle class that drew thousands of visitors. Pullman's vision grew alongside his company's productivity and profits.

Unfortunately, Pullman wasn't a collaborator. He rejected anything he didn't like, and the community soon bristled under his undemocratic leadership.

Fueled by economic downturns and unhappy union leaders, he set into motion a national confrontation that led to the famous Pullman strike. By the time it had run its course, the urban reformer's reputation lay in ruins. The town became a rundown, lower working-class neighborhood. Chicago ultimately engulfed and annexed the town but had little interest in its future. Recognized for its significant architecture as well as its impact on the history of labor, urban design, transportation, and race relations, Pullman's dream became a nightmare.

The New Kids on the Block

As the largest undeveloped land area in Chicago, efforts to reestablish Pullman surfaced through significant collaborations among government, private corporations, nonprofit initiatives, and community members. Chicago Neighborhood Initiatives (CNI) became the developer for Pullman Park, a 180-acre mixed-use development on the far south side of Chicago.

CNI started in 2010 with financial backing from U.S. Bank. CNI collaborates with low-income communities and neighborhood stakeholders, with specific focus on large-scale commercial real estate development and residential neighborhood preservation. They authorize micro lending in grants of up to $25,000 to entrepreneurs and small business owners to purchase equipment, update inventory, and obtain business licenses. CNI also receives funding from the City of Chicago Neighborhood Stabilization funds to transfer vacant, foreclosed properties into quality, affordable housing.

David Doig, president of CNI, has a background in community development, public housing, banking, and earlier Pullman Bank Initiatives. With the support of Ninth Ward Alderman Anthony Beale, CNI has a strong advocate within City Hall as well as within the largely African American community.

Doig and his team at CNI began their work by inviting stakeholders to extensive planning meetings, holding two workshops and more than 70 meetings over the course of a year. Community organizations, businesses, churches, and other stakeholders raised issues, clarified their positions, and passionately argued them. While the process of highlighting different and often opposing points of view can be threatening, the neutral stance of CNI and the cooperative spirit of these meetings served to establish common ground between stakeholders.

From this critical listening period, four essential needs were prioritized: food, employment, recreational spaces, and housing. Food was a critical concern because there were no accessible retail stores in the neighborhood. Pullman was a "food desert," with residents traveling nearly five miles to the closest grocery store. A second obvious problem was the high unemployment rate on the far south side of Chicago. Nearly 20 percent of the people in Pullman and its neighboring community of Roseland are unemployed. Therefore, a vision for a "big box" retail development space quickly rose as a solution. A large-scale commercial enterprise would provide a source of fresh food as well as jobs. The third component of redevelopment would provide a 10-acre park and repurposed recreation facility. This would provide a new "center" for the community and promote healthy lifestyles. Finally, community members petitioned for a variety of safe and affordable housing options for senior residents.

Pullman is located near major transportation routes within the city. Expressways, waterways, railroads, and commuter trains provide easy access to the center

(continued)

of the city, and the amount of undeveloped land is ideal for industry and business. These advantages received a major boost in 2013. As part of his commitment to create jobs and support economic growth, Governor Pat Quinn used federal money to reopen a critical roadway to the Pullman Park development. This created 300 construction jobs and access to new commercial space for private development. This infrastructure improvement laid the foundation for economic development.

The Proverbial Brick Wall

Phase one focused on bringing an "anchor" store into the neighborhood that included food, pharmacy, general merchandise, and a garden center. CNI contacted popular chain retail stores like Target and Home Depot. From the perspective of the retail stores, investing in this desolate area was risky. It was "not their demographic," a polite way of saying they didn't like the neighborhood, didn't know how to do merchandising in an urban setting, and had safety concerns. The project was untested, and retailers were reluctant pioneers. Only Walmart was eager to start an inner city initiative.

Efforts to secure a contract fizzled. Walmart's anti-union stance was at odds with pro-union labor practices in Chicago. The City Council rejected Walmart's offer. For six months, Doig was unable to move the project forward, until he convinced Walmart to negotiate its labor interests. A Community Benefit Agreement was signed, requiring specific concessions to operate in Pullman. Walmart agreed to hire all union construction workers, and 80 percent of the store's employees would be from the community. Walmart would donate $20 million to philanthropic causes, and use and sell local goods. The ability of CNI to leverage influence with Walmart lay in recognizing a hidden agenda. Walmart wanted to use this opportunity as their point of entry into the city.

City Hall stood firm until 400 community stakeholders showed up at the hearing to show support, and the negotiations between CNI, Walmart, and the City Council ended with store approval. But the quest didn't end. Chicago Transit Authority (CTA) demanded installation of a bus turnaround space and pedestrian walkway as part of the $125 million construction. Although Walmart complied with those demands, CTA reneged on their signed agreement to extend bus service to the store; the closest bus route ended nearly a mile from the store. In addition to customers, 250 of the 400 employees depended on public transportation to get to work. At the ribbon-cutting ceremony, the mayor showed his irritation and attributed his late arrival to the long walk from the bus stop. Within two days, the Pullman shuttle was operational.

The Best of Times

Phase one created positive change by bringing a retail "anchor" into the community. Two years later, the parking lot is filled, and sales are going well. Walmart's conflict with the city was resolved, and seven more stores opened in Chicago. Ross, Planet Fitness, and Subway stores followed, meeting phase two's employment goals. CNI invested $120 million, resulting in the first new industry in 30 years: Method Soap. This factory provided 100 jobs producing environmentally friendly cleaning products in an innovative building adjacent to Walmart. Using renewable energy for the plant's power, a rooftop greenhouse will eventually produce 500 tons of fresh food, allowing easier access to fresh, local, and healthy food options. Alderman Beale reveals the impact: 24 percent reduction in crime and 44 percent decline in violent crime.

Other collaborators have come forward. The Salvation Army's new community center was built on an abandoned industrial site. The completed facility projects 250 permanent full-time, part-time, and summer jobs and internship
opportunities in recreation. Mercy Housing, in partnership with business, government, and private foundations, renovated a historic factory from the original
company town into 210 affordable apartment units.

In 2015, President Obama established the Pullman historical district as a national
monument. This honor, along with the new Obama Presidential Library in neighboring Hyde Park, is likely to bring 300,000 visitors a year. The need for hotels, restaurants, and gift shops for tourists will provide additional jobs and opportunities,
recreating Pullman's ideal of a working middle class in a significant way.

Years of injustice, disrespect, and unemployment have perpetuated cycles of
poverty that are complex and enduring. Although finding resources and funds to
continue development activities are ongoing, the major challenge ahead is
keeping the community engaged with the process in order to sustain such
efforts. Perhaps the biggest lesson to learn from Pullman's resurgence lies in the
ethic of CNI. "Do well by doing good" means paying attention to the big picture
while listening to smaller voices. It reinforces the importance of marginalized
voices in collaboration. When that occurs, everyone wins.

QUESTIONS: What macro ethical issues were present in the Pullman
case? In what ways were the residents of Pullman marginalized? What did
the community leaders do to initiate a micro ethical context? What pragmatic ethical benefits came of the Pullman development?

Micro and Macro Context Tensions

In addition to considering the larger social and political context, as
well as the methods in which stakeholders will make decisions, stakeholders will be confronted with a variety of ethical decisions that do not always
present themselves as obvious and may even appear benign. Often these
decisions bridge the connection between micro and macro ethics; the
micro decisions made in the communication context of the group have
unforeseen ethical consequences in the macro context. For example, if the
collaboration is accumulating data (and most cross-sectoral collaborations
do in order to measure the impact their work is having),[54] consideration
must be paid as to who houses that information and who will have access
to it. What if the data do not show measurable changes in the work the
collaboration is doing? How will that be handled? It seems obvious that
transparency builds trust and credibility for collaboration. However, we
have worked with organizations that have chosen to bury reports commissioned and supported by grant money because they did not like the
results. Their leaders were good people and did not consider their own
actions to be unethical; they acted on the instinct to protect the work they
were doing. They also lacked a communication process that would foster

the ethical conditions of comprehension, truth, sincerity, and legitimacy—
an important check and balance that promotes accountability. Stakeholders encouraged to challenge one another against the backdrop of these
four conditions might challenge the sincerity and legitimacy of burying
data that were publically commissioned. Taking into account and considering how data will be handled in governance structures is just one of the
ethical dilemmas stakeholders will confront.

Funding is another area in which ethics may be tested. Are there
funders or organizations from which stakeholders will not take resources
based on moral grounds? Renee studied a collaboration focused on childhood obesity. Much discussion took place around whether the stakeholders
would accept funding from transnational corporations that made their profits from selling products laden with sugar and fat. Some stakeholder organizations may refuse to participate if certain stakeholders are invited to the
table because they do not want to "collude with the enemy." The reality for
many nonprofit stakeholders is that they have to adhere to particular missions, and their board members will hold them accountable to those missions, sometimes forbidding them to accept money from certain industries.

Consider the tenuous relationships among stakeholders immersed in
some of our biggest social problems such as those between the oil industry
and the environment, the beverage industry and water advocates, the pro-
cessed food industry and health care advocates. No dictum can prescribe
the answer for stakeholders in these situations. In the end, the group
Renee observed chose to take money from food industry partners based on
the justification that they could not solve the problem without the funding
of the for-profit sector, and this section of the for-profit sector was highly
motivated to align themselves with the mission of the collaboration. Space
does not allow enumerating the many ethical dilemmas that collaborative
stakeholders will confront, but we discuss a few to emphasize the need for
ethical processes. These ethical dilemmas demonstrate the link between
stakeholder interactions and the public sphere as decisions about contro-
versies such as sharing data and taking money from particular industries
relate back to questions of accountability in the macro context. They reinforce the idea that ethical discussion, dialogue, and decision making are
the best approach to navigating moral dilemmas.

CONCLUSION

This chapter focuses on the primary ethical contexts invoked in interorganizational collaboration. The macro ethical context is inextricably
linked to decisions and processes in the micro ethical context of the communication situation. Stakeholders and collaborating groups may erode
trust with the public and with each other if they do not take into account
the political and social significance of their actions. Trust is lost when marginalized voices are limited from participating in the process and when

collaborations appear to be more symbolic than authentic in their efforts to engage cross-sector organizational partners in decision making. The three chapters that follow address three additional cornerstones of ethics: diversity, shared power, and principled leadership.

CHAPTER TAKE-AWAYS

▶ Recognize the importance of ethics in collaboration
▶ Understand ethics as operating in macro and micro contexts
▶ Articulate how the public sphere becomes enacted
▶ Describe the ethical significance of marginalized perspectives
▶ Understand the four conditions of an ethical communication process—the ideal speech situation
▶ Consider the pragmatic benefits of collaborative ethics

ENDNOTES

[1] Online Etymology Dictionary, "Ethics," *Online Etymology Dictionary*, http://www.etymonline.com/index.php?term=ethics

[2] Garrett Hardin, "The Tragedy of the Commons," *Science* 162, no. 3859 (December 13, 1968): 1243–48, doi:10.1126/science.162.3859, p. 1243.

[3] John Charles Morris et al., *The Case for Grassroots Collaboration: Social Capital and Ecosystem Restoration at the Local Level* (Lanham, MD: Lexington Books, 2013), p. xxii.

[4] Jessica MacDonald Milam and Renee Guarriello Heath, "Participative Democracy and Voice: Rethinking Community Collaboration Beyond Neutral Structures," *Journal of Applied Communication Research* 42, no. 4 (October 2, 2014): 366–86, doi:10.1080/00909882.2014.911944.

[5] Rachel Carson, *Silent Spring*, Anniversary ed. (Boston: Houghton Mifflin Company, 2002).

[6] Archie B. Carroll, "The Pyramid of Corporate Social Responsibility: Toward the Moral Management of Organizational Stakeholders," *Business Horizons* 34, no. 4 (July 1, 1991): 39–48, doi:10.1016/0007-6813(91)90005-G, p. 43.

[7] Ibid.

[8] Jürgen Habermas, *Communication and the Evolution of Society*, trans. Thomas McCarthy (Boston: Beacon Press, 1979).

[9] Jürgen Habermas, Sara Lennox, and Frank Lennox, "The Public Sphere: An Encyclopedia Article (1964)," *New German Critique*, no. 3 (1974): 49–55, doi:10.2307/487737.

[10] Ibid., p. 49.

[11] Ted Bernard, *Hope and Hard Times: Communities, Collaboration and Sustainability* (Gabriola Island, BC, Canada: New Catalyst Books, 2013).

[12] Renee Guarriello Heath, "Rethinking Community Collaboration through a Dialogic Lens: Creativity, Democracy, and Diversity in Community Organizing," *Management Communication Quarterly* 21, no. 2 (November 1, 2007): 145–71, doi:10.1177/0893318907306032; Milam and Heath, "Participative Democracy and Voice."

[13] Eliana Garces, Duncan Thomas, and Janet Currie, "Longer-Term Effects of Head Start," *American Economic Review* 92, no. 4 (September 2002): 999–1012, doi:10.1257/00028280260344560.

[14] Ibid.

[15] David Schlosberg, *Defining Environmental Justice: Theories, Movements, and Nature: Theories, Movements, and Nature* (Oxford, UK: Oxford University Press, 2007).

16 Fraser M. Shilling, Jonathan K. London, and Raoul S. Liévanos, "Marginalization by Collabo-
    ration: Environmental Justice as a Third Party in and beyond CALFED," *Environmental Science
    & Policy*, Collaborative Governance and Adaptive Management: California's CALFED Water
    Program, 12, no. 6 (October 2009): 694–709, doi:10.1016/j.envsci.2009.03.003, p. 699.

17 Sherry J. Holladay, "Corporate Integrity and Social Responsibility," in *Business and Corpo-
    rate Integrity: Sustaining Organizational Compliance, Ethics, and Trust [2 Volumes]: Sustain-
    ing Organizational Compliance, Ethics, and Trust*, ed. Robert C. Chandler, vol. 1 (Santa
    Barbara, CA: ABC-CLIO, 2014), 53–77.

18 Bob Sallinger and Donna Murphy, "City, Port Disrupt Hayden Island Process," *The Portland
    Tribune*, June 28, 2012.

19 Port of Portland, "Traffic Impacts West Hayden Island Development,"
    http://cdn.portofportland.com/pdfs/WHI_Trffc_Impcts.pdf

20 Sallinger and Murphy, "City, Port Disrupt Hayden Island Process."

21 Judith E. Innes and David E. Booher, *Planning with Complexity: An Introduction to Collabor-
    ative Rationality for Public Policy* (Abingdon-on-Thames, UK/New York: Routledge, 2010).

22 Merriam-Webster, "Definition of CO–OPT," http://www.merriam-webster.com/dictionary/
    co-opt

23 Maude Barlow and Meera Karunananthan, "Save Our Water, End Investor Rights," *The
    Huffington Post*, May 13, 2015, http://www.huffingtonpost.ca/maude-barlow/
    water-crisis_b_7258782.html

24 Ibid. Reprinted with permission from the authors.

25 Eric Lowitt, *The Collaboration Economy: How to Meet Business, Social, and Environmental
    Needs and Gain Competitive Advantage* (Hoboken, NJ: Wiley, 2013).

26 Innes and Booher, *Planning with Complexity*.

27 Barlow and Karunananthan, "Save Our Water, End Investor Rights."

28 Sandor P. Schuman, "The Role of Facilitation in Collaborative Groups," in *Creating Collab-
    orative Advantage*, ed. Chris Huxham (Thousand Oaks, CA: Sage, 1996), 126–40, p. 128.

29 Jean Hillier, "'Agon'izing Over Consensus: Why Habermasian Ideals Cannot Be 'Real,'"
    Planning Theory 2, no. 1 (March 1, 2003): 37–59, doi:10.1177/1473095203002001005.

30 Habermas, *Communication and the Evolution of Society*.

31 Ibid.

32 Innes and Booher, *Planning with Complexity*.

33 Stanley Deetz, *Democracy in an Age of Corporate Colonization: Developments in Communi-
    cation and the Politics of Everyday Life* (Albany: SUNY Press, 1992), p. 174.

34 Innes and Booher, *Planning with Complexity*.

35 Deetz, *Democracy in an Age of Corporate Colonization*, p. 168.

36 Ibid.

37 Innes and Booher, *Planning with Complexity*.

38 Deetz, *Democracy in an Age of Corporate Colonization*, p. 170.

39 Ibid., p. 169.

40 Hillier, "'Agon'izing over Consensus," p. 41.

41 Deetz, *Democracy in an Age of Corporate Colonization*.

42 Timothy R. Kuhn and Stanley Deetz, "Critical Theory and Corporate Social Responsibility:
    Can/should We Get beyond Cynical Reasoning?" in *The Oxford Handbook of Corporate
    Social Responsibility*, ed. Andrew Crane et al. (Oxford, UK/New York: Oxford University
    Press, 2009), 173–96.

43 Morris et al., *The Case for Grassroots Collaboration*, p. 42.

44 Ann Marie Thomson and James L. Perry, "Collaboration Processes: Inside the Black Box,"
    Public Administration Review 66 (December 1, 2006): 20–32, doi:10.1111/
    j.1540-6210.2006.00663.x.

45 Ibid., p. 28.

46 William Leach and Paul A. Sabatier, "Are Trust and Social Capital the Key to Success?
    Watershed Partnerships in California and Washington," in *Swimming Upstream: Collabora-*

tive Approaches to Watershed Management, ed. Paul A. Sabatier et al. (Cambridge: MIT Press, 2005), 233–58.

[47] Morris et al., *The Case for Grassroots Collaboration*, p. 44.

[48] Robert D. Putnam, *Bowling Alone: The Collapse and Revival of American Community* (New York: Simon and Schuster, 2001), p. 19.

[49] Morris et al., *The Case for Grassroots Collaboration*.

[50] Carolyn J. Lukensmeyer and Steven Brigham, "Taking Democracy to Scale: Large Scale Interventions—for Citizens," *The Journal of Applied Behavioral Science* 41, no. 1 (March 1, 2005): 47–60, doi:10.1177/0021886304272656.

[51] Barbara Gray, *Collaborating: Finding Common Ground for Multiparty Problems* (San Francisco: Jossey-Bass, 1989).

[52] Ibid.

[53] Charlan Jeanne Nemeth and Margaret Ormiston, "Creative Idea Generation: Harmony versus Stimulation," *European Journal of Social Psychology* 37, no. 3 (May 1, 2007): 524–35, doi:10.1002/ejsp.373.

[54] John Kania and Mark Kramer, "Collective Impact," *Stanford Social Innovation Review*, Winter 2011.

5

Diversity

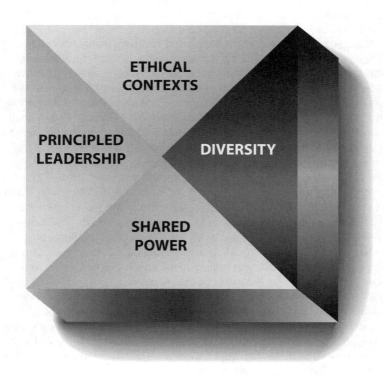

ETHICAL
CONTEXTS

PRINCIPLED
LEADERSHIP

DIVERSITY

SHARED
POWER

When You Don't Think Like Me

"I just don't understand."

"You don't understand what?"

"How can these be the responses we got from the exit survey on that exhibition? I mean it is like they didn't get it at all!"

"Well we knew it was a risk, it was a passive exhibit, nothing that was going to rock the boat."

"Yeah, but we all agreed that this would be the best way to go, an audio story to go with these black and white photos. Why did we think it was going to raise awareness about safe sex, and it did almost the opposite?"

This is what the members of Missoula's safe sex collaboration were trying to figure out after a two-week exhibit placed in the mall to raise awareness about safe sex was received with less than positive results in an exit survey. The collaboration had been working for six months to put together an exhibit that would raise awareness without making any waves in the community. The curriculum in the public school system in Missoula, Montana, is abstinence only, and the health department was trying to create a larger discussion on the topic without creating controversy in the school system or with the area religious sector that supported abstinence only education.

The collaboration included individuals from the public school system, health department, Planned Parenthood, and a few other area nonprofits that dealt directly with sex education and teen pregnancy. Missoula at the time was seeing a spike in the teen pregnancy rate, and many of the people in the collaboration believed that it was related to the recent move to abstinence only education. At the monthly meeting leading up to the decision to display a photo exhibit about the experiences of living as a teen parent, all the members were excited about what could be done. Routinely during the meetings, the discussions would get side-tracked regarding the K–12 curriculum changes. Almost all these "digressions" would end in: "But I am preaching to the choir." And it was true. Only stakeholders who represented the comprehensive-education approach to safe sex comprised the collaboration. The lack of diverse voices was acknowledged at the meetings, but members would say it was "too hard to get those people to attend." Some even privately stated that it was easier to make decisions when everyone agreed and didn't have to listen to opposing opinions.

When it came time for the exhibit (which took place during the spring break of the public school system), members set up photos with audio stories near the main entrance to the mall. Most people walked right by; only a few stayed long enough to pick up a headset and listen to the story of living as a teen parent. Of those that stayed, most were not the teenage group that the collaboration had intended to reach.

"How did we get this one so wrong?"

—Episode from Matt's work with Missoula Safe-Sex Collaboration

We live in an increasingly connected society; we cannot escape diversity. Stanley Deetz describes the related concept pluralism as, "a term that draws our attention to the increasing contact between people with different values, cultural heritages, and ways of living."[1] He adds that the consequences of pluralism, "are accentuated by increasing degrees of interdependence" with others worldwide.[2] In other words, we will never again live in a world where those who are different from us no longer cross our paths.[3] Instead, we are interdependently linked to diverse others because we share a planet together. Technology, geopolitical war, genocide, trade and industry, environmental degradation, and natural resources distribution are a few of the reasons we must learn to live and make decisions that account for diverse perspectives and positions in this world. Learning how to negotiate meaning with diverse others is integral to contemporary problem solving. Accordingly, this chapter will discuss the different ways we have learned to understand diversity and how these different conceptions are contingent on the collaboration context. Along these lines, we introduce the central belief that diversity is always dependent on the communication situation. We develop the idea of *requisite diversity* as the integral notion in collaboration. We also discuss the benefits of diversity and the challenges stakeholders face in the context of collaboration working with others who think differently than they do. Because diversity is so vital to interorganizational collaboration, we consider it the second cornerstone of the collaborative ethic.

Diversity's Central Role in Collaboration

The term "diversity" has existed in English from the late fifteenth century. It was defined as difference, unique features, and oddness as well as wickedness, perversity, contradiction, and disagreement. After the seventeenth century, the negative meanings were obsolete. With the rise of modern democracies in the 1790s, diversity was perceived as a virtue because it prevented one faction from seizing all the power. The focus on race and gender began in 1992.[4]

The good news is that the hopes and aspirations of interorganizational collaboration are predicated on the notion of diversity. Difference, unique features, and disagreement are often essential characteristics of creative thinking. If stakeholders working together to solve a problem already think alike, then there is simply no need for collaboration. Instead, collaboration is grounded in the idea that diversity among stakeholders will foster innovation, creativity, and/or resolution. Diversity and difference of ideas is thus the linchpin of creative collaboration. Yet attaining and incorporating diversity in collaboration is not easily done. In the case above, the participants struggled with diversity. They all acknowledged that there should be more people at the table, yet the effort to include diverse voices was minimal. The collaborators worried that diverse opinions would slow down the process of collaborating and achieving the goals of safe sex education. Diverse perspectives may be seen as perversions of our own preferred ways of seeing the world and imply that we will face difficulties trying to include and embrace diversity. Diversity in collaboration is further conceptualized as something that exists beyond simplistic categorizations of people. How we understand diversity can depend greatly on how stakeholders view the purpose of their collaboration.

Sources of Diversity

How we conceptualize diversity is complex and rooted in many things, including the social categories we use to define ourselves, how the collaboration is oriented, and ultimately the communication situation.

CartoonStock.com

WILOT

"So we agree: having attained diversity, we must now categorise, coordinate, and consolidate it."

As the cartoon depicts, diversity is often thought of as a fixed concept; our tendency is to think of diversity as social categories that compose our identity. How we see the world and our diverse perspectives are based on our experiences, education, religion, cultures, responsibilities, and much, much more. In chapter 3, we discussed how social identity helps us better understand who we are by comparison with other groups. At its most basic, concepts like race, gender, sexual orientation, and religion comprise the categories of similarity and difference.[5] More recently, geopolitical groups, the generational differences from the "greatest" generation to the millennials, and social conditions have also become common influence factors regarding who we are and how we perceive ourselves. While social identity theory tells us that we define ourselves in part by these social categories, diversity is more complex than simply organizing persons into social categories. It is not just the color of our skin or our cultural or religious orientations that influence how we think. Instead, our diversity manifests in the confluences of our identity and social experiences in specific communication situations. As the cartoon suggests, we are missing the point of diversity if we view it as a set of external categories that exist outside of the collaboration and communication process. When collaborating, we are likely to consider diversity in light of the context of those communication situations.

Collaboration Orientation and Diversity

Understandings of what counts as diversity to collaborative stakeholders varies depending on the collaboration's orientation.[6] Three major orientations to collaboration in part explain some of the primary impetuses for collaborating—(1) community reform, (2) conflict resolution, and (3) efficiency of resources.[7] Although collaborating organizations are likely to subscribe in some way to all of these orientations, it may be helpful to think of these orientations as foregrounding or backgrounding assumptions and values in interorganizational collaboration. If we understand what is foregrounded as important to stakeholders, we can make better sense of how diversity is understood in different contexts, what strengths and weaknesses exist around this thinking, and ways to fortify collaborative organizing.

Table 5.1 Collaborative orientations

Collaborative Orientation	Guiding Principles	Assumptions Regarding Diversity
Community Reform Collaboration as alternative to current government models	Democracy, accountability	Diversity is understood as liberal democratic "representation"
Conflict Resolution Collaboration as an alternative dispute resolution method	Difference will lead to acceptable resolutions	Conflicting viewpoints and ideologies compose diversity
Efficiency of Resources Collaboration to create programs, products, or innovative solutions	Functionality	Diversity is technical knowledge, resources, business type, etc. driven by needs of the project/program

Community Reform. Collaboration oriented toward *community reform* assumes democracy as a guiding principle and views collaboration as an alternative to current government models for solving social problems. In collaborations with this orientation, "representation" is the chief concern. Collaborations oriented toward community reform do not separate issues of diversity in representation from notions of democracy and accountability. Decisions must reflect the will of the community and the interests of key stakeholders. One of the chief barriers to this orientation is the inclusive paradox we discussed in chapter 3. The irony in representation is that the inclusion of potential stakeholders in a democracy can be infinite, and the presence of multiple stakeholders in a collaboration inherently impedes the process because of the number of voices that must be included. A study of a community reforming its discriminatory redlining practices in real estate illustrates this orientation in collaboration. A committee of "representatives from two major banks, two savings and loan associations, one mortgage banker, two appraisers, three realtors, four citizens and one member each from the city council and school board," was convened by the mayor and was charged "with the task of reviewing the data to come up with a plan to ensure continued investment in the community."[8] Frequently government leaders serve as the conveners or facilitators of collaborations in this orientation because the outcomes have the potential to transform policies and practices at social and political levels. Given these outcomes, diversity is considered present when representative groups and sectors of the community are participating. The heavy emphasis on representation in this orientation may encourage the participation of missing diverse stakeholders who do not have a large or vocal body of constituents.

Conflict Resolution. In the second orientation, *conflict resolution,* diversity is understood as conflicting viewpoints. Although conflict is present in all collaborations, the second orientation uses solving conflict as the driving force in making decisions about what counts as diverse stakeholders. Representative stakeholders are important to conceptualize the problem from a different, often conflicting, perspective and to move toward some type of resolution or to avoid expensive litigation.[9] Diversity in this orientation is fundamentally based on the assumption that difference leads to creativity, maximizing the ability for diverse others to see the problem in an alternate way. In other words, creative resolution—rather than democracy, accountability, or representation—drives what counts as diversity. A barrier in this orientation is the dilemma that surfaces when selecting stakeholder members based on their conflicting viewpoints. While alternative understandings of a problem can lead to creative solutions, conflict can be hard to overcome, especially with stakeholders entrenched in adversarial methods. This is an example of the mainstreamer paradox (chapter 3); collaborations struggle over whether to invite the very stakeholders who wish to impede their progress.[10] The dilemma arises in that if stakeholders are chosen because they share more mainstream views regarding the conflict area, uninvited stakeholders with more extreme positions may disrupt the implementation of resolutions. If those holding extreme positions are invited, they might work to sabotage the collaboration from the inside out. This paradox is especially evident in environmental collaboration where environmental advocacy depends on resistant tactics such as protests, community resistance, negative publicity, and litigation. Stakeholders often operate in two different worlds simultaneously. In one universe, they are battling one another in extended litigation or creating awareness about the evils of each other's rhetoric. At the same time, they may be seated across a table trying to come up with an alternative solution through gentler consensus decision-making processes.[11] The Applegate Watershed Partnership, a well-known collaboration among environmentalists, the timber industry, local ranchers, and indigenous people, is an excellent example of this orientation in which diversity (understood as conflicting viewpoints) fueled the creative solutions that arose out of stakeholder differences.[12] This partnership was so mired in conflict at the outset that participants chose to wear buttons with a line over the word "they" as a communication ground rule for how to speak about respective stakeholders.[13]

Resource Efficiency. Collaboration that is chiefly oriented toward an *efficient use of resources* conceptualizes diversity in terms of those resources. Collaboration, in this orientation more than any other, emphasizes functionality—diversity is the instrument by which the outcome will be achieved. Emphasis is placed on solving problems through more efficient uses of community resources. Creativity is arrived at through the capitalization of interdependent community resources, which may include tangible resources such as funding or intangible resources such as knowledge or political power. In its many forms, the outcomes of creativity serve instrumental purposes such as new products, programs, services, a particular knowledge, or unprecedented results. Discourse in collaborations oriented toward more efficient uses of resources focuses less on difference and more on what is held in common by collaborating partners. Diversity in this orientation is more likely to apply to the technical resources and organization types stakeholders represent rather than stakeholders' interests or ideologies. Resource dependency theory tells us stakeholders collaborate because they represent various scarce resources, knowledge, and expertise.[14] Stakeholders are also diverse in the sense that they represent different types of organizations such as for profit, nonprofit, and public organizations.

It is not uncommon that collaborations focused on social services and educational programs will adapt a resource orientation. Recall that Renee's first experience with interorganizational collaboration focused on at-risk prevention and was motivated by her organization's ability to fund high school job experiences (see chapter 2). The collaboration conveners viewed her participation initially in terms of the resources her organiza-

tion could offer. It is also not uncommon for funders such as foundations
to require similar organizations to collaborate in order to pool resources
more efficiently. One dilemma that surfaces in collaborations with a
resource orientation to diversity is that over time, stakeholder membership
tends to be homogenous rather than heterogeneous (as found in studies of
health care[15] and early care education[16]). Several studies document how
more diverse members dropped out the collaboration, for example, due to
a "jargony" technical language that was used by a majority of the nonprofit stakeholders.[17] This phenomenon is likely attributed to a membership focused on resources rather than democratic accountability or
conflicting viewpoints.

We do not advocate one particular orientation and subsequent understanding of diversity as more important or accurate than another. Rather,
the distinctions highlight assumptions about diversity in collaboration. We
articulate these different orientations not to suggest that there is no overlap
among them but as a way to think through diversity and its role in collaboration. Each orientation illuminate's particular strengths and weaknesses
associated with it. Collaborating stakeholders above all will need to recognize the assumptions of their partners regarding diversity as they strive
toward a particular goal. Recognizing different collaboration orientations
will help participants establish shared definitions and understandings of
the work they are doing.

> **QUESTION:** What are the possibilities and pitfalls associated with each
> orientation? For example, by foregrounding diversity as accountability,
> how will the collaboration be strengthened? What might be missed in
> this orientation?
>
> **QUESTION:** In the Safe Sex Collaboration, can you identify the collabora-
> tive orientation they used and potential issues that emerged from that
> orientation?

Rethinking Diversity as Dependent on the Communication Situation

In the context of collaborative decision making, it is important to
attend to the difference that makes a difference.[18] Ultimately our differences depend on the communication situation and subject matter.

Difference That Makes a Difference

A professor we know shows a picture of a cat, tree, dog, and squirrel
to his students and asks them, "Which one doesn't belong?"[19] Many students argue the tree does not belong because the tree is the only plant.
This would be accurate if the plant-animal distinction is the most impor-

tant difference that makes a difference. For any student preparing to take the SAT or GRE, this would be the difference that matters.

But what if the question was asked of students in Egypt where historically the cat is considered sacred? In this communication situation, students might then see the cat as the symbol of distinction—the one that doesn't belong among the others. The difference that makes a difference (the sacred status of the cat, rather than the plant-animal distinction) would potentially lead Egyptian students with this knowledge to an entirely different conclusion to the same question. Both answers are culturally grounded and contextually influenced. Both answers reflect a dominant way of thinking in each culture. By viewing diversity as the *difference that makes a difference,* we are brought back to the context of the communication situation and attention to why that difference is important. Dominant thinking is most often invisible to us. At first glance, it seems obvious that the plant-animal distinction is the one that matters. Only after further reflection and contrast to other cultural ways of thinking are we able to see that difference only matters in light of a certain context. Thus, the diversity that matters is the diversity required for the situation—or requisite diversity. To achieve requisite diversity, we will have to be willing to confront dominant ways of thinking and organizing.

Requisite Diversity

Requisite diversity is much more fluid and unfixed then other understandings of diversity and depends on the notion of the difference that makes a difference. Requisite diversity can be understood by reflecting on the following:

> Do we have the differences present that must dislodge commitment to existing positioning and give the greatest chance for creativity? In general, the more complex the problem, the more diversity that is needed. The question is not whether one or hundreds share the position but rather what is the difference that might make a difference? The legitimacy of a decision in this case does not rest on representation—that all had their say—but on reciprocity—that all differences contributed

to the possibility of an emergent solution. The quality of the emergent decision in terms of its ability to meet human needs is of key interest.[20]

Renee once noted in a conversation with a school administrator that the school advisory board was almost entirely composed of men. The board was primarily focused on finances and had attracted the participation of many businessmen. The school administrator agreed that the board lacked gender diversity and subsequently nominated Renee to join. Her participation influenced board conversations. For example, as a mother and primary caretaker, she persuaded the board to design events to be more inclusive, fostering greater participation from mothers and fathers who did most of the driving and caring for their children. In these cases, the difference that made a difference was her role as mother and caretaker—a primarily gendered role. However, her experience as an educator also brought a different perspective to the board's decisions. She advocated more often than her fellow board members for teacher training, knowing the important contribution continuing education had for her own career as a professor. Her frame for making financial decisions was different.[21] Her board colleagues achieved great financial success by approaching school decisions from a fiscal frame, which had been the dominant frame for making decisions. Renee's educator frame pushed the group to consider different reasons for financial commitments. Her experience as a professor was the difference that made a difference. In other words, the subject matter and decision-making situation drives what counts as diversity.

Consider how requisite diversity works in collaborations. Requisite diversity guides us in determining who should be participating in problem solving. Instead of focusing on what groups are underrepresented, who is likely to conflict with the solution, or what resources they bring, requisite diversity begins with the central idea of what difference of thought is needed to push the creative limits of this group? The concept also moves us away from ideas of representation that simply offer token opportunities for stakeholders with minority viewpoints to express their concern or "have their say."[22] Instead the focus is on how unique perspectives influence the quality of decisions.

In business forums, the focus on decision quality can drive who should participate. According to consultant Lindsay Degouve De Nuncques,

> When we talk about the value of having diverse workforces it is not the input—the "who"—that matters, it is the output—the "what" they bring—that makes the difference. Key to this new way of thinking about diversity is the idea that the value of diversity is through having a range of perspectives and experiences in a team.[23]

The focus on requisite diversity as key to collaborative organizing does not mean that stakeholders forming collaborative partnerships will not be concerned with accountability and democracy, conflict resolution, and resources. Certainly all of those concerns remain important in the organizing process. However, given the endless possibilities as to who counts as a stakeholder in a given position, requisite diversity focuses on the communication situation and the decision outcome as a guide for including participants. It provides a partial solution to the dilemmas of stakeholder and mainstreamer paradoxes.

Requisite diversity is also an important leveler to power that may be distorted or weighted in a collaboration in unseen ways. Deetz explained:

> Diversity is for me about materially embodied positionalities (subject positionings) that differ in saliencies. The diversity of interest at any moment are the ones that disrupt a dominant positionality thus opening contestation . . . or discussion where none seemed needed and opening interactive productivity where invention occurs. . . . In the problem solving (collaborative) situation relevant diversity cannot be set in advance. It is based on an analysis of positionality present, dominance, and choosing embodiments that create the optimal contestation and productivity." [24]

Deetz links embodied positionalities (understood in this text as identities) with power. Requisite diversity cannot be known in advance. It emerges in the communication situation when we attend to power and consider what perspectives (positions and identities) are needed to disrupt the dominant thinking that stunts our creativity, innovation, and accountability to one another. Accordingly, a focus on requisite diversity will lead to more democratic outcomes. Choosing stakeholders based on requisite diversity means inviting those who hold a viewpoint that will challenge the dominant thinking and persistent positions. In other words, inviting those that do not think like the "usual suspects" will address concerns with democracy, marginalization, and conflict resolution. Stakeholders whose views are not part of the dominant culture challenge collaboration members to be inclusive and to work through deeply held conflicts.

QUESTION: Think about what difference would have made the difference in the Safe Sex collaboration. What was the dominant thinking on the issue? How would requisite diversity guide members in selecting the needed voices for a better outcome?

QUESTION: How does the concept of requisite diversity influence how collaborations might identify stakeholders? Do you think requisite diversity is already included in the stakeholder criteria model introduced in chapter 3 considering power, urgency, and legitimacy? Explain.

In the spotlight box below, collaboration and diversity scholar Elizabeth Eger shares her ideas regarding how to teach the idea of requisite diversity.

Scholar Spotlight

Brainstorming and Creating
Requisite Diversity
Elizabeth K. Eger

A few years ago I had the fortune of working with a team of instructors to completely redesign a freshman-level group communication course. We created units on relational constructionism, liberal and participatory democracy, deliberation, dialogue, and collaboration. In our highly interactive class, each reading and assignment applied theories and skills building toward multi-day mock collaborations.

We divided students into groups of seven, and then the students chose a local problem topic that would require the involvement of stakeholders with diverse opinions and experiences. Before selecting a topic, students first took their time to consider local issues with complex layers, diversity of opinions, and problems centered in contexts of pluralism and interdependence. Students selected stakeholders who brought multi-layered positions to the collaboration with a willingness to dislodge those positions toward creative conversations and mutually beneficial solutions.

Let's look at one example that my students chose for their semester project: affordable housing in Boulder, Colorado. You may have heard about Boulder's beautiful sunny days and four seasons, its breathtaking Flatiron Mountains, and outstanding university. But have you heard about its exorbitant housing costs? Area Vibes, a cost of living calculator, estimates from a National Housing Index average of 100, Colorado housing as a whole has an index of 122. But Boulder has a housing index of 227, and it receives an "F" grade on cost of living. An average home price in Boulder is $489,500 compared to the national average of $184,400. As you can imagine, affordable housing is a prevalent issue in Boulder with complex stakeholders, which made this topic very worthwhile for students to pursue.

Once the group had their topic of affordable housing in Boulder, they had to brainstorm who needed a "seat at the table" of this collaboration. We followed the principles of requisite diversity, which you just read about in this chapter. The group had to ask themselves: Who are the key stakeholders, whose voices are echoing loudly in these conversations, and whose voices are often silenced but also are deserving of a seat at the table? What are the "differences that make a difference" for this collaboration context?

Students began by making lists separately at first and then together in their group of all the differences that made a difference for a Boulder collaboration on affordable housing. Themes they generated included: groups of people (e.g., landlords, renters, parents of college students, low income families), problematics (e.g., environmental concerns, gentrification, wealth disparities), and organizations and officials who should be involved (e.g., builders, realtors, city council members, housing counselors, lawyers, homeless representatives). The group did an awesome job of generating this list over a series of meetings, but they stumbled upon a new problem: There were about *one hundred* differences that made a difference on their final list, and they only had *seven* seats at their mock collaboration table. *What should they do?*

Their group was not alone with the problem of too many differences and not enough seats, given that each collaboration only had seven students. We decided that each group should thoughtfully combine their many differences into seven stakeholders. We reasoned that this made sense for the collaboration class exercises because in real world collaborations, people do not occupy only one position but are instead multifaceted, riddled with their own contradictions, and experience intersections of their diverse identities.

The affordable housing group attempted to represent varied stakes by choosing combinations that they felt were the differences that made a difference for their upcoming collaboration. Here is what they came up with together about the seven seats at their collaboration table:

Jakob: City Council member, high-income homeowner living in a particularly affluent Boulder neighborhood

Maarika: University of Colorado (CU) student, current Boulder renter and resident, attending CU from out of state

Edmundo: Landlord of multiple properties, real estate agent, parent of CU student

Mae: CU in-state student, Louisville (the closest neighboring city to Boulder) resident and renter, from a rural and poorer area of southern Colorado

Kacy: Low income single parent, head of her household, someone who requires affordable housing to remain working and living in Boulder

Adam: Builder with residential and commercial experience, stringent environmentalist

Caitlyn: Business woman, works to determine affordable housing requirements and laws, helps renters get placed in housing in Boulder

Once they selected these participants, students were then tasked with interviewing real locals from the variety of backgrounds, experiences, and stakes in the issue of affordable housing in Boulder, Colorado, that they had chosen. Each had to consider how to blend stakes from multiple real people, conduct research and interviews, and write a paper about how they would use the knowledge they gained in their actual collaboration activities. For example, Kacy (a student in this group) selected her stakeholder to be a person from a low-income family, the only adult in her household, a single mother with two children, and someone who relies on the strained affordable housing system to live and work in Boulder. Kacy first conducted online research to understand the intricacies of Section 8 and Public Housing and read stories in the local newspaper about gentrification and about families who relied on governmental programs to live in Boulder, such as a woman whose mobile home park was recently replaced by new, green affordable housing units.

(continued)

After her online searches, Kacy did a site visit to an affordable housing community and met with a program coordinator and a few residents who were eager to talk about their experiences, including a single father working for a retailer with two children beginning college and a single mother with two teenage children who taught in the Boulder County school district. Kacy used her online research and interviews to craft a backstory for this project based on her interviewees' hopes, dreams, and ideal worlds. All of Kacy's group members conducted similar research; after writing papers about their stakeholders, the group felt prepared to bring their complex, multi-layered stakeholders to life. Together, these activities taught all of us a lot about the complexities of requisite diversity and how students can embody requisite diverse principles in a classroom-based collaboration.

The Benefits of Diversity

Scholars across disciplines have studied the link between diversity and creativity. The results are mixed. Some studies identify the benefits of diversity in creative problem solving, while others illuminate the increased challenge of negotiating and making decisions in groups with very diverse memberships. Conflict inevitably surfaces and is not always managed effectively. We will address the issue of conflict in the next part of the book and summarize some of the more hopeful findings below. In particular, studies link diversity to greater innovation, increased accountability, and wider access to talent. Diversity will also help stakeholders avoid the dreaded problem of groupthink.

Diversity Leads to Innovation and Creativity

A diverse group of thinkers generates more ideas than do homogenous groups. Business scholars Charlan Nemeth and Margaret Ormiston argued, "Change, a lack of comfort, and the exposure to differing views may be the vehicle for actual production of ideas and for stimulating the most creative ideas."[25] The authors investigated idea generation in groups that had members that were stable versus groups that changed membership. The group that changed membership, ultimately exposing them to a greater diversity of thought and ideas, came up with a greater number of creative ideas than did the groups that maintained a stable membership.

Another study argued that exposure to multiple cultures enhanced creativity and reinforced the link between diversity and innovation.[26] This study found that multicultural experience enhances creativity by (a) providing access to novel ideas and concepts from other cultures, (b) fostering the ability to see multiple functions for the same form, (c) increasing accessibility to seemingly inaccessible knowledge, and (d) cultivating the bringing together of seemingly incompatible ideas. Multicultural experience may come from a variety of different sources. You may have been fortunate enough to travel to or live in a different culture. You may have made a move from a rural community to a larger city or vice-versa. You may have had an exchange student from another country live with you. When Renee's family had a visitor from Brazil stay with them for one year, they all became much more conscious of the amount of food they wasted. Andréa shocked Renee's children with her ability to eat an apple down to its seeds, rather than its core. Her presence in the Heath home gave the family access to knowledge that was not visible without her differing perspective.

> *QUESTION:* What multicultural experiences have you had that provided you with novel ideas, new knowledge, and or an ability to see something in a different form?

Thinking back to the story of the cat, tree, dog, and squirrel, access to different cultural understandings of what counts as important (dominant thinking) allows for multiple interpretations of what might be the "right" answer. Having numerous right answers at the table while problem solving brings forth a larger base of knowledge and potential outcomes. This chapter's opening case and the particular way a community or culture views safe sex serves as an example of how diversity matters in collaboration. This collaboration took place in the small mountain city of Missoula, Montana. The understanding of safe sex in Montana at the time was very much rooted in the political, cultural, and religious attitudes and perspectives prevalent throughout the state. Those understandings differed in urban areas versus rural parts of the state. In comparison, the safe sex collaboration in Montana might have seemed overly conservative if it had been located in Boston, Massachusetts, or relatively liberal compared to a collaborating group based in Indonesia. Stakeholders who articulate a different understanding of safe-sex education foster creative approaches to decision making in this context. Although it may not be important to have a person from Indonesia at the table in a western Montana collaboration, understanding that cultural experiences from across the state, region, and country can vary helps stakeholders identify requisite voices that will cultivate viewing the problem and solution in different forms.

Diversity Improves Accountability and Democracy

As discussed in the requisite diversity perspective (which calls for stakeholders to seek perspectives from those who do not hold the dominant position), diversity is important for its potential to enhance accountable and democratic decisions made by collaborative groups. Furthermore, some scholars argue that the collaborative process cannot be deemed ethical if representatives from marginalized groups are not present to influence decisions.[27] Matt's work on gentrification in East Austin (chapter 3) highlights how a diverse group of stakeholders in a collaboration can enhance accountability. OCEAN held monthly meetings to discuss the issues that were present in this culturally diverse, and traditionally African American, part of Austin. This group not only had members from the neighborhoods at the meeting but also business people, city officials, clergy, and developers. At these meetings, developers had to receive approval from the collaboration to build in the business corridors. While the developers and business people at the table may have had similar ideas on how to cultivate a vibrant and profitable East Austin business district, other members brought up concerns about the types of businesses that the buildings would cater to and how traffic might be affected in the surrounding neighborhoods. It was through this collaboration that a jointly agreed upon building plan would be created that took into account the concerns of all stakeholders in East Austin.

Renee also found that having diverse participants increased accountability to more vulnerable stakeholders. In her study of collaboration in the early care and education arena, Brittany, a business woman and stakeholder who jokingly referred to herself as a "token" among stakeholders mostly from the nonprofit and educational sectors of society, provoked the collaborative group to think more broadly of their constituents. Brittany convinced the other stakeholders to think beyond the "usual suspects" in terms of accountability of their programs. The other stakeholders were focused intently on winning politicians' endorsements of their preschool programs. Brittany instead encouraged the group to focus on the people who put the politicians in office. She advocated for a "grassroots" approach to educating the public and marketing the benefits of their programs, ultimately increasing accountability to a broader and less affluent audience.[28]

In another poignant example, Ted Bernard, professor of environmental studies, described a unique collaboration between the United States Forest Service and the College of the Menominee Nation in Wisconsin, called the Center for First American's Forestlands (CFAF).[29] Indigenous understandings of forest management combined with contemporary science to provide the most innovative solutions to fire, disease, and species diversification. The contribution of the Menominee people to forest management is invaluable and was readily apparent in 2007 after a devastating tornado toppled trees on federal lands and the tribe's adjacent forests. The trees, suddenly at risk for widespread disease and fire, interdependently linked the neighbors. The subsequent responses of each stakeholder demonstrated the wisdom and knowledge of the Menominee as they quickly harvested downed timber while the federal government remained mired in gridlock as to how to handle the destruction. Today, the Center honors the expertise of the Menominee in linking ancient philosophy and insight with modern forest science. This collaboration illustrates both the contribution of the diverse thinking of indigenous stakeholders to innovation in forest management and the increased accountability of the Forest Service to its historically marginalized neighbors.

Diversity Widens the Talent Pool

Diversity also fosters greater access to a wider array of talented people. Consider your university or workplace if professional women were absent. What might that feel like? What conversations, lessons, ideas, might you miss? Now consider other life experiences, traits, characteristics, and ways of thinking that contribute to our diversity. What might your classes or workplace be like without the viewpoint of people of color, those who have experienced economic depression, or those who are discriminated against because of their sexual orientation? By taking care to ensure our collaborative groups are diverse, we purposely cast a wider net that is bound to capture greater talent, experience, and problem-solving capacity.

In a blog for *Forbes* magazine, Selena Rezvani argued that the definition of diversity has changed.

> In addition to creating a workplace inclusive of race, gender, and sexual orientation (to name a few), many organizations are seeking value in something even simpler, diversity of thought. In some industries that are known for being insular—think law or high-tech companies—seeking out talent with different thinking and problem solving backgrounds is critical.

Rezvani reported that a lack of diversity led to groupthink in a corporate company she observed in her consulting practice. She claimed, "Future-thinking companies see the danger in this lack of diversity."[30] Rezvani reinforces the importance of access to diverse talent for organizations. *Groupthink* is a negative outcome that occurs when group members lack diversity; their efforts to achieve unanimity usually result in poor decisions.[31]

One way to decrease the tendency toward groupthink is to be sure your group is composed of diverse thinkers who are not likely to "go along to get along." We will discuss groupthink in greater detail in the context of conflict in group decision making (chapter 10). For now, it is safe to say diversity is not just a politically correct way of doing business. Scholars and practitioners are recognizing that diversity contributes to creativity, increases accountability, and provides connections to greater talent—those benefits beget further bonuses such as innovative techniques and protection against groupthink.

Challenges of Diversity

Although diversity is essential to interorganizational collaboration, we do not want to romanticize the challenges associated with honoring and including diverse perspectives. We will address a few of these challenges, including access, representation, prejudice, and conflict.

The Challenge of Access

One challenge facing stakeholders in the effort to include diverse perspectives is the difficulty of physically bringing people to the table. Renee found partners in an early care and education collaboration inadvertently left out parents of children from low-income families.[32] Although conveners had invited parents and grandparents to participate in the collaboration, the meetings were held during the day—a time convenient for stakeholders who were working on these issues as a part of their positions in their home organizations. But for the parents involved, daytime meetings meant they would have to take unpaid time off from their jobs to attend. The meetings were also held downtown in a large metropolitan city. This location once again served the stakeholders from businesses and nonprofits whose offices were primarily located downtown. The parents of participating children primarily worked and lived outside of the city and would have needed to take public transportation to and from meetings, precluding them from attending daytime meetings. Finally, parents felt isolated at the meetings because of the technical jargon used by childcare and education professionals. As mentioned above, jargon discourages those who are unfamiliar with terminology specific to certain professions from attending and participating—and important, diverse perspectives are lost.

Jargony Language

Do you know what these words mean?

- **Service provider**—those on the front-line of social services who work directly with the public or those receiving services.
- **Memorandum of Agreement (MOA)**—a formalized agreement outlining responsibilities and commitments of partners. Sometimes referred to as Memorandum of Understanding (MOU).
- **Governance Agreement**—formalized agreement or contract regarding fiscal responsibilities, decision methods, implementation responsibilities, data storage, etc., that guide the collaborative group's processes.
- **Capacity**—refers to the ability for organizations to provide services or programs based on their infrastructure, staffing, networked relationships, financial stability, funding potential, and more.
- **Fiscal Agent**—indicates the organization that receives and accounts for money coming into the collaboration, taking on responsibilities of taxes, payroll, and reporting.
- **501(c)(3)**—a legal nonprofit designation determined by the rules of the IRS. Often collaborative organizations cannot receive funds unless they are a designated 501(c)(3) (or one of their partners is and serves as the fiscal agent). Specific rules guide the governance of these types of organizations.
- **Request for Proposal (RFP)**—Granting foundations and the government typically provide RFPs that outline the requirements for applying for funding from their respective organizations. RFPs detail the terms and conditions of what should be included in a grant proposal.
- **Foundation**—an organization dedicated to distributing funds based on their mission. Money is typically distributed as grants.

Nonprofit and governmental partners are frequent members of inter-organizational collaboration. They bring a rich perspective but an equally rich vocabulary that is often hard to access if you are not immersed in their world. The words in the text box are commonly associated with nonprofit organizations. Unless you have worked in or with nonprofit organizations, the terms are probably unfamiliar and inhibiting. Every person and organization participates in unique languages, which limit access and discourage outsiders. These limits have benefits and consequences. By carefully attending to access issues, we can help lessen the reasons some stakeholders disengage or are excluded from collaboration.

> **QUESTION:** Think about jargony language in your own life. How does it limit access to other people? Do you have a "social media" language; a "friend-speak"; certain terms you use at work, school, or on your team? Why do we like to limit access to our language, and what are the consequences for others based on your examples?

The Challenge of Representation

Related to the problem of access is the problem of representation. One question scholars grapple with is the idea of embodied representation. Specifically, can others represent stakeholder groups who would not otherwise be physically present in the collaborative process? Critical scholar Sarah Dempsey explored the question of representation in collaborative partnerships between nongovernment organizations (NGOs) and the people they represent. Dempsey warned:

> Advocacy NGOs provide a particularly troubling example of the ideological functions of communicative labor. Here, personnel collect a wage for speaking and advocating on the behalf of groups without ready access to the public sphere. In so doing, they help constitute the identities of marginalized groups to broader publics across a variety of scales. Many times, the groups for whom they speak have never elected them to represent their interests.[33]

Hence, when the stakeholder is not an embodied participant, a plethora of ethical issues arise for those who speak on their behalf.

The issue of representation is especially pertinent to interorganizational collaboration taking place at the international level involving stakeholders from disadvantaged parts of the world. Dempsey points out that:

> NGOs and other civil society groups who speak on the behalf of others exist in a tension-filled relationship with those they represent. Despite the best of intentions, and by virtue of their ability to speak on the behalf of others, NGOs may further marginalize groups without access to the public sphere. As Linda Alcoff warns, although a speaker "may be trying to materially improve the situation of some lesser privileged group, the effects of [their] discourse [may] . . . reinforce racist,

imperialist conceptions and perhaps . . . silence the lesser- privileged group's own ability to speak and be heard."[34]

In the process of trying to represent diverse others, stakeholders may, in fact, be doing a disservice to those not present by cultivating particular identities for them that may not reflect the absent groups' beliefs. Accordingly, stakeholders must tangle with the ethic-riddled question of who gets to speak on behalf of diverse voices. The further representatives are from the stakeholder groups they claim to represent, the greater the burden they have to consider the identities they are actively constructing for others.

The Challenge of Prejudice

Stereotyping, and its ugly cousin prejudice, may be the elephant in the room when it comes to one of the greatest challenges involved with navigating diversity. While prejudice does exist, and will potentially unravel collaborative efforts, it is not easy to talk about; doing so sometimes comes at great risk. Professor Alexandra Murphy has been involved with an international collaboration between the global north and south with educators and health-care professionals in an HIV prevention project in Kenya, Africa. She speaks poignantly about her gay American colleagues who negotiate health-care policy in a religious culture that stringently punishes homosexuals.[35] Her case is riddled with complexity as dominant Western views must be balanced against local and religious values that are considered prejudiced and oppressive in other cultural contexts. Although our instincts may be to openly confront prejudice, Murphy's study demonstrates the limits of dialogue in certain social and political climates. She argued, "dialogue, and voice, though worthy goals in many situations, do not always lead to the opening up of stereotypes or the advancement of shared understandings . . . remaining silent is also a form of resistance against perceived, and real, dominant power structures."[36] In Murphy's case, the risk of dialogue had to be measured against her colleagues' safety. She claimed,

> While discussing frictions about sexuality may open a discursive space to challenge homophobic norms, there are significant material risks for gay men in Kenya. Gay men and lesbians are routinely beaten and even killed in Kenya, and are subject to a 14-year jail term if discovered.[37]

Murphy reminds us that in some collaborative contexts challenging prejudice can have detrimental, material consequences. Once again, the answer cannot be predetermined; it is found in praxis wholly contingent on the stakes of the situation. Murphy's case illuminates one of the most complex contexts of prejudice, including issues of culture and religion embedded in the larger context of white, Western hegemony. While the decision made by her gay colleagues to stay silent did not contest oppressive homophobic prejudice, it did allow for the collaborative goals around HIV education and health care to continue to be advanced in Kenya. Thus, dealing with prejudice illuminates how identity issues (i.e., sexuality, religion) are interwoven within collaborative problem domains (i.e., HIV prevention), amplifying the challenge of collaborating with those who hold diverse values and worldviews.

The Challenge of Conflict

Finally, as mentioned at the beginning of this chapter, conflict is an inherent challenge of navigating diversity. Conflict in collaboration is widely discussed and is the subject of chapter 10.[38] Conflict must and should occur in the collaboration given that you are bringing together voices from different and disparate bases of knowledge, experience, and understanding. A collaborative stakeholder once complained to Renee, "We are too polite," indicating they did not disagree enough to stimulate the types of discussions and directions they needed to capitalize on the different perspectives and talents around the table. Thus, the challenge that conflict presents regarding diversity is how to practice and capitalize on *constructive* conflict so that requisite differences may surface in a safe and ultimately creative environment. As we see with pluralism, "The world we live in has changed faster than our dominant communication concepts and practices, and these concepts are increasingly less likely to lead to mutually beneficial decisions."[39] Precisely because collaboration requires diversity, and precisely because conflict is inherent in diversity, participants must have the communication skills necessary to foster trust and relationships among people with diverse perspectives. Stakeholders must be able to have the types of conversations that will allow their different perspectives to authentically aid in problem solving.

QUESTION: Have you ever been a part of a diverse group that dealt with challenges of access, representation, prejudice, or constructive conflict? Do you think one of these challenges is more difficult to manage than any other? Why?

CONCLUSION

This chapter adds a second cornerstone in response to our question as to what counts as a collaborative ethic. The chapter continues to build the case for communication to match the complexity and commitments of ethical collaboration. As Facebook COO Sheryl Sandberg argued diversity among intraorganizational teams "have better results, so this is not only the right thing to do—it's also good for our business."[40] An ethical understanding of collaboration elevates the significance of diversity in collaborative processes.

Stakeholders need to reflect on how the membership of the collaboration will shape their understanding of the problem-domain. As stakeholders are invited into the process, discussions are ongoing as to what other voices/resources should be included related to the problem domain. The orientation of the collaboration—community reform, conflict resolution, or resource dependence—will initially influence what counts as diversity. But the lessons of this chapter should also guide decisions regarding what type of diverse perspectives are needed to disrupt the status-quo thinking of present stakeholders. Stakeholders also must consider how the diverse composition of the collaborative group will influence the types of decisions they will make and how the diversity of the group will influence the ability to implement decisions. How do conveners and stakeholders know what is the difference that will make a difference? Our research leads us to believe the process is iterative and, well, collaborative.

Additionally, collaborative stakeholders will need to reflect on the challenges presented with diversity. How can access, especially for those holding marginalized perspectives, be facilitated? How does the group's language include or occlude others? Who can speak for whom? Who gets to represent? How will we handle prejudice as it surfaces? What are the material risks to stakeholders and to the collaboration in the midst of confronting prejudice?

Understanding the complex ways diversity is defined and the important role it plays in collaborative problem solving begs us to consider how the thing that perhaps provides the greatest promise for collaborative problem solving—diversity—can also be the very thing that makes collaboration seem impossible at times. This chapter seeds future discussions on power and principled leadership, advancing the case for why we need to broaden our current repertoire of communication skills to better equip us to face diversity and power differentials in collaborative contexts.

CHAPTER TAKE-AWAYS

- Understand diversity as inseparable from the world we live in today
- Extend the definition of diversity beyond social categories
- Understand requisite diversity as focusing on the difference that makes a difference among dominant perspectives
- Articulate the benefits of diversity in collaboration
- Consider the challenges of diversity in collaboration

ENDNOTES

[1] Stanley Deetz, "Disarticulation and Conflict Transformation: Interactive Design, Collaborative Processes, and Generative Democracy," in *Communication and Conflict Transformation: Local to Global Engagements*, ed. T. G. Matyok and P. Kellett (Lanham, MD: Lexington Books, 2016).

[2] Ibid.

[3] Stanley Deetz and Elizabeth Eger, "Developing a Metatheoretical Perspective for Organizational Communication Studies," in *The Sage Handbook of Organizational Communication:*

Advances in Theory, Research, and Methods, ed. Linda L. Putnam and Dennis K. Mumby (Thousand Oaks, CA: Sage Publications, 2013), 27–48.

[4] Online Etymology Dictionary, "Diversity," http://www.etymonline.com/index.php?term= diversity

[5] Brenda J. Allen, *Difference Matters: Communicating Social Identity*, 2nd ed. (Long Grove, IL: Waveland Press, 2010).

[6] Renee Guarriello Heath, *Toward Social Problem Solving: Democracy and Creativity in Community Models of Collaboration* (University of Colorado at Boulder: Dissertation Abstracts International, 66-09A, 2005).

[7] Ibid.

[8] Barbara Gray, *Collaborating: Finding Common Ground for Multiparty Problems* (San Francisco: Jossey-Bass, 1989), pp. 97–99.

[9] Judith E. Innes and David E. Booher, *Planning with Complexity: An Introduction to Collaborative Rationality for Public Policy* (New York: Routledge, 2010).

[10] Jonathan Lange, "Environmental Collaboration and Constituency Communication," in *Group Communication in Context: Studies of Bona Fide Groups*, ed. Larry R. Frey (Mahwah, NJ: Lawrence Erlbaum, 2003), 209–34.

[11] Innes and Booher, *Planning with Complexity*.

[12] Ted Bernard, *Hope and Hard Times: Communities, Collaboration and Sustainability* (Gabriola Island, BC: New Catalyst Books, 2013).

[13] Cassandra Moseley, "The Applegate Partnership: Innovation in Crisis," in *Across the Great Divide: Explorations in Collaborative Conservation and the American West*, ed. Philip Brick, Donald Snow, and Sarah van de Wetering (Washington, DC: Island Press, 2001), 102–11.

[14] Jeffrey Pfeffer and Gerald R. Salancik, *The External Control of Organizations: A Resource Dependence Perspective* (Redwood City, CA: Stanford University Press, 1978).

[15] Caryn Medved et al., "Tensions in Community Health Improvement Initiatives: Communication and Collaboration in a Managed Care Environment," *Journal of Applied Communication Research* 29, no. 2 (January 1, 2001): 137–52, doi:10.1080/00909880128107.

[16] Renee Guarriello Heath, "Rethinking Community Collaboration through a Dialogic Lens: Creativity, Democracy, and Diversity in Community Organizing," *Management Communication Quarterly* 21, no. 2 (November 1, 2007): 145–71, doi:10.1177/0893318907306032.

[17] Medved et al., "Tensions in Community Health Improvement Initiatives"; Heath, "Rethinking Community Collaboration through a Dialogic Lens."

[18] Stanley Deetz, *Democracy in an Age of Corporate Colonization: Developments in Communication and the Politics of Everyday Life* (Albany, NY: SUNY Press, 1992).

[19] Ibid.

[20] Stanley Deetz, Personal Communication, interview by Renee Guarriello Heath, February 3, 2015.

[21] Innes and Booher, *Planning with Complexity*.

[22] For more on tokenism see Judith Long Laws, "The Psychology of Tokenism: An Analysis," *Sex Roles* 1, no. 1 (1975): 51–67, doi:10.1007/BF00287213; Linda Kathryn Larkey, "Toward a Theory of Communicative Interactions in Culturally Diverse Workgroups," *Academy of Management Review* 21, no. 2 (April 1, 1996): 463–91, doi:10.5465/AMR.1996.9605060219; Rosabeth Moss Kanter, *Men and Women of the Corporation* (New York: Basic Books, 1977).

[23] Lindsay Degouve De Nuncques, "Output Is Central to Diversity Debate," *The National*, February 5, 2015, http://www.thenational.ae/business/the-life/output-is-central-to-diversity-debate

[24] Deetz, Personal Communication.

[25] Charlan Jeanne Nemeth and Margaret Ormiston, "Creative Idea Generation: Harmony versus Stimulation," *European Journal of Social Psychology* 37, no. 3 (May 1, 2007): 524–35, doi:10.1002/ejsp, p. 373.

[26] Angela Ka-yee Leung et al., "Multicultural Experience Enhances Creativity: The When and How," *American Psychologist* 63, no. 3 (2008): 169–81, doi:10.1037/0003-066X.63.3.169.

[27] Innes and Booher, *Planning with Complexity*.

28 Heath, "Rethinking Community Collaboration through a Dialogic Lens."

29 Bernard, *Hope and Hard Times*.

30 Selena Rezvani, "Five Trends Driving Workplace Diversity in 2015," *Work in Progress: Career Talk for Women*, February 3, 2015, http://blogs.forbes.com/work-in-progress/author/selenarezvani/

31 Irving L. Janis, *Groupthink: Psychological Studies of Policy Decisions and Fiascoes*, 2nd ed. (Boston: Cengage Learning, 1982).

32 Heath, "Rethinking Community Collaboration through a Dialogic Lens."

33 Sarah E. Dempsey, "NGOs, Communicative Labor, and the Work of Grassroots Representation," *Communication and Critical/Cultural Studies* 6, no. 4 (December 1, 2009): 328–45, p. 330. doi:10.1080/14791420903348625.

34 Ibid., p. 331.

35 Alexandra G. Murphy, "Discursive Frictions: Power, Identity, and Culture in an International Working Partnership," *Journal of International and Intercultural Communication* 6, no. 1 (February 1, 2013): 1–20. doi:10.1080/17513057.2012.740683, p. 17.

36 Ibid., p. 17.

37 Ibid., p. 17.

38 Gray, *Collaborating*; Steven Daniels and Gregg Walker, *Working through Environmental Conflict: The Collaborative Learning Approach* (Westport, CT: Praeger Publishers, 2001), http://digitalcommons.usu.edu/sswa_facpubs/60

39 Deetz, "Disarticulation and Conflict Transformation."

40 Sheryl Sandberg, "Managing Unconscious Bias | Facebook Newsroom," *Facebook Newsroom*, July 28, 2015, http://newsroom.fb.com/news/2015/07/managing-unconscious-bias/

6

(Shared) Power

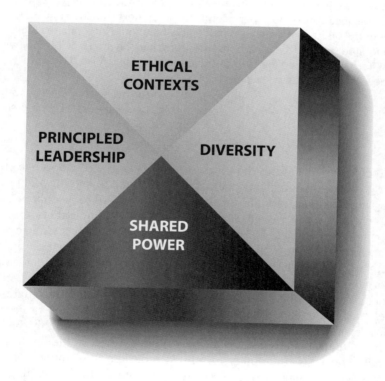

Out of My League

I felt a bit out of my league among the community leaders in this large county meeting room. Here I was sitting in a circle with Maggie, the assistant superintendent of schools, Mike, the county's chief financial officer (CFO), and Terry, a vice president from the local college, to name a few of the stakeholders. I was just out of college and only one year into my position at a nonprofit job training organization—their years of experience surpassed my age. I was invited to join them because I had the power to place high school students in job training positions as I saw fit. This group wanted my students to work in a new program aimed at making learning fun for young children at risk of dropping out. My organization was interested in aligning itself with these stakeholders in an innovative new project. Mike, the eternally optimistic and visionary convener of this group, coaxed, "Renee, we'd like your highschoolers to work in the classrooms with our children." Cautiously I countered, "Our students are at risk of dropping out of school themselves. That is why they are in our program. In order for this to be a successful placement, they will need very good supervision." The group next launched into a thoughtful discussion. They considered how they could integrate the high school students into the classroom and strengthen the model of job supervision. Terry approached me after the meeting, "I just told Mike, 'I like this Renee—she is not just a yes-person.'"[1]

—Renee reflecting on her first day meeting with
stakeholders of the Best SELF program

Shared power constitutes the third cornerstone of the collaborative ethic. Power is one of the most important concepts related to leading and participating in interorganizational collaboration. It is linked to just about every other central concept we have covered thus far, including structure, stakeholder interdependence, identity, ethics, and diversity. Successful collaborations hinge on the ability of stakeholders to share decision-making power. Indeed, scholars have argued for decades that the chief reason interorganizational collaboration fails is due to power inequities.[2] Cheryl Freeman, Director of Advocacy and Justice at World Vision International, argues that if a collaborating partner becomes dominant in a project, "it quickly reverts to a subcontract like arrangement—and invariably the benefits for all partners are lost."[3] Freeman defines power in the interorganizational context as "the ability to influence design, implementation, and ongoing decision making of projects and programs."[4] Understanding how power works in organizational structures and how power differences can be mitigated is foundational knowledge for stakeholders.

The excerpt from Renee's experience hints at many of the issues regarding power—including how it is relational and shared, as well as how to create parity among stakeholders. We will unpack these topics using this case throughout the chapter. We begin by examining power as it is understood in horizontal decision-making contexts. Next we articulate its relational features in collaboration and introduce a classic typology for understanding how stakeholders construct power from a variety of sources. Later, we discuss power in two contexts. First, we explore the macrocontext regarding the democratic responsibility of collaboration as well as how hegemony is sometimes embedded in its composition. Second, we examine how power can be shared in the microcontext of group behavior by aiming for egalitarianism and parity in systems and processes. We close the chapter by exploring the discursive enactment of hidden power in the group context, providing some suggestions that will contribute to shared decision making.

Hierarchy and Power Structures

Often when we begin to teach students or train stakeholders about collaborative leadership, they have a hard time conceptualizing the shared power concept of collaboration. That is probably because as a society we tend to conflate leadership with hierarchy. We imagine leaders at the top of a pyramid of employees who have ultimate authority regarding decisions (figure 6.1). Yet one of the ways we define collaboration is via its nonhierarchical attributes (figure 6.2 on p. 122).

Power is dispersed among organizations and stakeholder members—no one person or organization is solely accountable for the collaboration. Participating organizations do not work for one another; they have significant responsibilities to their own organizations; and their continued part-

Figure 6.1 Traditional model of leadership with a hierarchy of power.

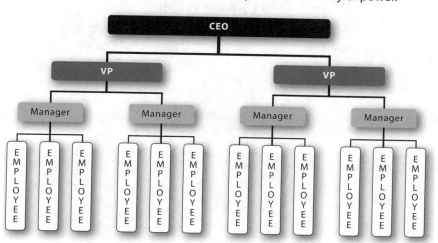

nership depends on the idea that the partnership is worth participating in and will yield benefits. Should partners feel dismissed, disrespected, or that their involvement does not provide any benefits, they are generally not compelled to continue participating. They will not lose pay or their jobs (provided there is no political cost to their organization) if they stop collaborating. This organizational structure then looks nothing like the typical top-down structure of leadership and power with the usual incentives of pay and promotion within the organization.

Instead, the metaphor of a round table characterizes how power works differently in collaboration. As discussed in chapter 2, collaborations are structured so that stakeholders share decision making—and therefore share accountability. The outcomes of the collaboration, whether successful or not, are the responsibility of its members and not the singular responsibility of any one organization. This feature demands that we reconceptualize leadership and power as something that does not originate from the top. It is negotiated, shared, and distributed among partners.

Figure 6.2   Collaborative model of leadership with shared power.

Power Is Relational and Constructed with Others

Power permeates our communication. In every conversation we are negotiating more than just the contents of our words—we are negotiating our identity, our relationships, and social orders (how the world works).[5] In the example above, Renee argued that her students were at risk of dropping out of school and would need supervision if they were placed in classrooms to work with younger children. The content (truth of her statement) could have been contested by others in the room. Because it wasn't, her fellow stakeholders granted her authority on the subject. This interaction also reinforced Renee's identity as a local expert on the at-risk children she placed in jobs; it worked to create and legitimate a particular relationship with the other stakeholders. She was respected for her knowledge on the subject matter, reinforcing an equality with others despite her young age and limited experience. Finally, this interaction reinforced a particular social order for this collaborative group—the interaction reinforced egalitarian *group* values. Power is always present when we interact with others. How we respond (or not) to others in decision-making situations influences how power is dispersed or challenged.

THE PEOPLE DON'T KNOW
THEIR TRUE POWER.

The cartoon is a fun illustration of how power is always enacted in relation to others. Power is never solely held or concentrated. Power is granted—either knowingly or unknowingly, willingly or unwillingly—by others.[6] Elections grant officials the power and influence to cast votes on our behalf, to control messages, and to shape narratives. However, we retain the power to vote them out of office; we pay attention to their voting records, and we can demand transparency from them. Even in feudal systems as depicted in *Game of Thrones*, power is tentative and dependent on others to honor or grant it. Hierarchical organizations (like figure 6.1) are not immune to the relational qualities of power. Consider the swift fall of Sony's chief executive officer, Amy Pascal. In late 2014, she refused to release the controversial movie, *The Interview,* which openly criticized North Korean leader, Kim Jong-un. In part, public outcry in defense of freedom of speech led to her firing, coupled with controversial personal emails leaked by hackers.[7] These examples illustrate that power is negotiated in concert with others.

Power Types in Interorganizational Collaboration

Power is not a possession. It is negotiated with others and is relational—a fluid concept that is tied to a plethora of sources in many complex ways. The classic typology of social power describes five bases—coercive power, reward power, legitimate power, expert power, and referent power.[8] The social power bases illuminate how stakeholders individually have access to different types of power. The five bases also explain how some collaborative groups become very powerful.

Coercive power is gained through punishments and threats. In collaboration, unwilling or unlikely stakeholders may be forced to the table via coercive power, as was the case with Shell Oil Inc. Relentless publicity launched by Greenpeace regarding the environmentally hazardous decommissioning of the Brent Spar oil platform (see chapter 2) nudged Shell to broaden stakeholder participation. Collaboration scholars call manipulative behavior that plays politics "collaborative thuggery" and argue that stakeholders must manage a tension between collaborative thuggery and a spirit of collaboration, switching between coercive and more nurturing behaviors.[9] Of course, coercive tactics are risky because stakeholders begin their collaborative problem solving with ill feelings and distrust caused by unequal power and thuggery. Coercive power is unlikely to keep stakeholders at the table, and stakeholders who complain of being mandated to participate by government or other authorities are usually the least cooperative.[10]

Reward power is also a strong motivator to participate in collaboration. For example, in the case that leads this chapter, Renee's nonprofit organization was willing to participate in the county's collaboration because leaders of her organization believed they would gain credibility, access, and strengthened relationships with key figures in the county and school district. Indeed, most collaborating stakeholders will need to believe that there is going to be some type of reward for participating. Sometimes that reward may be the altruistic joy of doing good, but most of the time stakeholders anticipate rewards at the organizational level (their organization will benefit from the collaboration) *and* the interorganizational level (they anticipate the reward of a joint mission accomplished). Organizational and interorganizational rewards are powerful enticers to collaborate and indeed constitute interdependent relationships among stakeholders. Each depends on the others for the success of the partnership and to realize the hopes of their own organization. In other words, if the county partnership failed to meet its goals of helping at risk children, Renee's organization would have something to lose as well; the loss is shared among partners. Accordingly, collaborative leaders are skilled at linking stakeholder participation to potential rewards.

Legitimate power is associated with a position or the particular authority of a position. In the case above, Mike enacted legitimate power by nature of his position as chief financial officer for the county. He controlled funding that would seed the program. Other stakeholders such as the assistant superintendent of schools and the college vice president were also granted authority to contribute resources and to make decisions in the collaborative partnership on behalf of their organizations. Their power to do so was embedded in the positions they held. Legitimate power is an important concept to consider in collaboration. At the stakeholder level, partners should be in positions that will permit them the flexibility to make decisions on behalf of their organizations. When partners are not decision makers and lacking legitimate power within their own organizations, processes will be slow and cumbersome due to the layers of communication that must take place between organizational stakeholder representatives and the leaders of the organizations they represent.[11]

Legitimate power is also important to consider at the level of the stakeholder group. Barbara Gray warned that when considering stakeholder membership, the collaboration must include partners who have the ability to implement whatever outcomes are determined by the collaboration.[12] In other words, does the collaboration have legitimate power to innovate or problem solve on the given task? Legitimate power may be gained by inviting key stakeholders such as government officials. Although government stakeholders frequently adopt neutral positions in collaboration, they are often key to the implementation of collaborative outcomes and therefore should be a part of the problem-solving process. Legitimate power may also be won based on the stature of particular stakeholders who may hold sway over public or political opinion, providing credibility to the work accomplished by the collaboration.

Expert power may also be attributed individually to stakeholders or collectively to a collaborative group. Individual stakeholders may be invited for their scientific, technical, social, political, or other expertise. Particularly in environmental collaboration, it is unlikely solutions will be found without the participation of expert stakeholders who understand the nuances of complex environmental problems. Their individual power is grounded in their expert knowledge of the issues. Collaborations may also gain expert power over time. Renee witnessed this in her study of a collaboration focused on early care and education for young children. The group of stakeholders became a go-to group for the school board, and their expertise was regularly solicited on issues associated with preschool education.[13]

Referent power, the last base of power, is typically associated with charismatic power or power earned by garnering the respect of followers. In the example that opens this chapter, Mike's optimism and vision for the possibilities of collaboration earned him great referent power. In the next chapter, we will discuss how his skilled knowledge of communication structures and practices contributed to his collaborative leadership and ultimately garnered him the admiration of the stakeholders he convened. While some may attribute referent power to particular, personality traits, we believe referent power can also be fostered through good communication.

In all of these mechanisms for gaining power, a relational quality is present. Coercive power and reward power require that the targets of that power care about the rewards or punishment. These types of power hold no sway if the sticks or carrots are meaningless. Legitimate power is most often tied to a position; however, membership is fluid in collaborations (just like organizations), and partners will be promoted, move, or leave their own organizations. Representatives may gain or lose legitimate power in the collaboration depending on their relationships with their stakeholder organizations. For example, Jonathon Lange, an environmental collaboration scholar, described a partnership in which a member left his position with Headwaters, the environmental stakeholder organization he represented; the member continued in the partnership because he belonged to other interested stakeholder groups.[14] However, his legitimate power to represent Headwaters was no longer viable. Indeed, Headwaters chose to end its participation after his departure from the organization. Expert power also depends on the stakeholder's relationship to the subject matter. Power is derived from stakeholder expertise as long as it is needed and as long as one's performance as an expert is accepted and "endorsed" by the other collaborative members. Once expertise or legitimacy is challenged, stakeholder power may be diminished.[15] Finally, referent power is perhaps most dependent on the idea that others' grant you power because of your persuasive, dialogic, and inclusive skills. By theorizing power as a fluid concept that is tied to many sources in many complex ways, we are better equipped to understand how to achieve power balances in collaboration. The typology of social power bases also helps to explain how different stakeholders individually negotiate different types of power and that power is not concentrated but dispersed, tentative, and interdependent within many contingencies.

QUESTION: Examine an interorganizational collaboration in your community. Who are the stakeholders? Using the social power typology, consider the ways stakeholders access power. Do some stakeholders have access to more power than others? Why?

Power and Democracy in Collaboration

Given that power imbalances are often at the heart of failed collaboration, collaborative leaders and stakeholders must learn how to foster and practice shared power and decision making in collaboration. As discussed in our chapter on ethics, there are other important reasons to share power—perhaps none more significant than the legitimacy of collaborative decisions. Environmental Attorney George Cameron Coggins was an early critic of collaborations. He felt that decisions made on behalf of communities were not legitimate or democratic when made by unelected or self-appointed partnerships.[16] Indeed, Renee's research found that collaboration stakeholders can lose track of the people to whom they are accountable. In one study she found most stakeholders identified each other as the constituents to whom they were most accountable rather than the public, even when they were receiving money from public entities.[17] This reaffirms the fear that collaborative stakeholders are not cognizant of their democratic responsibilities to the people on whose behalf they make decisions.

Unawareness of democratic accountability is problematic if we think back to some of the wicked problems that opened this book. Collaborative decisions have tremendous significance for a democratic public when the consequences of those decisions impact drug epidemics, safe drinking water, and the spread of infectious diseases. Parallel to our discussion on ethics, we see two primary contexts essential to understanding power in collaboration: the macro sociopolitical context and the microcontext of the collaborative group. In the macrocontext, we develop interorganizational collaboration as a forum for participative democracy, and as a departure from liberal democratic forums and native practices of communication.

The Problem with Liberal Democracy and Native Communication

Democracy is a contested term. Benjamin Barber, a political theorist, articulates several conceptions of democracy; two are particularly relevant to our discussion. First, "liberal democracy" is best illustrated in the US political system by voting and representative politics.[18] However, liberal democracy arguably steals voice from the individual by aggregating viewpoints that give credence to the majority but mute the minority. Instead, Barber advocates for "strong democracy," also called participative democracy. In participative democracy, individuals directly make decisions at local levels rather than abdicating this responsibility to representatives.[19] This model of decision making strongly resembles grass-roots interorganizational collaboration.

Communication manifests differently in these distinct models of democracy. Liberal democracy relies on norms of voting and persuasion, and forums to express diverse opinions. Professor Stanley Deetz calls these norms and practices *native communication*, our default settings for communicating and making decisions.[20] The problem with native communication is that while voting, persuasion, and expression support the adversarial system of liberal democracy, they do not foster participative democracy very well. For example, persuasion is appropriate when decision makers share definitions and assumptions regarding a particular subject. However, given the diversity involved in collaboration, if stakeholders cannot even agree on basic definitions or share values, persuasion is ineffective and likely to be harmful.

Voting also is appropriate when decision makers are elected, and constituents can assume some certainty in how they will be represented as well as some assurance that their seats at the table were legitimately won. However, when decision makers are voluntary or appointed without input from those on whose behalf they make decisions, as they frequently are in collaboration, voting is often inappropriate. The minority voices in a collaboration are not a result of fewer votes but the result of a capricious, volunteer process of invitation and stakeholder membership. Minority opinion voices could easily be outvoted in collaboration strictly determined by the composition of the collaboration.

Critiques that collaborations do not act democratically apply to the macrosociopolitical context, especially given the power of collaboration to affect environmental, political, and social policy; new legislation, and community planning. This worry may be especially relevant regarding collaborative groups that have become "institutionalized,"[21] meaning they have gained credibility and social capital in their communities. Recall from chapter 4 that social capital refers to "connections among individuals—social networks and the norms of reciprocity and trustworthiness that arise from them."[22] With social capital, collaborations are advising, writing, and leading policy in political and social arenas that have traditionally been the purview of elected officials and liberal (i.e., representative) democratic politics[23] in the United States. Because collaboration members are frequently self-selected, and may be the product of grassroots efforts, stakeholders must be mindful of their unelected power and its effects on other stakeholders who may not be included in the collaboration. Accordingly, many collaborations taking place in the public sphere have democratic obligations—whether they are aware of them or not.

In cases where collaboration is perceived to be making decisions on behalf of a greater public, it behooves stakeholders to adopt appropriate democratic processes that reflect participative democracy to legitimize decisions made.[24] Participative processes transform conflict into creative decisions through dialogue, eliciting and including diverse interests, gracious contestation, consensus decision making, and appreciative methods.

Conveners and stakeholders who attend to requisite diversity in their stake-holder membership will also be able to claim greater participative democracy in their collaborative structures (discussed in chapter 5). Participative democracy beckons new ways of communicating that are grounded in very different assumptions about sharing power and capitalizing on diversity.

> **QUESTION**: What are the communication processes associated with liberal democracy? Why don't they transfer well to collaborative decision making? How might the collaborative decision-making forum look and sound different from other political decision-making forums?

Spotlight scholar Stanley Deetz is chiefly concerned with the way power distorts the possibilities for organizations to generate creative and just outcomes. He explains the inadequacies of liberal democracy and posits his vision of generative democracy, which calls for organizational participation and accountability. His vision expands on the ideas of participative democracy and the potential of interorganizational collaboration regarding wicked problems.

SCHOLAR SPOTLIGHT

Generative Democracy
Stanley Deetz

Allow me to begin with the big picture. My work fits in a project to invent new ways to think about and practice communication and democracy. Neither can be deeply rethought without rethinking the other. The desire is to design new processes of human interaction and systems of governance enhancing the ability of the world to thrive in conditions characterized by fast rapid change, high degrees of pluralism and interdependency, and highly mediated (and sponsored) human experience. Without this, we and other species with us will at best merely survive the conflicts set in play by expected social and ecological changes.

I start with the big picture not because my work does all that but to keep in mind the end being sought. At best I have outlined a direction and detailed some pieces. The core issue in all of this is to understand the nature and consequences of power relations and productively work both within them and to reform them where they become harmful.

All interaction designs have to work with four basic questions central to democratic theory. These are answered differently based on larger concepts of human beings and their interaction. (1) What is the nature and source of human experi-

(continued)

ence, knowledge, and meaning? (2) How shall group and individual differences be presented or represented, or, in the case of democracies, how shall reciprocity be assured? (3) What shall be the preferred talk processes when we have differences, and how should the conflict around difference be adjudicated? (4) How shall we deal with the problem of scale given that decisions often involve large populations?

Liberal democratic conceptions and practices are based on particular answers to these four questions: (1) The autonomous individual is seen as the origin of perceptions, thoughts, and feelings. Communication study focuses on the expression of these. (2) Freedom of speech and speaking forums are considered to be adequate and adequately available for equitable participation in decision making. (3) Persuasion and advocacy are seen as the preferred mode of interaction when differences are present, leading to decisions by voting when differences and conflict remain. (4) Representation is used to overcome problems of scale. Representation may be based in lottery selection as in juries, elections as in representatives, or distribution as done in representing interests in community planning.

The difficulty of liberal democracy and the embedded/enabling communication theory for our contemporary and projected future is that is does not take into account actual power relations, assuming power can somehow be overcome by the force of reason and does not provide an interaction process that generates creativity.

The primary difficulty arises with the very first assumption that accepts a psychological rather than social/communication bases for experience production. If constructionism is accepted, democracy exists or does not in the systems of construction rather than expression. A critical interest in interaction has to focus on the interaction processes by which experiences came to be rather than simply on the manner of their expression and coordination. If experiences are socially constructed, they are always constructed within real historical conditions; hence, relations of power are always embedded within constructions, as well as relations of power determine who and how constructions can be used. All constructions benefit some more than others, but because they become a kind of commonsense, the disadvantaged come to unwittingly reproduce their disadvantage as they freely speak meanings produced by others. High degrees of mediation of experience and the absence of places for critical discussions accentuate this effect.

My work has spent considerable time discerning the complex processes of construction and the way it and its effects are rendered invisible in contemporary society. I'll be very brief here. I show that experience is a relational production. And to make the relation to power more precise I have shown that six interrelated relational constructions are present—constructions of (1) the inner world of the person, (2) personal identities in relation to others, (3) appropriate social behavior, (4) understanding of the external world, (5) stories of how the social world works, and (6) systems of appropriate justice and fairness. Each of these has a related politics when power is considered—authenticity, identity and recognition, social order, truth, the good and beautiful, and distribution.

To account for relations of power and to provide more creativity in human interactions, in contrast to liberal democracy, I propose a generative democracy, a democracy based on the potential productivity of difference in interaction. Generative democracy (1) describes experience as a power laden relational construction, (2) uses a strong sense of reciprocity as a normative ideal for the distribution of expression turns, (3) prefers *collaborative talk*, and (4) overcomes scale by the preservation and presentation of meaningful differences.

Within this general perspective, most of my specific studies have focused on workplaces and especially their corporate form. Corporations are very impactful in democracy. First they are powerful political actors in the traditional sense that can greatly distort the public decision-making process. This is why corporations were widely distrusted by the framers of the US constitution, and even Adam Smith treated them in a pejorative sense. Second, democracy to be meaningful needs to occur in the places most critical decisions are made. The corporate site is a key place decisions are being made regarding the use of natural and human resources, the distribution of income and wealth, identities production and family relations, and much more. From a moral standpoint, the public should be part of the processes that determine their future. Existing systems for getting social value into the decision chain such as leader stewardship, governmental regulation, and market pressures have tended to be only modestly effective, highly inefficient and often costly, and not productive of creative win-win choices. Finally, corporate organizations through internal training, media sponsorship and ownership, advertising, political messaging, and so on colonize the overall experience production process. The choices and activities of the corporate work site are a central issue of democracy.

But even beyond that, dominant power relations have hurt work productivity and the economic health of work organizations. *Managerialism* positively rationalizes the largely narrow self-interested value laden choice making of corporations. The myth of the "rational," "economic" organization hides the value system embedded in the monetary code (e.g., accounting practices) and the multiple ways values enter into social productions and decision making. Values are already present, the question is: Whose and which values enter where within the decision chain? And, do we have interaction design that enables productive gains from the tensions and differences?

Basically through my research and direct involvement in organizational change I have hoped to (1) provide a unified way of understanding the complex processes of organizational life through focusing on organizational constructions and embedded power relations; (2) direct the evaluation of existing organizational forms and activities through looking at distorting reproductive activities focusing on unwitting consent, systematically distorted communication, and forms of discursive closure; and (3) provide guidance for the education of members and redesign of organizational structures and practices that allow earlier and deeper inclusion of diverse values in the decision chain, thereby increasing organizational agility and innovation and the ability to increase economic, social, and ecological goods.

This later concern has been of most significance recently. It doesn't help much to know what organizations should do or even to identify what they do poorly. The critical issue is to develop design processes that lead to better meetings, more creative decisions, and better social impacts. Deficit guiding concepts of democracy and understanding of good practices has led many to feel that collaborative forms of management or what I call co-generative management can be inefficient or even costly. Generative forms of democracy need both good theory and positive practices.

Hegemony and Collaboration

As we consider power in collaboration from a macrodemocratic context, we must acknowledge that collaborative decision making takes place within and among hegemonic systems and structures. The concept of hegemony names the unseen and invisible power that orders the way we view and participate in (often oppressive) societal structures.[25] "Hegemony includes but is not limited to ideology."[26] It has been described as "when the leadership of one group dominates another group through the subjugated group's unwitting acquiescence or active participation."[27] This is what Deetz refers to when he discusses corporate colonization.

Hegemony bears great resemblance to systematic distortion—Jürgen Habermas's conception of invisible power—to which we consent by continuing to communicate and behave in ways that keep these power structures intact.[28] "Systematically distorted communication operates like strategic manipulation but without overt awareness."[29] In other words, our decision-making conversations are often laden with invisible and insidious influence. Ultimately, hegemony and systematically distorted communication name the ways dominant power structures and practices work to suppress marginalized groups. For example, a growing number of college campuses around the United States have joined Missouri State, Ithaca, and Yale universities to protest the "systematic oppression" of racism embedded in our higher education institutions. Consider how the application process for getting into college works as a gatekeeper to limit access for less advantaged students. The process is so complex and layered that those with greater resources (such as access to tutors/advisors and the funds to take multiple entrance exams) have advantages in gaining college acceptance over students without access to resources, thus perpetuating oppression in some communities. The process is systematically distorted to the point that we willingly and unwittingly accept these practices as the norm and do not see their inherent inequality, thus reproducing their hegemony.

An example of hegemonic power and systematic oppression can be seen in a study by Alessia Contu and Emanuela Girei of two collaborative international nongovernmental organization (INGO) partnerships working on issues of human rights and equality in Uganda.[30] Their study illuminates how hegemony works to distort power in partnerships and is reproduced in normative practices. They pointed out that the relationships between the primarily northern INGOs and community groups and governments in the global south were deemed "partnerships." INGO materials implied "positive values, such as mutuality, dialogue and reciprocity in decision making at all levels."[31] However, northern INGOs advised their southern "partners" as to what was missing from their proposals for projects in an effort to make the projects more attractive to donors. In other words, funders drove the parameters of needed projects in the south rather than the local stakeholders. Priorities of the funders, including "seeing results" and "showing [measurable] impact" rather than local need, became the drivers of the project designs. The authors argued,

> [The INGO] requests silence the needs, knowledge and work done by the local stakeholders who participated in the pilot project. [Their] requests are established by invoking donors' conditions, which legitimize (and are legitimized by) managerialist tendencies, that is, the need to comply to specific management imperatives (to show results established only by the INGO) and tools. . . . This is an aid chain that is shown to be more of an aid hierarchy: that is, the community is subordinated to Agandi, which is subordinated to [the INGO], which is subordinated to donor conditions.[32]

This study establishes how project design practices become systematically distorted by the power embedded in the interdependency of donor contributions. It provides a poignant example of how partnerships can be dominated by hegemonic, Western, practices that are accepted and uncontested as the norm for how collaboration is conducted in north/south "partnerships." Ultimately Western interests drive and define what counts as impact instead of the local community service providers. Hegemonic power can only be contested when stakeholders have access and influence to determine the values that drive funding and support for their projects.

Hegemonic power is not just limited to stakeholder relationships that cross international boundaries. Hegemony can be found in preferred processes, planning, funding requirements, and measurements of success. To make visible hegemonic power that unwittingly advantages some while working to suppress others, collaboration stakeholders should carefully consider how they will determine success. What are the indicators and the origins of those indicators? Considering that many collaborations are working on solving long-term social and environmental problems, concrete outcomes and change may not be visible for years. How will the collaboration know, learn, and adapt as its members seek their goals? What counts as important for funding, planning, and measurement cannot be determined outside the diverse needs, interests, and knowledge of stakeholder partners. The potential presence of hegemonic power reinforces the need for stakeholders to have equal access to influence collaboration decisions. Such access is constituted by communication practices and structures.

QUESTION: How does the case of hegemony in the INGO exemplify Deetz's concern with "managerialism"?

APPLICATION: Identify a grant application sponsored by a foundation or government. What are the expectations for measuring success? Do you recognize any hegemonic biases? Based on the requirements of the grant, are there marginalized groups that are not eligible to apply because they do not have the capacity (i.e., money, staff) to measure the outcomes required by the grant?

Sharing Power in the Collaborative Group

When we foreground the microcontext of interaction in the collaborative group, we see that power imbalances simply cannot be sustained over time. For instance, Matt observed that during major decisions, the stakeholders involved with OCEAN would swell, and an inordinate amount of people spoke and voted on behalf of the neighborhoods. This was problematic as the other stakeholder groups did not have the same number of representatives at the table; consequently, their voices were minimalized during discussion. The result was that fewer and fewer business and development stakeholders attended so that by the time a decision was voted on, it did not represent the views of the collaboration as a whole but rather a particular group of stakeholders in the collaboration.[33] Thus, the concept of sharing power was violated when one group decided to "pack the room" to crowd out the opinions of others. Consequently, not everyone had access to the same rights and influence in the collaboration. Overall, OCEAN began to be seen as the voice of one or two larger neighborhoods; it lost the legitimacy to represent the entirety of East Austin at city council meetings. In this section we examine how communicative structures and practices either foster or hinder sharing power because of their importance to collaborative sustainability.

Egalitarian Collaborative Spirit

Although sharing power and sharing decision making are imperative to collaboration, it is unrealistic to believe that equality will ever be fully attained in collaborative groups. Instead, stakeholders must rely on a *collaborative spirit* (general principles regarding acceptable goals, values, and behaviors that underlie and guide the collaboration) of shared power and the value of egalitarianism.[34] Egalitarianism is rooted in the principle of equality[35] and has also been described as a commitment to make decisions without hierarchy.[36]

For many reasons, collaborative stakeholders will have different or unequal access to negotiate or enact power. The organization that convenes the process has tremendous power (informal hierarchy) by being the first organization to invite or initiate partnerships with other stakeholders. Power is also influenced by the communication of the collaboration including who writes the agenda and the minutes. Power is constructed by an individual representative's ability to articulate an expert stance on the topic or to convey their message charismatically. Power is determined by who is most persuasive and who draws others to their ideas. Additionally, numerous structures and processes influence power, such as whose building hosts meetings and who has access to what resources.

The point is that power in collaboration will never be uniformly equal, thus egalitarianism must be constructed via group behavior and attitudes, guided by a collaborative spirit. For example, in the Best SELF case that began this chapter, the county became the fiscal agent for the collaboration. Any money brought into the project (i.e., grants and donations) and any money paid out (i.e., teacher salaries) was filtered through the accounting offices of the county. In the same collaboration, the school districts provided busses and buildings to facilitate summer programs and field trips. In each of these instances, the county and the school districts had tremendous power as chief contributors to the project. Had they withdrawn their resources, the viability of the program was at stake. Indeed, organizational capacity is frequently named as a contributor to uneven power distribution among collaborative stakeholders.[37] Despite the unequal distribution of power among stakeholders in the Best SELF program, a spirit of egalitarianism was constructed via the attitudes and behaviors of group leaders and members.

A spirit of egalitarianism can be generated through the micropractices of the group. For example, if a collaborative group depends on grants for funding, those funds will have to be housed in an organization that is registered as a nonprofit 501(c)(3) for tax purposes. This organization acts as the fiscal agent for the collaboration (unless the collaboration applies and is awarded 501(c)(3) status). Much is to be considered when choosing who will act as the fiscal agent for the collaboration. If the funding entails managing a payroll and/or distributing funds to other entities, it is wise to choose an experienced fiscal agent. The fiscal agent has a responsibility to the collaboration to be transparent and accountable for the funds. Given the power granted to fiscal agents, some collaborative groups have chosen less prominent stakeholder organizations as their fiscal agents. This helps maintain a balance of power when stakeholder groups include participants from resource-rich organizations such as government organizations or well-funded private for-profit corporations. If feasible, choosing a less powerful stakeholder as a fiscal agent can help foster structural equivalence among partners. If all members, and especially those who have unequal access to power, believe the group is committed to egalitarianism, stakeholders will feel they have equal access and ability to influence collaborative decisions regardless of the presence of experts or resource managers. Thus egalitarian values are produced and enacted in the structures and behaviors of stakeholders.

QUESTION: In your examination of a local collaboration, consider who convened the collaboration? How is it funded? Is there a spirit of egalitarianism present? Explain.

Parity Rather than Equality

Given that equality is never fully attainable in collaborations, stakeholders should instead strive for parity, which implies equality in the system or conditions of interacting rather than as an attribute of stakeholders.[38] Power parity is achieved when a stakeholder is unable to *impose* their proposed solution on the other collaborative members.[39] Stakeholders representing specific interests or interest groups may not impose their preferred solution for a variety of reasons. Stakeholders (a) may not wish to dominate and undermine the authority and responsibility of other stakeholders; (b) may want something related or unrelated to the collaboration from other stakeholders; and/or, (c) are uniquely interdependent—thus imposing their power in one situation would be unwise as it could affect future negotiations in other situations.

Similar to the notion of parity is the idea of "collaborative empowerment" where stakeholders grant one another "the capacity to set priorities and control resources."[40] When parity and collaborative empowerment are not present, collaborations will often devolve to coordination or disband altogether. For example, scholars JoAnn Keyton and Virginia Stallworth described how parity was never achieved in a crime watch partnership among the district attorney's (D.A.) office, a neighborhood watch program, and the sheriff's department.[41] The partnership had short-term success increasing the community's involvement in providing information to the crime watch program, but the partnership disintegrated for a number of reasons that affected parity among the partners. First, the stakeholders were composed of different representatives from the community and the D.A.'s office, but the D.A.'s office sent multiple members, while the other stakeholders had only single representatives from their respective organizations and groups. Much like the issues in East Austin's OCEAN collaboration, this overrepresentation of prosecutors dominated the opinions and perspectives of other stakeholders. Second, the D.A. facilitated the group, and the leadership style of the D.A.'s office was heavy-handed, hierarchical, and not conducive to sharing decision making with others. In this example the *structure* of the collaboration (who participates) and the communication *process* (input and decisions) greatly contributed to the D.A.'s concentrated power. Hence, thoughtful structures and processes are two ways we can construct (dis)parity.

In contrast, although Renee initially felt overwhelmed in the Best SELF project by the expertise of others in the room, she was quickly included in the decision-making process, with other members granting her expert and referent power (i.e., "she's not just a yes-person"), thus establishing parity and collaborative empowerment. This was accomplished communicatively when Mike, the collaborative convener, not only solicited her thoughts but also integrated her concerns into planning regarding the program. Parity among stakeholders is experienced when stakeholders achieve *voice*—the engagement of diverse perspectives—rather than *expression*—the public or semi-public sharing of diverse perspectives.[42] Had Renee's comments been solicited but then not incorporated into further discussion, she would have had the opportunity to express her thoughts but not gain the power of voice—the integration of her thoughts into the planning process. Fostering voice is a powerful mechanism for creating parity and will be further examined in future chapters.

Discursive Barriers to Sharing Power

Just as we constitute parity through communication, so can we foster disparity in collaboration through particular discursive practices. Building on the idea that power is systematically distorted in decision-making situations in the public sphere; Deetz described the ways in which power is hidden in the communication situation as *discursive closure* and argued that ethical communication processes help avoid ending discussion prematurely.[43] Discursive closure techniques are not strategic—they are not intentionally employed by communicators. Instead, they are micropractices that maintain systematically distorted communication. Over time, we have accepted these communicative mechanisms as normative; we fail to question the way they obscure power. Thus, the power in them becomes invisible to us. These closures include but are not limited to naturalization, neutralization, pacification, disqualification, and subjectification of experience. By recognizing the ways power is distorted in communication we can, as collaborative leaders and stakeholders, strive to open up conversations and to challenge discursive closure when we see it. Power is shared and parity is created when discursive closures are diminished.

Naturalization occurs when communicators do not challenge something that has been made to appear nature-given. Claiming something is natural is an effective way to close the conversation about the phenomenon's origins. For example, if we believe it is natural for boys to be violent, we accept the behavior without question. In doing so, we limit the opportunity to explore the phenomenon of violence—what its roots or origins are as well as the origins of why we accept a particular interpretation. In another example, the issue of global warming is naturalized when disbelievers attribute fluctuations in temperature and precipitation to be normal, natural, cyclical, weather patterns. By naturalizing the phenomenon, the conversation regarding the effect of human factors on the warming of the planet becomes irrelevant; the conversation is effectively closed. Stakeholders can counter naturalization by fostering a collaborative environment that encourages questioning and challenging taken-for-granted phenomena. Joint fact-finding can also help stakeholders reassess phenomena that tend to be naturalized.

Neutralization happens when we present potentially contestable ideas or knowledge as objective and unbiased. For example, statistics and numerical facts are often presented as neutral and therefore undisputable. Statistics can shut down a conversation by appearing to be the last word on a subject. The process of gathering statistics, however, is a human process. Researchers determine the scope of the study, the methods for gathering information, the methods for analyzing the information, and what to highlight or discuss from the information gathered and analyzed. Understanding how knowledge is created into seemingly neutral numbers or statistical "facts" requires in-depth understanding of the research process and knowledge production. This is a skill taught in many colleges and universities, but questioning statistics may seem unthinkable to many—especially if they are presented as uncontestable facts. Once again, this barrier is best overcome with joint fact-finding; that is, collaborating members must agree on the methods of collection and interpretation of data. For example, when a new high density apartment complex was going to be built in East Austin, the collaboration that oversaw the development in the area asked for an impact study that addressed the issues of all the stakeholders in the collaboration from neighborhood members to businesses, developers, and city planners. Joint fact-finding allows for the challenging of supposedly neutral statistics and builds a collective knowledge that is likely to be more just.

Pacification happens in conversations when we appear to engage the other's perspective without giving credence to their input. The classic example is the suggestion box in the workplace that solicits ideas but does not have an authentic mechanism for incorporating or engaging those ideas. In collaboration, pacification may happen by inviting particular stakeholders but not engaging their different viewpoints in a meaningful way.[44] Pacification is done when we give space to people to express their ideas but do not grant influence to their ideas. For example, in Matt's research on collaboration during times of crisis, he found smaller nonprofits routinely were asked to be a part of the collaboration, but when decisions were made, the voices of those from smaller nonprofits were not considered in the same way as those who came from organizations with more national recognition and clout.[45] Pacification is overcome by considering how to *integrate* opposing ideas and perspectives rather than only allowing expression. Rethinking how we can include stakeholder ideas, objections, knowledge, and preferences into our decision-making situations moves us toward inclusion rather than just representation. Defining inclusion as a mechanism for cultivating participation—not just attendance—can help counter pacification.[46]

Disqualification closes conversations when some stakeholders refrain from speaking up because they do not feel qualified to do so. For example, weighting a collaboration with "experts" who hold multiple degrees and speak in a technical language could work to disqualify stakeholders who bring different, perhaps marginalized, perspectives to the table. Some stakeholders may be too intimidated to speak. Others may feel a jargon-laden conversation is closed or too difficult to follow. During Matt's time with the East Austin collaboration, the development subcommittee routinely used development and engineering jargon during the meetings. It created an in-group/out-group mentality where anyone who did not have the education or experience to understand the terms used had to ask for an explanation in order to have even a basic understanding of the discussion. Consequently, members without the technical understanding eventually quit asking for clarification or stopped attending the meetings.

Disqualification may be countered with careful consideration of stakeholders. Groups with too many stakeholders from one particular sector (i.e., nonprofit, for-profit, or government) may structurally disqualify others from participating. In addition, setting ground rules about technical language can help lessen discursive closure by disqualification.

Finally, subjectification of experience is a complex way to say conversations become shut down when we attribute differences of opinion to a particular person (subject) rather than exploring the roots of those differences (experience). This type of discursive closure occurs when someone says, "Well, you're entitled to your opinion." This statement usually shuts the conversation down and appears to weight all opinions equally. However, all opinions are not equally relevant. Depending on the subject matter, one stakeholder's opinion may indeed be more important than another's. For instance, the example of the dispute as to whether and how to develop the land belonging to the Port of Portland came to a head when those who would be most affected by the development and ensuing traffic spoke up against it (chapter 4). The mobile home community stood to lose far more regarding their quality of life than any other stakeholder at the table. Their opinion was indeed more relevant than the opinions of others at the table. A more constructive communication mechanism would be to question why someone holds a particular opinion. Only after exploring the roots of that opinion are we in a position to judge its significance to the problem-solving process.

Discursive closure techniques are insidious in our communicative practices. We are better able to foster shared power among stakeholders when we recognize how power is enacted and when we consider alternative methods for constructing more egalitarian communication situations. Doing so may result in the sustainability of the collaboration as well as cultivating democratic accountability to less powerful stakeholders.

> **QUESTION:** Have you ever experienced discursive closure? Describe the content and the context of the conversation. What discursive closure technique did you experience? What was the effect on the discussion?

CONCLUSION

Power does not "belong" to an individual or leader; it is relationally constructed and has many potential sources. Because collaboration in its ideal form requires sharing power and decision making, traditional top-down methods of communicating and leading will not be effective in collaborative situations. The larger sociopolitical context of collaboration demands democratic responsibility. Liberal democracy and native communication practices are not well-suited to fostering the shared power that is essential in collaboration. Shared power is cultivated through a collaborative spirit of egalitarianism and parity. Power can be hidden in hegemonic systems. By recognizing discursive closure techniques, stakeholders are better positioned to counter systematically distorted communication and to cultivate horizontal hierarchical relationships.

Sharing power constitutes the third cornerstone of the collaborative ethic and informs communication behaviors and practices that demand new ways of thinking about how we interact with one another in decision-making contexts. Power will continue to be a central feature of this text and plays a role in the next chapter on principled leadership. Part 3 details a language of collaborative praxis that is grounded in the underlying assumption of shared power.

CHAPTER TAKE-AWAYS

- Understand the ways in which power is relational
- Recognize the sociopolitical context and the need for participative democracy in collaborative groups
- Acknowledge how hegemony and systematic distortion can be embedded in collaborative structures
- Distinguish equality from egalitarianism and parity
- Identify ways in which power is created discursively in collaborative groups

ENDNOTES

[1] Episode from Renee's work with Skagit County Best SELF program, 1991.
[2] Henry Mintzberg et al., "Some Surprising Things about Collaboration—Knowing How People Connect Makes It Work Better," *Organizational Dynamics* 25, no. 1 (1996): 60–71, doi:10.1016/S0090-2616(96)90041-8.
[3] The Intersector Project, "Lessons for Addressing Power Imbalance in Collaborations," *The Intersector Project*, July 10, 2015, http://intersector.com/examining-successful-and-failed-collaborations-for-lessons-addressing-power-imbalance/
[4] Ibid.
[5] Stanley Deetz, *Democracy in an Age of Corporate Colonization: Developments in Communication and the Politics of Everyday Life* (Albany, NY: SUNY Press, 1992).
[6] Chester I. Barnard, *The Functions of the Executive: 30th Anniversary Edition* (Cambridge, MA: Harvard University Press, 1971).
[7] Ellen Nakashima, "Why the Sony Hack Drew an Unprecedented U.S. Response against North Korea," *Washington Post*, January 15, 2015, https://www.washingtonpost.com/world/national-security/why-the-sony-hack-drew-an-unprecedented-us-response-against-north-korea/2015/01/14/679185d4-9a63-11e4-96cc-e858eba91ced_story.html
[8] John R. P. French Jr. and Bertram Raven, "The Bases of Social Power," in *Group Dynamics: Research and Theory*, ed. Dorwin Cartwright and Alvin Zander, 3rd ed. (New York: Harper & Row, 1968), 359–69.
[9] Chris Huxham and Siv Vangen, *Managing to Collaborate: The Theory and Practice of Collaborative Advantage*, (New York: Routledge, 2005), pp. 78–79.
[10] John Charles Morris et al., *The Case for Grassroots Collaboration: Social Capital and Ecosystem Restoration at the Local Level* (Lanham, MD: Lexington Books, 2013).
[11] Jonathan Lange, "Environmental Collaboration and Constituency Communication," in *Group Communication in Context: Studies of Bona Fide Groups*, ed. Larry R. Frey (Mahwah, NJ: Lawrence Erlbaum, 2003), 209–34.

[12] Barbara Gray, *Collaborating: Finding Common Ground for Multiparty Problems* (San Francisco: Jossey-Bass, 1989).

[13] Renee Guarriello Heath, "Rethinking Community Collaboration through a Dialogic Lens: Creativity, Democracy, and Diversity in Community Organizing," *Management Communication Quarterly* 21, no. 2 (November 1, 2007): 145–71, doi:10.1177/0893318907306032.

[14] Lange, "Environmental Collaboration and Constituency Communication."

[15] Johny T. Garner and Marshall Scott Poole, "Perspectives on Workgroup Conflict and Communication," in *The Sage Handbook of Conflict Communication: Integrating Theory, Research, and Practice*, ed. John G. Oetzel and Stella Ting-Toomey, 2nd ed. (Thousand Oaks, CA: Sage Publications, Inc, 2013), 321–48.

[16] George Coggins, "Of Californicators, Quislings, and Crazies: Some Perils of Devolved Collaboration," in *Across the Great Divide: Explorations in Collaborative Conservation and the American West*, 2nd ed., ed. Philip Brick, Donald Snow, and Sarah F. Van De Wetering (Washington, DC: Island Press, 2000), 163–71.

[17] Heath, "Rethinking Community Collaboration through a Dialogic Lens."

[18] Benjamin Barber, *Strong Democracy: Participatory Politics for a New Age*: Twentieth-Anniversary Edition (Berkeley: University of California Press, 2004).

[19] Morris et al., *The Case for Grassroots Collaboration*.

[20] Stanley Deetz and Lisa Irvin, "Governance, Stakeholder Involvement, and New Communication Models," in *Governance Reform Under Real World Conditions: Citizens, Stakeholders, and Voice*, ed. Sina Odugbemi and Thomas L. Jacobson (Washington, DC: World Bank Publications, 2008), 163–80.

[21] Thomas B. Lawrence, Cynthia Hardy, and Nelson Phillips, "Institutional Effects of Interorganizational Collaboration: The Emergence of Proto-Institutions," *The Academy of Management Journal* 45, no. 1 (February 1, 2002): 281–90, doi:10.2307/3069297.

[22] Robert D. Putnam, *Bowling Alone: The Collapse and Revival of American Community* (New York: Simon and Schuster, 2001).

[23] Barber, *Strong Democracy*.

[24] Jessica MacDonald Milam and Renee Guarriello Heath, "Participative Democracy and Voice: Rethinking Community Collaboration Beyond Neutral Structures," *Journal of Applied Communication Research* 42, no. 4 (October 2, 2014): 366–86, doi:10.1080/00909882.2014.911944.

[25] Antonio Gramsci, *Prison Notebooks*, vol. 1 (New York: Columbia University Press, 1992).

[26] Todd Norton and Chris Sadler, "Dialectical Hegemony and the Enactment of Contradictory Definitions in a Rural Community Planning Process," *Southern Communication Journal* 71, no. 4 (December 1, 2006): 363–82, doi:10.1080/10417940601000451, p. 366.

[27] Robin Patric Clair, "The Use of Framing Devices to Sequester Organizational Narratives: Hegemony and Harassment," *Communication Monographs* 60, no. 2 (June 1, 1993): 113–36, doi:10.1080/03637759309376304, p. 114.

[28] Jürgen Habermas, "On Systematically Distorted Communication," *Inquiry* 13, no. 1–4 (January 1, 1970): 205–18, doi:10.1080/00201747008601590.

[29] Deetz, *Democracy in an Age of Corporate Colonization*, p. 174.

[30] Alessia Contu and Emanuela Girei, "NGOs Management and the Value of 'Partnerships' for Equality in International Development: What's in a Name?" *Human Relations* 67, no. 2 (February 1, 2014): 205–32, doi:10.1177/0018726713489999.

[31] Ibid., p. 213.

[32] Ibid., p. 217.

[33] Matthew Gustave Isbell, "Communicating Social Identities: Exploring Boundary Spanners in Interorganizational Collaborations" (The University of Texas at Austin, 2009), http://gradworks.umi.com/33/89/3389918.html

[34] Renee Guarriello Heath and Patricia M. Sias, "Communicating Spirit in a Collaborative Alliance," *Journal of Applied Communication Research* 27, no. 4 (November 1, 1999): 356–76, doi:10.1080/00909889909365545.

35 Online Etymology Dictionary, "Egalitarian," http://www.etymonline.com/index.php?allowed_in_frame=0&search=egalitarian

36 Kathleen P. Iannello, *Decisions without Hierarchy: Feminist Interventions in Organization Theory and Practice* (New York: Routledge, 1992).

37 The Intersector Project, "Lessons for Addressing Power Imbalance in Collaborations."

38 Oxford Dictionary, "Parity," http://www.oxforddictionaries.com/us/definition/american_english/parity

39 Jane McCarthy, *Negotiating Settlements: A Guide to Environmental Mediation* (New York: American Arbitration Association, 1984), p. 13, emphasis added.

40 Arthur Turovh Himmelman, "On the Theory and Practice of Transformational Collaboration: From Social Service to Social Justice," in *Creating Collaborative Advantage*, ed. Chris Huxham (London: Sage, 1996), 19–43, p. 30.

41 Joann Keyton and Virginia Stallworth, "On the Verge of Collaboration: Interaction Processes versus Group Outcomes.," in *Group Communication in Context: Studies of Bona Fide Groups*, ed. Larry R. Frey (Mahwah, NJ: Lawrence Erlbaum, 2003), 235–60.

42 Stanley Deetz and Jennifer Simpson, "Critical Organizational Dialogue," in *Dialogue: Theorizing Difference in Communication Studies*, ed. Rob Anderson, Leslie A. Baxter, and Kenneth N. Cissna (Thousand Oaks, CA: Sage Publications, Inc, 2003), 141–58.

43 Deetz, *Democracy in an Age of Corporate Colonization*.

44 Milam and Heath, "Participative Democracy and Voice."

45 Matthew Gustave Isbell and Rachel Goldstein, "Communicating Crisis: Interorganizational Collaboration among Disaster Relief Agencies" (International Communication Association Conference, Dresden, Germany, 2006).

46 Milam and Heath, "Participative Democracy and Voice."

7

Principled Leadership

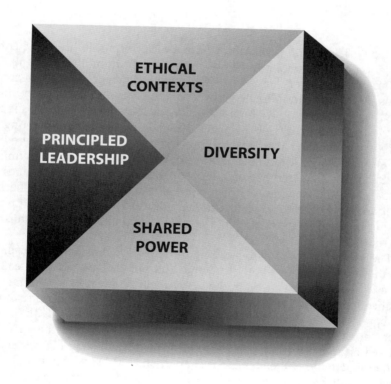

OCEAN in an Aquarium

In order to give access to as many stakeholders as possible, OCEAN conveners decided to hold their monthly meetings at the public library in East Austin. While the meeting space was centrally located, the room itself was small. Several meetings took place in which late arriving stakeholders had to sit in a chair against the wall or stand. When pushed together the tables created a rectangle, and the leader generally sat at the head. Although the room was not in the main part of the library, the library rules about talking affected the conduct of the meetings. People routinely talked in hushed tones. When the discussion became animated, someone in the collaboration would "shhhhh" the group, reminding them that "we may be disturbing the patrons." OCEAN members did their best to find a neutral space to conduct the meetings, but the space itself had certain norms associated with it that went against some of OCEAN's primary values, such as open dialogue and voice.

—Matt's observations of OCEAN meetings

Principled leadership is mindful of the ethical responsibilities and communication of the group, how to honor and benefit from diversity, and the need to share power among collaborative participants. Well-meaning actions by leaders can influence power and interaction in groups in unintended ways. A seemingly simple decision such as where to meet shapes the culture and practices of the group. The benign decision of meeting in the library can hinder trust and reciprocity as members are hampered in their attempts to build rapport because of the constraints on communication. Silencing animated stakeholders can work counter to the values of transparency and openness. Ethics, the valuing of diversity, and sharing power are embedded in a collaboration's culture. The structures and practices put in place by those guiding the collaboration affect relationships in the group.

The subject of leadership has long intrigued scholars and has inspired a plethora of literature—both academic and popular. We refer to leadership as it would be practiced in the very specific context of interorganizational collaboration. Principled leadership is the fourth cornerstone of the collaborative ethic and constitutes the final assumption that is the background for the language of collaborative praxis discussed in part III. We begin with three assertions specific to principled leadership: (1) leadership is a moral activity; (2) leadership is shared: and (3) leadership entails fostering the culture, structures, and processes needed to nurture a collaborative ethic.

First, principled leadership is a moral activity. Recall from chapter 4 that Sandor Schuman characterizes the practice of collaboration as a moral issue. "*How* we decide is subject to moral scrutiny just as *what* we decide."[1] Our vision of principled leadership adopts the assumptions put forth in the social change model of leadership: leadership is socially responsible and impacts change on behalf of others; it is collaborative; it is a process, not a position; it is inclusive and accessible to all people; it is values based; and it involves service to the community.[2] At the center of principled leadership are conceptions of sharing leadership, acting socially responsible, being guided by values, and recognizing the impact of leadership decisions on the communities in which collaborations are embedded. These conceptions guide our thinking throughout this text.

QUESTION: How do the claims of the social change model of leadership differ from your own conceptions of leadership? Where do they align? Where do they differ?

Second, principled leadership is shared leadership. Our conception of leadership departs from the idea of a lone, heroic leader.[3] Rather,

> Leadership is an interaction between two or more members of a group that often involves a structuring or restructuring of the situation and the perceptions and expectations of the members. Leaders are agents of change . . . any member of the group can exhibit some amount of leadership, and the members will vary in the extent to which they do.[4]

Throughout this chapter, we will discuss both the symbolic and tangible ways in which leadership is shared among collaborative participants.

Third, principled leadership is constructed through cultural structures and processes. Chris Huxham and Siv Vangen argue for a "collaborative leadership that is viewed as being not only enacted by key participants, but also by the structures and communication processes embedded within the partnership."[5] Consider the structures that will need to exist to sustain collaboration. Where will notes and other documents from meetings be stored if everyone participating works for a different organization? Where will the collaboration meet? How will meetings be structured in terms of time, who will run them? Collaborative leadership implies that delegation and responsibility are shared among participants. Without a defined "boss" or "supervisor," communication skills will be needed to motivate others to accomplish tasks and to negotiate difficult decisions.[6] Thus collaborative leadership is a tangle of sharing responsibilities and inventing structures and communication that foster collaborative goals.

In the remainder of this chapter, we presume that collaborative leadership is moral, shared, and embedded in structures and process—what we refer to as principled leadership. We introduce the concept of culture and consider the links between structures and processes as they relate to leadership. Culture is approached as both a manifestation of and a resource for collaborative values and practices. The latter half of the chapter presents Benjamin Barber's idea of participative leadership and considers the parallel communicative roles and practices that are conventional to collaborating. We view these leadership roles and practices as active generators and molders of the type of collaborative culture for which we advocate. Thus, this chapter begins the shift from identifying the assumptions on which a collaborative ethic rests to enacting ethical collaborative praxis through specific communicative activities.

Leadership and Collaborative Culture

A cultural approach to leading is consistent with the principled and egalitarian values of collaborative problem solving. Leaders do not emerge as authoritarian decision makers; rather, they guide structures and processes that constitute collaborative action.[7] Because collaborative stakeholders come from diverse organizational backgrounds, scholars have suggested developing a desired culture is essential to collaborative success.[8] Indeed, fostering culture has long been established as a leadership imperative.[9] Leaders who focus on culture will embed the values of collaborating in self-perpetuating structures that help cultivate respect and trust—and simultaneously empower stakeholders. Culture is not mutually exclusive of structures and processes; it is composed of them.

Focus on Culture

Culture has been described as three interrelated systems of meaning.[10] The first is a system of cultural abstractions including concepts, values, morals, and ideas about how things work together. The second system is composed of cultural artifacts. The third system is composed of language, practices, and communication. As an overarching system of meaning, culture defines what is in and outside of the boundaries of the collaboration, culls commitment from stakeholders to a particular collaborative identity, and aids in the predictability and control of member behavior.[11] Attention to these systems of culture can nurture a collaborative environment and prepare participants to participate in the appropriate interaction and processes between members. For instance, the opening vignette highlights the importance of the "table" in collaboration. The type of table at which collaboration members sit is the actual physical, visible artifact of the group. The table is something that can be seen, and it enables and constrains language and communication. Furthermore, the table is a representation of the power dynamics, the flow of communication, and potentially the pecking order of participants, thus symbolizing the deep values and morals of the culture. Something as simple as the shape of the table—round versus rectangle—can say much about collaboration and people and can be a powerful contributor to culture.

An inconsistent culture (one in which communication practices and artifacts do not match underlying values) will be less effective in terms of delineating its own boundaries (who are we and what do we stand for?), culling commitment, and influencing the behavior of its participants. An inconsistent culture also risks being disingenuous. For example, a collaboration that espouses shared decision making but practices unilateral decision making will feel inconsistent to its stakeholders. Participants will look to other cultural practices and artifacts to determine what is really true of the collaboration. If structures and practices do not foster shared decision making and instead reinforce hierarchy, the culture does not demonstrate a very strong collaborative ethic, one that is committed to ethical communication, diversity, and shared power. Even intelligent, capable stakeholders will feel confused when cultural practices do not match so-called cultural beliefs.[12] Thus the values and morals associated with a collaboration's culture will be visible in its language and communication as well as its norms, rituals, and artifacts.

Leaders' actions can help foster a collaborative ethic by attending thoughtfully to the practices of stakeholders that either contribute to, or detract from, a collaborative culture. For example, collaborative leaders and stakeholders can utilize artifacts to strengthen cultural values and assumptions. During the second year of the Best SELF collaboration, stakeholders tackled writing the mission statement. By this time, members had clarified their shared vision and could articulate their shared values. Some of those values were reinforced as aspects of the program were challenged. For instance, teachers hired in the program began to complain about the burden of supervising high school students who were themselves at risk of dropping out of school. However, their complaints were quelled when they were reminded of the guiding value, articulated in the mission statement, of fostering diverse students. Thus, the mission statement (an artifact) and its espoused values, cultivated the patience and tolerance needed to be an inclusive program. Recognizing the power of the mission statement, the first thing Renee did when she became the facilitator of Best SELF was to have billboard-sized posters of the mission statement and its guiding values displayed prominently in all seven of the Best SELF schools. This artifact aided in strengthening the values of the collaborative partnership and was used by school directors to guide decision making in tough situations. It was both a by-product and a cultivator of culture.

 QUESTION: Examine your work or school environment. What artifacts are visible? What values do they represent or imply?

That said, we are not proposing that collaborative leaders construct a monolithic culture that does not adapt to the needs and desires of the group and its decision-making contexts. Nor do we want collaborative groups to fix so rigidly on a particular set of values that they are not open to challenges to those values. For example, Renee studied the Occupy Portland social movement and found that the inclusive values of Occupy protestors became so dogmatic (unbending) that they were opposed to leaving out anyone, including those who were ultimately destructive to their movement by posing a physical threat to other participants. Their value of inclusivity over other values such as safety ultimately contributed to their demise. Although the value of inclusivity is important for diverse groups making decisions together, it also must be open to discussion and interpretation by members so that a value does not run counter to other values of the group. Given that collaboration hinges on the ability to learn from the diversity of stakeholders, we advocate that members think of culture as stable yet loosely constructed with differentiated values that will need to be considered on an ongoing basis.

> **QUESTION:** Occupy Portland created a monolithic culture that did not allow for challenging the value of inclusivity. Have you participated in a group that was dogmatic about its values? How did this dogmatism affect the group?

Leading through Structure and Process

Shared leadership, grounded in egalitarian values, manifests in structures and processes embedded in the culture of the collaborative group. Principled leadership focuses on the ways collaboration is led laterally, contemplating the moral implications of particular structures and processes and the importance of fostering an ethical collaborative culture. As depicted in the opening of this chapter, these structures and processes are clearly intertwined. When the East Austin collaboration met in the local library, the physical space altered interaction and the rules around that interaction. Sociologist Anthony Giddens' theory of structuration is useful for understanding the relationship between structure and process. He posited a duality of structure in which case actions by people (agency) create structures (rules and resources) that in turn influence people's actions.[13] For example, leaders in collaboration may design workshops to develop common understandings and vocabularies within a specific problem domain.[14] These workshops are based on the actions of people. The workshops themselves are a particular type of structure. The structure, in turn, shapes future actions (interactions) by facilitating common language, definitions, and understandings of issues. We are always engaged in creating structures, both physical (i.e., meeting spaces) and symbolic (i.e., language and rules), and are always influenced by those structures to some degree.

> **QUESTION:** What are the rules and resources that structure the classroom experience? How do they affect classroom interaction? How has classroom interaction influenced changes in rules or resources? For a hint, consider smartphones.

It is not a coincidence that the collaborations we have studied demonstrated power that mirrored their physical and symbolic structures. We have experienced the strong link between structure and action in our own departments. In one case, the new department chair enthusiastically changed the venue for department meetings from a conference room, which had to be scheduled and shared throughout the building and with other departments, to her office, where she had the luxury of a large meeting space and a round table.[15] In the spirit of generosity, she probably thought this would be easier than regularly scheduling the conference room. However, the unintended consequence was that instead of having professors meandering into the conference room early where they could enjoy their lunch and some banter with their colleagues, they were forced to wait in a line, like students on advising day, outside the office of their chair until she was prepared to let her colleagues enter. She frequently had students in her office right up to the time of the meeting. The hallway space was awkward, and lunch could not be eaten during the transition. The hallway was also public and thus did not encourage the types of conversations that colleagues might have in a private room. Without intending it, the chair had created an awkward differential in power and altered a cultural element of the department. She wisely changed the venue back to the conference room.

In another example, Renee found that a collaboration that struggled with power and hierarchy regularly met in a room with a very long table that seated more than 20 people comfortably. However, there was only room for two people to sit on the ends of the table that were visible to all. Of course, that is where the cochairs of the collaboration sat, symbolically reinforcing their positions of power. Indeed, participants complained that decision making took place among a select few.[16] Contrast this experience to that of another collaborative group that insisted everyone in attendance of the meeting (guest, reporter, observer, or stakeholder participant) sit at the round table and be visibly incorporated into the discussions and decision making.[17] This group cultivated collaborative empowerment among stakeholders, and every stakeholder felt they had the power to influence the group if they so chose.

Structures will help or hinder in cultivating rapport and trust with participants. Jack Shipley, the convener of the Applegate Watershed Partnership in southern Oregon, held the first meeting among stakeholders as a potluck.[18] He knew the importance of relationship building to the ranch owners he hoped would participate. The social event worked to humanize the government workers, timber representatives, and environmentalists who had previously only been known as adversaries. In this case the potluck, the front porch, and food all worked to symbolize a casual, informal setting that valued relationships.

Thoughtful structures and processes become essential in shaping collaborative values and practices. They contribute to the ability to share leadership because leadership is not centralized in a person. Thoughtful structures and processes generate and nurture the egalitarian and democratic principles of the group. As leaders contemplate decisions about structures (such as meeting spaces), they will need to consider what the already established values of those spaces may be and whether they complement or contradict the principles of the collaborative group. Is the meeting space in a big building? Do people have access to the meeting space, or does it require special key cards and passes? Are people free to express themselves in the space? Will laughing aloud disturb others who have space in the same building? Does the public have access to the meeting room? Is round table seating available? We take it for granted in sports games that playing on your own turf can have a great psychological advantage, so determining where to meet should also include thought as to how marginalized stakeholders may feel meeting in these spaces.

APPLICATION: Design the ideal meeting room for collaboration. What structures and artifacts will you include? Consider the effect you hope they have on your interaction processes. How does your design contribute to a particular culture for the group?

Participative Leadership and Collaboration

To understand how participative leadership is enacted in egalitarian decision-making environments, we turn to the work of Benjamin Barber.[19] Although the term participative leadership has been historically used to refer to political groups practicing participative democracy (chapter 6), Barber's work helps us conceptualize how leadership might take place with multiple persons fulfilling multiple roles, working side by side to make decisions that benefit their community. First, *transitional* leaders create participative institutions but do not linger in a leadership position. In interorganizational collaboration, transitional leadership is seen in the role of conveners—those with the authority to identify and bring stakeholders to the collaboration. Second, *natural* leaders possess communication skills and abilities that influence egalitarian communities, such as collaborative groups. Also often visible in conveners, natural leadership can be seen in those who enthusiastically keep the vision in the forefront—cheerlead, and inspire. *Facilitating* leadership is most concerned with egalitarian processes. This type of leadership is visible in those who design and execute the day-to-day of collaborative interaction. Facilitating leadership attends to meeting processes, structures, and other communicative practices of collaborating. In interorganizational collaboration, facilitators and process observers (both discussed in the next section) take on the duties of facilitative leadership. Finally, *moral* leadership is described as that which acts publicly but not politically. Moral leadership is enacted by those attending to the values and the principles of the group, specifically those stakeholders concerned with egalitarian decision making among diverse and sometimes marginalized stakeholders. Members in a collaboration may find themselves in the role of guardian of values associated with the pluralism of the group and the accountability of the group's decisions in the macroethical context. Although moral leaders may not be leading so obviously from the front, their stewardship of moral issues constitute leadership from the side.

In the remainder of this chapter we examine participative leadership as it manifests in the conventional roles and communicative practices of collaborating. We consider how participative leaders have the potential to nurture a collaborative culture. In particular, we discuss the leadership roles of convener, facilitator, process observer, and recorder—and the communicative practices associated with those roles.

Convener

In collaboration, the convener initiates the project or program and may or may not be a stakeholder.[20] They may serve as transitional leaders if they invite and motivate stakeholders to participate but do not continue in the collaboration or do not continue in a leadership role in the collaboration. The most significant contribution the convener makes is to recognize the value of collaborating and to identify and bring legitimate stakeholders to the table, demonstrating convening power.[21] The convener must have the authority and credibility to convene the group of stakeholders (see chapter 2 for a discussion on mandated collaboration). For example, Mike, Skagit County's chief financial officer, convened the Best SELF collaboration and brought substantial funding to the project. He had the political power to attract other resource-rich stakeholders such as the superintendents of two school districts and the executive directors of multiple nonprofit organizations. In the case of Best SELF, Mike not only initiated the group but he also stayed to facilitate the group—in part because he had tremendous "appreciative skills" to see the potential of collaborating.[22] These skills contributed to his role as a natural leader. Mike was famous among Best SELF stakeholders for his cheerleading. There was not a meeting that took place where Mike did not launch into a well-timed reminder about how Best SELF was "about the kids." His enthusiasm was contagious.

Facilitator

Facilitators have tremendous responsibility when it comes to fostering a collaborative culture through communicative behaviors. Facilitators help collaborative groups work together by focusing on processes; they are the primary actors of facilitative leadership. They do not have authority over the group and must remain neutral as they lead the communication practices and structures of the group.[23] Facilitators organize agendas, run meetings, help delegate tasks, and help guide groups toward consensus.[24] Collaborations come in all shapes and sizes, and they have varying capacities to hire professional facilitators. Yet, facilitation is so important that the federal government has recognized its integral role in multiparty, collaborative dispute resolution by allocating funding for stakeholders to utilize facilitative organizations such as the US Institute for Environmental Conflict Resolution.[25]

Many collaborative entities start out with little funding for formal facilitation processes; they must use their own experiences and skills to cultivate a collaborative environment. When facilitation and process expertise is the responsibility of stakeholders, it can be challenging to maintain parity. For example, if one organization is writing the agendas and minutes and facilitating the meetings, they exercise tremendous power and influence regarding discussion and decision items. We have often seen a hybrid model of facilitation where collaborating organizations apply for grant funding to help support their efforts and use the funds to provide infrastructure including a neutral coordinator or program director who assists the stakeholders with facilitation needs. While ideal, this is not common in most collaborations. The remainder of this section will proceed assuming the collaborative group does not have a professional facilitator.

Sharing procedural power is an excellent method for enacting principled leadership by fostering parity, trust, and transparency among stakeholders. One challenge with divvying up procedural responsibilities is that most stakeholders have very little time to be running meetings for a collaborative organization. They already hold multiple duties in their home organizations, and it is difficult to maintain neutrality while also representing a group or organization. We have witnessed (and scholars have suggested) collaborative groups that rotate the chairperson (facilitator) of the meeting on some type of agreed upon rotation, such as once a month.[26] This requires having the previous chairperson communicate closely with the present chairperson to formulate the agenda and to consider the direction of the meeting. This practice engages all stakeholders and fosters empathy and understanding of tasks such as joint fact finding. If this method seems laborious or chaotic for collaboration, the group might invite a neutral participant, such as a university professor/student or members from facilitative professional groups who may volunteer or accept a minimal fee for leading procedures. In fact, facilitation and deliberation has grown exponentially as a field. There are a number of universities who train upper division and graduate students to facilitate and may provide this service for the benefit of their students' experience.[27] The construction of the collaborative group should be considered. If the stakeholder with the greatest social capital is also the fiscal agent, then perhaps a stakeholder with less resources and power should be the facilitator. This would help share power among stakeholders and contribute to parity.

If facilitators are also stakeholders, they need to be mindful of when to talk and when to listen. If stakeholder facilitators share their own wishes too early in the meeting, they risk influencing the group's direction unfairly. However, there are times when facilitators must cheerlead, validate group members for the important work they are doing, and keep stakeholders focused on the big picture. Having said that, the facilitator should be listening more than talking; should be excellent at identifying spoken and unspoken interests and their potential overlap with other group members; should be skilled at fostering talk from quiet participants; and, perhaps most importantly, should be gracious and respectful in quelling dominators/interrupters.[28] Of course one of the most demanding tasks of the facilitator is to keep the meeting moving forward, balancing the desire to complete tasks while attending to the social and emotional needs of the stakeholders in the discussion.[29]

An agenda is a powerful facilitator tool that is not only indicative of the collaboration's cultural values but also influences communicative practices. A well-structured agenda will help a meeting run itself. One way to write an agenda is to think of yourself as a stranger about to attend a meeting for the first time. What would you want to know? Agendas should be written so that someone who did not attend the meeting could review it and have a pretty good idea of what happened. Agendas are not a list of bulleted items that are too cryptic to determine what will be done regarding those items. They are also not so wordy that the reader becomes lost in the content.

We have included the agenda from Renee's facilitation practice—note the times, titles, descriptions, and most importantly the order of presentation (see figure 7.1 on pp. 154–155). Agendas have an inherent logic. First, meeting participants enjoy knowing how much time they might be spending on a certain subject. This allows them to adjust their comments and weigh the importance of the topic. Most discussions are not allotted enough time on agendas, so careful assessment is required.[30] Times help facilitators direct meetings, and they also help the facilitators determine if the agenda has provided sufficient time to glean information, have deliberative discussions, and make decisions. Indeed, these are the three key functions of collaborative meetings: (1) sharing information or reporting, (2) dialogue and discussion, and (3) deliberation and decision making.[31]

Figure 7.1   Agenda example

ABC Collaboration Agenda
December 8   8:15 am to 3:30 pm
ABC Annual Board Retreat
ABC Offices, Alpha Street

8:15–8:45	**Arrivals/Breakfast**
8:45–9:00	**Welcome, Introduction and Context (Facilitator)** [A]
9:00–9:50	**YEAR IN REVIEW**

[B] Summary of year's activity
(Presented by ABC Staff led by the Executive Director)

Announcements:

Review of Market—How do we fit in?
Micro Lending vs. "The Missing Middle"

New Markets for Loans

Job Tracking

Capital Campaign Thus Far

BAS Program Updates

Loan Portfolio

9:50–10:00	**BREAK**
10:00–Noon	**DISCUSSION OF ABC'S VISION & MISSION**

[C] Purpose: To build consensus regarding the mission of ABC

[D] *The mission of ABC is to "Inspire business opportunities and create jobs and wealth for underserved small businesses and distressed neighborhoods." ABC provides loans to women, immigrant, minority, and disabled-owned small businesses.*

Ground Rules (Facilitator)

What motivates you to be part of ABC?

What do we do well now?

What are our dreams for this organization?

Noon–1:00	**BREAK & LUNCH**
1:00–1:30	**MOTIONS FOR APPROVAL** (Executive Director)

CARS Shadow Analysis Project Submission

[E_1] **Discussion of Budget**

ACTION: (Post Retreat) the Finance Committee will present proposed Budget to full board for approval

| 1:30–2:30 | **ABC LOAN CRITERIA** |

Discussion to Advise the *Loan Committee* (LC Chair)

Collect Ideas about what businesses ABC should be lending to

ACTION: (Post Retreat) the Loan Committee will present policy with new information to full board for approval

Discussion to Advise the *Finance Committee* (FC Chair)

Collect ideas about continuing "Lines of Credit" as an ABC loan product

F *ACTION: (Post Retreat) the Finance Committee will present policy with new information to full board for approval*

2:30–3:30 **ACTION PLAN DISCUSSION AND PRESENTATION**

E₂ **Role of Board/Committees**—*Utilizing Our Time and Talents* (Founder)

Capital Campaign Moving Forward (Founder and Executive Director)

ACTION: (Post Retreat) the Capital Committee will present proposed Capitalization Plan for full board approval

Agenda Key:

A Person responsible for leading the agenda item

B Set times for discussing each item

C Title and purpose of each item

D Additional description as needed for items

E Ordering of meeting—Notice more important items are placed when most people should be in attendance (**E₁**). Items that may not need every stakeholder are placed at the beginning and ends of meetings (**E₂**).

F Actions expected for certain items

Although times may be adjusted as needed depending on the goals and success of the meeting, we recommend not making a habit of altering two important times; the start and ending of the meeting. Most stakeholders must make time for collaboration while also carrying out their responsibilities to their home organizations. Thus, collaborations may find themselves meeting during the lunch hour or other less than ideal times of the day. Consider how the culture of the collaboration changes if facilitators reward those who come in late by waiting for them. Instead, starting meetings on time will constitute desired group norms, and early arrivers will appreciate having their time honored. Along the same lines, regularly running meetings past the specified time will affect the group's culture. If meetings consistently run late, the group needs to examine the use of meeting time. Are stakeholders spending too much time on reports? Do members need more time to accomplish collaborative business? Keeping people longer than scheduled eventually is interpreted as not honoring their time. With rare exceptions, *start on time, end on time,* is an excellent ethos for acknowledging and appreciating busy stakeholders and fostering a culture of respect.

Next, sections of the agenda are titled so that participants are clear regarding the purpose of this portion of the meeting. Is it a report? Is it a discussion? Is it a decision? Collaborations spend too much time reporting.[32] If the reporting activity is an effort to share participants' testimony, which has been linked to positively reinforcing the group's mission,[33] name it as such. Specificity with the agenda will help meeting participants understand the importance of the agenda items. For example, a report may be named, "Reinvigorating the Mission—Mary's story." A brief description will inform meeting participants of the purpose of their time, for instance, "Mary Allen, a ten-year-old in our after-school program, will share her journey."

Ordering the agenda is essential to collaborative problem solving, a process that often feels unwieldy. Note in the sample agenda, Renee allotted the most time for the discussion of the mission. It might not always be appropriate to spend so much time on the mission; in this case, conflict had ensued regarding the direction of the organization. A discussion was needed and appropriately placed in the group's annual retreat to clarify the values to new and old board members. Once the values of members had been discussed, the meeting could progress to the decision items, which would be more easily made once the stakeholders collectively clarified their mission. Clarifying values and interests (discussed in chapter 9) before decisions are made save the group from recycling the same debates regarding every important decision.[34]

Discussions identified as important take place on the agenda when all key members are likely to be present—and when they have enough energy to interact. Therefore, important discussion and decision items are not placed at the beginning of the meeting, when people are likely to wander in late, or at the end of the meeting, when participants are more likely to experience meeting fatigue or need to leave early. In an ideal world, all stakeholders would attend all parts of the meetings. However, given that stakeholders work for different organizations, it is likely their work schedules will at times conflict with collaboration meetings.

While agendas can take on a predictable format, the content of the agendas is a shared leadership endeavor . . . to a point. Stakeholder input is solicited prior to the meeting. If their suggestions cannot reasonably be included in the agenda, facilitators can offer alternate methods or dates. Rarely is it appropriate to alter the agenda to include a major discussion or decision that was not discussed prior to formulating the agenda. However, having an opportunity for stakeholders to share brief announcements is a good way to share the floor with other stakeholders. A purposeful and thoughtful agenda will be an excellent tool for the facilitator, a guide for stakeholders, and an organizing structure for the recorder. A well-structured agenda helps enact behaviors that foster a collaborative culture.

JoAnn Keyton has worked extensively with collaborative groups. Her research examines the importance of communication skills as leaders of collaboration foster relationships and trust among stakeholders. Keyton distinguishes between task-oriented communication skills and relationship-oriented communication skills—both essential for leading collaboration.

SCHOLAR SPOTLIGHT

Why Take the Risk of Collaborating?
JoAnn Keyton

Interorganizational collaboration not only occurs at multiple structural levels—individual representative, organizational, collaboration, and public—but it also has effects at multiple levels. Thus, organizational leaders have to weigh the benefits and challenges when they are asked to collaborate with other organizations. Potential organizational benefits include having access to needed resources, creating potential partnerships that can open up market shares, and moving products and services into new parts of the world. On the other hand, collaborating always comes with risks. Will employees learn about the other organization's employee policies, prefer those, and become disenchanted with your organization's policies? Could increasing demand for your organization's products create too much overtime and disturb the work/life balance you and your employees have come to expect? Will collaborating with another organization to move into new markets expose your organization to a potential take-over or buy-out with the potential that you will lose your job?

Too often, interorganizational collaborations begin with the assumption that all parties to the collaboration know and fully understand the other collaborators' positions. But, working from a basis of assumption is not helpful. Collaborators may hold dated or biased views of other collaborators' motives. Collaborators may mistake their lack of information about the other collaborators as the collaborators' unwillingness to share information. Simply, collaboration is a communication process, and it is challenging.

(continued)

Even well planned interorganizational collaborations will result in unexpected tensions and unplanned changes. As a member of an interorganizational collaboration, you will need a variety of communication skills. Being able to participate in collaborative discussions to describe and explain your position is key. You will also need to listen carefully and keep track of what topics or issues are not being fully addressed, so you can compose thoughtful and clear introductions of these topics. Finally, you need to be able to ask open-ended questions to help collaborators move on from a stuck or contested position. Displaying these task communication skills will allow others to recognize the important role of communication in collaboration. In turn, you will be perceived as a valuable member of the team.

Using these communication skills to help the collaborating group understand and work toward its goal should be complimented by several relational communication skills. When you first meet the other members of the collaborating group, be sure to introduce yourself and explain why you and your organization are part of the collaboration. This is the essential first step in creating a sense of trust among the collaborative partners. When there is time and opportunity before the meeting begins, and after the meeting is over, continue to find opportunities to create relationships with other collaborators. As the group is discussing, be sure to pay attention to those members who are *not* participating. When it is appropriate, ask a question to draw them into the conversation. A collaboration can only be successful when all partners are working together and contributing to the discussion. Finally, when the group's discussion gets stuck and is not moving forward, you can draw upon these relationships to redirect the group's conversations by asking those you know for their opinion or point of view.

Interorganizational collaboration can be risky and difficult. But as an effective communicator, you can help create a climate of relationship building and trust that makes it easier for the collaboration to accomplish its work. An effective communicator will *work* all levels of the collaboration. He or she will use his or her personal communication skills to make a good impression on other collaborators, represent their organization in a positive and constructive manner, become a valuable and contributing member of the collaborating team, and represent the interorganizational collaboration in a positive way to the various publics.

Process Observer Role

In our experience, the process observer is an underused option to manage the task and social/emotional needs of stakeholders in collaborative meetings and to cultivate a culture of egalitarianism. Process observers may be any stakeholder other than the facilitator or recorder during a meeting. Process observers are concerned with the process aspects of the meeting and share a facilitative leadership role. However, unlike the facilitators, process observers are not focused on moving through the agenda. They also serve as moral leaders when it comes to the group's values regarding processes.[35] If, for example, the group has asked that stakeholders fully listen and avoid interrupting one another, the process observer will attend to this desire. Process observers may choose to jump in when ground rules (discussed below) are being violated and gently point out the violation. Or facilitators may systematically take breaks to check in with the process observer and publicly question how the meeting is progressing. At that time, the process observer would say something like, "I noticed Justin has been very quiet during this discussion, Justin would you be willing to weigh in at this time?" It would not be unusual that the facilitator did not notice Justin's unusually quiet behavior, or perhaps the facilitator read the quiet behavior as approval when the root of Justin's withdrawal is actually disapproval of the direction the group is going. By normalizing the role of the process observer to check in with participants, guide stakeholders back to their ground rules, and assist the facilitator with another set of eyes and (mostly) ears, the stakeholder group will learn to attend to the processes that matter to the group, further cultivating a collaborative culture.

Utilizing process observers creates two additional advantages. First, process observers quickly learn the ground rules of the group; they thus become more mindful stakeholders themselves when they are not in the process observer role. Second, and perhaps more importantly, utilizing process observers is another tool to share power. While the facilitator is handling the logistics of the meeting, the process observer is a quiet leader and listener for the group that day. Thus, rotating the process observer role is an excellent method for fostering parity among stakeholders and educating stakeholders to be attuned to their communication behaviors.

A final note of caution to process observers and facilitators: while facilitative processes are key to fostering a collaborative culture and integrative decision making, they can also quickly turn off stakeholders. Renee once interviewed a banker who was part of a collaboration focused on prevention. He complained that the heavily nonprofit-weighted group discussed things "ad nauseam" and were not particularly skilled at directly stating what they wanted—a communication skill he valued in his for-profit world. The moral of the story is that while attending to processes and ensuring everyone has voice is important, we cannot lose sight of achieving tangible outcomes.[36] When it seems like what is being stated in the collaboration is getting redundant, facilitators must move the process forward, close the topic, and/or make a decision. Overdoing processes can keep important stakeholders from coming back.

Process observers are the chief guardians of the group's ground rules, which play an integral role in running a smooth meeting and fostering a collaborative environment. Ground rules outline acceptable and unacceptable behavior for stakeholders.[37] Importantly, ground rules are decided by the group.[38] We mentioned in chapter 5 that in the Applegate Partnership in Oregon, one of the ground rules was to avoid using the word "they" when speaking.[39] This rule forced the previously conflicting group members to use more inclusive language. It fostered a collaborative culture, which was reinforced with the artifact of a chest pin with the word "they" crossed out. In a grassroots collaboration located in the Chesapeake Bay area, successful partnerships between industry, the military, and environmentalists were made possible according to many involved because the organizers employed a "no blame" ground rule. As stakeholders worked to improve the ecology and livability of important watersheds in that area, they were careful not to point fingers—in fact, some organizations claimed that this ground rule was a factor in their choice to get involved.[40] Ground rules are powerful indicators of the values of the group and the guidelines for interaction.

Examples of Ground Rules

- Do not use the word "they"
- No blaming
- Turn off your cell phones during the meeting
- Listen to understand before responding

In contrast, the absence of ground rules can encourage chaotic practices. For example, while researching a collaboration addressing homelessness, Matt found that it was not only important to get collaborative members to the table but it was also important that the appropriate members were there. Surrogates for people who originally committed to participate (in one case an organization sent an intern) attended key meetings. Surrogates typically lacked the decision-making power to commit their organization to a collaborative decision. Even more problematic, the surrogate often did not have the experience or skills needed from that member organization to add a diverse viewpoint. In the homeless collaboration, the surrogates began to slow down the collaborative process because they needed to report back to the home organization, solicit a response, and bring it back to the collaboration. This was even more difficult if the organization sent a different person (whomever was available at the time) to each meeting. In some cases, certain organizations used a rotating surrogate (a tactic referred to as obfuscation)[41] to slow down the collaboration or to derail the process entirely. In this case, the group greatly needed clarification in the ground rules at to what counted as acceptable attendance. In each of the cases mentioned in this section, the ground rules fit the needs and reflect the behaviors and habits of the particular collaboration.

Designing and implementing ground rules can be tricky. Even using the terminology of "ground rules" may sound authoritarian to some stakeholders, so developing a language particular to the collaborative group is key. A facilitator might say, "We want to encourage some tough discussions, and we definitely want to make sure everyone has an opportunity to voice their input, so let's identify your rules for how our meetings should proceed." Next, they may offer an example of a ground rule that makes sense to the group. Renee facilitated an annual meeting of very busy community leaders belonging to a nonprofit board of directors. The executive director requested that she ask the participants to refrain from using their cell phones. As she opened the meeting, almost every participant was already busy typing away on their cell phone. To navigate this awkward moment she used humor to introduce the ground rules: "Don't groan!" she joked, "But we would be so grateful if you refrain from using your cell phone if possible."

At that same meeting, the executive director was anticipating a heated debate. In the past, dominant stakeholders spoke over others, and it was hard to determine if the group had consensus or not. Therefore, Renee introduced the common facilitation method of turning your name card up on its side when one wished to speak. She then wrote down the names of those who turned their cards in the order they turned them, freeing participants from having to jump into the conversation in order to be heard. She provided pens and paper and encouraged people to write their thoughts down so they could listen more fully to one another. She also checked occasionally to make sure the upcoming comments were relevant to the present point to avoid the comment taking the group in a new direction. The executive director was thrilled with the civility of the meeting and noted that an important debate surfaced regarding the group's priorities. However, this same technique backfired in a collaborative group where the facilitator demanded a strict chronological order among the speakers. The result was a disjointed and incoherent discussion.[42] The differing results with this technique remind us that praxis demands that we draw on those communicative techniques that fit the moral obligation of the situation. A prescriptive method of turning cards on their side does not suffice as good communication if conversation is stifled.

Ground rules are not overly elaborate.[43] They may grow out of the group's experience and may be altered as different issues arise. Keeping in mind collaborative interaction, ground rules should not stifle communication—for example, limiting speaking time or storytelling may make it more difficult to establish trust and rapport. Also, ground rules should not demonize conflict, as constructive conflict is needed in order to capitalize on stakeholder differences. Instead, ground rules cultivate the types of conversations stakeholders need for their collaboration. For example, the facilitation convener, New Hampshire Listens, states in their ground rules, (which they call group agreements), "It's okay to put issues like race and class on the table," in an effort to make sure important discussions surface.

One of the elements ground rules should cover is when and how the group will make decisions, especially in the context of contributing to an egalitarian collaborative culture. Parliamentary procedures are formal and have a special language associated with them.[44] They prepare groups for voting, thus creating winners and losers. While voting may be necessary at times in collaboration, stakeholders must consider and model how their communication fosters an environment of discussion, transparency, and trust. Ground rules should address these important factors to some extent. A final note about ground rules: given that collaborations do not meet as often as other types of organizational entities, ground rules are best captured visibly, either on the agenda or in meeting materials so that they can be periodically reviewed and are always available for stakeholders. By doing so, they become an important artifact to sustain the group's values.

> **APPLICATION:** In your next group experience, whether writing a paper together, or implementing a project, begin by constructing a brief set of ground rules you will use to guide your interaction. They may cover how you will communicate, turnaround times on work, or even how to avoid some of your pet peeves. Be sure they are not overly elaborate and that everyone in the group has contributed to them.

Typical Leadership Roles in Collaboration

Convener: Initiates collaboration. Invites participants by articulating what they may gain from participating and how they can help achieve improvements in the problem domain.

Facilitator: Guides the collaborative meetings, writes agendas, stays neutral as much as possible (although may be a stakeholder in the absence of funding). Seeks consensus on collaborative decisions.

Process Observer: Guardian of the ground rules, observes collaborative processes and advises the group and facilitator on how to encourage egalitarian values.

Recorder: Records collaboration's activities. Constructs a collaborative history through texts as well as prompts future collaborative activity through written documents such as minutes. Encourages transparency and accountability.

Recorder

Recorders provide an essential service to the collaboration by keeping records of the meeting. What gets recorded or not also reflects group values and norms regarding transparency; therefore, the recorder operates under the assumptions of principled leadership. Yet, little formal training exists regarding this skill. When Renee became the development director for a newly formed nonprofit foundation board, she was assigned an assistant to take minutes for the meetings. Although the assistant had more than a decade of clerical experience in her position, she had never been trained formerly in minute-taking. The result for the first board of directors' meeting was a nonspecific and general accounting of the meeting. It was not clear who spoke, what was decided, or who had taken responsibility for what action items. Spending some time to clarify what stakeholders' expectations are for those who are writing the minutes will help avoid this problem. Recorders are the archivists of a meeting's activities.[45] They have very little time to participate in the meeting, so it is not ideal to have a stakeholder fulfill the recorder role. However, if this is the only option, those talking will need to be prepared to slow down to allow recorders to catch up and participate when necessary.

Minutes are the communicative tool produced by recorders. Basic tips for writing minutes focus on: topics of discussion and general points; decisions of the team and action items or assigned tasks; persons responsible for completing the task, and deadlines for completing the task.[46] Minutes detail who attended, who was absent, where the meeting was held, and for how long stakeholders met.[47] In interorganizational collaboration, recording some of these details can be challenging. As discussed in chapter 3, knowing which stakeholders are absent from the meeting can be difficult to determine. Important discussions and decisions are chronicled with the necessary details of those items. Robert's Rules of Order establishes the following general rule about the contents of minutes: "except when they are published outside the organization, [minutes] should record what is done by the assembly, not what is said by the members."[48] Although it may be appropriate at times to provide a direct quote, minutes are not transcripts, which are important documents on their own. That said, groups may want to record the meeting (especially if the group is small) so that everyone can be involved; the recorder can later go back and create minutes from the recording.

The interorganizational context creates additional challenges regarding minute writing. For instance, if an organization is a registered 501(c)(3), minutes are legal documents that provide evidence of the collaboration's work. Stakeholders may need to provide copies of the minutes to federal and state governments in order to maintain nonprofit, tax-exempt status. Minutes can also be subpoenaed should any legal conflict arise regarding collaborative business. Given this, the recorder has tremendous power as to what is said, as well as what is left out of the minutes.[49] Consequently, minutes should always be shared and approved by the stakeholders even if the group is not using a formal parliamentary procedure. Sharing and approving fosters transparency and shared power.

In collaboration, minutes also serve as a very useful tool for reminding stakeholders of the commitments they made during the meeting. Best SELF facilitators always sent the minutes and a proposed agenda out one week before the next monthly meeting. In the text, actions volunteered by stakeholders would be marked so that readers could quickly peruse the minutes (bolded, italicized, underlined, etc.), find their names and be reminded of their responsibilities before the next meeting. For example, *"Renee will gather statistics from DMV on number of teen-related accidents."*

Figure 7.2   Meeting minutes example*

MINUTES**
Rocktown Bike Walk Summit
July 29, 9:00–11:00 am
127 Bryce St., Rocktown—107 Conference Room (first floor)
Fifth Planning Meeting

Attending: Ian Laws, Pete Troust, Mark Cyphert, Kevin Clancy,
John Montiss, Amanda Yang, Nathan Price, Lori Britt, Ron Helms

The following guests attended the meeting:
Stephanie Sallton, Director, Rocktown Tourism[†]
John Yang, Concierge Manager, Cove Mountain Resort[†]
Ken Clince, Director of Sports and Risk Management, Cove Mountain Resort[†]

[†]Rocktown Tourism and Cove Mountain Resort are members of Rocktown Valley Travel
Association

Discussion with members of local tourism industry

An hour-long discussion followed regarding bicycle/walking tourism needs in
the city/county and how they could best be incorporated into the Summit keynote address. Here is a summary of what was discussed and will be communicated to the keynote speaker from Missoula, Montana. (Ian and Lori took notes
and may want to add to this list.)

- The need to provide safe routes for tourists and residents.
  — Organized rides.
- The importance of connectivity—"Visitors do not see boundaries."
- The need for more bike and walking information (mapping, facilities, food
  options, points of interest, etc.) that tourists can access before and when
  they arrive in our community.
  — Mapping system (for all levels, indicate incline, intensity/comfort level).

  C — What do Missoula's maps look like?

  — Include where to park, closest restrooms, etc.
- Highlight that a large number of Canadian bicyclists are already coming to
  our area.
  — How can we improve and build on this?
  — How do we market and measure the return?
- Provide examples of tourism successes that our community can learn from.
  — <u>Collect data from Cove Mountain</u>—why people are coming (capture not
  only resort but those renting from VRBO).

*Adapted and provided by Lori Britt, Bike Walk Summit facilitator
**Note that the minute headers should parallel the agenda headers for that meeting.

- Ways to collect and use bike and walking data to promote and find funding for tourism development.
  — City Tourism is currently compiling a database, using Google analytics.
  — They are looking to write a grant to fund a kiosk/online system for tourism information 24/7.
  — Need the trackable data for the grant.
  — Grant will be written in fall.
  — Stephanie indicated needing help with an Asset Inventory.
  — Note that we can't promote what "could be" needed to promote what is on the ground.
  — Identified a need for someone in the bike coalition to facilitate the relationship with Stephanie to work on this grant.
  — Utilize professors, students, and classes for data collection.
- The benefits of greenways, multiuse paths, and rails to trails to tourism.
- How to bring diverse organizations together to develop biking and walking tourism.
- How to involve businesses in advocating for bike/walk tourism.
  — Look to Missoula for examples of "We've invested in X with these goals and have yielded Y return."
- Ways to involve JMU in bike and walking tourism.
- Educating the non-cycling population to the benefits of bicycling and tourism.
  — Reduce animosity of rural residents.
- <u>Explore the possibility of having the keynote speaker facilitate a data collection workshop</u> for select advocates and tourism staff before the Summit.
- Need to work on talking about the tourism benefits beyond the city borders; county thinks of tourism as only benefitting the city.
  — Locally, we need to get restaurants off 33 to buy in.
- In terms of building connections to Cove Park, connect bike trail to Albert Lutz Park from Rocktown as first step, then you are a third of the way to Cove Mountain.
- <u>Inquire about Greenway tourism</u> in Missoula/separate use trailheads (Virginia Creeper).
- Ask the speaker to describe "If you are a cyclist coming to Missoula, how are you greeted, what kind of amenities are available to you, what are the main sources of communication about biking/the community, etc."

Preparing the Year in Review Presentation   D

The second hour was devoted to developing the Year in Review presentation for the Summit. Headings were generated and specific information was added. <u>Kevin will coordinate</u> the committee members to continue to add more information between this meeting and our August 28 meeting. Kevin provided a Google link to the committee members to collaboratively add more details.

(continued)

New Award Development

   Mark gave a quick update on the advocacy award—He <u>will present the idea to</u> <u>the Rocktown Bike Coalition</u> board at their August meeting. If they agree to sponsor the award, RBC will develop the details, and the award process will be announced at this year's Summit with the first award to be given the following year. <u>Mark will provide another update</u> at our next meeting.

Summit Logistics Updates

a. Speakers

   • Ebbett Jones cannot do the University partner welcome—He will attend the keynote and year in review. The University President will do the university partner welcome.

b. <u>Developing and printing the Summit Program—Denise.</u>

c. Year in Review—see notes above.

d. <u>University Location Liaison—Steve.</u>

   • Meal—<u>Lori will make recommendations</u> and send them to Ron for the final meal choices.

   • Parking- in progress.

e. Registration—<u>Kevin will send out a registration</u> e-mail to all those on the invitation list the first week of August. The registration will be open only to those on the invitation list. If someone not on the list wants to register, they need to contact Kevin to do so. This will be included in the e-mail. Kevin will also send a separate e-mail to the members of the planning committee asking that they personally contact those they want to attend the Summit.

f. Publicity—<u>Kevin will coordinate the sending out of press releases</u> about the Summit the week before Oct. 10.

g. SVBC website—<u>Amanda will continue to update as needed.</u>

h. Pre and Post-summit activities.

   • The keynote speaker is meeting with the Rocktown Co. Board of Supervisors and Town Managers on Wednesday, October 8—<u>Ron will continue to</u> <u>coordinate this with Supervisor Bill Jones.</u>

   • The invited speaker will be meeting with tourism officials about bike and walking data collection—<u>Ian will coordinate this with Stephanie Sallton</u>, Director, Rocktown Tourism.

   • Post-Summit Social at The Local Pub's Lounge—3:30–5:30 PM—confirmed by Pete.

i. Budget and paying the bills—<u>Kevin will contact Ian</u> to see if Ian or Mary Cummings should coordinate the keynote speaker's travel arrangements and communicate today's tourism information.

Next meeting—Thursday, August 28 from 9–11 AM at 127 Bryce St., Rocktown—104 conference room

Meeting Key:

A	Where the meeting was held, and for how long stakeholders met.
B	Who attended.
C	Record what is done by the assembly, not what is said by the members.
D	Topics of discussion and general points.
E	Decisions of the team and action items or assigned tasks.
F	Persons responsible for completing the task.
G	Plans for next meeting.

By distributing the minutes one week before the meeting, stakeholders had enough time to complete their tasks as well as an opportunity to review the minutes and give input as to what they hoped would be included in the agenda for the coming meeting. We have included a copy of the minutes from Professor Lori Britt's facilitation work to demonstrate some of the best practices in minute taking (figure 7.2). Note that important actions or duties to be completed are underlined, including who will be completing the action.

Balancing specificity with summary is an ongoing tension in minute writing. Minute writers do not project adjectives or opinion into their summary; they state the facts.[50] Collaboration meetings are a safe place where organizations can speak frankly, be transparent, and educate their partners regarding details of their own organizations. Stakeholders may share information that they do not wish to be shared publicly in the minutes. Stakeholders may want to declare particular conversations off-the-record, provided no legal violations have taken place. If this is the case, the procedures for sharing of confidential information should be outlined in the collaboration ground rules.

Minutes are not just a procedural practice. They should be considered in light of their contribution to the culture of the collaboration. They can stimulate joint fact-finding, summarize shared interests, and respect stakeholder needs to balance the tension of transparency with confidentiality. The writing and handling of minutes in collaboration is a communicative norm that shapes, and is evidence of, the collaboration's culture.

Participative leadership surfaces in many roles, and collaboration has specific needs that facilitate sharing power and responsibility. Principled leadership keeps values associated with the collaborative ethic (such as transparency and sharing power) at the forefront of communication practices and conventions. Every leadership role in collaboration provides an opportunity to steer the culture so that it becomes a symbolic structure that influences and is influenced by collaborative interaction.

CONCLUSION

This chapter conceptualizes principled leadership as moral, shared, and grounded in cultural structures and practices. Principled leadership creates the conditions by which ethics are considered, difference is appreciated, conflict is useful, and where new meanings can emerge in conversations with others that were not possible before to help address wicked problems. We develop the concept of culture as a mechanism for leadership that embeds the values and practices of collaborating. By aligning cultural artifacts, languages, and values, stakeholders can share leadership responsibilities that foster the group's core values. In this view, collaborative behavior is guided by the values and norms that are embedded in structures and processes, rather than by authoritarian leadership or the vision of the vocal few. We also introduced Barber's vision of participative leadership and demonstrate how it is enacted in the typical roles and communication conventions of collaboration. Principled leadership is the fourth cornerstone of ethical collaboration and concludes the section on collaborative ethics. Part III focuses on the language of collaborative praxis—a language built on the four cornerstones of ethical contexts, diversity, shared power, and principled leadership.

CHAPTER TAKE-AWAYS

- Understand principled leadership as moral, shared, and embedded in culture
- Recognize culture as a producer and product of ethical collaboration
- Identify the link among leadership culture, structures, and processes
- Distinguish conventional roles and communicative practices in collaboration and how they relate to participative leadership

ENDNOTES

[1] Sandor P. Shuman, "The Role of Facilitation in Collaborative Groups," in *Creating Collaborative Advantage*, ed. Chris Huxham (London: Sage, 1996), 126–40, p. 137.

[2] Susan R. Komives and Wendy Wagner, *Leadership for a Better World: Understanding the Social Change Model of Leadership Development*, 2nd ed. (San Francisco, CA: Jossey-Bass, 2009).

[3] See Garry Wills, *Certain Trumpets: The Nature of Leadership* (New York: Simon & Schuster, 1995).

[4] Bernard M. Bass, *Bass & Stogdill's Handbook of Leadership: Theory, Research & Managerial Applications*, 3rd ed. (New York: Free Press, 1990), pp. 19-20.

[5] Chris Huxham and Siv Vangen, *Managing to Collaborate: The Theory and Practice of Collaborative Advantage* (New York: Routledge, 2005).

[6] Ibid.

[7] Joann Keyton and Virginia Stallworth, "On the Verge of Collaboration: Interaction Processes versus Group Outcomes.," in *Group Communication in Context: Studies of Bona Fide Groups*, ed. Larry R. Frey (Mahwah, NJ: Lawrence Erlbaum, 2003), 235–60.

[8] Ibid.

[9] Thomas J. Peters and Robert H. Waterman Jr., *In Search of Excellence: Lessons from America's Best-Run Companies*, Reprint ed. (New York: HarperBusiness, 2006).

[10] Stephen W. Littlejohn and Kathy Domenici, *Communication, Conflict, and the Management of Difference* (Long Grove, IL: Waveland, 2007). p. 94.

[11] Edgar H. Schein, *Organizational Culture and Leadership*, 4th ed. (San Francisco: Jossey-Bass, 2010).

[12] Jessica MacDonald Milam and Renee Guarriello Heath, "Participative Democracy and Voice: Rethinking Community Collaboration Beyond Neutral Structures," *Journal of Applied Communication Research* 42, no. 4 (October 2, 2014): 366–86, doi:10.1080/00909882.2014.911944.

[13] Anthony Giddens, *The Constitution of Society: Outline of the Theory of Structuration* (Berkeley: University of California Press, 1986).

[14] Huxham and Vangen, *Managing to Collaborate*.

[15] Descriptive details have been altered to provide anonymity to the participants.

[16] Milam and Heath, "Participative Democracy and Voice."

[17] Renee Guarriello Heath and Patricia M. Sias, "Communicating Spirit in a Collaborative Alliance," *Journal of Applied Communication Research* 27, no. 4 (November 1, 1999): 356–76, doi:10.1080/00909889909365545.

[18] Cassandra Moseley, "The Applegate Partnership: Innovation in Crisis," in *Across the Great Divide: Explorations in Collaborative Conservation and the American West*, ed. Philip Brick, Donald Snow, and Sarah van de Wetering (Washington DC: Island Press, 2001), 102–11.

[19] Benjamin Barber, *Strong Democracy: Participatory Politics for a New Age: Twentieth-Anniversary Edition* (Berkeley: University of California Press, 2004).

[20] Barbara Gray, *Collaborating: Finding Common Ground for Multiparty Problems* (San Francisco: Jossey-Bass, 1989).

[21] Ibid.

[22] Ibid., p. 72.

[23] Shuman, "The Role of Facilitation in Collaborative Groups."

[24] Deborah Harrington Mackin, *The Team Building Tool Kit: Tips, Tactics, and Rules for Effective Workplace Teams* (AMACOM Div. American Mgmt. Assn., 1994).

[25] "U.S. Institution for Environmental Conflict Resolution: FAQs," *Udall Foundation*, http://udall.gov

[26] Heath and Sias, "Communicating Spirit in a Collaborative Alliance"; Keyton and Stallworth, "On the Verge of Collaboration."

[27] See, for example, James Madison University's Institute for Constructive Advocacy and Dialogue at http://www.jmu.edu/icad/ ; also, National Coalition for Dialogue at ncdd.org

[28] Mackin, *The Team Building Tool Kit*.

[29] See the scholar spotlight box, Why Take the Risk of Collaborating? by Joann Keyton in this chapter for more information.

[30] Mackin, *The Team Building Tool Kit*.

[31] Ralph Brody and Murali D. Nair, *Effectively Managing and Leading Human Service Organizations*, 4th ed. (Thousand Oaks, CA: Sage, 2013).

[32] Milam and Heath, "Participative Democracy and Voice."

[33] Heath and Sias, "Communicating Spirit in a Collaborative Alliance."

[34] Mary Ann Renz, "Paving Consensus: Enacting, Challenging, and Revising the Consensus Process in a Cohousing Community," *Journal of Applied Communication Research* 34, no. 2 (May 1, 2006): 163–90, doi:10.1080/00909880600574088.

[35] Mackin, *The Team Building Tool Kit*.

[36] Heather M. Zoller, "'A Place You Haven't Visited Before': Creating the Conditions for Community Dialogue," *Southern Communication Journal* 65, no. 2–3 (March 1, 2000): 191–207, doi:10.1080/10417940009373167.

37 Gray, *Collaborating*.
38 Ibid.; Matthew J. McKinney, "What Do We Mean by Consensus? Some Defining Principles," in *Across the Great Divide: Explorations in Collaborative Conservation and the American West*, ed. Philip Brick, Donald Snow, and Sarah van de Wetering (Washington DC: Island Press, 2001), 33–40.
39 Moseley, "The Applegate Partnership."
40 John Charles Morris et al., *The Case for Grassroots Collaboration: Social Capital and Ecosystem Restoration at the Local Level* (Lanham, MD: Lexington Books, 2013).
41 Laurie Lewis, Matthew G. Isbell, and Matt Koschmann, "Collaborative Tensions: Practitioners' Experiences of Interorganizational Relationships," *Communication Monographs* 77, no. 4 (December 1, 2010): 460–79, doi:10.1080/03637751.2010.523605.
42 Matthew A. Koschmann, "The Communicative Accomplishment of Failed Collaboration," *Journal of Communication* 66, no. 3 (2016).
43 Gray, *Collaborating*.
44 J. Kevin Barge, "Enlarging the Meaning of Group Deliberation: From Discussion to Dialogue," in *New Directions in Group Communication*, ed. Lawrence R. Frey (Thousand Oaks, CA: Sage, 2002), 159–78.
45 Mackin, *The Team Building Tool Kit*.
46 Ibid., p. 18.
47 Darwin Patnode and Henry M. Robert III, *Robert's Rules of Order* (Nashville, TN: Thomas Nelson Publishers, 1989).
48 Ibid., p. 116.
49 Renee Guarriello Heath, *Toward Social Problem Solving: Democracy and Creativity in Community Models of Collaboration* (University of Colorado at Boulder: Dissertation Abstracts International, 66-09A, 2005).
50 Patnode and Robert, *Robert's Rules of Order*.

PART III
Language of Collaborative Praxis

Part III explores five orientations to communication practices and decision making—dialogue, interests, conflict, consensus, and solutions. We refer to this ethical approach to stakeholder interaction as the language of collaborative praxis.

A language is a system of distinctions[1] that puts into play particular values; it is thus both ideological and political.[2] Language does not just represent a particular reality or experience—it is an active producer of that experience.[3] Accordingly language constitutes a particular way of speaking, interpreting, and organizing the world around us. Part III articulates the language needed to approach collaboration ethically.

The language of collaborative praxis loosely follows the pioneering work of Roger Fisher, William Ury, and Bruce Patton through the Harvard Negotiation Project.[4] They posited a principled negotiation process as an alternative dispute method for arriving at solutions in conflict situations.[5] Their stages of principled negotiation call for separating people from the problem, focusing on interests as opposed to positions, inventing options for mutual gain, and using objective criteria.

We see these stages of principled negotiation closely aligning with the way collaborative groups move from learning about one another to articulating a common vision that will frame the strategies and solutions they implement as they work toward solving wicked problems.[6] Communicatively collaborative groups practice dialogue and interest-based talk; they experience conflict and engage in consensus-building around values while generating solutions.

We depict the concepts in part III as a pyramid of communication practices, vocabulary, and structures that build on each other. Each component is not mutually exclusive to a particular stage of collaborating. The layers build, and movement upward is important (as opposed to hierarchy). The wide, base levels of the pyramid are dialogue and interest-oriented communication, which are an important foundation for navigating through conflict to consensus. To be effective, solutions must be built on a solid foundation. The pyramid reflects *ideal* movement as stakeholders interact and communication moves toward solutions.

We envision stakeholders revisiting areas of the pyramid as collaboration ebbs and flows, membership changes, and external stimuli (such as legal challenges) alter the context. It would be naïve to think that collaboration proceeds in a linear manner. Our model is not intended as a rigid prescription for how to do collaboration. Rather, as participants move from getting to know one another to making decisions together, it is a heuristic of communication practices associated with collaborative problem solving.

Chapter 8, "Communication Oriented toward Dialogue," establishes a process of openness, transparency, and vulnerability as central to the practice of ethical communication. We distinguish dialogue from debate explaining why it is well-suited to collaborative problem solving. The chapter identifies specific communication mechanisms for fostering dialogue—from gentle inquiry, to curious listening, to story telling, to perspective taking. Dialogue is presented as the substance of collaborative communication.

Chapter 9 illuminates interests that drive the preferred solutions of stakeholders. "Communication Oriented toward Interests" distinguishes positions from interests and demonstrates the way identity and power intersect with our most basic interests to complicate decision-making situations. This chapter provides descriptions of various communication tools as shared representations of collaborative members' interests and mechanisms for identifying commonality and overlap among participants.

Chapter 10, "Communication Oriented toward Conflict," recognizes conflict as normative to collaborative learning and decision making. Conflict is likely to emerge as stakeholders are forced to make decisions and agree on priorities. The chapter describes common communication practices that serve as barriers to constructive conflict.

Chapter 11 articulates the relationship between constructive conflict and consensus decision making. "Communication Oriented toward Consensus" describes the ways stakeholders can move from individual interests to establishing a collective identity to crafting a vision from their shared values. Stakeholders build consensus on interests before deciding on solutions.

The final chapter in part III, "Communication Oriented toward Solutions," explains why solution-generation *follows* foundational communication orientated toward dialogue, interests, conflict and consensus. It introduces the concept of appreciative inquiry (AI) as an *ethic* for thinking and communicating with others and articulates the possibilities and challenges of adopting an AI methodology for interorganizational collaboration. It also explores other communication strategies for arriving at solutions such as generative brainstorming.

NOTES

[1] Ferdinand De Saussure, *Courses in General Linguistics*, 2nd Revised ed. (Peter Owen Publishers, 1974).

[2] Stanley Deetz, *Transforming Communication, Transforming Business: Building Responsive and Responsible Workplaces* (Cresskill, NJ: Hampton Pr, 1994).

[3] Ibid.

[4] Roger Fisher, William L. Ury, and Bruce M. Patton, *Getting to Yes: Negotiating Agreement Without Giving In*, 2nd ed. (Boston: Houghton Mifflin Harcourt, 1992).

[5] Ibid.

[6] We note within chapter 9 on interests, an exception to the order in which collaborative groups move through principled negotiation processes.

Communication Oriented toward Dialogue

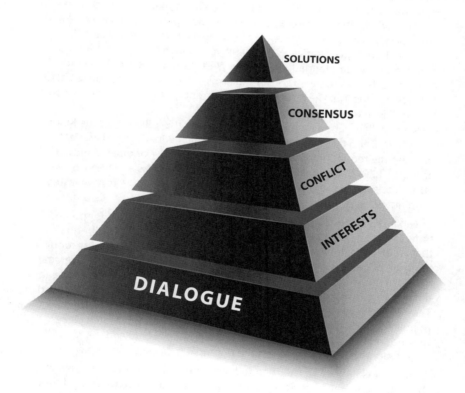

Slackers or Experts?

During their annual retreat, a small group of community stakeholders belonging to West Early Care Collaboration sat in a circle discussing the problems associated with a research project they outsourced to a consulting firm, "Latina Forward." Marcos, the director of the consulting firm, is not present at the meeting, but the meeting follows a tension-filled conference call between him and West's coordinator (Nicole) and grant writer (Julie). During the call, Marcos defended his firm's refusal to write a literature review of best practices and to meet the deadlines outlined in the contract for the research project.

The goal of West's stakeholders was to design a project that would benefit Latina children in their city. West stakeholders chose the Latina Forward firm through a competitive bid process that ultimately was influenced by their primary funder, the King Foundation, whose mission included the enrichment and support of Latina lives. The bid processes required a proposal that articulated how the research firm would meet the benchmarks of the project—including a literature review of best practices in early care and education for Latina children. After providing a literature review, the firm was to conduct quantitative and qualitative research in the geographic area and to make recommendations for how West should proceed toward its goal. More than 20 research consulting firms submitted a competitive bid for the research job, but the King Foundation strongly advocated that the contract be given to Latina Forward.

Some collaboration members felt trapped by the influence of the King Foundation, and they were now dissatisfied that Latina Forward was not meeting the requirements of the job as outlined in the original request for proposal (RFP). Some stakeholders wanted to fire Marcos and his firm, while others considered the complexity of the dilemma. The conversation lasted 45 minutes, but these are the highlights:

Nicole (Collaboration Coordinator): Well, we held a meeting for potential firms to bid on this project; we wanted a balance of technical skill, and by that I mean qualitative and quantitative research expertise. And a second thing we hoped for was a cultural understanding of the families we were targeting in our study. We narrowed it from about 30 to a handful of good candidates, but the King Foundation really pushed for us to hire Latina Forward. They are Latina and have a very strong cultural understanding of our target population. And now if they can't do a quality job on this research piece, they not only make us look very bad, but this reflects badly on the King Foundation. The whole thing has the potential to backfire politically.

Tom (Stakeholder 1): They handed over one page of a literature review that wasn't a literature review at all. It's been a month since we started this. I'm not sure they know what a literature review is!

Aimee (Stakeholder 2): I just don't understand why they are doing the project in this way when the RFP clearly stated an order for how things needed to be done. We could have hired a lot of other very qualified consulting firms.

Nicole: Yes, this is very complex. I mean really, this firm was hired because of their sensitivity to the target population. Part of what Marcos has made clear is that they don't believe prior literature and best practices were based on programs that showed exemplary cultural sensitivity. You know they don't give these studies a lot of credence, and he is right. There is a lot of stuff out there that really didn't acknowledge what we are trying to be sensitive to. For example, some of those studies labeled children who did not maintain eye contact with the teacher as developmentally delayed, but for children in our target community, that behavior is a sign of respect—a cultural practice.

Julie (Grant writer): They aren't following our set protocol because they don't really agree with it philosophically, and we did choose this group for their cultural understanding of the population we are targeting.

Nicole: I propose we give this a little more time. Although they are not following the typical protocol, I'd like to see where their expertise takes us.

The group agreed to continue the contract relationship with Marcos and the Latina Forward Consulting Group.[1]

—Based on the unpublished research of Renee

Built on the ethical cornerstones of contexts, diversity, power, and principled leadership, dialogue is the foundation from which all other collaborative interaction skills are generated—the base of collaborative praxis. Dialogue is at the root of the other communication orientations presented throughout this text. It is an element of behaviors that are oriented toward identifying interests (chapter 9), navigating constructive conflict (chapter 10), building consensus (chapter 11), and arriving at solutions (chapter 12). In an ethical approach to collaboration, communication is thus grounded firmly in dialogue.

We believe collaborative groups will not feel like they are moving forward unless they listen to one another and foster opportunities for dialogue. We have noticed in our research and practice that meetings become stymied when people do not feel heard. This pattern is recognizable when it seems that you are hearing the same story from the same person again and again. What is probably happening is that the stakeholder has had the opportunity to express their concerns, but their concerns have not been granted influence or legitimacy—voice.[2] Only, when the speaker feels understood and validated will they not feel the need to repeat their story or issues[3]. They will continue to reiterate their position if they fear their perspective has been lost, dismissed, or misunderstood.

Our emphasis on communication oriented toward dialogue coincides with the first step in Fisher, Ury, and Patton's principled negotiation method, which advises communicators to seek win-win solutions to problems by first separating the people from the problem.[4] The authors posit that separating people from substantive problems requires listening, perspective taking, and legitimizing the emotions that people feel. Talk at this stage of problem solving is likely to be positional. Most of us tend to think in terms of our positions; thus, it is important to create a safe format in which stakeholders will share their positions. In the interorganizational context, stakeholders are also initially getting to know one another, establishing cultural norms, and building trust—all of these are more easily facilitated with a dialogic process.

That said, dialogue is much more than having a conversation with another person. Indeed, we've all encountered conversations with other people that felt very unfulfilling. We might have described it as being talked *at* rather than talking *with* someone. Dialogue is also much more than a back and forth transaction of conversation. We transact in conversations all the time without experiencing what will be described in this chapter as the inventive, destructive, dialogic moments that allow us to more fully experience the other. We also cannot conflate collaborating and dialogue. Interorganizational collaboration is goal oriented, and dialogue is not (unless you count understanding and learning as a goal). Ultimately in interorganizational collaboration stakeholders will need to make decisions together just as the group of stakeholders in the vignette that opens this chapter tried to decide whether they should continue working with the research consulting firm they hired. Dialogue is essential to working with diverse participants; through dialogue, stakeholders begin to appreciate the strengths and challenges each encounter in the context of the problem domain. But dialogue does not guarantee a particular decision outcome. It is the practice of relating that facilitates learning and understanding throughout the process.

During all stages of collaborating, stakeholders will draw on dialogue skills. Dialogue is not a sequential or linear process (that would be prescription). It is also not a new age concept nor an ideal that can never be attained. Indeed, business scholar and consultant William Isaacs illuminated the relevancy of dialogic skills.[5] "Thinking together implies that you no longer take your own position as final. You relax your grip on certainty and listen to the possibilities that result simply from being in a relationship with others—possibilities that might not otherwise have occurred."[6] Isaacs placed dialogue at the center of creativity and innovation, characterizing it as a practical concept in the context of business and decision making. These are some of the reasons why dialogue constitutes the foundation of the language of collaborative praxis.

This chapter first distinguishes dialogue from debate and the assumptions and skills that accompany each approach. Having established dialogue as a vastly different communication skill than debate, we then trace the origins of dialogic scholarship from influential thinkers summarizing key themes including dialogic moments, the I-Thou ethic, and dialogue as generative and critical of dominant thinking. The latter part of the chapter considers the praxis of dialogue as an element of interorganizational collaboration. It outlines the preparation needed to cultivate dialogue, as well as key principles and practices associated with it. Finally, we develop listening and storytelling as elements of dialogic praxis in collaborative contexts.

Distinguishing Dialogue from Debate

While she was writing this chapter, Renee's 11-year old son, Kennedy, came home from school one day very excited about a project he had been assigned. The class had been divided into various groups including loggers, environmentalists, and rubber-tappers (those dependent on the sap from trees for their livelihood); the assignment was generating rules for managing the Amazon forests of Brazil. Each group of students was to: conduct research on their group's preferred solution, construct winning arguments for their positions, and anticipate and undermine the arguments of the other groups. The students were asked to prepare for a *debate*. Given the composition of this project (various stakeholder groups approaching a problem domain from different perspectives) and Renee's collaborative bias, she was surprised. "A debate?" she inquired, thinking surely the teacher meant for the students to focus on problem solving. "Yes a debate, Mom," Kennedy insisted. Sure enough, for the next several weeks the animated talk among the sixth graders regarding their project hovered around who won and who lost the debate. Facts were tossed at one another's groups. Students from one class section shared tips with students from the other sections, saying things such as, "Oh that argument won in our debate, use that!" From a very young age, we are socialized in the United States to think of environmental and social problems as a debate that can be won or lost, rather than as issues that must be solved jointly. With a focus on debate, rather than collaborative problem solving, we are preparing children for polarizing discussions and an adversarial process that have not been successful in dealing with wicked problems.

One way we can foster the skills needed for complex problem solving is to teach dialogue. Dialogue is as important as debate as a leadership skill in the twenty-first century. As depicted below, dialogue and debate operate on very different assumptions with very different outcomes. J. Kevin Barge reminds us that familiar and traditional communication practices are inadequate for problem solving that is grounded in differences among stakeholders.[7] Debate falls short in complex problem solving, especially given our tendency to polarize diverse perspectives.[8]

Drawing on the works of many authors and projects, political theorist Oliver Escobar provides a thorough comparison of the two types of communication often practiced in public decision making (table 8.1 on pp. 180–181). Escobar notes the etymological root of the word: de = down and batre = to beat; thus, debate means to fight—to resolve by beating down.[9] Yet, debate is not without value and purpose. Scholars have argued

Table 8.1   Comparing dialogue to debate as a means of problem solving[10]

Dialogue	Debate
Dialogue is collaborative; participants work together towards shared understanding of issues and perspectives	Debate is oppositional: various sides oppose each other and try to prove each other wrong
Participants speak to each other	Participants speak to their own constituencies and the undecided middle
The atmosphere is one of safety: facilitators implement ground rules agreed by the participants in order to enhance safe and respectful exchange	The atmosphere is threatening: attacks and interruptions are expected and usually permitted
The goal is exploring common ground and differences	The goal is winning by beating down
Participants listen to understand and gain insight into the beliefs and concerns of others. They try to find their strengths, rather than only weaknesses	Participants listen in order to refute, to find flaws, and to counter arguments
Questions are asked from a position of curiosity that serve the purpose of shared inquiry	Questions are asked from a position of certainty. They are often rhetorical challenges or disguised statement
Participants reveal and investigate their own and others' underlying assumptions	Participants defend their own assumptions as truth
Participants aim to learn through inquiry and disclosure	Participants aim to convince through advocacy and persuasion
Dialogue fosters an open-minded attitude; an openness to being wrong and an openness to change	Debate fosters a closed-minded attitude; a determination to be right
Participants express uncertainties, as well as deeply held beliefs	Participants express unwavering commitment to a point of view, approach, or idea
Differences among participants on the same "side" are revealed, as individual and personal beliefs and values are explored	Difference within "sides" are denied or minimized
Participants share their ideas knowing that other people's reflections will help improve them rather than destroy them	Participants share their ideas and defend them against challenges in order to show that they are right
Dialogue calls for temporarily suspending one's beliefs	Debate calls for investing wholeheartedly in one's beliefs
Dialogue involves a real concern for the other person and seeks to avoid alienating or offending	Debate ignores feelings or relationships, and often allows belittling or deprecating

Dialogue	Debate
Participants are encouraged to question the dominant public discourse, to express needs that may not often be reflected in that discourse, and to explore various options for problem definition and resolution. Participants may discover inadequacies in the usual language and concepts used in public debate	Debates operate with constraints of the dominant public discourse. That discourse defines the problem and the options for resolution. It assumes that fundamental needs and values are already clearly understood
Participants strive to overcome ritualized exchanges, allowing new information to surface	Participants' statements are predictable and offer little new information
Dialogue enlarges and possibly changes a participant's point of view	Debate entrenches a participants own point of view
Dialogue assumes that many people have pieces of the answer and that together they can make them into a workable solution	Debate assumes that there is a right answer and that someone has it
Success requires exploration of the complexities of the issue	Success requires simple impassioned statements
Dialogue remains open-ended	Debate seeks a conclusion

Reprinted with permission from Oliver Escobar, *Public Dialogue and Deliberation: A Communication Perspective for Public Engagement Practitioners* (Edinburgh, Scotland: The Edinburgh Beltane- Beacon for Public Engagement, 2011), https://oliversdialogue.wordpress.com/2013/08/01/public-dialogue-and-deliberation-a-communication-perspective-for-public-engagement-practitioners/

debate is appropriately utilized in the decision-making process, which follows getting to know stakeholder's differences and eliciting their underlying interests.[11] Debate can help stakeholders choose workable solutions from worthy options. Debate is better matched to communication situations where: it is not necessary to preserve relationships (i.e., adversarial situations) or relationships and understandings of one another's differences have been established that will withstand the effects of debate. In interorganizational collaboration, dialogue is initially better suited for understanding differences among stakeholders.

If the concepts presented in table 8.1 sound familiar to you, it's because the communication practices of dialogue and debate parallel the methods associated with collaborative problem solving and adversarial problem solving presented in chapter 2. You might recall that the typical forum for adversarial problem solving is the legal system. The debate Kennedy's class was asked to have regarding the rules and regulations of the Amazon forests prepares students to think of problem solving in terms of legal battles to be won or lost. How often as young students were we required to consider complex issues such as forest management in terms of collaborative problem solving? It is no wonder we have been accused of being an overly litigious society; our education prepares us to litigate.[12] How do we formulate the dialogic skills needed for collaborative leadership and practice?

Even though debate remains the dominant form of communication in the United States, the future is not bleak. For example, in parts of the United States and Canada, the restorative justice movement is gaining ground in the court system, and its principles are making their way into conflict management systems in schools.[13] At the core, restorative justice is a dialogic process in which victims and perpetrators confront one another face-to-face to gain understanding, including the loss experienced by victims and their families. Together they determine what counts as justice given the context of their situation. A building block of the movement is forgiveness, which can only come out of understanding.

The process of understanding is outlined in the practices listed in table 8.1. Listening, gentle inquiry out of curiosity as opposed to certainty, self-disclosure, and open-mindedness contribute to understanding. Those who favor the restorative justice system find it has greater promise for rehabilitation and can ease the costs and energy spent on endless appeals and battles in the court system. As the movement trickles into schools it focuses on having students physically sit in circles, listen and explore each other's contributions, and dialogically work through conflict. Programs such as these do not replace the need for skilled debate and adversarial options, but they do work to cultivate the dialogic skills needed to broaden our complex problem-solving skills.[14] Dialogic skills will initially, and quite often, be more important to stakeholders than debate skills as members work to bring together diverse participants.

"I Get It"

The language of dialogue encompasses the importance of perspective taking in conversation with others. Many theoretical streams influence contemporary understandings of dialogue. Literary scholar Mikhail Bakhtin saw the world as dialogic interactions of relations and texts that draw our attention to the plurality of many voices. He referred to these voices as "multivocalic" and understood the world as endless texts of voices in dialogic tension.[15] Bakhtin describes rather than prescribes dialogue as a particular ideal or condition of communication. Emmanuel Levinas and Jürgen Habermas, though representing different philosophical traditions (i.e., Jewish, critical), speak of dialogue as part of an ethical responsibility in conversation with the other (i.e., the other perspective). Martin Buber, a Jewish philosopher, also developed an ethical understanding of dialogue as conditional on a particular type of human experience. Unlike Levinas (who did not believe dialogue took place in the context of equality but rather as a way to overcome inequality), Buber believed that dialogue was based on reciprocity in conversation.

> This experiencing of the other side is essential to the distinction Buber makes between "dialogue," in which I open myself to the otherness of

the person I meet, and "monologue," in which even when I converse with her at length, I allow her to exist only as a content of my experience. . . . Only when I risk and reveal myself as she risks and reveals herself will I grasp her uniqueness and she mine.[16]

We frequently use this quotation about Buber's philosophy in our teaching. What does it mean that, "even when I converse with her at length, I allow her to exist only as a content of my experience?" It is natural in conversation to find commonality with someone, especially when demonstrating empathy for another's experience. Consider that your friend just ended a three-year relationship with her partner. To show you understand her pain, you may say, "I'm sorry. I know how you feel. I felt the same when I broke up with Jordan." Although you are genuinely interested in comforting your friend, have you really understood her from the content of *her* experience? Your relationship, your break-up, is the content of *your* experience. It is possible that your friend will feel you understand her pain when you share your own story. However, she may instead feel that her experience is different— that you could not possibly know her pain—that you and Jordan were never as close as she was with her partner. Quite simply you will not know if you stop short of trying to understand her experience through her eyes.

To understand the content of someone else's experience we will need to explore it *with* them. As Martin Buber would say, we need to be present in the experience of trying to understand the other. It may be that you ask gentle questions to understand her experience. Ask her how she is doing. Has she ever experienced something like this before? Connect with *her* experience. We are not suggesting you should not offer your own experience as a way of building commonality; we are instead drawing attention to the inadequacy of our conversations when we are not open to understanding the other from their unique perspective. Knowing when to ask questions, when to offer a story of shared experience, or when to say nothing but nod your head, is the skill you develop as you attend to the praxis of dialogue. If we must think in terms of goals with dialogue, then the primary goal is to genuinely and sincerely reach the point of "I get it." When *she feels* that you as the listener "get" her, and you find your understanding of her or the subject exceeds your singular understanding, you have most likely experienced a dialogic moment.

QUESTION: In the case that opens this chapter, who sees the problem only as a content of their own experiences? What is their perspective? Who sees the problem from the experience of the other? What is the other's perspective? Which stakeholder(s) seem to "get" the other?

Dialogic Moments

As practitioners of dialogue, we seek dialogic moments. We do not experience dialogue as uninterrupted; dialogic moments are not continuous. The etymological definition of dialogue defines "dia" not as two but as through, between, or across.[17] Thus dialogic moments are not an individual experience but the sum of an experience between individuals. Dialogic scholars Kenneth Cissna and Rob Anderson described dialogic moments as temporal moments in conversation with others.

> The basic character of such a dialogic moment, therefore, is the experience of inventive surprise shared by the dialogic partners as each "turns toward" the other and both mutually perceive the impact of each other's turning. It is a brief interlude of focused awareness and acceptance of otherness and difference that somehow simultaneously transcends the perception of difference itself.[18]

In dialogic moments, individuals experience learning and understanding as the sphere between one another through the process of disclosure and listening. And the expansion of viewpoint might not even take place in the conversation but after individual reflection. As Cissna and Anderson argued, "Dialogue, in other words, is more likely to be surprising, raucous, and momentary than predictable, orderly, and sustained."[19]

An Ethic of I and Thou

Communication oriented toward dialogue is not strategic. Buber theorized that when we approach the other in communication situations as someone to understand, we experience them as "I-Thou" in the dialogic moment.[20] In this communicative experience we are not strategic; we do not communicate for the purpose of achieving something (goal-oriented), which he called the "I-It" relationship. When we approach the other as it, we communicate for our own purposes rather than theirs, or ours together. Dialogue, in Buber's vision requires that we approach the other in an I-Thou relationship requiring humility and the setting aside of goals for communication. The I-Thou relationship is an authentic experience of dialogue that demands reflexivity, transparency, openness, and vulnerability.[21] Consider how the stakeholders in the opening vignette begin by talking about the Latina Forward consulting firm strictly in terms of what they expected to get from them—a literature review of best practices. The initial conversation that takes place among West stakeholders approaches Marcos and Latina Forward from an "I-It" perspective. As the conversation proceeds, we begin to see some of the members of the collaboration consider Marcos from an "I-Thou" perspective. They demonstrate openness and reflexivity to his viewpoint as a marginalized person who does not agree with the methods of research that the collaboration has demanded.

Dialogue as Destruction and Invention

Dialogue is destructive of our singular perspectives. Although the idea of dialogue as destruction sounds counterintuitive to what we hope to accomplish with dialogue, drawing heavily on the idea of the "genuine conversation"[22] and the ideal speech situation,[23] Stanley Deetz and Jennifer Simpson explain:

> In contrast to the common sense view, we develop a concept of dialogic communication that is aimed less at self-expression and more at self-destruction. . . . The point of communication as a social act is to overcome one's fixed subjectivity, one's conceptions, one's strategies— to be open-ended to the indeterminance of people and the external environment to form an open redetermination. This we believe is the basis for "voice." Communication in this dialogic form is productive rather than reproductive.[24]

Accordingly, dialogue is destructive in that our singular, monologic understanding of the other is replaced with a new understanding that could not have been known prior to the dialogic situation. Rather than *reproducing* ideas, understandings, stereotypes, and conclusions that we already knew prior to dialogue, we *produce*, generate, and invent fuller meaning in dialogue together with the other. When we experience dialogue, we create a new understanding of a person or phenomenon. We do not replace our understanding with that of others—we integrate their understanding with ours and ours with theirs.

Deetz and Simpson are careful to differentiate between what they call "having say" and "having voice." Having say is reproductive in that it permits us to share or reproduce verbally concepts and constructions we already own. When we have say, we are expressing something. As critical scholars, the authors are concerned about the suppression of marginalized others. They claim marginalized perspectives are often silenced when people with dominant, hegemonic viewpoints have say. For this reason, they warn against rooting dialogue in the conception of common ground, arguing, "Dialogic models that favor a quest for common ground inherently favor the already-dominant position of institutional privilege."[25] Instead, their conception of dialogue as both destructive and generative emphasizes the importance of creating the opportunity for dialogic moments among stakeholders. It elucidates the potential for marginalized voices to contribute to fuller understandings of complex problems and to contribute richly to potential, albeit temporary solutions.[26]

> **QUESTION:** Consider opening vignette of the chapter. In what ways is hegemony present in this example? What role does marginalization play in the interaction? How does power become leveled in the example?

> **QUESTION:** How did the arguments of the coordinator and grant writer work to be destructive of commonly held assumptions about the Latino Forward firm held by Tom and Nicole?

Dialogue as Collaborative Praxis

The act of "getting" another's perspective does not mean that you will replace your perspective with theirs. It does not mean that you will agree. Josina Makau and Debian Marty describe the well-known Public Conversations Project, which took on the topic of abortion in the early 2000s.[27] Persons from both sides of this topic took part in facilitated dialogic conversations that fostered a more complex understanding of abortion and humanized the persons behind the positions.[28] This is an important distinction to make in interorganizational collaboration. Dialogic moments may influence interorganizational decision making, but they are not strategic (I-It), or intended to be so. That is why we refer to dialogue as the foundation of conversation. Dialogue opens the possibility for other forms of communication and decisions that would be hard to enact without it. For example, consensus decision making depends on dialogue because stakeholders must understand how others perceive the problem and possible solutions. Appreciative Inquiry is a dialogic practice of building a shared vision for what works best in a community or organization.

The possibilities for dialogue for interorganizational collaboration are immense. We introduced in chapter 4 a theory of collaborative rationality, which posits that collaboration is grounded in diversity, interdependence, and authentic dialogue (DIAD).[29] Listening to someone who holds vastly different opinions, experiences, and values than you do until the point where you can say, "I get it," furthers collaborative problem solving. Dialogue enables us to have difficult conversations with those different from us. Given that interorganizational collaboration hinges on the ideas of ethics, diversity, sharing power, and principled leadership, dialogue is the core of a communication praxis. Developing a language of collaboration compels us to think about how we prepare diverse stakeholders to encounter one another in authentic dialogue.

Praxis through Preparation and Reflexivity

Collaborative leaders foster the setting and context needed to have authentic dialogic moments in the context of interorganizational collaboration. The microprocess of communication and the structures we build regarding how we communicate influence the types of conversations we will have. Sheila McNamee, scholar and family therapist, argues we must prepare so that a dialogic experience is more likely to develop.

> Our focus should be on how we craft livable futures together. This is a very important issue. In the simplest, and probably also vaguest terms, this question suggests the need to create the conversational space, where different kinds of conversations can transpire. For me this implies that planning is not the central feature but, rather, the preparation for generative dialogue should be central. What I mean by this is that we must engage in reflexive inquiry where we consider how to invite participants to engage in the dialogue with different voices.[30]

But what does it mean to engage in reflexive inquiry? McNamee offers practical advice.

Preparing Dialogue

To prepare to engage in dialogue stakeholders should
- avoid speaking from abstractions
- be present to the immediate situation
- set ground rules
- practice the imaginative
- make the other reasonable

Avoid Speaking from Abstractions. Often we speak in abstractions regarding difficult subjects. We might say, "This is what I believe," or "This is true. This is wrong." Instead, McNamee suggests we "root abstractions in a life story of their own." By doing so, the other may disagree with our position, but they cannot tell us that our story is wrong. In our opening case, West Early Care Collaboration members may not agree with the assertion by Marcos that research on Latina children lacks credibility, but they cannot dispute specific stories about children who were labeled developmentally delayed because they did not demonstrate eye contact. They cannot dispute his claim that eye contact in his culture has a different meaning. This concrete anecdote is more powerful and less open to dispute than the general abstraction that studies of Latina children lack credence. By sharing the concrete concerns of Marcos, the conversation moved from an abstract judgment of research to a tangible story of how children were mislabeled, ultimately fostering greater empathy.

Be Present to the Immediate Situation. In conversation, it is difficult to avoid getting stuck on our past experiences and hurts. McNamee suggests that "rather than let the history dominate the relational experience" we focus on being present to the immediate situation and the immediacy of the person we encounter. In this sense, presence refers to time. In our opening case, Nicole redirects the conversation away from Aimee's concerns of the past, "we could have hired a lot of very qualified consulting firms," to the present contribution made by the Latina Forward firm. Nicole argued, ". . . this firm was hired *because* of their sensitivity to the target population." The shift to the present forces the group to be reflexive about their criteria for hiring the consulting firm and not dwell on historical definitions for what counts as quality work.[31]

Set Ground Rules. In the last chapter, we discussed the importance of ground rules to structure conversation in collaboration. McNamee points out that ground rules can also help prepare us to encounter the other dialogically.[32] In this sense, ground rules are also very personal and should reflect the communication needs of the individuals. For example, in the case of a husband and wife, a wife may request as a ground rule that her husband not respond in a manner in which he tries to "fix" her concerns. Such a ground rule organically grows out the native, typical communication habits of the couple—their triggers and emotional buttons. The same is true for collaborative stakeholders attending to how they can craft a communication environment that brings out the best in participants and helps overcome some of the communication habits that typically stifle thoughtful conversation. These rules are likely to vary with stakeholders.

Go Beyond Expected Roles in Conversation.   McNamee suggests that particular questions help us avoid certainty. For example, "pause at the moment we know we are correct and ask, how else might this be? Is there another way to make sense out of a person's actions? Or comments?"[33] These techniques help us appreciate and make sense of the other's position. Be prepared to respond not from your role—CEO, executive director, scientist—but as an empathic human. For example, after an extended conflict Renee and a colleague had reached an impasse regarding a new faculty hire. Renee began their next meeting by embracing her colleague—who had been a dear mentor and friend. The embrace was a human reaction, perhaps not expected or even considered appropriate in a work setting. But they began the meeting by sharing that each felt that their relationship as colleagues and friends was more important to preserve and mattered more than the outcome of their disagreement. We cannot prescribe this technique, because the reason it was effective was because it was organic, spontaneous, and authentic. However, we can urge you to be open to authentic moments that allow you to abandon expected roles and embrace your common humanity.

Practice the Imaginative.   We can also practice reflexivity by imagining "as if" or "what if." When you imagine "as if," you talk as if you were in another situation. For example, can you talk to this person *as if* you were a spouse rather than a colleague? How might that change the tone and tenor of the conversation? Similarly, when you talk in "what if" mode, you focus on an idealized future rather than speaking in the certainties of the past. McNamee argues that "what if" fosters constructive questions such as, "How do we do this together?" It cultivates the thought that, "My actions are not wholly mine; they are ours."[34] In many ways the conversation at the beginning of this chapter demonstrates "what if?"-thinking. Nicole proposes that the collaboration suspend their instinct to fire the Latina Forward firm and consider what if Marcos is right? What if the studies really aren't inclusive of Latina children and do not represent best practices? What if the benchmarks are wrong? By engaging on some level with these questions, stakeholders could look forward to the possibilities illuminated by the Latina perspective rather than concentrating on defending the certainties regarding preferred methods for conducting research.

Make the Other Reasonable.   We add to McNamee's list the notion of reasonableness. Communication scholars Karen Tracy and Kristen

Standerfer remind us to rethink communicative behavior that appears unreasonable and ask, "what if I were to assume they were acting reasonable?"[35] Sometimes the response of another might be construed as manipulative or conniving. When we contemplate what would make their behavior seem reasonable, we have to consider their identity needs (are they trying to save face?), their emotional needs (is their response in relation to a perceived hurt?), and their power needs (do they feel like they are losing control?) By trying to understand what appears to be irrational communication as reasoned response, we build empathy and appreciation for the other rather than react from a positional stance. We can help meet the unspoken needs of our dialogic partners.

Spotlight scholar Sheila McNamee speaks worldwide on the topic of dialogue and its constructive potential for transforming conflict. She shares her insights in the scholar spotlight below.

SCHOLAR SPOTLIGHT

Dialogue and Transformation
Sheila McNamee

I would like to invite you to reflect on some issues that I think are crucial for us to consider today. We live in a world of differences and conflict. We are globally connected in ways that have not been previously possible, highlighting differences and conflicts of significant proportion. I believe an understanding of the process of constructing the social order and the process of dialogue—as a special form of communication—offers us a way to step into and embrace the diversity of moral stances we confront.

Richard Rorty says, "Intractable moral conflicts are not easily resolved and, in many cases, may not be resolvable. Indeed, many such conflicts should not be resolved, but they can be argued in more humane, enlightening, and respectful ways, at least 'continuing the conversation.'"[36] There are two issues I would like to address here that resonate with Rorty's idea of "continuing the conversation." These two issues are framed as questions: What is dialogue? and How can dialogue be useful in moving beyond moral conflict? In order to explore these questions, it is important to first consider the topic of moral conflict.

Daily, we confront conflicting moralities ranging from the diverse values of Western modernity and traditional cultures to local campus or community politics, not to mention the clashing moralities we encounter in some of our most intimate relationships. Let us refer to these moral stances as moral orders—that is, ways of being in the world that are taken for granted as necessary for main-

(continued)

taining "goodness." Moral orders emerge out of the unwritten social conventions that serve to maintain social order. We operate within moral orders every time we utter to ourselves or others the "oughtness" or "shouldness" of a given action or set of actions. To that end, the exploration of diverse moralities should be a common focus for us all since every morality is constructed in our day-to-day interactions with one another. Our attention should be directed to the situated activities of people. With our stories, and in our interactions with others, we craft our worlds. The moral orders within which we live are emergent products of the flux and flow of daily engagement. That one person or another might respond differently to our actions is always a possibility. To this end, the moral character of everyday life rests on the contingent quality of communication—therefore, communication becomes our necessary focus of attention.

I often think about the offhanded ways that we justify our actions: "It's written in the rule book," or "This is the way we've always done it," or even more popular, "These are the procedures and I cannot make exceptions." But from where do these rule books, ritualized patterns, and procedures materialize? Each represents its own moral order—the taken for granted expectations we have for "how things should be." And each is no more permanent or solid than the patterns of communication that create them. Moral orders arise out of our interaction with others. They are made not found.

When you confront difference, do you think long and hard about how to craft your argument, what persuasive tactics to employ, and privately rehearse the anticipated conversation? Many people do, and I would like to suggest that this is precisely the focus that traps us in unending conflict. There is no possibility to successfully persuade the other because when we compare what is coherent for each conflicting party, we are comparing apples and oranges. Your good reasons and compelling evidence are discounted as irrational by my standards and vice versa. We are trapped in a debate of "my good" over yours.

What if, instead of—or at least in addition to—careful crafting of our argument, we entertain how we would like to "meet" the other and what sort of conversation we would like to have? What if our vision of winning was reframed as an opportunity to be in extended conversation with the other in which new understanding—not agreement, validation, or consensus—could be constructed? This is the difference of dialogue.

Undoubtedly, moving beyond our own passionate positions is a seemingly impossible task. It requires a dramatic yet simple refocusing of attention away from the carefully planned sequence of actions that we imagine might secure a firm place for our own moral order. Our focus is better placed on what people do together and what their "doing" makes. Put differently, I am proposing that we shift from a focus on the "rightness" of any person's or group's actions—temporarily—to consider what conditions might generate more humane ways of confronting difference. It is in our coordinated activities with others that we make meaning. And, it is these coordinations with others that place our focus on the social, relational aspects of what we come to assume is or is not moral.

Let's examine, for example, the various moral positions constructed around the issue of same-sex marriage. No one is born with a position for or against this issue. Rather, the positions we all adopt are worked out in the give and take of our conversations with others—family, friends, acquaintances, and media. Our position on this issue emerges from those relational coordinations that are most central to us. And, while discussing this topic with others who share the same opinion, we experience a particular form of coordinated action that confirms and substantiates our view.

Think for a minute now of this process of coordination occurring every time we interact with another. The smallest and most insignificant of moments becomes a moment of confirming or reconstructing meaning. Furthermore, every time we interact with another, we are constructing meanings that have implications not only for the present relationship and/or the present moment, but also for other relationships in which we are engaged. Additionally, our moment-to-moment engagements with others have important implications for the expectations we impose upon ourselves and others. By extension, there are implications for what we come to see as moral. In other words, in every encounter we are crafting moral orders with others.

Reflect for a moment on the various issues about which you are passionate. Think about some of your strongest beliefs. Perhaps your intensity is focused on issues of social justice, racial equality, abortion, polygamy, war, euthanasia, substance abuse, pornography. Over what issue or issues would others claim you lose your "objectivity?" What are the topics you have a difficult time discussing in a civil manner? Now think about the conversations, the coordinations, and the relational histories where you feel supported and virtuous for your stance on these heated issues. These are the very moments within which you create, confirm, and solidify your moral stance. And, as mentioned earlier, this process is occurring every time we engage with others. It is a moment full of potential in that new "positions" or meaning can emerge at any moment because of the contingent quality of our situated activities with others; it could also be a moment further amplifying a dogmatic stance. We are no longer talking about universal good or bad but good and bad that are worked out at a very local level—in our coordinations with others. They can be generalized into patterns and rituals that we come to expect. It is in this process that our "moral orders" are born.

Now let us consider the fully functioning, well coordinated moral order of same-sex marriage advocates as well as the moral order of those who oppose it. The moral stances are completely coherent within their communities (i.e., they are relationally crafted). Yet, there is no point of contact between them—no way to bridge their incommensurate beliefs. The first thing to note here is the clarity of oppositional moralities. The second important point is that social processes have produced these very specific moral orders. And finally, the division between the two moral orders is readily apparent. In other words, they are both internally coherent; they are both rooted in patterns of social coordination; and they are incommensurate. Why should we expect either group in this conflict to think they are morally wrong? How do we choose which morality to employ as the evaluative standard? Even as a potential third party to this moral conflict, would it be possible for any of us to stand outside one of these two moral orders? Are not all of us already embedded within one or the other?

Is persuasion our only recourse in the face of competing moralities? Persuasion, in these moments, is an easy defense. I can argue you are wrong and evil and I can tell you why (i.e., you don't share my values). You can do the same. Yet,

(continued)

we have accomplished nothing but the further construction of pain and anger without locating a way of "going on together."[37] More challenging and more humane is finding a way to bridge these differences.

The challenge we face is to take this understanding of how communication processes construct moral orders and use this same attention to process—not content and not individual moral character—so we might bridge these moralities thereby providing some way to continue the conversation. Clearly, if moral orders are crafted out of ordinary coordinations among people, the diversity, and thus incommensurability, of these orders is inevitable. How could we ever imagine a single, unquestioned moral order? Dialogue, as a very special form of communication, places our attention on coordinating multiple moral orders. I would like to suggest that dialogue is a way to move beyond the oppression of one moral order over another.

Praxis through Listening

We often make the claim to our clients and students that the key to interorganizational collaboration is to become an excellent listener—and that this skill is just as, if not more, important than being an excellent speaker for stakeholders. Julia Wood reminds us that we listen for various reasons, such as to listen for information.[38] In subsequent chapters we will discuss listening for that which is not said, such as listening for unspoken interests and listening for identity needs that will likely never be said aloud. These purposes—to unearth interests and identity needs—are a part of listening to try and understand the other's position or perspective. We are listening to learn and to destroy our singular perspectives. In addition to the critical reflexivity we need to prepare for dialogue, dialogic listening is composed of sincerity, appreciation, embodied presence, and genuine curiosity.

Sincerity. Dialogic listening requires being genuine. Many books and lessons exist to assist one to become a better listener. They often offer prescriptive practical advice that can indeed help you hone your listening skills, such as make eye contact, paraphrase what the speaker has said, use their words when possible. That said, listening can only be approached as a praxis and not a practice. The rote, rehearsed responses exchanged with the speaker will feel disingenuous. Renee once worked with a woman who frequently responded to her suggestions with, "So what I hear you saying is . . . ." Renee easily recognized the paraphrasing technique from her undergraduate communication courses. While her colleague may have been sincere, the phrase lost its meaning over time, and Renee interpreted it to be condescending. Listening in the context of interorganizational collaboration requires that listening be approached with hearts as well as minds and bodies. Praxis demands that a sense of moral obligation meets with local wisdom to navigate a communication experience. Moral obligation in listening manifests in our reflexivity, openness, transparency, and vulnerability in the speaking situation. Memorizing a particular method for paraphrasing, or intensely looking into another's eyes, does not necessarily make us great listeners.

Appreciating. Listening allows us to appreciate the diversity of others. An association of women lawyers asked Renee to do a workshop about intergenerational conflict. A few weeks before the training was to happen, she had a worrisome call from the workshop organizers. Their association had recently hosted a related lecture that devolved into a confrontational and divisive talk leaving many in the room unsettled and polarized on the issue—the organizers were concerned this might happen again. Although Renee was mindful that many of the same women would also be a part of her training and might be presupposed to divisive talk, she also felt confident that her method for training would not invite such polarization. Renee and her partner had designed the training around dialogue grounded in the ethic of Appreciative Inquiry (AI).[39] An entire methodology exists around AI techniques that are useful in organizational change (see chapter 12), but at the heart of the methodology is an ethic of appreciation and the belief that what we focus on is what we see in others.[40] Listening appreciatively allows you to see the strengths in people and situations. Asking appreciative questions influences the direction of our conversations.[41] Instead of griping about intergenerational conflicts, workshop-goers were asked to identify the strengths they see in each generation and each other. The workshop left participants with a greater understanding of one another and greater appreciation for the skills and abilities of their colleagues. Listening appreciatively is part of a dialogic ethic and can move people with conflicting viewpoints toward understanding.

Embodied Presence. Dialogic listening requires being present. Contrary to what we have convinced ourselves about multitasking, you cannot listen well while you are doing other things. Studies have found that college students who text and use social media during class perform poorer on tests and other assignments, despite their perception that they can do both well.[42] Listening requires being mentally and physically present. As our bodies turn toward those we try and understand and our eyes meet theirs, our conversational partners slow down the speed of their talk; they may be more articulate as they realize they do not have to vie for our attention in the moment. For example, Mike, the chief financial officer for the county and the facilitator for the Best SELF collaboration, held the highest, nonelected position one could in local government. Not surprisingly, many people competed for his time. Yet when Renee stopped by his office, unscheduled, the first thing Mike did was to unplug his phone (yes, this was quite some time ago). He invited her to sit down, folded his hands on his desk, and leaned toward her chair to listen. His behavior made Renee (and many others) feel as if they were important. It created reciprocity in the speaking situation, despite his high-ranking position. Making ourselves present to others in this hurried society signals our minds and bodies to engage more fully with the other.

> **QUESTION:** In the case of the Latina Forward firm, Marcos was actually not present for the discussion among stakeholders. Instead, Nicole and Julie represented his viewpoint. Do you think physical presence is a requirement for interorganizational collaboration? Can representatives speak on behalf of marginalized stakeholders? Consider the discussion in our chapters on diversity and power as you contemplate your response.

Genuine Curiosity.   Demonstrating genuine curiosity requires listening receptively; scholars argue sincere curiosity is central to engaged listening.[43] Makau and Marty claim, "this nonjudgmental quality is what we experience in a toddler who continuously asks 'why?' . . . The child is not evaluating. She simply wants to know and understand what she is experiencing in her world."[44] When asked questions from a stance of genuine curiosity, the speaker does not feel interrogated but instead is relieved or delighted at the opportunity to have someone focused and curious regarding his or her experience. The difference between asking questions that feel judgmental versus asking questions that the speaker experiences as curious is grounded in the communicators' ability to create reciprocity through reflexivity, openness, transparency, and vulnerability. For example, making yourself vulnerable to the other through disclosure may help assure the other that you are asking questions from a stance of sincere curiosity.

> **QUESTION:** What techniques besides disclosure might foster openness, transparency, and vulnerability as you engage in genuine curiosity?

Praxis through Storytelling

Storytelling provides an opportunity for interorganizational stakeholders to engage dialogically. While stories are not necessarily dialogic on their own, they can invite dialogic moments.[45] Stories follow a narrative format (a beginning, middle, and end) and center on a theme or problem that is resolved and gives meaning to the story.[46] Laura Black studied storytelling in deliberative contexts and found it invites perspective taking, negotiates identity, and helps others be present to one another by bringing their experiences into the conversation.[47]

For example, Renee was engaged in a conversation with an acquaintance who lived most of his life in a small country in the Middle East, near Afghanistan. To her dismay he countered the widespread belief in the brutality of the Taliban by saying, "Renee, all of my culture is brutal." He could see that she did not grasp his assessment, so he told two stories. The first story was about the kidnapping of his son. He threatened to punish the kidnappers should they not promptly return his son but reward them once the son was safely at home. As a result, his son was returned. He explained that his wife called him at work to report the kidnapping. As he told this story, it struck Renee that he spoke of this event as if his wife had called and asked him to pick up groceries from the store on his way home from work. An act that strikes terror in the hearts of parents was a transaction—part of the fabric of living—in his culture. He reinforced the lesson with another story about a visit from an American friend. After picking up his fair skinned, red-headed companion at the airport, they were followed home by an aggressive driver whose vehicle continually edged closer to his car. He instructed his driver to "hang the A.K. out the window" so the car following them would not try and kidnap his fair friend. The driver held the gun out the window, and the harassing car retreated. Having heard these stories Renee had a very different understanding of "brutal" and how hard it must be for her friend to separate one brutal force from other random acts that had become a way of life for him and his family. In the United States, her friend mowed his yard, hosted backyard barbecues, and lived an ordinary suburban lifestyle. In his country, he had a driver who carried an automatic assault rifle at all times. It is doubtful she could have grasped his perspective without the poignancy of his stories.

Invites Perspective Taking.   Storytelling has the potential to elicit dialogic moments because it fosters perspective taking. By building a space for storytelling, stakeholders invite others to move from abstract levels of preferred policies and positions to concrete examples of how those policies and positions play out in the lives of individuals. The story told by Renee's acquaintance was in the midst of a larger discussion about US military policy. The explanation of the complexity of violence in her friend's culture provided a greater context for understanding the outcomes of policies overseas. As Black argues,

> Storytelling enables a kind of perspective taking that is fruitful for deliberation because it allows participants to understand the reasonableness of another's perspective, even during a disagreement. In dialogic terms, storytelling can allow participants to "imagine the real[ity] of the other" in a profound and meaningful way. If this kind of dialogic understanding is achieved, it can promote a fairer consideration of reasons arising from different viewpoints and help participants engage in collaborative conflict management and deliberative decision making.[48]

Accordingly, stakeholders in collaboration must carve out a space for storytelling in the processes of crafting solutions for complex problems that require deep understandings.

Negotiates Identity.   Stories also work to help us negotiate our singular and collective identities. Black found storytellers negotiate their identities in relation to each other by building on each other's stories, expressing individual values, and bringing listeners into their story world. The stories of a particular Middle Eastern culture told to Renee portrayed very distinct identity characteristics of the culture's people. Renee's acquaintance was a survivor in one sense, having navigated life and raised a family in what he claimed, and his stories portrayed, as a brutal culture. His stories change our views of A.K.-carrying civilians from violent people to people merely trying to survive. His stories carved a collective identity of brutality for his lived culture versus an identity reserved solely for the Taliban.

Collective identities of groups can also be developed through story chaining, which happens when one person's narrative launches another's story, and that person's story builds on the preceding narrative. Story chaining and storytelling in interorganizational collaboration can help stakeholders build a collective identity as they "attempt to understand and take on aspects of each other's perspectives."[49] In the context of interorganizational collaboration, stakeholders' stories may help negotiate the values that the group will take on as part of its mission. For example, in one case study of interorganizational collaboration, Renee and her colleague Patricia Sias identified testimony as a strategy used by stakeholders to reinforce their collective values and mission.[50] Testimonies from the people who benefit from the collaboration are stories told in their own words that work to foster and cement the collective values, identity, and mission of the stakeholders. These stories can also be told and brought to the interorganizational experience through video, blogging, and print media. Testimonies can work to launch dialogic conversations among stakeholders.

Makes the Other Present through Experience.   Black argues that a story "makes it easier for listeners to understand and take on the reality of another in a powerful way."[51] Renee connected viscerally with the kidnapping story of her friend's son. She knew the boy. She has a son the same age. She could not think of anything worse than receiving that phone call. The story made poignant the fear and threat with which her friend lived. She could not possibly fully grasp his experience without his humanizing story. She could not minimize the claim, "all of my culture is brutal," once she learned his experience as he lived it. The story was the vehicle in which Renee's experiences as a mother and relatively safe American met her friend's experiences; in a dialogic moment, she understood his claims and he understood her.

Storytelling Considerations.   Although telling stories can initiate dialogue, storytelling time should not be limited to introductions.[52] Consider the level of trust and dialogic preparation that may need to be in place before stakeholders will feel safe enough to share their stories. The purpose and content of storytelling should drive the decision of where to time this activity in the meeting process. Storytelling can lead to dialogic moments because it requires openness, transparency, and vulnerability. For these reasons, storytelling can be risky and can reinforce differences among stakeholders.[53] Accordingly, stakeholders should be mindful of the preparation and reflexivity needed to facilitate dialogic moments and foster respect and trust among stakeholders.

Finally, storytelling also takes time. If storytelling is meant to foster dialogue among stakeholders, space will need to be allotted both for expressive (linear, monologic) and dialogic types of communication in interorganizational meetings. This can be accomplished in a number of ways. An individual stakeholder could be invited to share testimony at each meeting, tilting the focus of the dialogue that day toward that stakeholder's unique experiences. A longer retreat day could be planned to carve out space for storytelling from multiple or all stakeholders. Facilitated dialogues could follow the storytelling. Storytelling could take place in an atypical venue, such as a stakeholder's home or an outdoor facility that disrupts the expected norms of meetings. Or storytelling could become a cultural norm for the interorganizational collaboration by leaving plenty of time on the agenda and encouraging stories at each meeting.

Rather than thinking of dialogue as an ideal "aha" moment that you encountered with another, or the accomplishment of a particular outcome, it is more useful to think of dialogue as an iterative process. In dialogue with others, you are practicing a principled interaction that changes in the act of communicating. Dialogue allows us to understand a phenomenon, another person, or rich subject in iterations, meaning the subject changes as soon as we engage it. The phenomenon, person, or subject grows ever more complex and rich as we practice reflexivity, listening, and storytelling, and by attending to our own openness, transparency, and vulnerability. These practices do not always happen in the same conversation, or in concert with others. Thus, practicing dialogue does not end when the conversation ends.

CONCLUSION

We began this chapter by unpacking the ways in which we understand dialogue—as a practice of (not a synonym for) collaborating; as distinct from debate; and as a means of dismantling singular viewpoints. Effective dialogue is marked by openness, transparency, and vulnerability. In dialogue we seek the opportunity to "get" the other in ways we could not previously. Developing a dialogic praxis enables stakeholders to engage with others who hold diverse perspectives. Dialogue levels power differentials communicatively because it focuses on reciprocity in interaction. It is a foundational tool for principled leadership; it cultivates egalitarian ways of knowing and understanding interorganizational problems. Dialogue rests at the base of our communicative model for the language of collaborative praxis because we cannot envision how stakeholders will authentically arrive at solutions to wicked problems without engaging in it. It seeds all other communication goals and orientations presented in this text.

CHAPTER TAKE-AWAYS

• Recognize dialogue as the foundation to a collaborative communication ethic and understand what dialogue is not—collaboration, goal oriented, or debate

- Understand dialogic moments as destructive of singular perspectives and a turn toward the other
- Comprehend how openness, transparency, and vulnerability are practiced in dialogue
- Articulate how to prepare for dialogic experiences
- Discern the roles of sincerity, embodiment, and genuine curiosity in listening
- Understand the role of storytelling in dialogue as perspective taking, negotiating identity, and an invitation to presence

ENDNOTES

1 Based on the unpublished research of Renee Guarriello Heath. Names, places, and dialogue have been altered to provide anonymity to the participants.

2 Stanley Deetz and Jennifer Simpson, "Critical Organizational Dialogue," in *Dialogue: Theorizing Difference in Communication Studies*, ed. Rob Anderson, Leslie A. Baxter, and Kenneth N. Cissna (Thousand Oaks, CA: Sage, 2003), 141–58.

3 By validation we are not insinuating "agreement."

4 Roger Fisher, William L. Ury, and Bruce M. Patton, *Getting to Yes: Negotiating Agreement Without Giving In*, 2nd ed. (Boston: Houghton Mifflin Harcourt, 1992).

5 William Isaacs, *Dialogue: The Art of Thinking Together* (New York: Crown Business, 1999).

6 Ibid., p. 18.

7 Kevin Barge, "Enlarging the Meaning of Group Deliberation: From Discussion to Dialogue," in *New Directions in Group Communication*, ed. Lawrence R. Frey (Thousand Oaks, CA: Sage, 2002), 159–78.

8 Ibid.

9 Oliver Escobar, *Public Dialogue and Deliberation: A Communication Perspective for Public Engagement Practitioners* (Edinburgh, Scotland: The Edinburgh Beltane-Beacon for Public Engagement, 2011), p. 19; https://oliversdialogue.wordpress.com/2013/08/01/public-dialogue-and-deliberation-a-communication-perspective-for-public-engagement-practitioners/

10 Reprinted with permission from Ibid.

11 Barge, "Enlarging the Meaning of Group Deliberation."

12 Paul Rubin, "More Money into Bad Suits," *The New York Times*, November 16, 2010, http://www.nytimes.com/roomfordebate/2010/11/15/investing-in-someone-elses-lawsuit/more-money-into-bad-suits

13 *Restorative Practices to Resolve Conflict/Build Relationships: Katy Hutchison at TEDxWestVancouverED*, http://tedxtalks.ted.com/video.mason/Restorative-Practices-to-Resolv?

14 Ibid.

15 Mikhail M. Bakhtin, *The Dialogic Imagination: Four Essays*, ed. Michael Holquist, trans. Caryl Emerson, Revised ed. (Austin: University of Texas Press, 1982).

16 Peter Atterton, Matthew Calarco, and Maurice Friedman, eds., *Levinas and Buber: Dialogue and Difference* (Pittsburgh, PA: Duquesne University Press, 2004), p. 3.

17 Escobar, *Public Dialogue and Deliberation,* p. 19.

18 Kenneth N. Cissna and Rob Anderson, "Theorizing about Dialogic Moments: The Buber-Rogers Position and Postmodern Themes," *Communication Theory* 8, no. 1 (February 1, 1998): 63–104, doi:10.1111/j.1468-2885.1998.tb00211.x, p. 74.

19 Ibid., pp. 79–80.

20 Martin Buber, *I and Thou* (Mansfield Centre, CT: Martino Publishing, 2010).

21 Ibid.

22 Hans-Georg Gadamer, *Truth and Method*, 2nd Revised ed. (London/New York: Bloomsbury Academic, 2004).

[23] Jürgen Habermas, *The Theory of Communicative Action, Volume 1: Reason and the Rationalization of Society*, trans. Thomas McCarthy (Boston: Beacon Press, 1985); Jürgen Habermas, *The Theory of Communicative Action, Volume 2: Lifeworld and System: A Critique of Functionalist Reason*, trans. Thomas McCarthy (Boston: Beacon Press, 1985).

[24] Deetz and Simpson, "Critical Organizational Dialogue," p. 143.

[25] Ibid., p. 143.

[26] We say temporary because decisions affecting social and environmental issues must eventually be open to re-examination in a democratic society.

[27] Josina M. Makau and Debian L. Marty, *Dialogue and Deliberation* (Long Grove, IL: Waveland Press, Inc., 2013).

[28] Ibid., pp. 70–71.

[29] Judith E. Innes and David E. Booher, *Planning with Complexity: An Introduction to Collaborative Rationality for Public Policy* (New York: Routledge, 2010), p. 17.

[30] Sheila McNamee and John Shotter, "Dialogue, Creativity, and Change," in *Dialogue: Theorizing Difference in Communication Studies*, ed. Rob Anderson, Leslie A. Baxter, and Kenneth N. Cissna (Thousand Oaks, CA: Sage 2003), 91–104, p. 93.

[31] Ibid.

[32] Ibid.; Sheila McNamee and Dian Marie Hosking, *Research and Social Change: A Relational Constructionist Approach*, Reprint ed. (New York: Routledge, 2013).

[33] McNamee and Shotter, "Dialogue, Creativity, and Change," p. 103.

[34] Ibid.

[35] Karen Tracy and Christina Standerfer, "Selecting a School Superintendent: Sensitivities in Group Deliberation," in *Group Communication in Context: Studies of Bona Fide Groups*, ed. Larry R. Frey, 2nd ed. (Mahwah, NJ: Psychology Press, 2002), 109–36.

[36] Richard Rorty, *Philosophy and the Mirror of Nature* (Princeton, NJ: Princeton University Press, 1981), p. 394.

[37] Ludwig Wittgenstein, *Philosophical Investigations*, ed. P. M. S. Hacker and Joachim Schulte, 4th ed. (Hoboken, NJ: Wiley-Blackwell, 2009).

[38] Julia T. Wood, *Interpersonal Communication: Everyday Encounters*, 8th ed. (Boston: Cengage, 2016).

[39] David L. Cooperrider and Diana Whitney, *Appreciative Inquiry: A Positive Revolution in Change* (San Francisco: Berrett-Koehler Publishers, 2005).

[40] Ibid.

[41] Ibid.

[42] Louis-Philippe Beland and Richard Murphy, "Ill Communication: Technology, Distraction & Student Performance," CEP Discussion Paper (Centre for Economic Performance, LSE, 2015), https://ideas.repec.org/p/cep/cepdps/dp1350.html

[43] Makau and Marty, *Dialogue and Deliberation,* p. 113.

[44] Ibid., p. 113.

[45] Laura W. Black, "Deliberation, Storytelling, and Dialogic Moments," *Communication Theory* 18, no. 1 (February 1, 2008): 93–116, doi:10.1111/j.1468-2885.2007.00315.x.

[46] David M. Ryfe, "Narrative and Deliberation in Small Group Forums," *Journal of Applied Communication Research* 34, no. 1 (February 1, 2006): 72–93, doi:10.1080/00909880500420226.

[47] Black, "Deliberation, Storytelling, and Dialogic Moments."

[48] Ibid., p. 96.

[49] Ibid., p. 107.

[50] Renee Guarriello Heath and Patricia M. Sias, "Communicating Spirit in a Collaborative Alliance," *Journal of Applied Communication Research* 27, no. 4 (November 1, 1999): 356–76, doi:10.1080/00909889909365545.

[51] Black, "Deliberation, Storytelling, and Dialogic Moments," p. 109.

[52] Ibid.

[53] Ibid.

Communication Oriented toward Interests

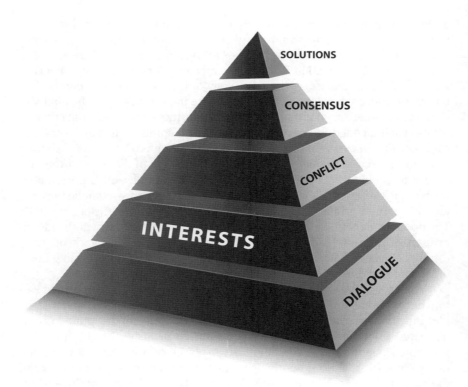

Reconciling Differences

Olivia had been at home for eight years raising her children while her husband, Jack, supported the family as the primary income-earner. They had both decided on this path while their children were young. Now that their youngest was starting first grade, Olivia wanted to return to school to get her MBA. She didn't realize how much she had missed having colleagues and felt ready to reenter the workforce and continue her career path toward Certified Public Accountant (CPA). She believed the MBA would give her greater options regarding where she might work and would result in greater flexibility, which she desired as a working mother. Jack was vehemently opposed to Olivia's return to school. He believed the family was fine on one income and did not want her to return to school or work while their children were still at home.[1]

—An aggregate of several interpersonal true-life stories

Identifying people's interests, as well as our own often unexplored interests, can be a powerful mechanism toward solving interorganizational problems. The noun use of Latin *interresse* means, "to concern, make a difference, be of importance"; the derivation is from *inter* meaning "between" and *esse* meaning "to be" (as in *essence*).[2] The etymology of the word *interests* emphasizes that these concerns make a difference and are important to us. The ability to discover the interests that motivate people's positions is an essential communication skill needed in interorganizational collaboration. It may be the key to succeeding in every relationship we hold dear in life. The praxis of shifting to interests from positions is grounded in the concept of dialogue; it requires excellent listening for both what is said and what is unsaid. Unfortunately, people don't often speak in the language of their interests—complicating the identification of primary concerns that will affect making decisions together. The opening vignette describes an interpersonal example in which the identification of interests is critical for Olivia and Jack. We will work our way through Olivia and Jack's differences as a starting point for unraveling interorganizational differences among stakeholders.

The groundbreaking work by Roger Fisher, William Ury, and Bruce Patton helps frame our theories of how communication works toward the identification and negotiation of interests in problem-solving contexts.[3] As discussed in chapter 8, a primary contribution of Fisher et al.'s model of principled negotiation is the emphasis it places on moving from position talk to interest talk. Frequently, the word "negotiation" triggers images of the exchange one encounters at a car dealership. In this competitive negotiation, we have learned not to disclose our bottom line. In fact, we've been socialized not to be forthright about how much we are prepared to spend. Similarly, we anticipate the dealership will not be forthright. The result is a bartering situation where, after an exhausting deceit-riddled exchange, we eventually arrive at an acceptable price for the vehicle.

This is not what we mean by negotiation in interorganizational collaboration. Indeed, competitive negotiation works counter to constructing the trust and culture you will need to collaborate. Barbara Gray best describes interest-based negotiation for the purposes of this text. She counsels that negotiation "refers to conversational interactions among collaborating parties as they try to define a problem, agree on recommendations, or design action steps."[4] This is a much broader, communicative conception of negotiation that does not refer to a specific type of haggling—rather, it denotes the everyday encounters we have. We are always negotiating something.[5] As emphasized in this chapter, we are often negotiating interests that seem to have little to do with the content of our conversations, such as our identity and power needs.

We begin our discussion by defining positions and interests, attending to the most basic and most common interests encountered in human interaction and interorganizational collaboration. We unpack the conflict brewing between Olivia and Jack to demonstrate expressed and unexpressed interests. We next identify practical communication tools that capture the collective interests and values of collaborative groups. We close by considering how communication in collaboration is both aligned with, and departs from, the principled negotiation process as stakeholders move from individual interests to shared values. Communication oriented toward interests not only relies on dialogue, but it also constitutes a fundamental shift in the way we talk. Accordingly, interest-talk composes the second, vital layer, in the construction of a language of collaborative praxis.

Positions versus Interests

We tend to frame problems in the language of our own positions. Yet if we were to peel the layers back regarding what we think we want from a particular problem-solving situation, we would find our position—often our preferred solution—is driven by other interests. For example, a college campus suffered, as many do, from high numbers of sexual assaults. To combat the problem, a group of students and faculty diligently campaigned to have lighting installed along the dark pathways around campus. The group had come to define the problem of sexual assault as a lack of safely lit, pathways. With such a narrow definition of the sexual assault problem, the solutions were narrow and simplified. The group eventually (and unwittingly) narrowed the problem of sexual assaults to the *absence of their preferred solution*—i.e., the problem is a lack of lighting.[6] However, their position, "we need better lit walkways" was not the significant underlying interest driving their campaign.

Position-based language and framing of the problem prematurely limit a fuller understanding of the problem, thus limiting options for resolution.[7] In contrast, interests "are the silent movers behind the hubbub of positions. Your position is something you have decided upon. Your interests are what caused you to so decide."[8] Interests can often be identified

Table 9.1   Position-based versus interest-based language

Position	Interest
Often a *preferred* solution: "The campus needs to light dark paths."	What causes you to decide your position? Interests define the problem. "We need to decrease sexual assault."
Positions force people to take a stance one way or another; they are what we have decided.	Interests motivate people and our decisions.
Positions unnecessarily narrow the problem and possible solutions.	For every interest, several possible positions exist.
Competing positions are usually not reconcilable.	Different interests do not have to be competing and can be reconcilable.

by trying to determine why a particular position exists (or why not).[9] If we dig deeper to determine "why" the group would want pathways lit, one of their main interests would be that it is because they want women and men to be safe from sexual assault. Accordingly, decreasing sexual assault is a primary interest driving their campaign. If our understanding of the problem is reframed from a position to an interest—*why* we want to solve the problem, we will have many more avenues for solutions. By redefining the problem as an interest—decrease sexual assault—we are not limited to lighting as the only solution. Understanding problems from an interest framework facilitates a greater number of options for solutions.

Interest framing cultivates broader thinking about a problem. Continuing with the assault example, if we reframe the problem as an interest of decreasing sexual assault, we are not locked into taking a stance (position) on lighting. Freeing us of the lighting dilemma, we can explore more fully the facts around sexual assault on campuses. Most likely we would learn that sexual assaults of college students more frequently occur off campus with acquaintances than on dark campus pathways by strangers.[10] Thus our solutions for decreasing sexual assault could focus on the binge drinking culture as a greater contributor to sexual assault than dark pathways. We would miss the opportunity to solve the problem if we focus too quickly and narrowly on our preferred solution.

People also hold many interests at one time; therefore, we are more likely to find overlapping interests among the parties. In contrast, positions force us to take a stance one way or another; they are often irreconcilable if we disagree. Many interests may surface in the context of decreasing sexual assault on campus—safety, education, and the ability to facilitate something effective. By speaking and focusing on interests, we have a better chance of identifying solutions that will meet a broader array of interests and appeal to more people. Thus, learning how to recognize and talk about interests are essential skills for collaborative communication. Table 9.2 presents a list of stakeholders involved in the problem domain of decreasing gang violence. Their positions are listed as possible preferred solutions. Consider their underlying interests.

Table 9.2   Stakeholders and positions in problem domain

Stakeholders involved in problem domain of gang violence	Interests	Positions (and sometimes preferred solutions)
Police Department		We need more officers in this area to combat violent crime.
Schools		We need after school programs to keep kids from dropping out and joining gangs.
Local Church		We need better spiritual guidance for young people. They lack a moral compass.
Local Business Bureau		We need safer streets for our businesses.
Parents		We need decent jobs for our kids that will keep them out of trouble and give them some money.

APPLICATION: Identify the possible missing interests for each of these stakeholders. List as many as you can and circle the interests that you think will serve as strong motivators. Identify the positions that are really preferred solutions. Hone your ability to recognize problems framed as preferred solutions. Practice this skill in other relationships.

The earlier stakeholders begin speaking in terms of interests, the better; they will be less committed publicly to specific positions. Interest talk can help stakeholders identify what is truly more important to them. However, this is not a native skill for many of us. Rather, we too often subscribe to the garbage-can theory of decision making—a metaphor for the chaotic swirl of predetermined solutions that are often applied to problems without taking the time to assess interests and applicability.[11] In other words, we are going to have to rewire the way we think and talk about problems in collaboration. Speaking (and thinking) in terms of our interests is a learned communication behavior.

Basic Needs

Fisher, Ury, and Patton described five basic human needs that are powerful interests motivating people one direction or another—security, economic well-being, a sense of belonging, recognition, and control over one's life.[12] In the opening vignette of this chapter, we can see all of these fundamental needs in play. Jack's sense of *security* is disrupted when Olivia proposes she go back to school. He has a million questions running through his mind, such as will she be home when the kids are home from school? How will the family function when she is not around as much? He is probably also feeling a loss of *control*. What will this decision mean for his routine? How will he manage to pick up the slack given his demanding job? On the other hand, Olivia remembers when she used to bring an income into the home, and she would like the ability to purchase things without worrying about what Jack might think. She desires her own sense of *economic security*. She also remembers how she felt a part of something when she worked in an office. She missed the busy buzz of tax season and even the simple things such as sharing a cup of coffee with her colleagues. She missed a sense of *belonging*. She was also a very good bookkeeper and remembers the bonuses she earned for her diligent work. She would love that sense of *recognition* she achieved when working outside the home. Jack and Olivia have each taken positions over her proposal to return to school. He does not want her to go—she is determined to go. It is easy to see that these positions are irreconcilable. However, if Jack and Olivia focus on the interests driving each of their positions, they are likely to come up with some solutions of which neither had thought. The point is that basic needs are usually the foundation of other interests—Olivia's desire for more education is an interest based on her needs for recognition and a sense of belonging. Her desire to achieve an MBA is a preferred solution that she thinks might help her attain flexibility and control over her life.

Although we have used an interpersonal example to illustrate the point, stakeholders need to understand the basic needs that drive stated interests and positions so that they might help their colleagues meet their needs with mutually satisfying solutions. Whether in groups or interpersonal communication situations, we are always negotiating multiple needs and interests. Stanley Deetz (building on the work of Jürgen Habermas[13]) argued that every time we communicate we are negotiating meaning with one another in at least four contexts—knowledge (what we count as true), our own identity (who we think we are), relationships (who we are in relation to each other), and social orders (what do we legitimize as society?).[14] The concepts of identity and power are tightly woven with basic needs; they underlie the interests that drive our everyday negotiations.

Identity. In the case of Olivia and Jack, Olivia's desire for economic well-being, a sense of belonging, recognition, and control are tightly connected with her identity. Early in her career, she had always planned on earning both a CPA and an MBA. She believes these achievements will help her gain greater flexibility in her career. Her identity is associated with those goals, and the fact that she put them on hold has left her feeling a loss of control and loss of self. By expressing her desire to continue her education and to have control over her work hours, she is negotiating who she believes she is or wants to be. Identity strongly motivates her position.

Table 9.3   Latent or unexpressed basic needs

Negotiation is happening simultaneously within multiple contexts	Olivia's Expressed Position "I would like to return to school for my MBA and CPA license."	Jack's Expressed Position "But this will be very disruptive to our lives and we don't need you to work outside of the home."
Knowledge/what we believe is true	Unexpressed: "I believe these achievements will grant our family greater control and flexibility."	Unexpressed: "I don't believe she needs these things."
Identity	Unexpressed: "I always saw myself as having completed these things. I enjoyed my career. I was good at it."	Unexpressed: "She is a good mom. I don't understand why she needs these things."
Relationship (power)	Unexpressed: "I am equal in this relationship and should be supported to pursue my dreams."	Unexpressed: "We agreed it was best for her to stay home and put the children first. She can't just change her mind now. This is not just her decision."
Social order (ideological power)	Unexpressed: "I don't believe there is only one model for raising a family."	Unexpressed: "I always thought I would work while my wife takes care of our home and family needs. I thought these were *our* values."

Power. The communication between Olivia and Jack negotiates power in two contexts—their relationship with one another and their beliefs about power and equality in the context of marriage (ideological social order). Their negotiation is further complicated by Jack's opposition to her plan. Olivia feels a greater sense of powerlessness with his determination to see her stay home. She is likely to cling more strongly to her position than she would if Jack did not oppose it. She wants to assert her own sense of power and control over her life as well as a sense of equality in her marriage.[15] At this point the negotiation appears to be about her position—going back to school—but the more important issues are identity and power. Jack reacts strongly precisely because he also feels a loss of control. He is negotiating who they are in relationship to one another and the subtle rules of that relationship. Is one partner entitled to change the agreed upon plan when the alteration threatens to throw the relationship into upheaval? One way out of this dilemma is to back out of the positions by identifying the basic needs and interests motivating them. Collaboration members not only recognize basic interests, but they validate them. What Olivia and Jack are both feeling are legitimate fears, concerns, and desires. Getting each to recognize them as legitimate is the first step toward collaborative problem solving. This is why dialogue is the foundational skill of collaborative praxis.

As table 9.3 makes clear, throughout our communication (negotiation) with one another in the midst of conflict, our basic needs and especially those related to identity and power are frequently unexpressed. Consider the amount of trust and vulnerability it takes to express your identity and relationship needs in an interpersonal relationship and now consider how much more difficult such expression would be among a group of stakeholders. Therefore, stakeholders must learn how to listen for said and *unsaid needs* in every communication situation. One way to do this is to consider what a stakeholder has expressed and then consider related questions such as the ones in the text box below. To the extent that collaborative stakeholders recognize and can help meet the basic needs of their peer members, they will be more successful at moving beyond expressed positions.

Identifying Latent Identity and Power Needs

When trying to identify unspoken identity and power needs consider:

(a) What is this expression saying about the stakeholder's identity needs? How might these be identified and met?

(b) What is this expression saying about the stakeholder's relationship to me, or to our group? Are they drawing distinctions? Expressing solidarity? Seeking affirmation?

(c) What is this expression saying about this stakeholder's ideological beliefs? Do we need to validate that this stakeholder's particular worldview is understandable and legitimate?

It is not appropriate to express every interest pertaining to identity and power. For example, if you have an elected official participating as a stakeholder in your collaboration, they undoubtedly are interested in getting reelected and maintaining a particular image based on their expressed positions. Keeping in mind how these interests motivate stakeholder behavior is important. But not all stakeholder interests are important for the group to share, and stakeholders need to exercise political savvy when deciding whether and how to validate identity and power needs. For example, some stakeholders may need to publicly oppose the work of interorganizational collaboration (even if they privately support it) in an effort to navigate their identity among their constituents.

From Individual Interests to Shared Values

One method we have developed for moving beyond the impasse of positions and toward interests is constructing a shared values list, which in turn fosters commitment. Ralph Keeney argued that values are "the principles for evaluating the desirability of any possible alternatives or consequences. They define all that you care about in a specific decision situation."[16] Keeney used the word *value* interchangeably with Fisher et al.'s concept of interests. Once Olivia and Jack acknowledge and recognize one another's basic needs and interests, they can start listing values that each would like to be honored in the process of decision making. For example, Jack may add to the list that the children's well-being is a critical value.

Olivia and Jack's Shared Values List

1. Our children's well-being
2. Equality in taking care of the home
3. Equality in earning an income
4. Equality in decision making in the marriage

This is a value that Olivia shares. Olivia may add to the list that she values feeling more equal in the home. Framing Olivia's interest as a value of equality rather than as a position (i.e., Jack needs to share in more of the domestic duties) gives the couple greater freedom to design solutions to meet their values and to validate Olivia's power needs. Thus, agreed upon values will drive the decision making of the couple. By stating values, and letting them drive solutions, each person feels their basic needs are being honored in the process. Focusing on interests and values sets the stage for creative solutions. Olivia may agree to find a program that offers daytime classes to lessen the disruption to the children. Jack may not be able to help more around the house if his job is too demanding, but he might agree to hiring a housekeeper or promising to do so when Olivia finishes her MBA. In the interim, the kids can pick up some of the slack, and he can lower his expectations of Olivia in an effort to honor her equally busy life. Because Jack and Olivia share the commitment to the values list, they are more willing to keep searching for solutions that honor their shared values. Stakeholders in interorganizational collaboration replicate this process of trying to understand one another's interests, basic needs, and shared values so that they can think more creatively and openly about solutions. Keeney warns against stopping short and identifying values that are "motherhood and apple pie objectives that anyone can agree to."[17] Instead, he encourages parties to go deeper by continuously asking one another, "Why is that important?"[18] This question fosters the revelation of bedrock values.

Naming and listing interests does several important things. First, by writing down the interests of a stakeholder in a visible location for all to see, he or she is less likely to repeat their interests because they are publicly represented to the group. They will feel heard and repetitive conversations in the group will be minimized, as a collective memory is being formed.[19] Second, listing interests will help the group identify their *shared* interests and values. Third, writing down stakeholder's interests allows the contribution to be refined, questioned, and better understood as stakeholders struggle together for the best wording regarding their interests. Fourth, many times stakeholders believe they are speaking in interests, but they are really speaking in positions. Recording interests helps stakeholders learn how to develop the collaborative skill of moving from position-speak to interest-speak. For example, a stakeholder representing the Veteran's Association in a mock interorganizational collaboration on homeless veterans, repeatedly said his interest was "educating the public about the stigma attached to the homeless." Once this contribution was written in a visible place, the group could determine that education in this context was actually a preferred solution. The stakeholder was expressing a desire to combat stigma associated with homelessness—educating the public was just one method for solving the stigma problem. By reworking the wording of the contribution from a position to an interest, more stakeholders were able to agree that stigma is an important interest because they were not locked into a specific method for solving the stigma problem.

The early stages of the list may include every interest contributed by each one of the stakeholders. Group members work together to reword and strengthen the articulation of interests and begin to identify *shared* interests. Values underlying those interests can also be identified as the group works toward translating their publicly stated interests into a shared values list. Stakeholders should be careful to use one another's specific words and to honor the contributions of one another as much as possible.

As stakeholders become more familiar and comfortable with one another, they may disclose more and may be willing to share things that they did not in the beginning stages of collaboration. Their stories, emotions, and fears may not surface until this stage (or even later stages) of collaborating. Stakeholders will recognize that they may need to encourage emotions and to validate at later stages of problem solving in order to move the group forward again. That said, if the group has made great progress identifying interests, "going back" to a venting and validating stage ideally fostered through dialogue, may be disruptive and may lead some stakeholders to believe the collaboration is too process-heavy.[20] Once again, contingency and the moral obligation of the communication context should guide stakeholder decisions regarding processes.

> **APPLICATION:** Return to the list of interests you created for the interorganizational collaboration example listed in table 9.2. Underline the values that are most likely shared among several stakeholders and rewrite them in a shared values list.

> **APPLICATION:** Watch the documentary produced by the BASEL Action Network, Exporting Harm, the Trashing of Asia.[21] Identify the *major* stakeholders who most likely would need to be involved in a decision regarding this wicked problem. Once you have listed the stakeholders, identify their interests and needs. In a final step, identify their overlapping interests by creating a shared values list.

Shared Representations as Collaborative Praxis

A shared values list captures the group's interests; it can lead to more formal communication to express the group's vision. David Perkins refers to such formal communication as "shared representations," which he claims "are often underused [yet] matter a lot."[22] In this section we consider the different communication representations that may result from identifying shared values in collaboration, whether mission and/or vision statements, guiding values statements, or collective identity statements.[23]

Shared Representations

Several communication options exist for groups to capture the shared representations of their values. Values statements publicly state the beliefs, concepts, and principles of the collaborative group.[24] They describe how the organization will behave and become criteria for decision making.[25] Many value statements may later be refined into group objectives.[26] A mission statement, "tells two things about a company: who it is and what it does."[27] A sample mission statement and its corresponding guiding values are provided in table 9.4 (on pp. 212–213) from Best SELF. Interestingly, neither the mission nor values statements were written during the first year of the collaboration. It took months of meetings, dialogue, discussion, debate, deliberation, and negotiation before the stakeholders felt prepared to write a statement and the guiding values that encapsulated their group's purpose. A vision statement "describes the organization as it would appear in a future successful state. When developing a vision statement, organizations answer this question: 'If the [collaboration] were to achieve all of its strategic goals, what would it look like 10 years from now?'"[28] Another shared representation involves developing a collectivity identity statement. How groups communicatively arrive at such a statement is explored in the next section.

Table 9.4   Communication developed from shared values

Communication Tool	Definition	Example
Shared Values List	Statements of value (interests and the values that drive those interests) that are elicited from individual stakeholders and are made public and visible to the group as they formulate, tweak, and refine their shared values. Later the group will prioritize the values through consensus decision making; they will then formalize the results in writing. Formal statements could be values statements, mission statements, vision statements, identity statements, or all of the above.	1. Education that is also fun 2. Diversity in students 3. Diversity in staff 4. Connecting with the community 5. Keeping focused on children
Values Statement	Values statements publicly state the beliefs, concepts, and principles of the collaborative group.	Best SELF Guiding Principles Best SELF values diversity and promotes understanding by providing multicultural education. Best SELF includes children and staff with a broad range of backgrounds, talents, interests, and abilities who can share and learn from each other. Best SELF believes in service learning in an environment that is safe, nurturing, positive, challenging, child-centered, and fun.

Communication Tool	Definition	Example
Values Statement *(continued)*		The staff and students of Best SELF continue to extend their vision beyond the traditional and recognize that learning takes place not just in the classroom but also in interactions with one another and with the community.
Mission Statement	A mission statement announces who a collaboration is and what it does.	It is the mission of Best SELF to provide an enriching summer experience for children, to serve families and to foster community involvement and collaboration.
Vision Statement	Vision statements articulate how the collaboration would appear in its most successful state.	To be the premier summer educational resource for all children in the Skagit County geographic area.
Collective Identity Statement	Collective identity statements develop a "we" identity for the group.	Best SELF is Best Summer Education Learning Fun Program Other examples: "We are the 99%" Occupy Movement Protestors We are the "dashboard" for the community.

Fostering Collective Identity

Collective identity statements refer to the "we-ness" of a group,[29] or a collective's sense of itself—"a communal property that cannot be reduced to any particular individual."[30] Matthew Koschmann's work explains how collaborative groups cultivate collective identity. Ultimately, forming a collective identity is a communicative activity. Drawing on organizational communication scholar Timothy Kuhn's concept of authoritative text,[31] Koschmann explains a text is a "network of meanings" that "become imbued with shared qualities that a collective respects and is willing to coalesce around."[32] Shared representations can serve as authoritative texts, meaning they do more than represent a group's values—they influence communicative and other behavior. They "shape future conversations, direct members' attention, and discipline their actions."[33]

Koschmann demonstrated how a community–based collaboration struggling with disparate individual understandings of its purpose created a collective identity around the metaphor of a "dashboard." Although the collaboration's director serendipitously invented the dashboard metaphor, over time, this coalescing theme was adopted and owned by all stakeholders. Stakeholders eventually forgot the origins of the word. The dashboard trope gave stakeholders a sense of how to describe their work and, consequentially who they thought they were as a collaboration in the community. Perhaps a more public example of authoritative texts is provided by the Occupy social movement, which peaked in 2011.[34] Despite deep differences rooted in education, socioeconomic class, gender, age, and profession, Occupy protestors coalesced under the collective identity of being part of the "99 percent." This symbolic discourse worked as an authoritative text to foster a shared identity for those who lacked wealth and power in the United States (and beyond). One of the characteristic features of these texts is that they were ambiguous, yet meaningful enough, to connect disparate stakeholders.

Ambiguity in Stakeholder Communication

Throughout studies of identity in collaboration, ambiguity in communication is a prevalent theme.[35] Accordingly, stakeholders must learn when and how to appropriately and ethically use ambiguity. For example, one study of a collaboration working on establishing a charter school found meeting participants managed "cultural identities in part by challenging fixed membership categories as they [went] about doing the business of collaborating."[36] This study showed how the interests of one stakeholder in a collaboration discussing charter school curricula was reflected in exclusive language that referred to not wanting students to be learning from "dead European white males" but to be connected with "Spanish writer[s]," and "Latino Caribbean heritage." These interests were restated by another stakeholder in more ambiguous terms: "I don't want kids studying [in] a social study group that there is no reflection of themselves . . . learn the history that they were never a part of while their ancestors has [sic] contributed a lot." The second stakeholder "identifies students in relation to ethnic categories without ascribing to them particular categories."[37] The study found ambiguity in stating interests and values was essential to winning community support for the charter school.

This type of communicative move is called *strategic authenticity*—"communicating in ways that are appropriate for a particular audience, but also true to personal beliefs and convictions."[38] In their study of a religious nonprofit, Arianna Molloy and Renee found participants used what they termed "bridge discourses" to manage competing belief systems. They found for example, a term like "excellence" allowed for commitments to business, while maintaining the values of faith. The careful selection of words can ultimately make space for multiple and competing interpretations, thus allowing for several meanings and values to coexist. Although strategic ambiguity is not a new concept in organizing,[39] we believe the emphasis on authenticity (as evident in the above studies) is an important step toward developing collaborative communication and principled leadership.

> **APPLICATION:** Take the following interests and rewrite them in a language that is strategically authentic, yet ambiguous and inclusive:
> - Help African American children fight institutional racism in their access to colleges
> - Keep businesses from abusing and polluting our waters
> - Stop discrimination of transgendered students

The research of collaboration scholar Matthew Koschmann explores how language works to represent shared values and constitute the collective identity of, and shared power among, collaborative members. In the scholar spotlight box below, Koschmann explains his work on authoritative texts. Through their ambiguity, these texts coalesce a particular identity for the collaboration that influences its stakeholders' actions and interactions.

Scholar Spotlight

Collaboration and Authoritative Texts
Matthew Koschmann

If you have ever participated in a collaboration at any level, you probably realized very quickly that one of the main difficulties is the issue of authority. The problem is that collaboration complicates the straightforward authority relations that are assumed in traditional management systems. Collaboration brings together people who represent several aspects of an issue in order to do something together that they could not do on their own. But how do you coordinate voluntary collective action in a group of organizational or community representatives when no one has any formal power over others? Collaboration is all about integrating different kinds of knowledge, expertise, practices, and experiences. But how do you reconcile differences when you cannot defer to conventional means of control associated with bureaucratic and hierarchical forms of organizing? Although collaboration is different, we still need some system of authority to ensure accountability and to manage the diversity of interests and ideas of the people involved.

(continued)

Therefore, a key issue for collaboration is developing a system of authority that has the power to coordinate multiple stakeholders apart from hierarchical mechanisms of control. This requires a shift from traditional thinking about authority toward more organic forms of influence that arise as people interact with each other.

Many scholars now explain authority as a *negotiated phenomenon* that is distributed among organizational or collaboration members, emphasizing more emergent forms of influence and accountability that transcend boundaries. This shifts the emphasis away from hierarchical positions and toward the meanings and interpretations that are worked out among organizational members in practice. Authority is thus a *social accomplishment* that is achieved as people interact with each other and make decisions about the scope of power they have over each other and their tasks. Of course, this raises the question of how these kinds of interactions can actually create the authority needed to coordinate and manage work across domains of knowledge and expertise. To address this question, we need to get a bit theoretical . . .

Communication scholars have made important contributions to this issue by articulating a unique approach to authority based on a *constitutive model of communication*. From this perspective, communication literally constitutes our social realities, not merely expresses or transmits preexisting information. Accordingly, scholars theorize authority as a process of *authoring* (note the etymological similarity), where people coordinate to "write" an official version of the organization or collaboration that conveys specific notions of purpose, intent, direction or, identity. This happens as people interact with each other and the outcomes of their interactions "stick" in such a way that they inform subsequent interactions and decisions. These interactional outcomes are conceived as *texts*, which can range from the concrete (like memos or policies) to the figurative (like unwritten norms or values). This is why sometimes we refer to organizing as "being on the same page" or having a "good read" of the situation, even though we're not necessarily referring to any official paper or tangible document. The key point is that texts—both concrete and figurative—can become sources of authority for collective action in collaboration. Here's how it works . . .

Collaborating and organizing involve countless "local" interactions among various stakeholders in particular situations, and these local interactions gain distance from their original contexts as they are referenced and repeated in successive conversations. Inevitably this "distancing" generalizes and simplifies the depth and complexity of the initial conversations. More and more ambiguity is introduced until all that remains is an abstract representation of the original interactions—not just a scattered collection of texts, but instead an organizational abstraction that is interpreted as representing all the interactions it refers to. For example, when the current US American presidential administration makes a decision about a specific policy, we don't talk about all the people and conversations that make up the administration and led to the decision; we simply say "Today the White House decided . . . " Or when Google develops a new invention, we don't explain all the details of every meeting or the contributions of every employee, we just say "Google introduced a new application . . . " In both of these instances, we refer to an abstract representation of all the interactions that constitute the organization, which has a way of sounding—and actually being—much more authoritative. So how does this happen?

Through the process of distancing, the resulting abstract representations shed any trace of authorship, meaning that the actions and intentions of specific people are left out of subsequent interactions. The *abstraction itself* becomes the center of our conversation. The contributions of individuals get lost in the distancing of texts, and more power is attributed to the abstraction. This "vanishing" of individual authorship enables textual abstractions to develop authority because it (the abstraction) is now the focal point of our communication and it is not reducible to any particular interaction or individual contribution—it now conveys a sense of power such that "it" is in control, "it" motivates us to act, we answer to "it." In contemporary language, we might even say *it's like a thing*, referring to how some social practices—not simply the people who perform them—develop a more authoritative status in our culture.

Bring it all together and you get what scholars call an *authoritative text*—an abstract depiction of the "official" organization or collaboration that embodies prevailing values and norms while also indicating relations of power and legitimacy. Thus, authority is not in a person who gives commands or a hierarchical position but is instead in the *process* of "authoring" a definitive representation of the collective. Authoritative texts have the power to *do* things in collaboration because they develop a degree of *agency* through the processes I described above. And authoritative texts are powerful because they are simultaneously present and absent in collaboration. They tend to "lurk" in the background of day-to-day interactions, shaping conversations and decisions in ways that we often take for granted. Authoritative texts are sort of like the operating system on your computer, always there humming along in the background, enabling you to run all your various programs and providing the means for you to accomplish your work, but often without your immediate awareness.

My colleague Timothy Kuhn at the University of Colorado has done the most to develop the concept of authoritative texts for the broader fields of management organizational studies. In my empirical research, I use the concept of authoritative text to understand and explain collaboration and organizing in a variety of contexts. Let me give you some examples . . .

In one study, I explored how the term "community dashboard" emerged as an authoritative text for a social services collaboration, providing a renewed sense of identity and purpose to organize their work. In another project, my coauthor and I studied how a "wild-wild west" mentality became an authoritative text that shaped the collaborative work—or lack thereof—in a large scientific laboratory.[40] And in one more study, another coauthor and I demonstrate how the concept of "inclusiveness" evolved into an authoritative text at a nonprofit organization, shaping their work in a variety of areas. In all these case studies, I trace how a series of interactions and communication practices "scale up" to an authoritative text that has the power to influence and discipline collaborative work, apart from hierarchies and bureaucratic control mechanisms.

All this relates to the textual existence of organizations, where organizations are understood as networks of meaning that are "read" in ways that convey authority and facilitate coordinated action. Texts are thus a *mode of being* for organizations, and authority is not in a position or a person who gives commands but rather in the continual process of authoring a definitive representa-

(continued)

tion of the collective. This is especially relevant for collaboration, where negotiated authority is even more important because of the absence of hierarchical control. Collaborative partners are not necessarily bound to prior authority relations so they constantly negotiate to write and rewrite (i.e., author) systems of authority to coordinate their work. Thus, *authoritative texts* are an insightful way to understand and explain the issue of authority in collaborative work.

QUESTION: What does Koschmann mean when he says authoritative texts have the power to discipline collaborative work?

Groups may choose to develop some or all of these forms of public statements about who they are and what they do. The point is that shared representations capture the group's values and interests—and importantly and potentially serve as authoritative texts. Utilizing strategic authenticity is important. Contrarily, writing these statements in terms of *specific* goals and objectives is likely to hinder forming a collective identity because at this stage of communication stakeholders will have different goals and objectives for participating. Strategic planning that outlines specific goals, objectives, and methods of measuring success can be done at later stages of collaboration once the broader values and identity of the group have been made explicit.

Principled Negotiation in Collaboration

Thus far in this chapter we have identified two key shifts in communication that will aid in ethical collaborative praxis. The first is to orient talk toward interests rather than positions. The second is the move from individual interests to shared representations (authoritative texts) of interests and values. We have introduced the shared representations that aid collaborative groups in navigating diverse interests, identity, and power differences. However, we have not said much about how groups will arrive at those shared representations. Conflict will inevitably surface when constructing shared representations. Consensus-oriented communication is essential because all stakeholders must agree to the articulated values that represent their group. If one or more stakeholders do not see at least one (or some of) their values represented in the group's publicly shared representations, they will likely not continue in the collaboration. However, it is not likely that all individual stakeholder interests and values will be included. Therefore, identifying multiple and overlapping interests for each stakeholder assists members as they prioritize the values of the interorganizational group. In the latter stages of collaborating, communication orientations depart from the types and methods of communication that facilitate the principled negotiation process.

The communication orientations that take place in the early stages of collaborating parallel the early stages of the principled negotiation method. Communication oriented toward dialogue facilitates separating people from problems, the first stage of the principled negotiation method. Communication oriented toward interests coincides with moving from positions to interests in the second stage of the principled negotiation model. In the third stage, participants invent options for mutual gain. The orientations in this stage—conflict, consensus-decision making, and solutions—depart from the principled negotiation process.[41] Because stakeholders hold such diverse experiences and values in interorganizational collaboration, they should not focus on options and solutions until they have developed a stronger collective identity.

In collaboration, we believe the third and fourth stages of the principled negotiation model are reversed. A case in point: Renee once facilitated a group that balked at having to discuss their mission before making decisions. Although they had been working together for a while, they had new members and began to drift from the vision of the founders. Eventual decisions would depend on the group's values and priorities—thus the mission discussion was essential prior to making decisions. Groups must know who they are and what is important to them before they invent solutions.[42] The goal of the third stage of communication in collaboration is to hone shared values that are gleaned from the interests of stakeholders.

The fourth stage in principled negotiation is to use objective criteria.[43] However, the collaboration communication model differs in an important way. One of the assumptions underlying interorganizational collaboration

Table 9.5   Collaborative communication praxis and principled negotiation

The Language of Collaborative Praxis	Goals of Communication in Collaboration	Stages of Principled Negotiation Method
Dialogue oriented	Learning, validation, understanding	Separate the people from the problem
Interest oriented	Reframing, speaking from interests rather than preferred solutions, eliciting the interests/values of stakeholders	Focus on interests not positions
Conflict oriented and Consensus oriented	Prioritizing/deciding group's shared values that will serve as decision criteria	*Invent options for mutual gain
Solution oriented	Invention, creativity, solution generation	*Insist on using objective criteria

*Order is reversed in collaborative praxis

is that there are no objective standards for making decisions. So-called objective standards tend to privilege dominant perspectives and perpetuate hegemony.[44] Precisely for these reasons, collaboration that rests on the cornerstones of ethical decision making takes into account lesser voices, histories, and emotion. These criteria are just as relevant as reason, science, and agreed upon measurements. Instead of invoking objective criteria in the last stage of the process, as the principled negotiation method suggests, a stakeholder group must first define what is meant by "mutual gain" (see table 9.5). Mutual gain will be determined by articulating shared values and interests rather than objective measures. The values that are prioritized by stakeholders will become the "objective" criteria that guide the group's decision making. These values, in the form of authoritative texts, influence the constraints and possibilities of inventing options. Thus, the third stage in our model focuses on eliciting constructive conflict and garnering consensus around values and interests.

Although our model loosely follows the principled negotiation process, we do not envision it as a linear model. Ideally, groups will have determined their values and collective identity before embarking on a large project or decision; however, we cannot expect stakeholder interaction to work prescriptively through dialogue, interests, conflict, consensus, and solutions. Ideas for solutions sometimes work in tandem with the third stage of communication. Groups form identities and are sometimes prompted to identify their values based on ideas they are willing or not willing to support. For example, they may see themselves as service providers and envision after-school programs that need designing—this is how Best SELF began. One stakeholder may bring an idea for a grant to others. Or they may have no idea what they can accomplish together. The point is that consensus around values will be important for helping collaborations set the scope of their work, understand their limitations, and seek grants and other funding while working toward their dreams. Yet the impetus for collaboration sometimes comes from solution-oriented communication. The key is to leave the idea soft around the edges and moldable with stakeholder input until shared values have been articulated.

CONCLUSION

This chapter develops communication practices oriented toward interests as opposed to positions. We build on the foundation of dialogue. Recognizing interests is primarily a dialogic endeavor that depends on listening both for what *is* said and what is *not* said. Key to this skill is understanding how power and identity function as strong interests that affect our communicative behavior. The principled negotiation process serves as a model for the turn stakeholders make when they move from expressing individual interests to coalescing around shared representations of the group's values. The next chapter discusses constructive conflict and its centrality in moving groups toward shared understandings. It tackles the messy communicative space between articulating individual interests and deciding on shared representations. Communication oriented toward constructive conflict thus joins dialogue and interest-based talk as part of a larger language system comprising ethical collaborative praxis.

CHAPTER TAKE-AWAYS

- Understand negotiation as a broader communication concept of mutually determining meaning
- Recognize the difference between a position and an interest (listen for what is *not* said)
- Discern basic needs and the ways in which they underlie interests, including the way identity and power intersect with interests
- Understand the role of shared representations as communication statements expressing shared values
- Identify the constitutive power of shared representations that serve as authoritative texts
- Distinguish the ways in which collaborative praxis aligns with and departs from the principled negotiation method

ENDNOTES

[1] This extended example is based loosely on true events.
[2] Online Etymology Dictionary, "interest" http://www.etymonline.com/index.php?term=interest
[3] Roger Fisher, William L. Ury, and Bruce M. Patton, *Getting to Yes: Negotiating Agreement Without Giving In*, 2nd ed. (Boston: Houghton Mifflin Harcourt, 1992).
[4] Barbara Gray, *Collaborating: Finding Common Ground for Multiparty Problems* (San Francisco: Jossey-Bass, 1989), p. 25.
[5] Fisher, Ury, and Patton, *Getting to Yes*.
[6] Ibid.
[7] Gray, *Collaborating*.
[8] Fisher, Ury, and Patton, *Getting to Yes*. p. 41.
[9] Ibid.
[10] National Sexual Violence Resource Center (NSVRC), "Campus Sexual Violence Resource List," *Sexual Assault Awareness Month*, http://www.nsvrc.org/saam/campus-resource-list
[11] Michael D. Cohen, James G. March, and Johan P. Olsen, "A Garbage Can Model of Organizational Choice," *Administrative Science Quarterly* 17, no. 1 (1972): 1–25, doi:10.2307/2392088.
[12] Fisher, Ury, and Patton, *Getting to Yes*, p. 48.
[13] Jürgen Habermas, *The Theory of Communicative Action, Volume 1: Reason and the Rationalization of Society*, trans. Thomas McCarthy (Boston: Beacon Press, 1985); Jürgen Habermas, *The Theory of Communicative Action, Volume 2: Lifeworld and System: A Critique of Functionalist Reason*, trans. Thomas McCarthy (Boston: Beacon Press, 1985).
[14] Stanley Deetz, *Transforming Communication, Transforming Business: Building Responsive and Responsible Workplaces* (Cresskill, NJ: Hampton Pr, 1994).
[15] Fisher, Ury, and Patton, *Getting to Yes*.

16 Ralph L. Keeney, "Creativity in Decision Making with Value-Focused Thinking," *Sloan Management Review* 35, no. 4 (June 22, 1994): 33–42, p. 33.

17 Ibid., p. 36.

18 Ibid., p. 35.

19 David Perkins, *King Arthur's Round Table: How Collaborative Conversations Create Smart Organizations* (New York: Wiley, 2002).

20 See Heather M. Zoller, "'A Place You Haven't Visited Before': Creating the Conditions for Community Dialogue," *Southern Communication Journal* 65, no. 2–3 (March 1, 2000): 191–207, doi:10.1080/10417940009373167.

21 *Exporting Harm: The High-Tech Trashing of Asia*, http://archive.ban.org/films/ExportingHarm.html

22 Perkins, *King Arthur's Round Table*, p. 151.

23 Society for Human Resource Management, "Mission & Vision Statements: What Is the Difference between Mission, Vision and Values Statements?" https://www.shrm.org/templatestools/hrqa/pages/isthereadifferencebetweenacompany%e2%80%99smission,visionandvaluestatements.aspx

24 Krista Jaackson, "Engagement of Organizational Stakeholders in the Process of Formulating Values Statements," *Atlantic Journal of Communication*, 18: 158–76, p. 159.

25 Society for Human Resource Management, "Mission & Vision Statements."

26 Keeney, "Creativity in Decision Making with Value-Focused Thinking."

27 Thomas A. Falsey, *Corporate Philosophies and Mission Statements: A Survey and Guide for Corporate Communicators and Management* (New York: Praeger, 1989), p. 3.

28 Society for Human Resource Management, "Mission & Vision Statements."

29 Karen A. Cerulo, "Identity Construction: New Issues, New Directions," *Annual Review of Sociology* 23 (1997): 385–409.

30 Matthew A. Koschmann, "The Communicative Constitution of Collective Identity in Interorganizational Collaboration," *Management Communication Quarterly* 27, no. 1 (February 1, 2013): 61–89, doi:10.1177/0893318912449314, p. 62.

31 Timothy Kuhn, "A Communicative Theory of the Firm: Developing an Alternative Perspective on Intra-Organizational Power and Stakeholder Relationships," *Organization Studies* 29, no. 8–9 (August 1, 2008): 1227–54, doi:10.1177/0170840608094778.

32 Koschmann, "The Communicative Constitution of Collective Identity in Interorganizational Collaboration," p. 69.

33 Ibid., p. 69.

34 Courtney Vail Fletcher, "(De) Colonization and Collective Identity: Intersections and Negotiations of Gender, Race, and Class in Occupy," in *Understanding Occupy from Wall Street to Portland: Applied Studies in Communication Theory*, ed. Renee Guarriello Heath, Courtney Vail Fletcher, and Ricardo Munoz (Lanham, MD: Lexington Books, 2013), 121–44.

35 Laurie Lewis, Matthew G. Isbell, and Matt Koschmann, "Collaborative Tensions: Practitioners' Experiences of Interorganizational Relationships," *Communication Monographs* 77, no. 4 (December 1, 2010): 460–79, doi:10.1080/03637751.2010.523605; Michael W. Kramer, "Toward a Communication Theory of Group Dialectics: An Ethnographic Study of a Community Theater Group," *Communication Monographs* 71, no. 3 (September 1, 2004): 311–32, doi:10.1080/0363452042000288292; Michael W. Kramer, "Communication in a Community Theater Group: Managing Multiple Group Roles," *Communication Studies* 53, no. 2 (June 1, 2002): 151–70, doi:10.1080/10510970209388582.

36 Alan Hansen and Trudy Milburn, "Enacting Cultural Identities in Conversation: Managing Collaboration in Two Nonprofit Organizations," *Journal of International and Intercultural Communication* 8, no. 3 (July 3, 2015): 224–36, doi:10.1080/17513057.2015.1057906, p. 232.

37 Ibid., p. 231.

38 Matthew A. Koschmann, "Human Rights Collaboration and the Communicative Practice of Religious Identity," *Journal of Communication & Religion* 36, no. 2 (August 2013): 107–33, p. 116.

[39] Eric M. Eisenberg, "Ambiguity as Strategy in Organizational Communication," *Communication Monographs* 51, no. 3 (September 1, 1984): 227–42, doi:10.1080/03637758409390197.

[40] Matthew A. Koschmann and Nicholas R. Burk, "Accomplishing Authority in Collaborative Work," *Western Journal of Communication* 80, no. 4 (August 7, 2016): 393–413, doi:10.1080/10570314.2016.1159728.

[41] Fisher, Ury, and Patton, *Getting to Yes*.

[42] Mary Ann Renz, "Paving Consensus: Enacting, Challenging, and Revising the Consensus Process in a Cohousing Community," *Journal of Applied Communication Research* 34, no. 2 (May 1, 2006): 163–90, doi:10.1080/00909880600574088; Mary Ann Renz, "The Meaning of Consensus and Blocking for Cohousing Groups," *Small Group Research* 37, no. 4 (August 1, 2006): 351–76, doi:10.1177/1046496406291184.

[43] Fisher, Ury, and Patton, *Getting to Yes*, p. 81.

[44] Judith E. Innes and David E. Booher, *Planning with Complexity: An Introduction to Collaborative Rationality for Public Policy* (New York: Routledge, 2010); Stanley Deetz and Jennifer Simpson, "Critical Organizational Dialogue," in *Dialogue: Theorizing Difference in Communication Studies*, ed. Rob Anderson, Leslie A. Baxter, and Kenneth N. Cissna (Thousand Oaks, CA: Sage, 2003), 141–58.

Communication Oriented toward Conflict

"But I Don't Agree with You!"

It was early spring when Karen from the school board visited our monthly meeting at Metro Collaboration, an influential coalition of professionals focused on early child care and education. The agenda for the meeting was pushed aside and Maggie, the cochair of the collaboration, gave Karen the floor to discuss a controversial new policy, which she had helped to craft and the school board was about to implement regarding preschool education. The district is suffering from budget cuts and seeks to charge for the formerly free half-day preschool program. It has some limited funding to offer free preschool to selective schools and seeks a fair way to do so. School board and city officials have endured an uproar of protests from community members who believe this cut is unfair and that the methods for determining need appear capricious. The other cochair of the collaboration, Lynn, works as an administrator for the school district. She explained to the group the formula for determining how the limited resources would be distributed to "at-risk kids . . . with the greatest needs."

The room went silent.

I realized how important the topic was when the next woman to speak was a Metro city council member. While her name appears on the roster of collaboration members, I had never seen her before at a meeting, nor would I again in my 14 months of observation. Her office had been bombarded with emails from families who claimed that although they live in a nice area of the city, they bought their houses years ago when housing prices were lower, and they do not have the means to pay for preschool. The first fifteen minutes of conversation centered around a fair method for identifying families that would have the most need for scholarships. The focus shifted when Annette, a longtime member of the early child care community and a current employee of the mayor, questioned not the method of the cut but the philosophy of the cut.

Annette protested, "I think it's more than the proposed fee of $185.00 and whether or not that is a reasonable amount for preschool. I think it's a time when we're trying to establish early child education as a part of the public trust, along with K–12 education. To say that we're going to charge is to say: 'We know preschool's important with public education but if you have money and you're coming to Metro Public Schools, you have to pay for your preschools.'" She presented the analogy of asking parents to pay for preschool with a what-if scenario: "'We know there are some wonderful private schools out there for high school too, so conversely, if you're a senior, and you've done really well, and your parents can afford it, why not pay for your senior year in high school?' It's partially the philosophical question to me and what we want to create as Metro Public Schools—we've been a cutting-edge city."

Karen offered a justification that illustrated her viewpoint that those with economic advantages should not expect to send their children to preschool for free. "You know part of my thinking, maybe it wasn't good thinking, but part of my thinking . . . is that regardless of income, if there are slots available, you can send your kid, which means I can send my kid free to pre-school. I don't think that's right. I think I should pay! I mean this is how I feel personally, but the intent was never to penalize those who couldn't pay. So my thinking was . . . those who can pay, pay. Those who can't pay, don't pay."

Annette responded with, "It's almost defeating the purpose to say to middle income families that 'Metro Public School isn't for you. We don't offer the same programs that we offer if you're a poor child.'"

But Karen continued to defend her position from a logical, budgetary stance, "Yeah, I'm sorry that didn't make too much sense to me—remember, every other school district does charge."

Annette countered, "But that doesn't make it right and that doesn't make it what we want to strive for."

Karen responded, "Well it's right if there's no funding stream."

The room went silent again.

After a pause, Karen seemed to back off her argument and proceeded to break the tension in the room with a joke about her differences with Annette. She invited others to weigh in, "We can debate it. We can debate it. I mean I'm open to being convinced, although I don't know if the rest of the board members are," she chuckled.

With the invitation to weigh in, Danielle, a visitor from a local foundation and a regular attendee of the meetings, spoke next. "You know it's a classic signal of bureaucracy that you can't do something because it's an administrative mechanism rather than what's right and good for the kids. My larger point is the signal this is sending to the community, which I guess you've heard from obviously. In terms of higher Metro city leadership I do believe the image in the community is that, 'We're about K–12, and we do early childhood education (ECE) when there's a little bit of money in the bank to do it, but that is not where our heart is, we do not fundamentally believe and understand what a powerful school reform ECE is. We do not fundamentally believe it is a powerful recruiting tool for middle- and upper-class families and therefore we don't invest in it. And we'll do what we can when we can, but if we don't, tough beans!' And that's the image that I've been getting for years. This is the wrong direction."

Karen asked Danielle, "So what would you recommend?"

Danielle answered, "I'm with Annette, leave it alone."

—Unpublished exemplar from Renee's field notes

In the last chapter, we introduced a number of communication options (such as mission statements and guiding values) that collaborative groups can create to guide decision making. These possibilities are predicated on the idea that stakeholders can reach agreement about their shared values and collective identity. Until now, we have said very little about how that happens because detailing how groups arrive at shared representations entails addressing how stakeholders manage conflict. What happens when values clash or groups cannot seem to identify shared priorities? The opening vignette illustrates these problems vividly. Annette fiercely defends what she believes to be a "cutting edge" identity for the city and school; cutting-edge school districts do not cut preschool education for middle class families. In part this conflict is about what Metro Collaboration stands for and who they are. We will continue to dissect this conflict throughout the chapter. The ability to communicate amidst conflict is an essential skill needed to harness the innovation catalyzed through difference.

Our hope with this chapter is that you will view constructive conflict as normative—meaning that it is both typical and valued behavior in interorganizational collaboration. Creativity and innovation are unlikely to surface if stakeholders already agree on assumptions, definitions, interests and values, methods, and outcomes. Only through the airing of differences will perspectives grow as stakeholders are challenged and inspired. Although communication that is oriented toward constructive conflict may potentially take place at any time during collaboration, it is especially likely to surface at the stage of the collaborative process when groups move from learning about one another (dialogue and interests) to the identification of shared interests and values and eventually making decisions together. Communication oriented toward constructive conflict adds the next layer of ethical praxis to our language of collaboration.

We begin the chapter by examining some of the ways we think about conflict in collaboration. Next we explore how native understandings of how to work together thwart an acceptance of conflict as a normative and generative part of collaboration. In the latter part of the chapter we turn to praxis and consider how collaborations can start to build agreement. Grounded in our cornerstone ethical assumptions, and building on our praxis of dialogue and interest-oriented communication, we advocate for a language of gracious contestation that facilitates constructive conflict. We further develop the concept of voice and articulate the significance of going beyond expressive modes of communication. By practicing ethical communication, conflict can be used to stimulate creativity and steward authenticity and accountability among stakeholders. Learning the vocabulary and communicative practices that allow collaborative members to disagree while maintaining constructive relationships is the focus of communication in this orientation.

Conflict in Collaboration

Conflict has long captured the interest of scholars and practitioners and has thus generated a number of theoretical definitions. Charles Conrad's definition of conflict fits the interorganizational context well: "communicative interactions among people who are interdependent and who perceive that their interests are incompatible, inconsistent, or in tension."[1] His definition not only emphasizes the communicative center of conflict but it also reinforces our understanding of conflict as something that results from our interdependence—the heart of the collaborative relationship. Conflict matters when we are linked to one another through our wants or needs. William Wilmot and Joyce Hocker identified common metaphors that reveal our own assumptions about conflict.[2] For example, conflict as warlike, violent, or explosive reveals a perception of conflict as destructive. They also found neutral metaphors such as a game, or balancing act, which emphasize a skillful approach to conflict. Finally, positive metaphors referred to conflict as a tide or dance, or a garden. A tide ebbs and flows; a dance takes many turns; and things grow in gardens. These positive metaphors illuminate the possibility that arises from conflict.

> **QUESTION:** When you hear the word "conflict," what metaphors come to mind? Are your own assumptions about conflict negative, positive, or neutral? What experiences have led you to those assumptions?

Environmental collaboration experts Steven Daniels and Gregg Walker refer to the management of conflict as making progress and describe management as the "generation and implementation of tangible improvements in a conflict situation."[3] Accordingly, we embrace conflict as the *origin of possibility* for interorganizational collaboration. Interorganizational partnerships are either stimulated by the opportunity to advance a vision or by conflict (chapter 2).[4] Thus, one of the primary impetuses to interorganizational collaboration is conflict—the presence of conflict is the reason for collaborative problem solving. However, even interorganizational groups that form to advance a vision will encounter conflict. Think of all of the different contexts and natures of conflict that may arise in interorganizational collaboration, including conflicts of facts, conflicts of how the history of the community may be understood, and conflicts of cultural or religious values.[5] Conflict is an inevitable part of collaborative relationships.

In some collaboration, conflict is deeply rooted and likely ongoing. Scholars refer to this as intractable conflict in which multiparty "disputants with dissimilar framing repertoires differ from and frequently oppose each other for extended periods of time."[6] In other words, conflicting parties have come to understand the issues in very different ways and continue to frame their narratives about the conflict in such a way that their interpretation is reinforced. Intractable conflicts are especially difficult because these different frames are cemented in stakeholders' ways of thinking. Researcher Boris Brummans and colleagues argued conflict in collaboration manifests around the frames that different stakeholders hold.[7] We will consider the way intractable conflicts may be communicatively addressed later in the chapter.

Framing is the "communicative process through which people foreground and background certain aspects of experience and apply a set of categories and labels to develop 'coherent stories of what is going on and make decisions about what should be done' given the stories their frames have created."[8] Frames are neither good nor bad; they can be examined for how they organize the way particular stakeholders think. For example, in studies on environmental conflict, stakeholders foregrounded particular frames regarding their identity, power, and ways to manage conflict.[9] Stakeholders' stories illuminated the frames in which they viewed collaboration and that framing contributed to things such as trust among parties. In the opening vignette, the dispute between Karen and Annette looms largely around their different frames for understanding the problem. Karen views preschool education from the historical knowledge that families pay for prekindergarten schooling. She wants the privilege of preschool education to be available to all families, so she proposes that those who cannot afford it should not have to pay while those with means should pay. Her understanding of the problem foregrounds it as a budget and financial issue. Annette, on the other hand is not disputing the price families should have to pay for preschool, she is disputing the fundamental assumption that preschool is less important than K–12 education. She is disputing the philosophy that early education is a privilege. She instead views it as a right—as part of the "public trust." Therefore, she believes charging anyone for preschool is a step backward in legitimizing preschool. Communication—the interpretive act of framing—contributes to ways stakeholders understand their conflict. Storytelling and other dialogic practices can help stakeholders create more consistent frames among the group. Frame conflict is one way to understand how stakeholders understand and reinforce their differences in the communication situation.

 QUESTION: How do the frames of viewing preschool as a "privilege" to be afforded versus "right" shape the conflict? What assumptions come with each frame? How does each frame work to limit what the other sees?

Other conceptualizations exist to help make sense of the types of conflict interorganizational collaboration encounters. For example, Daniels and Walker developed assessment tools to measure what they refer to as "The Progress Triangle"[10] (see scholar spotlight box on pp. 231–234). Their tools measure environmental conflict on three interrelated dimensions: substance, procedure, and relationship. The substantive dimension includes understanding existing tensions, information needs based on the complexity of the issue, and language concerns. In this dimension facilitators might assess: What are the issues? What are the likely sources of tension over these issues? Are issues complex? Technical? What are the mutual gain options? The procedural dimension includes determining decision space, resources, jurisdiction, and procedural preferences. Procedural conflict assessment asks: Is mutual learning desired? Who has jurisdiction? What management approaches have been used in the past? Are resources sufficient? Are key constituents supportive? Relational conflict can be determined by questions such as: Who are the parties/stakeholders? Do any parties have a unique status? What are the parties' relational histories?

Stated positions? Interests? Worldviews? Values? The authors have designed a number of questions to help understand where conflict lies among stakeholders in order to address it and manage it.

Spotlight scholar and environmental collaboration expert Gregg Walker describes his research and practice and the life lessons he has gleaned from attending to conflict in collaborative groups.

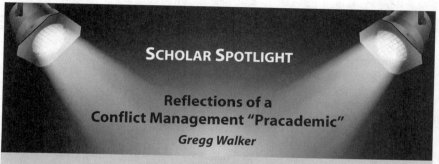

SCHOLAR SPOTLIGHT

Reflections of a
Conflict Management "Pracademic"
Gregg Walker

Throughout much of my time as a university professor, I have mixed work on campus with work in communities; integrated theory and practice; and engaged people and issues as an academic and a practitioner. In doing so, I have pursued a career as a "pracademic," a term a colleague assigned to me many years ago. The label applies well. There is a strong relationship between the practitioner and academic roles in the field of conflict management. In my case, what I learn from communities, agencies, and stakeholders informs my teaching. Correspondingly, what I have introduced in my classes often provides a foundation for ideas and techniques I present in the field. Consequently, through my work as a "pracademic," I have learned numerous lessons about managing conflicts, negotiating collaboratively, mediating disputes, and facilitating multi-stakeholder interaction. In this short essay, I will draw on both scholarship and field experience to feature five of those lessons.

Lesson One: Constructive Conflict Management Begins with Assessment

In any given conflict or decision situation, assessment before action is essential. Assessment is fundamentally a research activity; those conducting an assessment collect relevant data and analyze that information.[11] A conflict situation assessment provides the foundation for developing a conflict management plan or strategy.

Data gathering activities that are typically part of an assessment include surveys, interviews, focus groups, and artifact analysis (such as community, organization, and agency websites; blogs, newspapers, and documents).[12] Assessments often employ frameworks that structure the analysis. My colleagues and I have developed two: The Progress Triangle,[13] and the Unifying Framework.[14] Other useful frameworks exist, such as the Conflict Assessment Guide[15] and the Conflict Dynamics Continuum.[16]

Assessment work can feature innovation—new techniques and new ways of applying conventional tools. Interviews, for example, may start with influential or

(continued)

prominent community members. When working on a community-based project, my colleagues and I have often talked first with Tribal elders, local school administrators, clergy, elected officials (e.g., mayor, county commissioners), health care professionals, and newspaper publishers. These local citizens are knowledgeable about community issues (past and present) and the spirit or morale of the area. They may be an excellent source for referrals.[17]

Lesson Two: Constructive Conflict Management Is Strategic

Conflicts, regardless of scope and scale, are often complex and controversial, needing thoughtful attention.[18] Such attention is strategic—an intentional plan to achieve desired outcomes. Parties in conflict and negotiation situations may employ a strategy that is competitive, collaborative, or a mixed approach of competition and cooperation actions.[19]

Based on an assessment, a party may determine that a competitive strategy makes sense (e.g., when buying a car). A collaborative approach, though, may be warranted as complexity and controversy increase. The assessment can evaluate collaborative potential (the potential for a collaborative strategy to be successful) and collaborative capacity (the capacity of the parties to engage in a collaborative effort).[20] By evaluating collaborative potential and collaborative capacity, parties can include in their strategic approach appropriate techniques for strengthening collaboration.

Lesson Three: Constructive Conflict Management Is Principled

Regardless of the strategy employed, conflict management should be ethical.[21] Ethics, though, for some negotiators, may be relative or situational.[22] My work with colleagues has emphasized collaboration, specifically an approach we call "Collaborative Learning."[23] Collaborative Learning (and ideally other collaborative methods) ascribes to the principles of FAAITH.[24] Colleagues and I developed this set of principles during a collaborative learning (CL) project with a National Forest. While presenting a CL training, a National Forest staff member asked us what principles guided CL. We reflected on our CL projects and generated the six principles.

Fairness. Parties should treat one another with respect, even as they disagree significantly on the issues at hand. They need to be fair—to the other parties, the issues, and the situation.

Accountability. Parties need to be accountable and responsible for their participation, positions, and decisions. Accountability extends beyond oneself and one's own group, organization, or agency. Parties should be accountable to one another as well as to those they represent.

Access. A collaborative process emphasizes accessibility for all relevant parties. Information needs to be available and understandable. Community meetings need to be offered when citizens and stakeholders can attend.[25]

Inclusion. Efforts should be made to include all relevant parties, including typically underserved and marginal communities. These may include youth, urban residents, and communities of color. Inclusion extends to communication, participation opportunities that emphasize interaction and shared learning.[26]

Transparency. In a collaborative process, parties, including decision makers, need to clarify their expectations, resources, and options. Decision makers, such as government agencies, should clarify decision space, that is, what can be negotiated among the parties.[27]

Honesty. While collaborative negotiation does not require full disclosure, parties should be honest with one another about both substantive and procedural matters; what they can or cannot commit to; what information they can provide.

Lesson Four: Skilled Leadership Is Essential

In order to manage interpersonal conflicts constructively, parties need to share accountability, responsibility, and decisions.[28] Multi-party conflicts (such as organizational, community, and international conflicts) require something else: skilled, capable leadership. Steve Daniels and I, based on extensive work with government agencies, nongovernment organizations, advocacy groups, and communities, have proposed "unifying leadership" as a construct for collaboration. Unifying leadership combines distributive and collaborative leadership. It draws on the skills of different people to lead specific parts of a collaborative effort[29] and to promote collaborative governance.[30]

Lesson Five: Relationship and Procedural Factors Matter

When conflicts occur, parties typically focus on the substantive aspects of the situation—the concrete, tangible, or observable components (e.g., an employee is often late for work; a labor organization seeks better employee benefits; a community protests the site of a landfill). As Steve Daniels and I developed the Collaborative Learning approach, we realized that focusing on substantive matters alone was not sufficient to manage conflicts, resolve disputes, and make good decisions. Procedural (e.g., rules) and relationship (e.g., trust) aspects were potentially just as important. If parties could not agree on procedures or did not address relationship elements, progress or agreements on substance were unlikely.

Consequently, we created the "Progress Triangle" with substance, procedure, and relationship dimensions.[31] Progress (or lack thereof) on one dimension affects progress on all. Akin to an iceberg, the procedure and relationship dimensions may be hard to see, with only the substance of the conflict above the water line (see figure 10.1).

Parties need to pay as much attention to procedure and substance as they do to matters of substance. Conflict management is not just about the visible and concrete issues. A process that all parties regard as appropriate and fair and essential relationship factors such as trust and respect are just as important.

Figure 10.1

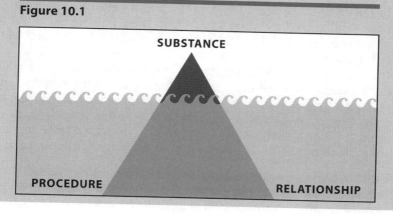

(continued)

Other Lessons

In my work as a "pracademic," I have experienced the importance of competent communication among parties, cultural sensitivity and responsiveness, systems or holistic thinking, and adult, experiential learning.[32] Similarly, I have discovered that most people want to work through conflict situations positively and peacefully. By drawing on my work as an academic and my experiences as a practitioner I have learned that by integrating the two roles I better understand and can guide conflict management processes. Learning how to manage conflicts, negotiate constructively, and make decisions collaboratively involves more than theories and studies. The greatest value is in the impact of people–their relationships, their organizations, and their communities.

QUESTION: How do the principles of FAAITH align with the ethical cornerstones of this text? What might they offer that has not yet been considered in this text?

Walker offers us much to think about regarding conflict in collaboration. Some people believe the language of "managing" conflict might work to diminish the importance of conflict and contribute to the assumption that conflict is negative. Tricia Jones and Andrea Bodtker studied collaboration in post-Apartheid Africa.

> Our experiences . . . have heightened our appreciation for the power of conflict to be positive, not just to be managed positively. Our experience has energized us to explore, conceptually and practically, conditions in which the stimulation of conflict may bear unexpected results in social justice situations. We need to ask ourselves when "managing" conflict becomes counterproductive and be ready to provide thoughtful answers for scholars and practitioners. We should explore the points of interface between group and community tensions where conflict is a generative force.[33]

In the spirit of valuing conflict as integral to and capable of birthing creativity (and in the best cases, social justice), the framing of conflict as a learning process is a useful metaphor for its potential.[34] Daniels and Walker remind us that, "While some people may assume that conflict is overwhelmingly negative, conflict scholars do not hold this view. . . . Conflict is neither inherently positive nor negative. Rather, it has the potential to be either."[35] Our approach is to construct a communicative environment that generates productive outcomes for stakeholders as they inevitably encounter conflict. Unfortunately, we will first need to overcome some ingrained communication behaviors that limit the potential for constructive conflict.

QUESTION: How does conceptualizing conflict as a learning process change your understanding of conflict? What might we expect to encounter when we are going through a learning process?

Native Communication Expounded

Research has found that conflict is often viewed as a disruption to collaborative processes rather than embraced as a part of the process.[36] Studies conducted by Renee and her colleague Jessica Milam found similar communicative practices in two interorganizational collaborations that limited constructive conflict.[37] Decision-making processes were not transparent; therefore, stakeholders were not invited to engage in their differences. Stakeholders were also found to view collaboration as something harmonious and thus avoided conflict. We consider these practices and attitudes native, meaning they are the default setting for how groups communicate and make decisions. You may recall from chapter 6 that native communication practices are a product of liberal decision-making models and organizing bodies (such as our representative political system) that operate differently than does interorganizational collaboration.[38] Unfortunately, familiar, deep-seated communication processes and structures often do not often facilitate the constructive conflict environment needed in interorganizational collaboration.

Native Meeting Practices

Our native and normative ways of organizing a meeting can limit constructive conflict. For example, the collaborations studied by Renee and Jessica organized their meetings in a format that prioritized *information*. This practice is deeply rooted in our representative political system that prioritizes expression, providing forums for speech and subsequent voting.[39] Expression is a native communication practice resulting from a liberal democratic emphasis on giving people "their say" (see table 10.1). Think about how our political system works. Candidates are positioned to express their viewpoints. Ideally, constituents weigh those viewpoints and vote for the candidates who best represent their own viewpoints. Expression is given priority over engagement. Even in candidate debates, we rarely see a meaningful engagement of difference and ideas. Rather, we are more likely to witness candidates use the format to express their positions, even when the moderator directs a question that has nothing to do with that position (see chapter 6 for a discussion of liberal democracy). David Perkins, named this linear type of group communication "coblaboration" as opposed to collaboration.[40]

The practice of expression is so tacit in our understanding of how to communicate that the groups studied provided little space or room on the agenda to facilitate time or foster a forum that allowed for constructive disagreement, meaningful debate, or deliberation. Instead, the agenda served to cover committee reports. Time to debate ideas, procedures, and group identity had to be worked in before the committee reports or were initiated at the end of the meeting under "other." These native meeting structures and practices diminished the possibilities for constructive disagreement.

Native Decision Making

Native decision-making practices also limit constructive conflict and tend to be largely invisible.[41] Collaborations were found to make decisions with the familiar techniques of (a) authoritative decision making—a leader or small committee does not open the decision to discussion or constructive conflict[42] or (b) parliamentary procedure—arguably a native practice well-matched to liberal democratic modes of decision making (where elected officials are expected to represent the voice of their constituents).[43] Authoritative decision making in collaboration, especially practiced under the guise that decision making is shared among stakeholders, can be problematic for many reasons. It may erode the trust of stakeholders not included in the decision, and it puts the relationships of peer stakeholders who have lent the credibility of their names and their organization's names to support the decisions put forth by the partnership at risk. Argued throughout this book, parliamentary procedures that culminate in voting reproduce majority viewpoints and are therefore not well-suited to the unelected, often voluntary nature of interorganizational stakeholder collaboration that depends on the minority viewpoint as the linchpin of different thought, diversity of perspective, innovation, and creativity. Only when stakeholders are voting on options that already honor the group's collective identity, values, and interests is voting appropriate. However, the pull to move a group toward a vote is often second nature. Unfortunately, authoritative decision making and parliamentary decision making are not good processes for encouraging suppressed or marginalized conflict to surface.

 QUESTION: How do authoritative decision making and parliamentary procedure suppress conflict?

Native Conceptions of Collaboration

Another barrier to constructive conflict is that stakeholders sometimes focus too heavily on harmony and relationships, diminishing their willingness to engage in disagreement.[44] An emphasis on harmony may be more frequent in interorganizational collaboration that originates for the purpose of advancing a vision (such as drop-out prevention) as opposed to collaborations that form to manage conflict (such as environmental disputes).[45] In Renee and Jessica's studies, stakeholders complained about tense moments—revealing the viewpoint that conflict is a disruption rather than a part of collaborating. For example, one stakeholder said, "I've never been on the side of dissenters, so maybe it's not fair, but I'd feel like what was being asked for was out of line with what everybody else had already talked about and agreed upon. That even though it didn't look collaborative, I don't know what else you can do if you want to move things along."[46] Another stakeholder referred to the tense argument portrayed in the opening of this chapter, "It did feel like to me that the school district was interested in ideas and feedback but I didn't have any sense that there would be a shift . . . . that felt tense to me."[47] Both of these stakeholders emphasize a harmonious view of collaboration, equating collaboration with agreement and moving the agenda along. Conceptions of collaboration characterized by harmony, agreement, and accomplishment is not surprising considering that the most prevalent lay definition of collaboration is "working together."

Groupthink

The idea that overly harmonious conceptions can be harmful to groups is well-documented. Irving Janis developed the groupthink hypothesis based on case studies of "fiascoes" (such as the Watergate break in and the US Bay of Pigs invasion). In those cases, intelligent decision makers failed to elicit or engage alternative viewpoints. Janis argued that the "more amiability" and "greater esprit de corps" among group members, the more likely groupthink would replace independent critical thinking. When groupthink occurs, collaborative members try to minimize conflict and reach consensus without critical evaluation through suppression of alternative viewpoints. Janis claimed the effect of groupthink would result in "irrational and dehumanizing actions directed against out-groups."[48] His work illuminates the need for formalizing disagreement as a part of the decision-making process.

QUESTION: Have you ever encountered groupthink? What were the communicative behaviors that contributed to groupthink? What were the implications of your experience?

Gracious Contestation as Collaborative Praxis

The opening of this chapter depicted a constructive conflict about preschool education. The short-term result was that the district changed its policy to charge for preschool. However, the staunch advocacy for preschool education by Metro Collaboration resulted in a line item for preschool and kindergarten on the next district bond. The district passed the bond, and Metro Collaboration was credited by school district officials with having won the dollars for ECE funding. Thus, the group's conflict seeded a win-win for the district and for preschool education in the long-run. Conflict made visible stakeholders' taken for granted values around preschool as a privilege. With successful argumentation, Annette and Danielle altered the conflict frame by convincing stakeholders to see preschool as a right on par with K–12 public school education.

Group research has established the value of conflict especially as it relates to generating creativity and innovation.[49] Scholars have argued, "a normative environment that permits—even encourages—debate, dissent, and criticism may liberate people to freely generate ideas. This . . . may be superior to emphasis on harmony, which is often at the expense of authentic differences."[50] At this point we see the value that our traditional modes and practices of communication, such as debate and argumentation, contribute to collaborating. However, there are a couple of caveats to constructive conflict. First, conflict that is related to tasks (such as whether to charge for preschool) is found to be valuable as opposed to conflict attributed to persons or identity.[51] This can make collaborating tricky, as we discussed in the last chapter on interests. Sometimes people's positions (i.e., I don't want to charge for preschool) are not about the procedure or task but about identity (i.e., we are a cutting edge school system). If the challenge is to an *individual's* identity, the conflict might do harm, as differences may be perceived as personal attacks. Therefore, stakeholders need to listen for those spoken and unspoken interests that clue each other as to what the disagreement is really about. The second caveat, is that the challenges proposed to the group will be more successful if they are authentic rather than seeded in "devil's advocate" role-playing. Some research has found that devil's advocacy actually increases commitments to the stated position rather than questioning its efficacy. In contrast, authentic disagreement can be effective in moving groups to consider problems from varied angles.[52]

So how do we make constructive conflict normative? If working together also means tension and disagreement, how do we embrace conflict with the same enthusiasm as getting along? The challenge is not just limited to collaboration contexts. Renee once had a class erupt in a heated discussion of feminism and working mothers. Some students were very uncomfortable with the fact that open disagreement, conflict, and tension were a part of the discussion. Renee was disappointed with this assessment because she believed the discussion was healthy, constructive, and challenged assumptions without personal attacks. One of her graduate students, an attorney, wrote her and said she believed the class was the most outstanding that semester, and indeed the best class of her graduate career! What if we all embraced the clashing of perspectives with such openness? Daniels and Walker provide clues for how to do so. "Argument is an essential dimension of communication competence in collaborative public participation. Constructive argument can be critical to a collaborative process' success.[53] They posit these key features of collaborative argument: valuing and respecting disagreement; a desire to learn; a willingness to risk; open-mindedness; distinguishing between arguers and arguments; a positive regard for the other; and ethical responsibility.[54] We believe these features of collaborative argument are facilitated through dialogue (discussed repeatedly in this text) and gracious contestation.

Gracious Contestation

Whereas dialogue primarily regards understanding, gracious contestation is our language for engaging in communicative behaviors that challenge, argue, debate, and invite dissent from others. Understanding is still a part of the process, but disagreement is also vital. An emphasis on graciousness asks us to be mindful of how we challenge one another. The meaning of grace derives from the concepts merciful and benevolent, thus gracious contestation fosters reflexivity (a dialogic practice) as we challenge differing viewpoints.[55] In our opening case, we see Karen model this graciousness when she invites others to weigh in on the decision the school board proposes to make regarding charging for preschool. Graciousness also means that we can disagree while still being courteous, pleasant, kind, and friendly.[56] Though there were some tense moments in the preschool discussion, Karen is humble, admitting her thinking might have been flawed. She uses humor to relieve the tense moment without discrediting her primary challenger, Annette. The praxis of gracious contestation is grounded in a collaborative ethic and draws on all of the dispositions and skills associated with dialogue and appreciation. Several chapters in this book contribute to a conception of what it means to enact gracious contestation. They include considering marginalized viewpoints (chapter 4), embracing diverse perspectives (chapter 5), recognizing how power is present in the decision-making situation (chapter 6) creating egalitarian discussion spaces (chapter 7), listening critically, and reflectively (chapter 8), separating positions from interests (chapter 9), and appreciating one another's' unique contributions (chapter 12). Together, the attitudes and skills emphasized in the other chapters prepare us to practice gracious contestation—cultivating the respect and trust that encourage us to disagree without damaging one another.

Contestation implies public disputation. The work of Jürgen Habermas addresses contestation. [57] He posited that participants must be free to challenge one another in the pursuit of consensus outcomes in decision-making situations in order to avoid distorted power (chapter 6).[58] Contestation serves a different purpose than being adversarial. Building on earlier scholarship, Cynthia Hardy and Nelson Phillips, likened being adversarial to "not merely a hard-fought contest to see who wins a particular chess game; [but] a threat to the game itself. It is one thing to fight hard to win a game; it is another thing to overturn the chess board."[59] Contestation is also hard-fought but leaves the chess pieces and players intact. It is apparent in the preschool discussion that the differences are not about tearing down the school board or the city but encouraging reflexivity on the part of both to consider their symbolic messages to the community. No person or entity at the meetings is interested in dismantling the people or organizations that are working on behalf of children. Gracious contestation facilitates respectful and openly transparent disagreement.

 QUESTION: Reflect on a situation where you witnessed or participated in gracious contestation. What were the communicative behaviors that facilitated the conversation? What was the result?

Creating VOICE

Fostering gracious contestation is one challenge facing interorganizational collaboration, especially if groups subscribe to overly harmonious
conceptions of collaboration and tend to create forums that promote
expression as opposed to voice.[60] Voice, defined as "the communication
microprocesses and structures that constitute civic legitimacy by fostering
access to, and participation in, influential discussions in collaborative decision-making situations,"[61] constitutes a mode of communication that
emerges from contestation. Voice is the theoretical antonym to expression.[62] The communication microprocesses associated with voice are dialogic in that they encourage practices such as openness, critical listening,
and genuine inquiry.[63] But voice also implies power and influence in the
communication situation. Voice does not exist if stakeholders do not have
access to participate in and influence discussions and decisions.[64] Voice
thus goes beyond expressing ideas; it implies the challenging, mulling,
accepting, rejecting, and integrating of ideas. As such, voice includes
debate among participants that is not focused on winning the argument,
as much as it is intended to shape and influence the argument and the
frames that stakeholders use to understand the problem (table 10.1).

Table 10.1   Expression versus voice

Expression	Voice
Associated with liberal democracy, where representatives make decisions on behalf of constituents	Associated with participative democracy, where decision making lies directly with stakeholders
Goal is to "have a say"	Goal is to influence the decision making content and process and to integrate one another's thinking
Serves voting processes where suppression of minority viewpoints is acceptable and democratic	Serves consensus processes where suppression of minority viewpoints is consequential and lacks accountability
Manifests in linear communication such as speeches, persuasion, formal rules-oriented debate	Manifests in dialogue, contestation, debate oriented toward consensus rather than winning

Given our tendency to rely on native modes and forums of expression,
Renee and Jessica's research led to the creation of the heuristic provided in
table 10.2. This heuristic prompts stakeholders to consider their communication processes and structures in light of sowing the seeds for constructive conflict and contestation by focusing on voice.

Collaborative VOICE begins with V for visible stakeholder decision-
making processes that reveal how decisions were accomplished, who was

involved, and who might be missing. Stakeholders consider: when decisions should be sent to smaller committees; how subcommittees will make deliberative discussions transparent; and how the larger collaborating group can access information that will facilitate informed decision making. By emphasizing visible processes, transparency and accountability are fostered, ultimately creating new inclusive and collaborative norms of communication. In our preschool case, the school board made their decision-making process visible by bringing it to Metro Collaboration to discuss in a public meeting. This move encouraged voice among early care and education stakeholders by giving them access to, and influence in, the decision-making process.

The O in the VOICE heuristic reminds stakeholders to own their political power and to frame their activities as accountable to the public. Ownership prompts stakeholders to practice communication and decision-making processes with accountability in mind, thinking explicitly about access, civic legitimacy, and influence—thus attending to the political implications of their work. In our preschool case, Annette's contesting of the board's decision draws attention to the larger community and to the implications the board's decisions will have for middle income families

Table 10.2   A heuristic to foster collaborative VOICE

V Visible decision processes draw attention to:	how do we arrive at this decision? what process will we use? who is involved and who needs to be involved? how will others be informed?
O Ownership of political power asks that we:	acknowledge civic responsibility; consider the larger community affected by decisions; commit to participative processes.
I Information balanced with deliberation considers:	are our processes overemphasizing information exchange? is this the best use of peoples' time? is this taking up time we need to be deliberating? how should we best use meeting time?
C Contestation requires that we consider:	collaborations a safe place for contestation; how we encourage quiet voices; how we draw out dissenters and diverse viewpoints; whether we overemphasize harmony.
E Expression reminds us to limit expression and increase discussion by considering:	the structures and practices we use. Do they foster expression or voice? Are our forums expressing or integrating diverse views?

Reprinted with permission from Jessica MacDonald Milam and Renee Guarriello Heath, "Participative Democracy and Voice: Rethinking Community Collaboration Beyond Neutral Structures," *Journal of Applied Communication Research* 42, no. 4 (October 2, 2014): 366–86, doi:10.1080/00909882.2014.911944.

and even wealthier families that are left out of the proposed decision. Ownership in collaboration prevents marginalized stakeholders from being overlooked and thus invites difference into the conversation.

The I in VOICE stands for keeping information in balance with deliberation and other methods of communication. Ann Marie Thomson and James Perry argue: "Although information sharing is necessary for collaboration, it is not sufficient for it to thrive."[65] We see the decision made by cochairs Maggie and Lynn to table the meeting's proposed agenda and to make room for discussion and deliberation regarding the urgent budget cuts and proposed preschool fees as fostering opportunities to deliberate and debate. We can also see that the meeting balanced information presented by Karen about the proposed cuts with deliberation time to discuss the implications of those cuts. Both information and deliberation were vital to the group's decision making.

The C in the VOICE model normalizes gracious contestation as expected and accepted in collaborative interaction and as an important counterweight to concentrated power. Rethinking collaboration from conceptions of harmony to conceptions of safe arenas to confront alternative viewpoints will help guide collaborative members as they design communication processes that integrate constructive conflict. Focusing on contestation asks stakeholders to consider the quiet voices and dissenters, and it invites diverse viewpoints. In the preschool example, Karen invited challenges to the proposal several times: first by bringing the proposal to the stakeholder group; next by engaging in a discussion with Annette; and later when she invited more of the group to join the discussion. Explicitly acknowledging contestation as a part of the collaborative process will contribute to normative expectations around conflict.

The E in the heuristic is for expression and is preceded by a request to limit the focus on expression and to increase the focus on stakeholder voice and participation. With this prompt, collaborative participants can collectively discern whether their forums, structures, and practices foster expression or create space for authentic influence in the decision-making situation. Although, the preschool case exemplifies many of the practices associated with the VOICE heuristic, the conflict that took place was one of only two witnessed throughout 14 months of observation. Indeed, rarely were Metro's meetings dialogic, let alone conflict-oriented. To promote normative constructive conflict, Metro could have learned from its own example and limited the monologic reporting that characterized many other meetings. The VOICE mnemonic aids collaborative stakeholders in designing processes and structures that foreground constructive conflicts in a shared decision-making context. VOICE reproduces a collaborative ethic aimed at fostering egalitarianism and participation from all stakeholders.

Prolonged Conflict

Although some collaborations struggle to elicit conflict (depending on the motivations for collaborating) other collaborations become mired in prolonged, intractable conflict. Being immersed in long-standing adversarial relationships (often visible in environmental collaboration situations for example) calls for different communication skills. The problem is not making conflict normative but rather encouraging stakeholders to engage one another constructively. Barbara Gray and Jill Purdy's research provides several recommendations for stakeholders involved in intractable conflict, including: synchronized de-escalation, telling identity stories, developing shared frames, and shuttle diplomacy.[66]

Synchronized de-escalation encourages small concessions by the conflicting parties to signal "good faith."[67] The parties simultaneously commit to concessions without knowing if the other party will also concede, thus communicating trust to each other. This incremental approach to conflict encourages the good will and graciousness needed to encounter each other's differences. Gray and Purdy argue that having stakeholders tell their own story in the midst of conflict can help promote deep and reflective listening, which is consistent with what we know about storytelling in dialogic situations. The authors also promote developing shared frames as a way of working through prolonged conflict. Although different frames are not always obvious, they can be exposed by using techniques such as asking stakeholders to participate in role reversals or imagining processes "in which parties share views of themselves and how they appear to others."[68] Storytelling frames contribute to how differing stakeholders understand their own conflict. Finally, shuttle diplomacy can be used in cases where stakeholders are not able to meet without escalation. Shuttle diplomacy uses a mediator (though this could be a convener, facilitator, or respected stakeholder) to meet separately with each partner and to convey their concerns to each other in a subsequent private meeting, thus opening up the communication lines and helping each stakeholder foster empathy for the other's concerns.

Collaborative praxis revolving around conflict will vary depending on the impetus and orientation of collaboration. In the cases of collaborations born out of the hope to advance opportunities and visions, an explicit case may need to be made for making conflict normative. The VOICE heuristic offers one mechanism for making gracious contestation explicit and expected in collaboration. However, intractable conflict invites its own challenges, which may include getting stakeholders into the same room. In this case, the dialogic skills advocated in previous chapters can help stakeholders move to a place of understanding.

CONCLUSION

Conflict is an unavoidable and important part of collaborating. Without conflict, stakeholders are not likely to arrive at creative resolutions and innovations. However, conflict in collaboration will vary depending on whether it is the impetus of collaboration (to solve a problem) or it is the result of collaboration (advancing a vision). In many cases, stakeholders have valued harmony over conflict, sometimes to the detriment of advancing collaborative business. This chapter reviewed some of the ways we understand conflict and methods for measuring it. We also examined some of the native communication practices and attitudes visible in collaboration that hinder constructive conflict and discourage stakeholder participation. Instead, we advocate that stakeholders enact gracious contestation and consider structures and processes that will normalize contestation in their communication. This chapter contends that communication oriented toward conflict is a normal and necessary part of collaborating. The next chapter takes conflict for granted and considers how stakeholders can begin to build agreement out of their differences.

CHAPTER TAKE-AWAYS

- Understand conflict as normal and vital to the learning process in collaboration

- Recognize the native communication practices employed that suppress constructive conflict in collaborative groups

- Comprehend gracious contestation as a mechanism for embracing conflict while maintaining relationships

- Articulate how the VOICE heuristic fosters contestation in collaborative group processes

- Identify the different communication strategies that may be needed when conflict is prolonged

ENDNOTES

[1] Charles Conrad, *Strategic Organizational Communication: An Integrated Perspective*, 2nd ed. (Fort Worth, TX: Harcourt School, 1990).

[2] William Wilmot and Joyce Hocker, *Interpersonal Conflict*, 9th ed. (New York: McGraw-Hill Education, 2013).

[3] Steven Daniels and Gregg Walker, *Working through Environmental Conflict: The Collaborative Learning Approach* (Westport, CT: Praeger, 2001), p. 35.

[4] Barbara Gray and Jill Purdy, "Conflict in Cross-Sector Partnerships," in *Social Partnerships and Responsible Business: A Research Handbook*, ed. M. May Seitanidi and Andrew Crane (New York: Routledge, 2014), 205–26.

[5] Daniels and Walker, *Working through Environmental Conflict,* p. 30.

[6] Boris H. J. M. Brummans et al., "Making Sense of Intractable Multiparty Conflict: A Study of Framing in Four Environmental Disputes," *Communication Monographs* 75, no. 1 (March 1, 2008): 25–51, doi:10.1080/03637750801952735, p. 29.

[7] Ibid.

[8] Ibid., p. 28.

[9] Ibid.

[10] Daniels and Walker, *Working through Environmental Conflict*.

[11] Gregg Walker, Steven Daniels, and Jens Emborg, "Public Participation in Environmental Policy Decision-Making: Insights from Twenty Years of Collaborative Learning Fieldwork,"

in *The Routledge Handbook of Environment and Communication*, ed. Alan Hansen and Robert Cox (New York: Routledge, 2015), 111–30.

[12] Ibid.

[13] Daniels and Walker, *Working through Environmental Conflict*; Walker, Daniels, and Emborg, "Public Participation in Environmental Policy Decision-Making."

[14] Steven E. Daniels, Gregg B. Walker, and Jens Emborg, "The Unifying Negotiation Framework: A Model of Policy Discourse," *Conflict Resolution Quarterly* 30, no. 1 (September 1, 2012): 3–31, doi:10.1002/crq.21045.

[15] Wilmot and Hocker, *Interpersonal Conflict*.

[16] Susan L. Carpenter and W. J. D. Kennedy, *Managing Public Disputes: A Practical Guide for Professionals in Government, Business and Citizens Groups* (San Francisco: Jossey-Bass, 2001).

[17] Walker, Daniels, and Emborg, "Public Participation in Environmental Policy Decision-Making."

[18] Gregg B. Walker, Steven E. Daniels, and Anthony Cheng, "Facilitating Dialogue and Deliberation in Environmental Conflict: The Use of Groups in Collaborative Learning," in *Facilitating Group Communication: Innovations and Applications with Natural Groups*, ed. Larry R. Frey (Cresskill, NJ: Hampton Press, 2006).

[19] Roy Lewicki, David Saunders, and Bruce Barry, *Negotiation*, 7th ed. (New York: McGraw-Hill Education, 2014).

[20] Walker, Daniels, and Emborg, "Public Participation in Environmental Policy Decision-Making"; Antony S. Cheng and Victoria E. Sturtevant, "A Framework for Assessing Collaborative Capacity in Community-Based Public Forest Management," *Environmental Management* 49, no. 3 (December 31, 2011): 675–89.

[21] Lewicki, Saunders, and Barry, *Negotiation*.

[22] Ibid.

[23] Daniels and Walker, *Working through Environmental Conflict*; Walker, Daniels, and Emborg, "Public Participation in Environmental Policy Decision-Making"; Steven E. Daniels and Gregg B. Walker, "Collaborative Learning: Improving Public Deliberation in Ecosystem-Based Management," *Environmental Impact Assessment Review* 16, no. 2 (March 1, 1996): 71–102; Gregg B. Walker, Susan L. Senecah, and Steven E. Daniels, "From the Forest to the River: Citizens' Views of Stakeholder Engagement," *Human Ecology Review* 13, no. 2 (2006): 193–202.

[24] Gregg B. Walker, Susan L. Senecah, and Steven E. Daniels, "Reflections from the Road: New and Improved Concepts, Tools, and Lessons for Community-Based Collaboration," in *Proceedings of the 8th Biennial Conference on Communication and the Environment*, ed. L. S. Volkening (Athens: University of Georgia Department of Speech Communication, 2007), 213–34.

[25] Susan L. Senecah, "The Trinity of Voice: The Role of Practical Theory in Planning and Evaluating the Effectiveness of Environmental Participatory Processes," in *Communication and Public Participation in Environmental Decision Making*, ed. Stephen P. Depoe, John W. Delicath, and Marie-France Aepli Elsenbeer (Albany: SUNY Press, 2004), 13–33.

[26] Gregg B. Walker, "Public Participation as Participatory Communication in Environmental Policy Decision-Making: From Concepts to Structured Conversations," *Environmental Communication* 1, no. 1 (May 1, 2007): 99–110, doi:10.1080/17524030701334342.

[27] Gregg B. Walker, "The Roadless Areas Initiative as National Policy: Is Public Participation an Oxymoron?" in *Communication and Public Participation in Environmental Decision Making*, ed. Stephen P. Depoe, John W. Delicath, and Marie-France Aepli Elsenbeer (Albany: SUNY Press, 2004), 113–36.

[28] Wilmot and Hocker, *Interpersonal Conflict*.

[29] Gregg B. Walker and Steven E. Daniels, "The Nature and Role of Agency Leadership: Building and Sustaining Collaboration in Natural Resource Management and Environmental Policy Decision-Making," in *Environmental Leadership: A Reference Handbook*, ed. D. Rigling Gallagher (Thousand Oaks, CA: Sage, 2012), 147–58.

[30] Gregg B. Walker and Susan L. Senecah, "Collaborative Governance: Integrating Institutions, Communities, and People," in *Community-Based Collaboration: Bridging Socio-Ecolog-*

ical Research and Practice, ed. E. F. Dukes, K. E. Firehock, and J. E. Birkhoff (Charlottesville: University of Virginia Press, 2011).

31 Daniels and Walker, *Working through Environmental Conflict*; Gregg B. Walker and Steven E. Daniels, "Assessing the Promise and Potential for Collaboration: The Progress Triangle Framework," in *Finding Our Way(s) in Environmental Communication: Proceedings of the Seventh Biennial Conference on Communication and the Environment*, ed. Gregg B. Walker and W. J. Kinsella (Corvallis: Oregon State University Department of Speech Communication, 2005), 188–201.

32 Daniels and Walker, *Working through Environmental Conflict*; Walker and Daniels, "The Nature and Role of Agency Leadership"; Walker and Daniels, "Assessing the Promise and Potential for Collaboration."

33 Tricia Jones and Andrea Bodtker, "A Dialectical Analysis of a Social Justice Process: International Collaboration in South Africa," *Journal of Applied Communication Research* 26, no. 4 (1998): 357–73;

34 Daniels and Walker, *Working through Environmental Conflict*.

35 Ibid., p. 28.

36 Jones and Bodtker, "A Dialectical Analysis of a Social Justice Process"; Mary Ann Renz, "Paving Consensus: Enacting, Challenging, and Revising the Consensus Process in a Cohousing Community," *Journal of Applied Communication Research* 34, no. 2 (May 1, 2006): 163–90, doi:10.1080/00909880600574088; Mary Ann Renz, "The Meaning of Consensus and Blocking for Cohousing Groups," *Small Group Research* 37, no. 4 (August 1, 2006): 351–76, doi:10.1177/1046496406291184.

37 Jessica MacDonald Milam and Renee Guarriello Heath, "Participative Democracy and Voice: Rethinking Community Collaboration Beyond Neutral Structures," *Journal of Applied Communication Research* 42, no. 4 (October 2, 2014): 366–86, doi:10.1080/00909882.2014.911944.

38 Ibid.; Stanley Deetz and Lisa Irvin, "Governance, Stakeholder Involvement, and New Communication Models," in *Governance Reform Under Real World Conditions: Citizens, Stakeholders, and Voice*, ed. Sina Odugbemi and Thomas L. Jacobson (Washington, DC: World Bank Publications, 2008), 163–80.

39 See Deetz Scholar Spotlight in Shared Power (chapter 6)

40 David Perkins, *King Arthur's Round Table: How Collaborative Conversations Create Smart Organizations* (New York: Wiley, 2002).

41 Ibid.

42 Christoph Haug, "What Is Consensus and How It Is Achieved in Meetings? Four Types of Consensus Decision Making," in *The Cambridge Handbook of Meeting Science*, ed. Joseph A. Allen, Nale Lehmann-Willenbrock, and Steven G. Rogelberg (New York: Cambridge University Press, 2015), 556–84.

43 Benjamin Barber, *Strong Democracy: Participatory Politics for a New Age: Twentieth-Anniversary Edition* (Oakland: University of California Press, 2004).

44 Milam and Heath, "Participative Democracy and Voice."

45 Gray and Purdy, "Conflict in Cross-Sector Partnerships."

46 Milam and Heath, "Participative Democracy and Voice," p. 377.

47 Ibid., p. 377.

48 Irving L. Janis, *Groupthink: Psychological Studies of Policy Decisions and Fiascoes*, 2nd ed. (Boston: Cengage Learning, 1982), p. 13.

49 Charlan J. Nemeth et al., "The Liberating Role of Conflict in Group Creativity: A Study in Two Countries," *European Journal of Social Psychology* 34, no. 4 (July 1, 2004): 365–74, doi:10.1002/ejsp.210.

50 Ibid., p. 367.

51 Karen A. Jehn and Elizabeth A. Mannix, "The Dynamic Nature of Conflict: A Longitudinal Study of Intragroup Conflict and Group Performance," *Academy of Management Journal* 44, no. 2 (April 1, 2001): 238–51, doi:10.2307/3069453.

[52] Charlan Nemeth, Keith Brown, and John Rogers, "Devil's Advocate versus Authentic Dissent: Stimulating Quantity and Quality," *European Journal of Social Psychology* 31, no. 6 (November 1, 2001): 707–20, doi:10.1002/ejsp.58.

[53] Daniels and Walker, *Working through Environmental Conflict,* p. 142.

[54] Ibid., p. 142.

[55] Online Etymology Dictionary, "Grace," http://www.etymonline.com/index.php?term=grace

[56] Ibid.

[57] Jürgen Habermas, *Communication and the Evolution of Society,* trans. Thomas McCarthy (Boston: Beacon Press, 1979).

[58] See also Stanley Deetz, *Democracy in an Age of Corporate Colonization: Developments in Communication and the Politics of Everyday Life* (Albany: SUNY Press, 1992). Page 76 for detailed discussion.

[59] Roland Leslie Warren, Stephen M. Rose, and Ann F. Bergunder, *The Structure of Urban Reform: Community Decision Organizations in Stability and Change* (Lexington, MA: Lexington Books, 1974), p. 51.

[60] Milam and Heath, "Participative Democracy and Voice."

[61] Ibid., p. 370.

[62] Stanley Deetz and Jennifer Simpson, "Critical Organizational Dialogue," in *Dialogue: Theorizing Difference in Communication Studies*, ed. Rob Anderson, Leslie A. Baxter, and Kenneth N. Cissna (Thousand Oaks, CA: Sage, 2003), 141–58.

[63] Ibid.

[64] Senecah, "The Trinity of Voice."

[65] Ann Marie Thomson and James L. Perry, "Collaboration Processes: Inside the Black Box," *Public Administration Review* 66 (December 1, 2006): 20–32, doi:10.1111/j.1540-6210.2006.00663.x, p. 27.

[66] Gray and Purdy, "Conflict in Cross-Sector Partnerships."

[67] Charles E. Osgood, *An Alternative to War or Surrender* (Champaign: University of Illinois Press, 1965).

[68] Gray and Purdy, "Conflict in Cross-Sector Partnerships," p. 219.

11

Communication Oriented toward Consensus

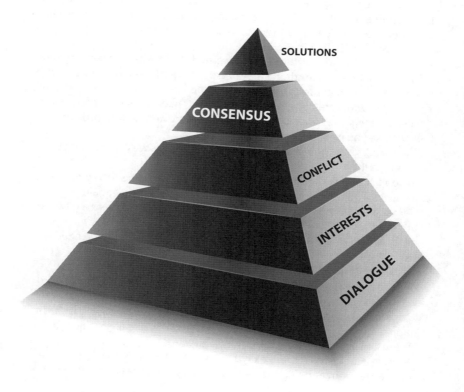

A Confusing Case of Consensus

Dana recently left Metro Collaboration, a network of professionals devoted to improving and delivering high quality early care and education. She was a founding stakeholder representing State University for the 12 years the partnership had been in existence. Described as a visionary by her peers, Dana resigned as a director at State University, leaving the continuation of the partnership with Metro Collaboration unclear. She historically wielded undisputed freedom within State University to contribute organizational resources to Metro. In return, Metro contracted with the university to gather and house data. Her departure destabilized the sustainability of the partnership with the stakeholder organization. Suddenly questions surfaced regarding who owned the data—Metro or State? The organizational relationship with State was important to the group because many of the grants won by Metro Collaboration required that outcomes for children be tracked. At a collaboration meeting, cochairs Lynn and Maggie led a discussion on what to do regarding the university partnership. The meeting began with a brief report about the findings of a subcommittee that had convened at an earlier date to consider how to proceed after Dana's departure.

Lynn began, "So hearing . . ."

James, a long-term partner, was concerned about what the subcommittee had decided and the criteria they had used. He suspected that the group would be asked to approve the subcommittee's recommendations. He interrupted Lynn with carefully chosen words: "Well I'm only hearing information. I'm not sure what specific questions we'll be approving or disapproving, it seemed like you were heading toward a motion."

Lynn said, "I was going to say, 'Hearing no changes we'll go forward.'"

James, "Okay."

Maggie jumped in. Turning to the subcommittee chair, she asked, "Rena, can you very quickly summarize what you just went through again?"

James interrupted the process again, "Are you moving toward a motion? That's my question."

Maggie said to James, "I'm asking Rena to review the things we need to consider."

James continued, "The only thing I'm saying is to do that by consensus, to allow it to move forward. I think the general consensus on all of those, and don't make that so formal, . . . for example, there are some aspects that aren't tied down real specifically. And that's the only thing that I'm saying is that a motion might be giving consensus to something that's really not tied down with consensus that's, 'That's good, move forward.'"

Maggie acquiesced, "That's okay. I mean that's fine if that's what people want. I see [voting] as being the same, but that's okay. We can say it's by consensus."

—*Exemplar adapted from Renee's transcripts of Metro Collaboration*

Thus far we have indicated that we need to move past native conceptions of conflict in order to understand its role in collaboration of eliciting the differences that will help groups meet their creative potential. We've identified several ways of understanding and supporting conflict in collaborative groups. So how do groups communicatively move from conflict to shared values and decisions? The answer lies in the decision-making process. Consensus decision-making processes encourage the constructive conflict needed to legitimize decisions. Consider being a part of a collaboration that must defend its decision to a larger community, such as Metro Collaboration stakeholders who advised the school board on a number of issues including the cut off age for kindergarten. The group's decision has much greater credibility if arriving at that decision involved processes that elicit participation from all stakeholders. The ability to defend the decision and to understand the consequences of the decision are greater because the group encouraged minority viewpoints and possibly lone dissenters. It did not move forward until conflicts were aired and all parties could accept the decision. In addition, the sustainability of the collaborative group rests on whether stakeholders believe they were heard and influential in the process—whether they exercised voice. Should they believe their input is not valued or necessary to the decision-making process, they have little incentive to continue to participate. Accordingly, eliciting conflict and working through conflict honors the ethical assumptions on which collaborative praxis is built.

Having established the inevitability of conflict, we introduce consensus as the preferred decision-making method for collaboration; conflict is a necessary and valuable component of the process. As illustrated in the opening vignette, consensus decision making is not always clear to groups; stakeholders often don't know what consensus means. Maggie described it as "the same" as voting. This chapter distinguishes why and how consensus decision making is different from voting and other types of decision making—and why that distinction is relevant to collaborative decision making. Developing a shared definition for consensus-processes among stakeholders provides a vehicle to embrace conflict and cultivates a constructive culture for harnessing difference toward creative and accountable decisions. Consensus decision making adds to our repertoire of skills and practices in communication oriented toward arriving at solutions. It is a part of the language of collaborative praxis.

Consensus and Collaboration

Not surprisingly, community collaboration and consensus decision-making processes are often linked in the literature.[1] Matthew McKinney, environmental collaboration scholar and practitioner argued, "Consensus building is perhaps best understood as a particular form of collaborative problem solving, meaning that consensus shares many of the same traits as collaborative processes."[2] Judith Innes and David Booher found consensus decision making assisted stakeholders in maintaining shared power and building trust and claimed consensus as both a legitimate process and decision outcome of collaboration.[3] Renee and her colleague Patricia Sias found specific consensus practices and structures facilitated sharing power among collaborating stakeholders.[4] Yet Douglas Kenney remained skeptical regarding the quality of decision making accomplished by consensus processes in community collaboration.[5] Although consensus decision making is often linked to collaborating as an appropriate method of decision making, it is not well defined as a decision making process.[6] This section will develop the difference between consensus outcomes and consensus processes that in part explain why people are sometimes skeptical of consensus. As a part of that distinction, we will emphasize the importance of expressed disagreement and gracious contestation (chapter 10) as essential to consensus building demonstrating the important relationship between conflict and consensus decision making.

The vignette that opens this chapter is difficult to follow; we chose it precisely to illustrate the struggles of stakeholders regarding consensus decision making. James, a nonprofit stakeholder, seems to be asking for consensus, but a close examination of the conversation shows that he used the word consensus in multiple ways, invoking multiple meanings. Maggie, the collaboration cochair, responds in a confusing manner as well conflating consensus decision making with voting. This section of the chapter is in part about clearing up the confusion of consensus. The dilemma of losing State University has something to teach us about how we define and understand consensus decision making. It also gives us a window into the dynamics of power and the necessity of well-defined and agreed upon decision-making processes.

Lay Definitions

We often encounter business leaders and professionals who hold a skeptical view of consensus decision making. This is probably because they conceptualize consensus as agreement, overemphasizing the conception of consensus as a particular decision outcome. In her study of Metro Collaboration featured in the opening of this chapter, Renee found several lay definitions of consensus in use by different stakeholders including consensus as something to be done before voting, pseudo consensus, and consensus as laboring. The difference in their conceptions of consensus helps explain why some people are reticent to engage in consensus processes and gives context to the confusion in the opening vignette.

Maggie's View: Trying Consensus before Voting.   Frequently we encounter groups that decide to "try" reaching consensus (conceived as unanimous agreement); however, if they do not reach agreement, they vote. This understanding of consensus is visible in the excerpt above where Maggie conflates making a motion (the parliamentary procedure precursor to voting) with consensus. In an interview with Renee, Maggie revealed her reticence to use consensus as a legitimate decision-making process. She said, "I mean I think that if we're going to go public on a position, we have to vote. Because I do think that otherwise we'd leave too much to assumption, and sometimes silence around the table is affirmation and sometimes it's not. It's resistance. And we need to know that."[7] Maggie's comment indicated she viewed consensus decision making as less transparent than voting processes. In her claim, "We'd leave too much to assumption," it is clear she views consensus as an outcome of agreement rather than a process of sorting through the "silence around the table." Another stakeholder, Sherry, confirmed,

> Maggie wants everyone to vote so they feel like they have a say in things. [At a meeting Maggie chaired] I could see her struggling, like "Okay, I know we need consensus, but I need to make them know that they do have authority." She said to me afterwards, "I'm sorry we voted but I felt like we had to vote because I had to feel like I knew that people felt like they were involved in the decision."

Maggie's tendency to see consensus decision making as less authoritative, or official than voting, is not uncommon.[8] While her comment exposes the assumption that consensus decision making is an expected decision process, it also demonstrates an understanding of consensus as an outcome. Neither Maggie nor Sherry demonstrated confidence in consensus decision making as an effective process that could be utilized to build the inclusiveness Maggie hoped to create by involving everyone in the decision.

As argued in the last chapter, many groups we encounter rely on their native communication practices of voting and parliamentary procedure. We believe this has much to do with the confusing and multiple interpretations of consensus decision making. Stakeholders skeptical of consensus tend to overemphasize consensus outcomes. The problem with this view is that consensus and voting are not the same. Voting will always overrule the minority viewpoint, which is problematic in interorganizational collaboration that is often weighted heavily with representatives from a particular sector (such as industry or nonprofits). The problem with "trying" consensus is that groups are not committed to consensus processes and too easily fall back on the familiar, native voting process, undermining their creative potential. With voting lurking as a possibility, groups will short circuit their consensus process in favor of the less tedious and time-consuming process of voting. However, with a richer conception of consensus decision making, groups will find consensus processes can be more transparent and legitimate than voting in interorganizational contexts. While voting initially may save time, latent disagreement and conflict is bound to resurface, causing groups to retread ground they thought they had covered.

Julia Wood distinguished among different methods of group decision making. Table 11.1 reflects some of the constraints and conditions groups should consider before choosing a decision-making method and describes the strengths and weaknesses of particular methods in particular contexts. Wood uses the guiding terms "agreement" and "participation" to describe consensus; negotiation is guided by "settlement" and "bargaining" (as in the competitive type of negotiation described in chapter 9); and voting is demarcated by "resolution" and "partisanship." In each case, determining the method for decision making depends on the constraints posed by

Table 11.1   Different methods of group decision making

Constraint	Alternative Methods		
	Voting	**Negotiation**	**Consensus**
Member	strong initial commitments to specific outcomes	commitments to planks of outcomes	no strong initial commitments
	uncommitted to membership in group	dependence on group	highly committed to group
	combative orientation	compromise orientation	cooperative orientation
Task	emergency or time limited	some regard for time	extended time available
	single views permitted	safeguard individual interdependency	meld diverse perspectives
	members' support irrelevant to implementation	some support required for implementation	solid support essential to implementation
	unambiguous task	limited ambiguity	highly ambiguous
Outcome	decision quality a moot issue	decision quality a priority	decision quality a priority
	members' satisfaction is unimportant	each member must be satisfied with what she/he deems crucial	members' satisfaction a priority
	ad hoc groups	ongoing groups as long as conditions producing inter-dependency exist	ongoing groups

Reprinted with permission from Julia T. Wood, "Alternative Methods of Group Decision Making: A Comparative Examination of Consensus, Negotiation, and Voting," in *Emergent Issues in Human Decision Making*, ed. Gerald Phillips and Julia T. Wood (Carbondale: Southern Illinois University Press, 1984), 3–18.

membership, task, and outcome. Wood's table makes clear the reasons consensus is so well-matched to interorganizational collaboration—that is; its cooperative orientation, its need to meld diverse perspectives, and its intent to arrive at a quality decision that will satisfy stakeholders.

QUESTION: Consider scenarios where it might be appropriate to use different decision-making processes in interorganizational collaboration. What are the conditions you took into account?

Sherry's View: "Pseudo" Consensus.   Another reason groups shy away from consensus decision making is that they view consensus as a diluted process of agreement. At its worst, consensus devolves to "watered-down decisions that mark the least common denominator among members."[9] Sherry, a staff member at Metro, argued that what is mostly practiced is a pseudo consensus. She said, "Decisions are made by pseudo-consensus. Well, I shouldn't say pseudo . . . soft, soft consensus." She clarified her choice of words, "Sometimes they vote literally and sometimes they kind of look around, all nodding, like okay. Soft decisions—again." Sherry's depiction of consensus decision making paints a view of a less-than-authentic process—"look around, all nodding" stands for the process of gaining consensus. Sherry thus calls it pseudo consensus. Instinctively Sherry knows that consensus involves more than looking around the room of stakeholders "nodding." Unfortunately, consensus decision making does get practiced in this watered-down manner; conflicts are not drawn out, differences do not surface, and those who might challenge the decision do not speak up in the wake of nodding heads. Pseudo consensus sets the conditions for groupthink (discussed in chapter 10) where disagreement and contestation are quelled or silenced without a rich process of eliciting different viewpoints.[10]

Manuel's View: Consensus as "Laboring."   An alternative view of consensus decision making more aligned with the conception we posit in this chapter also existed among Metro stakeholders. Manuel held a more enthusiastic view of consensus based on his previous group experience. He said,

> We arrived at consensus through collaboration. I mean we labored on it [laughing] and stuff like that and got something everybody could agree with. Now it wasn't always 100 percent your way or sometimes you might win in something over here, but the finished project benefited everybody. And I think that's the way I see this thing [Metro Collaboration] should go.

Manuel held a more process-oriented understanding of consensus decision making, invoking the word "labored" to depict it. Laboring conjures up images of struggle and work to arrive at a decision. The laboring metaphor is also a telling, evaluative description—consensus decision making is hard.

Theoretical Definitions

The lay definitions swimming around the membership of an interorganizational collaboration reflect the distinction between theoretical definitions of consensus as an outcome and consensus as a process. Theoretical definitions mirror lay definitions as scholars tend to foreground consensus decision outcomes (agreement to move forward) over consensus processes (laboring). The distinctions are important because they give us a vocabulary to understand our processes in our efforts to implement them.

Little "c" consensus: Consensus as an Outcome. Scholars have long distinguished between consensus outcomes and consensus decision-making processes, yet studies and people we meet tend to emphasize the former— consensus as an outcome of agreement[11] leaving underdeveloped a complex understanding of consensus decision making as a process in which underlying conflicts surface and are negotiated.[12] We have labeled agreement, little c consensus, because it is the less complex definition of consensus, and probably the most readily associated colloquial definition. Deliberation scholars Kevin Sager and John Gastil explain that a consensus outcome "refers to group members' unanimous agreement on a particular issue or course of action."[13] Wood's definition demonstrates the emphasis on agreement and cooperation.

> Consensual decision making regards the function of talk as forging agreements acceptable to all members. In turn, this implies that only certain forms of communication are appropriate (e.g., review, clarification), certain forms are praiseworthy (e.g., support of others' ideas, coordination of views, reconciliation), and certain forms are patently unacceptable (e.g., grandstanding, creating divisions, negativism toward others' ideas).[14]

Similarly, supportive communication (courteous, trusting, and sympathetic), was found to be linked to group satisfaction with consensus rules.[15] Cooperation,[16] collaboration,[17] and supportive communication,[18] all associated with consensus processes, foreground agreement and unwittingly downplay the important role dissent plays in reaching consensus outcomes.

Christoph Haug refers to the outcome orientation of consensus as mental consensus, in which case the degree of agreement is measured and often aggregated.[19] He claims mental consensus may be achieved "*regardless of how the decision was actually made.* In this view, it is entirely possible that there is a high degree of group consensus on a decision made, for example through majority voting."[20] We see this understanding of consensus in the excerpt—both James and Maggie refer to consensus when it appears that they are actually referring to agreement. James said, "And that's the only thing that I'm saying is that a motion might be giving consensus to something that's really not tied down with consensus that's, 'that's good, move forward.'" In the first use of the word consensus he refers to agreement. In the second use of the word he seems to be referring to consensus as a process.

Big C Consensus: Consensus as Process.   Consensus as a *process* is not the same as agreement, or a consensus outcome. Although agreement has been at the forefront of the literature, scholars recognize the important roles the processes of disagreement (nonconformity), dissent (difference of feelings or thoughts), and contestation (public challenge) play in consensus decision making.[21] Haug refers to several types of communication behaviors associated with consensus processes as interactional consensus and reminds us consensus is "ultimately about creating a situation where opposition is absent."[22] In other words, "Consensus decision making . . . is not about expression of agreement with a particular option, but about the absence of expressions of disagreement."[23] In order to claim opposition does not exist, ethical communication demands we design an interactional context that is transparent and free of hidden power.[24] This is what we refer to as Big C Consensus—consensus that encourages disagreement, allows expressed dissent, and fosters contestation until the group of stakeholders is willing to go forward on a proposal *without opposition*. However, not all communication processes observed in consensus decision-making situations lead to Big C Consensus.

Haug outlines four types of interactional consensus—imposed, acclaimed, basic, and deliberative.[25] In the first three types of interactional consensus, consensus is claimed by a leader (facilitator or chair) and participants have the burden of arguing in opposition to the claim. In *imposed consensus,* the leader leaves no room in the discussion for disagreement—claiming consensus is present and thus requiring and perhaps implying disagreeing participants risk much to express their thoughts because there is no built-in space in the interaction to express dissent. Dissenting stakeholders would have to interrupt the meeting and openly disagree with the leader in order to express their concerns. In *acclaimed consensus,* discussion does leave space for participants to express their views, such as a pause or intentional silence, "but its official purpose is not to express dissent but consent."[26] For example, participants might be asked, "Does everyone agree?" Although a space is present for disagreement, the design of the space and question encourages agreement and discourages dissent. This type of consensus is visible in the description offered by Sherry of pseudo consensus. The third type of interactional consensus, *basic consensus,* explicitly asks participants if there is anyone who disagrees. The leader might ask, "Is there anyone who cannot live with this decision?" or "Anyone against?" Consensus is presumed only after a lengthy pause of silence, which is built into the interaction as the measurement of the presence of opposition. Should no opposition occur, consensus is presumed. All three of these types of interactional consensus fall short of leveling power differentials (one of the cornerstones of a collaborative ethic) because they put the onus of disagreement on participants who may or may not feel they have the influence or ability to disrupt and/or disagree with the proceedings.

The final type of interactional consensus described in Haug's typology reflects the processes of Big C Consensus. *Deliberative consensus* "not only gives participants the opportunity to express dissent, but actively encourages that dissent is articulated in order to make sure that no one is silenced."[27] The purpose of deliberative consensus is to bring forth concerns and objections to a proposal so that they can be integrated into a future consensus decision. In deliberative consensus, integration of dissenting opinions is of greater importance then the speed of decision making. Stakeholders might follow the lead of Alfred Sloan, the Chairman of General Motors, who upon leaving a meeting gave his employees the homework of developing challenges to the relevant proposal that could be discussed in future interactions.[28] Communication processes in deliberative consensus align well with the ethical communication described in chapter 4, in which case stakeholders incorporate (1) reciprocity for expression, (2) some equality in communication skills, (3) setting aside of authority relations, (4) open investigation of stakeholder positions, (5) open sharing of information and transparency of decision processes, and (6) opening of fact and knowledge claims to contestation.[29] These practices lead to consensus building.

> **QUESTION:** Think about the difference between agreement and the absence of disagreement in group decision making. Describe a scenario where the absence of disagreement does not reflect agreement. What might that look like? Sound like? How is acceptance different than agreement in the consensus process?

Laurie Lewis has an extensive history of studying and working with nonprofit organizations. In the scholar spotlight box, she reminds us that collaboration, more often than we think, has to navigate what appear to be insurmountable challenges. She argues we cannot "overstate the critical need" for communication processes that build trust and foster commitment.

SCHOLAR SPOTLIGHT

Collaborating with Frenemies
Laurie Lewis

Collaboration has come to be held as a 'god term' amid associations with positivity; surrendering of self-interests for joint benefit; resolution of negative feelings; and imbued with mutual respect, if not genuine friendship, among partners. However, we often find ourselves in situations where moving forward with a plan, decision, activity, or obtaining a vital resource or desirable outcome requires that we work with others who we may not always like or with whom we have serious disagreement. Sometimes those disagreements are due to personality clashes, past bad behavior, or a sense of being out negotiated or cheated in the past. We sometimes have to make "deals with the devil" or at least with our "frenemies."

The Urban Dictionary defines a "frenemy" as an enemy disguised as a friend. The term can be described as "a relationship that is mutually beneficial or dependent while being competitive, fraught with risk and mistrust." So, how do you collaborate in such a relationship? This problem is further complicated if a collaboration involves several partners, all of whom share some mutual mistrust or past conflict and disappointments.

An important component of collaborative engagement concerns the ways in which partners regard each other. In an earlier review of collaboration literature, it was clear that most definitions of collaboration involve a theme of defining partners in terms of equality or equal footing.[30] Consideration of the standing of the partners in collaboration is a critical part of doing collaboration. Interestingly, some definitions of collaboration involve an assumption that participants start at a point of difference and move closer together. Collaboration is often described as involving reconciling parties' divergent interests or coming together after acknowledging diverse perspectives.

In reality, many collaborative engagements involve participants who have both selfish as well as joint/shared goals, and where initial trust may be quite low. In communities where partners have a previous history and are working in environments with scarce resources, if not competitive circumstances, there are often existing tensions, disparate values and goals, and perceptions of past harm or disappointments. Further, collaborative engagements that involve partners of mixed power (by virtue of status, resources, reputation, or structure) can often involve potential tension and conflict.

So, how can one engage in collaboration with one's frenemies? This strikes me as an essential question to answer given that many, if not most, of the complex and intractable problems in our communities, nation, and world will require "frenemies" if not enemies to engage in collaboration. Much of our theorizing and conceptual work about collaboration seems to me to focus on assumptions of a willingness to engage in good-faith efforts to come together and contribute to a "third way" (rather than rigidly advocate for one's own side or compromise away bits and pieces of what one wants). This is typically described as a creative process that involves a set of communication skills such as integrative behaviors, expression of concern for others, emphasis of joint goals, use of problem-solving structures, conflict resolution skills among others. While positive and certainly possible in some settings, it is less likely and perhaps unrealistic in highly charged contexts with deeply entrenched beliefs and long-held grudges. In such contexts, commitment to the relational maintenance dimensions of collaboration, the time-consuming process of building or reestablishing lost trust, and fostering of commitment to a joint set of goals and singular vision of a future may not be possible—at least in a short-term.

It seems an additional perspective on collaboration is needed to address less than ideal contexts in need of collaborative communication. Such a perspective needs to address negative history, low trust, scarce resources, power differences, and conflicted goals, in a context of crisis, urgency, and high stakes. This "worst

(continued)

case" scenario for collaboration is more common than our literature suggests and is likely the most important one. Examples abound from a local dispute about policing, to our congressional discourses around a plethora of policies and law, to international and interethnic war and hatred. It is hard to overstate the critical need for development of communication tools and approaches that would equip collaborative partners in such circumstances.

Consensus Building as Collaborative Praxis

Consensus processes draw out disagreement and dissent, give voice to the minority viewpoint, and lead to deliberation—combining a number of processes that may or may not result in unanimous agreement but are vital to shared decision making. Together these practices help stakeholder groups build consensus among partners, which in the long run can foster stronger relationships and trust. We believe consensus processes, in part, address that "critical need" to which Lewis refers. Yet, consensus building is still aimed at the absence of disagreement rather than the presence of unanimous agreement. We once interviewed a stakeholder who represented a community college. She explained that the consensus processes they used sometimes meant that stakeholders would choose their battles knowing that they may barter and negotiate to achieve consensus. If something meant more to one of her partners than it did to her, she might back down knowing that she could gain support for the initiatives that meant more to her by supporting her partners now.[31] We point to a few other practices that guide communication regarding consensus building including consensus-decision rules, encouraging lone dissenters, and transparency. Together these practices contribute to communication conventions oriented toward consensus and compose the larger vocabulary of collaborative praxis.

Implement Consensus Decision-Rules

A decision-rule is "a complex, time-consuming social process during which members must reach full agreement prior to coming to a final decision."[32] Decision-rules in the consensus process address how consensus will be determined. They are designed and decided by the stakeholder group; therefore, a set of decision rules that work for one group should not be assumed to work for another. There are, however some general rules regarding consensus that would apply in many different situations. For example, "the rule of non-opposition" is a decision rule that states consensus is not achieved until the group can claim there is no opposition to the proposal.[33] That said, defining non-opposition will require its own decision-rules, such as non-opposition exists after every stakeholder has had a chance to read, question, and reflect on the proposal. Other decision rules may determine if everyone is required to speak before consensus is presumed. Some groups employ consensus cards to determine the degree of support or dissent for a proposal. For example, cards may be red, green, or yellow (indicating dissent, acceptance, or acquiescence, respectively).[34] The meaning of the cards is determined by the group's decision rules. Similar to the ground rules that guide collaborative communication behavior, consensus-decision rules clarify the processes that are acceptable to stakeholders and determine what counts as a consensus decision. In the opening case of the chapter, stakeholders were confused about the process being implemented. James objects, "It looked like you were moving toward a motion." Maggie believes that consensus and moving toward a motion are the same thing. What is lacking is a clear discussion about the rules regarding the group's decision making. When should the group vote on a motion (if ever)? What types of decisions demand consensus? What counts as consensus?

These questions are answered in the collaboration's discussion and consideration of their own decision-making standards. Importantly, consensus decision rules must also be open to scrutiny. Studies have found that groups can focus too rigidly on their rules and that they will sometimes need to revisit those rules. For example, a consensus group in a cohousing community found their rules regarding what counted as a legitimate "block" of the decision needed to be revised.[35] In the same case, the group revisited whether there would be times that, after thoughtful deliberation, they might need to accept a majority vote. They decided that they would accept an 85 percent majority in rare instances, if indeed consensus processes had been enacted but they could not overcome an impasse. Like any process or practice advocated in this text, we claim no panacea for group decision making. Consensus, like any other process, is filled with dialectical tensions. One issue particular to consensus is balancing time for open discussion with the urgent need to make decisions.[36]

Encourage Dissenters

One of the reasons consensus processes are so well-matched to interorganizational collaboration is because of the power of the lone dissenter. Previous studies conducted on Quakers,[37] (who historically practice consensus decision making within their communities),[38] found "lone dissenters can force groups to recognize and consider alternatives that might have never come into discussion had the group acted after reaching a simple majority."[39] Unlike a vote, the lone dissenter has the power not only to block a decision from moving forward but also to influence the thinking of other stakeholders as they are forced to consider the minority viewpoint. Kendal Phillips argues, "Dissent, though motivated by a sense of difference from and resistance to the background consensus, exists ultimately in the service of this consensus."[40] Therefore, consensus prizes dissent and embraces its creative potential by making space for the expression and integration of dissenting viewpoints. In the opening vignette of the last chapter, Metro Collaboration fostered dissent by opening up the conversation regarding preschool fees. Annette's protests began as a lone voice in a quiet room. By encouraging her feedback, more stakeholders were emboldened to share their concerns with the decision to charge for preschool.

Yet enacted dissent is not without consequences.[41] Even when the dissenting position led to more creative outcomes, dissenters are viewed as having created conflict in the group.[42] Another study found that dissent was deemed appropriate by other stakeholders earlier in the process but bred resentment when the group had committed toward a particular decision.[43] This is all the more reason collaborative groups will need to make space for dissent. As Haug's research suggests, deliberative consensus often must be explicitly invited and normalized to the point that the process of dissent can be naturalized and separated from attributing conflict to a specific person. In this way, it is not that Annette (chapter 10) or James (this chapter) are "stirring the pot." Instead, their alternative viewpoints are an expected and valued part of the process. Creating safe conversational spaces and a culture that encourages dissent (chapter 7) in turn may prevent suppressed opposition from surfacing at a later time when the group already thought they had made a decision. Consensus scholarship has also suggested that face-to-face interaction with the dissenters between meetings can also help facilitate consensus in the larger group.[44]

 QUESTION: How might stakeholders encourage dissent in a way that protects dissenters from being blamed for the conflict? What can be done to create a safe space for dissent?

Foster Transparency

Transparency is an important part of leveling power in shared decision-making situations. Johnson and Johnson argue that consensus processes demand public acknowledgement of disagreement.

> When a decision is made by consensus, all members understand the decision and are prepared to support it. That means that all members can rephrase the decision to show that they understand it, that all members have had a chance to tell the group how they feel about the decision, and that those members who continue to disagree or have doubts will nevertheless say publicly that they are willing to give the decision a try for a period of time.[45]

The assumption that disagreements will be made public and acknowledged (giving stakeholders the opportunity to voice their level of support or not) builds transparency, and potentially trust, as a part of consensus processes.

James' protests against moving toward a motion are about more than a preference for consensus versus voting. Metro Collaboration leaders had a history of making decisions outside of the stakeholder group.[46] At the time of Dana's sudden departure from State University, many questions remained about why she was leaving and what effect her departure would have on the collaboration. James protested the idea of leaving that discussion to a subcommittee. He contests the procedure of granting the subcommittee decision-making power around the replacing of a stakeholder when he is not really sure what specific details the subcommittee considered. He is asking for transparency in processes by claiming the group is not ready to give "consensus," meaning agreement, "to something that's not really tied down with consensus," in this case he means a transparent process. James is protesting power.

One of our professors once remarked that any theory taken to the extreme is ludicrous. That notion rings true for any of the theoretical ideas we have presented thus far and underscores the reason we have emphasized praxis over prescription. Consensus decision making, like collaboration, cannot be practiced with rigid loyalty to any single concept or rule. Although transparency is associated with accountability, democracy, and has the potential to level power, it is also laden with dialectic tensions that mean transparency is not simple to implement without unintended consequences.[47] Some organizations must bridle the tension between confidentiality and transparency in the decision-making context. Consider the sensitive work of police officers or human trafficking social workers and lawyers who may not be at liberty to share information openly with a large stakeholder group. Too much emphasis on transparency and open communication can lead to concealment.[48] In such cases, accountability and transparency in decision making may call for more time to be spent on informal communication practices, such as conversations, smaller group discussions, and personal storytelling[49] between stakeholders, as opposed to formal communication with the entire stakeholder group that includes enacting procedures, rules, regulations, and policies and is captured in public documents such as minutes.

Another unintended consequence of increased norms and rules about transparency is that workloads for data and information may or may not be feasible. When transparency is fetishized,[50] groups and organizations sometimes give "obsessive attention to measures and means of transparency themselves."[51] In the case above, Maggie was operating on the assumption that it would be more efficient for a committee to gather the information and work through the details of Dana's departure and subsequent replacement. Therefore, while constructing a transparent decision making-process like consensus decision making can be a powerful method for sharing authority among stakeholders, the contexts of the decision-making situation should dictate the expectations as to what counts as reasonable transparency.

QUESTION: What informal communication could have taken place between Maggie and James to prevent James public protests of the decision-making process? Do you think James protests were appropriate? Why or why not?

Dialogue is the communication foundation of consensus decision making. One consensus scholar argued, "Discussions of value differences are important for all groups, but for consensus groups they are crucial."[52] Gracious contestation and other communication methods for experiencing constructive group conflict, such as informal communication techniques like shuttle diplomacy, can begin to move groups toward consensus. Consensus decision-rules, encouraging dissenters, and transparency are other considerations for how consensus might be achieved in interorganizational collaboration.

CONCLUSION

In the previous chapter, we argued that rethinking conflict as normative and practicing it in a gracious and constructive manner is our best hope for achieving the potential of diversity. This chapter builds on that foundation by providing a better understanding of how to do so. It challenges our lay thinking about consensus decision making and advocates for deliberative, big C-Consensus. Consensus decision-making processes, when practiced in a deliberative format with a focus on process rather than outcome, are well-suited to collaborative decision making because they encourage participation from all stakeholders, developing a collaborative ethic of egalitarianism. Some scholars argue that consensus processes do a better job of promoting the conditions for deliberation than do voting processes.[53] Maggie's assumption that voting is more legitimate than consensus is definitely not the case if disagreements were not aired and stakeholders' positions were not made public. Because interorganizational collaboration arises from a commitment to diversity and the belief that diverse perspectives will lead to innovation and resolution, stakeholders must be prepared for the conflict that accompanies difference. By matching our ethic of egalitarianism and shared power with a decision-making process that fosters participation and transparency, we further develop our fluency in the language of collaborative praxis. The final chapter in this part of the book will explore communication when it is oriented toward solutions and idea generation.

CHAPTER TAKE-AWAYS

- Understand the relationship between constructive conflict and consensus decision making
- Differentiate between consensus decision making as an outcome of agreement and as a process
- Understand the different ways consensus decision making is practiced and why deliberative Consensus suits collaboration
- Discern how commitments to consensus decision rules, lone dissenters, and transparency contribute to consensus decision making

ENDNOTES

1 Edward M. Marshall, "The Collaborative Workplace," *Management Review* 84, no. 6 (June 1, 1995): 13–18; John Charles Morris et al., *The Case for Grassroots Collaboration: Social Capital and Ecosystem Restoration at the Local Level* (Lanham, MD: Lexington Books, 2013).

2 Matthew J. McKinney, "What Do We Mean by Consensus? Some Defining Principles," in *Across the Great Divide: Explorations in Collaborative Conservation and the American West*, ed. Philip Brick, Donald Snow, and Sarah van de Wetering (Washington, DC: Island Press, 2001), 33–40.

3 Judith E. Innes and David E. Booher, "Consensus Building and Complex Adaptive Systems: A Framework for Evaluating Collaborative Planning," *Journal of the American Planning Association* 65, no. 4 (September 1999): 412–27.

4 Renee Guarriello Heath and Patricia M. Sias, "Communicating Spirit in a Collaborative Alliance," *Journal of Applied Communication Research* 27, no. 4 (November 1, 1999): 356–76, doi:10.1080/00909889909365545.

5 Douglas S. Kenney, "Are Community Watershed Groups Effective? Confronting the Thorny Issue of Measuring Success," in *Across the Great Divide: Explorations in Collaborative Conservation and the American West*, 2nd ed., ed. Philip Brick, Donald Snow, and Sarah F. Bates (Washington, DC: Island Press, 2000), 188–93.

6 Christoph Haug, "What Is Consensus and How It Is Achieved in Meetings? Four Types of Consensus Decision Making," in *The Cambridge Handbook of Meeting Science*, ed. Joseph A. Allen, Nale Lehmann-Willenbrock, and Steven G. Rogelberg (New York: Cambridge University Press, 2015), 556–84.

7 Renee Guarriello Heath, Contestation in Community Collaboration: Consensus and the Consequences of a Relationship Emphasis (Western States Communication Association, Boulder, CO, February 2008).

8 See Philippe Urfalino, "La décision par consensus apparent. Nature et propriétés," *Revue européenne des sciences sociales. European Journal of Social Sciences*, no. XLV, 136 (February 1, 2007): 47–70, doi:10.4000/ress.86.

9 Julia T. Wood, "Alternative Methods of Group Decision Making: A Comparative Examination of Consensus, Negotiation, and Voting," in *Emergent Issues in Human Decision Making*, ed. Gerald Phillips and Julia T. Wood (Carbondale: Southern Illinois University Press, 1984), 3–18, p. 5.

10 Irving L. Janis, *Groupthink: Psychological Studies of Policy Decisions and Fiascoes*, 2nd ed. (Boston: Cengage Learning, 1982).

11 Albert V. Carron et al., "Using Consensus as a Criterion for Groupness Implications for the Cohesion–Group Success Relationship," *Small Group Research* 35, no. 4 (August 1, 2004): 466–91, doi:10.1177/1046496404263923; McKinney, "What Do We Mean by Consensus?"; Kevin L. Sager and John Gastil, "The Origins and Consequences of Consensus Decision Making: A Test of the Social Consensus Model," *Southern Communication Journal* 71, no. 1 (April 1, 2006): 1–24, doi:10.1080/10417940500503464.

12 Stanley Deetz and Jennifer Simpson, "Critical Organizational Dialogue," in *Dialogue: Theorizing Difference in Communication Studies*, ed. Rob Anderson, Leslie A. Baxter, and Kenneth N. Cissna (Thousand Oaks, CA: Sage, 2003), 141–58; Seyla Benhabib, *Situating the Self: Gender, Community, and Postmodernism in Contemporary Ethics* (New York: Routledge, 1992).

13 Sager and Gastil, "The Origins and Consequences of Consensus Decision Making."

14 Robert V. Harnack, Thorrel B. Fest, and Barbara Jones, *Group Discussion: Theory and Technique* (Englewood Cliffs, NJ: Prentice-Hall, 1977); R. Likert, *New Patterns of Management* (New York: McGraw-Hill, 1961); Wood, "Alternative Methods of Group Decision Making," p. 5.

15 Kevin L. Sager and John Gastil, "Reaching Consensus on Consensus: A Study of the Relationships between Individual Decision-Making Styles and Use of the Consensus Decision Rule," *Communication Quarterly* 47, no. 1 (January 1, 1999): 67–79, doi:10.1080/01463379909370124.

16 Wood, "Alternative Methods of Group Decision Making."

17 Innes and Booher, "Consensus Building and Complex Adaptive Systems"; McKinney, "What Do We Mean by Consensus?"

18 Sager and Gastil, "The Origins and Consequences of Consensus Decision Making."

19 Haug, "What Is Consensus and How It Is Achieved in Meetings?"

20 Ibid. Emphasis is in the original, p. 8.

21 Distinctions among these words derive from their etymological origins found at http://www.etymonline.com

22 Haug, "What Is Consensus and How It Is Achieved in Meetings?" p. 22.

23 Urfalino, "La décision par consensus apparent. Nature et propriétés," p. 65.

24 Timothy R. Kuhn and Stanley Deetz, "Critical Theory and Corporate Social Responsibility: Can/Should We Get beyond Cynical Reasoning?" in *The Oxford Handbook of Corporate Social Responsibility*, ed. Andrew Crane et al. (New York: Oxford University Press, 2009), 173–96.

25 Haug, "What Is Consensus and How It Is Achieved in Meetings?"

26 Ibid., p. 25.

27 Ibid., p. 28.

28 David H. Johnson and Frank P. Johnson, *Joining Together: Group Theory and Group Skills*, 11th ed. (London: Pearson, 2012), p. 287.

29 Kuhn and Deetz, "Critical Theory and Corporate Social Responsibility."

30 Laurie Lewis, "Collaborative Interaction: Review of Communication Scholarship and a Research Agenda," in *Communication Yearbook 30*, ed. C. Beck (Thousand Oaks, CA: Sage, 2006), 197–247.

31 Heath and Sias, "Communicating Spirit in a Collaborative Alliance."

32 John Gastil, *Democracy in Small Groups: Participation, Decision-Making and Communication* (Philadelphia, PA: New Society Publishers, 1998); Sager and Gastil, "The Origins and Consequences of Consensus Decision Making," p. 3.

33 Philippe Urfalino, "The Rule of Non-Opposition: Opening Up Decision-Making by Consensus," *Journal of Political Philosophy* 22, no. 3 (September 1, 2014): 320–41, doi:10.1111/jopp.12037, p. 321.

34 See Mary Ann Renz, "Paving Consensus: Enacting, Challenging, and Revising the Consensus Process in a Cohousing Community," *Journal of Applied Communication Research* 34, no. 2 (May 1, 2006): 163–90, doi:10.1080/00909880600574088; Mary Ann Renz, "The Meaning of Consensus and Blocking for Cohousing Groups," *Small Group Research* 37, no. 4 (August 1, 2006): 351–76, doi:10.1177/1046496406291184.

35 Renz, "Paving Consensus."

36 Ibid.

37 Michael J. Sheeran, *Beyond Majority Rule: Voteless Decisions in the Religious Society of Friends* (Philadelphia, PA: Philadelphia Yearly Meeting of Religious Society of Friends, 1983).

38 Gastil, *Democracy in Small Groups*.

39 Sager and Gastil, "Reaching Consensus on Consensus," p. 78.

40 Kendall R. Phillips, "The Spaces of Public Dissension: Reconsidering the Public Sphere," *Communication Monographs* 63, no. 3 (September 1, 1996): 231–48, doi:10.1080/03637759609376391, p. 233.

41 John M. Levine, "Reaction to Opinion in Small Groups," in *Psychology of Group Influence*, 2nd ed., ed. Paul B. Paulus (Hilldale, NJ: Psychology Press, 1989), 187–232.

42 Charlan Jeanne Nemeth and Joel Wachtler, "Creative Problem Solving as a Result of Majority vs Minority Influence," *European Journal of Social Psychology* 13, no. 1 (January 1, 1983): 45–55, doi:10.1002/ejsp.2420130103.

43 Renz, "Paving Consensus."

44 Ibid.

45 David H. Johnson and Frank P. Johnson, *Joining Together: Group Theory and Group Skills*, 6th ed. (London: Pearson, 1997), p. 250.

[46] Jessica MacDonald Milam and Renee Guarriello Heath, "Participative Democracy and Voice: Rethinking Community Collaboration Beyond Neutral Structures," *Journal of Applied Communication Research* 42, no. 4 (October 2, 2014): 366–86, doi:10.1080/00909882.2014.911944; Renee Guarriello Heath, "Rethinking Community Collaboration through a Dialogic Lens: Creativity, Democracy, and Diversity in Community Organizing," *Management Communication Quarterly* 21, no. 2 (November 1, 2007): 145–71, doi:10.1177/0893318907306032.

[47] Lars Thøger Christensen and George Cheney, "Peering into Transparency: Challenging Ideals, Proxies, and Organizational Practices," *Communication Theory* 25, no. 1 (February 1, 2015): 70–90, doi:10.1111/comt.12052.

[48] Ibid.

[49] Eric M. Eisenberg, "Ambiguity as Strategy in Organizational Communication," *Communication Monographs* 51, no. 3 (September 1, 1984): 227–42, doi:10.1080/03637758409390197.

[50] Christensen and Cheney, "Peering into Transparency," p. 82.

[51] Ibid., p. 84.

[52] Renz, "Paving Consensus," p. 184.

[53] Sager and Gastil, "The Origins and Consequences of Consensus Decision Making"; Kevin Barge, "Enlarging the Meaning of Group Deliberation: From Discussion to Dialogue," in *New Directions in Group Communication*, ed. Lawrence R. Frey (Thousand Oaks, CA: Sage, 2002), 159–78; Kevin Barge, "Dialogue, Conflict, and Community," in *The Sage Handbook of Conflict Communication: Integrating Theory, Research, and Practice*, ed. John G. Oetzel and Stella Ting-Toomey (Thousand Oaks, CA: Sage, 2006), 517–44; Edna F. Einsiedel and Deborah L. Eastlick, "Consensus Conferences as Deliberative Democracy A Communications Perspective," *Science Communication* 21, no. 4 (June 1, 2000): 323–43, doi:10.1177/1075547000021004001.

12

Communication Oriented toward Solutions

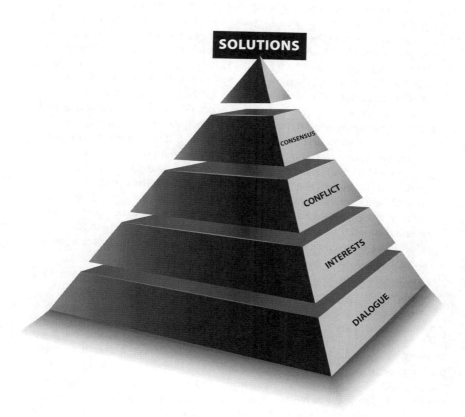

What You See Is What You Get

"What is one thing we are doing well?"

That was the question to the group and for a minute the people in the room just stared blankly at each other. One thing we do well?

This question had turned the whole idea of why we were all here together and pointed us in a different direction. We were at a planning day with various state-level and nonprofit employees all working on nutrition and family services in the state of Texas. While many people arrived assuming this would just be another, "What is missing?" and "Why aren't we doing it?" as soon as this question was asked, you could tell that the room's energy changed. Smiles started to break out on peoples' faces. There was a buzz that seemed to swell in the room. After a brief pause to consider the question people, started pouring out examples. It was as if a barrier had broken away, and people were finally allowed to talk about the parts of their jobs they enjoyed.

Over the course of the rest of that half-day meeting, people were encouraged to tell stories about what they did well, to share those stories in small groups, and to enjoy the positivity that those conversations created within the group. After lunch another wrinkle in the day was introduced when we rolled out a large piece of paper on the floor. The paper was easily five feet wide by fifty feet long. When the employees came back from lunch, we asked them to think about what they had talked about prior to lunch.

"Now imagine we are river and that all of your stories feed into that river and at the river's terminus we achieve the vision we have for our work together."

Again our prompt was met with blank stares. But slowly, one by one, people started grabbing coloring pencils, crayons, and markers. A group of people drew a long river down the center of the paper and put the vision as the opening of the river to the sea. People started putting their positive strengths and stories as tributaries to the river. At the end of the drawing we had a mural of who we were together, what we brought to our vision, and we could see all the other strengths that led into our river and out to the vision. From there, we just had to start using what worked to create a better future than we could ever have achieved individually.

—Matt's field notes on an appreciative experience with the WIC Program

Given that a primary reason people collaborate is for the purpose of arriving at a solution and/or innovation that advances a vision or solves a problem, you might be wondering why we place solution-oriented communication in our model as the small, top of the pyramid as opposed to the base. Indeed, we advocate a solution orientation only after stakeholders in the collaboration have already demonstrated a strong praxis of collaborative communication grounded in the other orientations. Some groups may already be very skilled in collaborative praxis and may move very quickly to solutions. Others may need more time to build a communicative foundation—getting to know and understand one another then prioritizing group interests and values before directing resources toward solutions. The point is not how fast groups move toward solutions but whether or not they skipped important communicative steps. This chapter addresses the processes and talk geared toward solution and idea generation—determining what the collaboration wants to do (i.e., what are our strategies and tactics for addressing the problem domain?). Communication behavior at this stage in collaborating is task-oriented and geared generally toward strategic planning (i.e., what are our goals and measurable objectives?). Our communication praxis model depicts visioning around group values (i.e., shared values list, chapter 9) before visioning around tasks. As we have repeated multiple times, however, collaboration is not a linear process but a contingent one. Collaborative groups may find themselves revisiting their values and interests as their focus shifts and they accomplish goals and projects. We believe the key to movement through different stages of collaboration is mastering communication that comprises the language of collaborative praxis.

The remainder of this chapter asserts that solution-oriented communication emerges most successfully when grounded in the other orientations of communication—dialogue, interests, conflict, and consensus—that compose collaborative praxis. We begin with a discussion of why stakeholders will want to hold off on solution-talk until they have mastered the foundational components of a language of collaborative praxis. Next, we introduce a transformative process, appreciative inquiry, that purposely avoids the problem-solution framing of accomplishing shared visions as a viable methodology for interorganizational collaboration. Appreciative inquiry honors the cornerstone ethical assumptions that underlay collaborative praxis. The final part of the chapter touches on general guidelines for brainstorming as a method that most groups utilize in some form or another as they move toward operationalizing their shared vision.

The Problem with Shortcutting to Solutions

Groups that shortcut to solutions—that is, make decisions without an understanding of stakeholders' interests and values—run the risk of having their solutions viewed as *compromise* (a lose-lose model of conflict resolution)[1] by some members because the solutions fail to meet the collective values of the group or because the collective values were not articulated. An interpersonal example illustrates the problem with shortcutting to solutions. Kate is a senior in college who wants to spend her spring break in Mexico with her closest friends. Kate's mom is adamant that Kate not go. Kate and her mom compromise; she can go as long as she calls her mother every single morning so that her mom knows she is safe—and if she picks up the cell phone no matter what time her mother calls.

Without a discussion about the interests and values driving each person's position, the solution is vulnerable, teetering on an unstable pyramid of assumptions regarding what motivates their positions. Kate might view her mother as not trusting her and ultimately resent the fact that she has to "check in" every day, even though she is a legal adult.

If Kate and her mother spend some time exploring the interests driving their preferred solutions and integrating each other's interests into their plan, their shared solution is less likely to be seen as a compromise. For example, Kate could learn through dialogue and interest-oriented talk that it's not that her mother does not trust her, but that she is very worried for her daughter's safety. In other words, her mother's interests do not come from a place of control but from a place of security. Such a discussion would allow Kate to reframe her thinking around the solution of calling every morning as a small act that she can do to assure her mother she is safe. On the other hand, through discussion, Kate's mother may come to understand her daughter's natural interest in exerting control over her own life. She may see that requiring her daughter to be accessible by phone every minute of the day violates this important value of Kate's. The solution to this dilemma in the end may be similar to the one they decided on initially with very important differences. Each believes their values are being met, and *because they value the other's interests too, they no longer feel like they are compromising.* They have integrated one another's interests into a solution that will not breed resentment, regret, or possibly sabotage. They have a solution that strengthens their relationship over time because it is grounded in understanding and acknowledgement fostered by a solid base built on the communication orientations of collaborative praxis.

The hope for collaboration is to integrate one another's interests into solutions that will strengthen relationships, foster understanding, and cultivate trust. Our interpersonal example is not nearly as complicated as interorganizational collaborative solutions will be, but the same principles apply. Imagine that a community is working on its relationships between those suffering from mental illness and the police department. Should the group shortcut to solutions and decide the answer is in sensitivity training for the police, it is likely the police will resent the implication that the solution involves "fixing them." They may oppose the solution or half-heartedly implement it. Some may view it as an empty "public relations" tactic. However, the police department may be very amenable to agreeing, and perhaps even helping to design, a sensitivity training if they had the opportunity to listen to stories that explain some of the experiences community members with mental illness have had in their encounters with the police. With this broader understanding, the stakeholders from the police department will work with mental health advocates in their community to determine their shared values. With joint ownership of the group's shared values, the police department is more likely to support solutions that are in line with those values. As such they can reframe the solution of training from "fixing the police department" to seeing it as one mechanism toward accomplishing their shared vision of better community-police relationships.

You may still be wondering, if the solutions arrived at through dialogue, constructive conflict, and consensus around values and interests may end up being similar to solutions that are generated without those labor-intensive processes. Isn't it more efficient to just skip to the solution part of collaboration? While collaborative groups might think they are being efficient in the short run, shortcutting to solutions will likely unravel because the solutions are disconnected from *shared* values. In the long run, groups are likely to recycle through the same arguments and debates and may ultimately be less committed to implementing solutions. Our communication model takes into account the need to build trust and to develop strong relationships among stakeholders, increasing the likelihood that solutions will be implemented and have enduring results. Solutions that do not honor the individual and shared interests of the group are untethered to a foundation of understanding and prioritizing; they are therefore less likely to galvanize stakeholder action and accountability. Having positioned solutions as a particular type of talk that should follow dialogue, constructive conflict, and consensus around values and interests, we next introduce an all-inclusive process that shares this book's basic cornerstone ethical assumptions, appreciative inquiry.

Appreciative Inquiry

A radical process that can be used to move groups toward innovation is found in appreciative inquiry (AI).[2] In the chapter on dialogue, we mentioned the power of appreciation as a mechanism for listening and understanding. AI approaches an area of interest from a different lens. Instead of using a problem-solution structure that roots out what is wrong and needs to be fixed, AI takes for granted that all organizations and communities have successes and processes they do well. These strengths can be the starting point for change that value the collective and the will of the collaboration.[3] Instead of paying attention to a problem and thus highlighting it, AI focuses on what works, assuming that an organization (or a collaboration) is "a solution to be embraced."[4] As creators David Cooperrider and Suresh Srivastva argue, AI's purpose is to gain "knowledge to promote egalitarian dialogue leading to social-system effectiveness and integrity,"[5] making it a well-suited communication methodology for uncovering solutions in interorganizational collaboration. This positive shift in thinking as a driver of solutions and innovation is visible in the case that opens this chapter. Many of us arrive at strategic planning meetings expecting to focus on problems, so much so that encountering this positive shift in thinking feels unfamiliar at first—"blank stares" as Matt recalled. But as Matt experienced, a focus on things that work can ultimately be liberating for groups.

Our purpose for introducing AI in this text is to enhance a language of collaborative praxis: First, we believe the principles and assumptions of AI compose an *appreciative ethic,* which is complementary to the communication orientations presented thus far and can be practiced throughout collaboration at every stage. This ethic is vital to understanding those who hold different perspectives; it directs us toward each other's strengths and contributions. It reminds us of the power of our language and questions as we move toward resolutions. An ethic of AI constitutes a worldview for how to approach others. Second, the well-developed *methodology* of AI and its four stages—discovery, dreaming, design, and destiny (4-D Cycle)—can be used as a facilitation tool to move groups toward tangible innovations that are rooted in past successes.[6] After introducing AI principles and explaining how they relate to collaborative praxis, we will briefly explore the 4-D methodology, highlighting communication techniques that can be used to help stakeholders innovate toward their shared vision.

Appreciative inquiry is a mode of discovery that fosters innovation in a group. Cooperrider and Diana Whitney emphasize that a focus on value is the first part of adopting an ethic of AI. "Valuing [is] the act of recognizing the best in people or the world around us; affirming past and present strengths, successes, and potential; to perceive those things that give life (health, vitality, excellence to living systems)."[7] Cooperrider and Whitney further define valuing as prizing, esteeming, and honoring. We believe this inspires a fundamental shift in thinking as stakeholders encounter those who hold different perspectives than themselves. The act of valuing is very different than the act of "tolerating"—language that is commonly associated with encountering diversity. Tolerating has etymological roots dating back to European religious freedom in the sixteenth and seventeenth centuries. The derivation is from Latin, meaning "bearing, supporting, enduring," as well as, "to sustain, support, suffer."[8] Whereas valuing calls for honoring and affirming, and adding value, tolerating suggests we are sacrificing something as we endure or suffer. Appreciating is a decidedly different lens from which to see the other.

The second profound shift generated by an AI perspective is the reverence granted to questioning. AI questions can be transformative as they turn the focus of groups toward what works. The core of an AI ethic can be further understood by considering its five theoretical principles: constructionist, simultaneity, poetic, anticipatory, and positive.[9]

The *constructionist principle* is the basis for AI and understanding how our realities are created. Rooted in the power of interaction, the constructionist principle articulates how the relationships we have with others create our sense of what *is*—what is true.[10] Consequently, we must master the ability to listen and interpret organizations as living entities evolving through our interactions with one another. In doing so, we come to see

> ## Core Theoretical Principles of Appreciative Inquiry
> - Constructionist principle: understanding organizing as living, human constructions
> - Simultaneity principle: inquiry and change are not necessarily separate activities
> - Poetic principle: (collaborative) organizing as a coauthored book to be studied
> - Anticipatory principle: images of the future guide our present behavior
> - Positive principle: affirmative language begets positivity

that questioning is just a part of the evolution of the organization and that AI is a generative process of moving forward the best parts of the organization's realities through our communal knowledge of what works.

The *simultaneity principle* builds on the generative nature of AI by emphasizing that there is no difference between questioning and change; in doing one, you are already creating the other.[11] As we question and communicate, we are already discovering and thinking about a future different than our current vision. Simultaneity focuses us on the importance of the question and the effect the question has on the respondent and the person asking the question. Crafting the question becomes just as important as the answer. Questions become part of the change, and asking questions that get to the strengths of the individuals (and thus the organization) allows for visions based on the positive core of what we can do together.

The third principle, *poetic*, posits that our organizational scripts are constantly being "coauthored" and rewritten.[12] As the question is also part of the change, our pasts, presents, and futures are a constant source of information and inspiration. Highlighting this ever-present source of knowledge reminds AI participants that all parts of our lives can be explored for positive growth and strengths. The poetic principle encourages us to seek new ways of understanding continually and to avoid recreating what we already know. Inquiry should be about moving forward, not reaffirming the present or past; otherwise, growth can be stunted.

The fourth principle of AI, the *anticipatory principle,* emphasizes that taking a positive look forward helps create positive action toward that future.[13] The principle could also be labeled the self-fulfilling prophesy; it is an important part of AI interventions. When we think about change and creating a joint vision for what we can do collectively, the basis of that dreaming needs to be positive. Why envision a negative scenario when envisioning positive results sets the tone and action for a road map to success?

The *positive principle* is the fifth and final theoretical principle. Affirmative language begets positivity. Thus, stakeholders in collaboration are encouraged to talk openly about what excites them or brings them hope. This type of communication builds camaraderie. When we ask questions, we need to craft those questions to elicit strengths and positive thinking.

Hope and relationship building are important elements in successfully implementing AI in collaboration. They help create solutions for which all members will feel the pride of accomplishment.

Eight basic assumptions of AI are derived from these five principles.

1. In every organization [or community] something works.
2. What we focus on becomes our reality.
3. Reality is created in the moment, and there are multiple realities.
4. The act of asking questions of an organization influences the group in some way.
5. People have more confidence and comfort in their journey to the future (unknown) when they carry forward parts of the past (known).
6. If we carry parts of the past forward, they should be what is best about the past.
7. It is important to value difference.
8. The language we use creates our realities.[14]

Consider how the five principles inform collaborative practice. For example, a collaboration focused on the health of a local watershed could take a more traditional approach to solution generation by first focusing on defining the problem—pollution and the unhealthy state of the watershed. If the stakeholders were to instead take an AI approach to generating solutions, they would begin with different assumptions and thus a different set of questions. They would start by considering what makes the watershed (and perhaps other watersheds) healthy? The language frame is positive and begins to focus the group on success. With the AI approach, the group would ask questions that build upon best practices when it comes to watershed restoration. The solutions around which they coalesce as a group would eventually grow out of a methodological process of collecting ideas that have already been known to work but are not yet systemically applied. As the group continues to focus on the things that work in their community and in other locations, they begin to build a hopeful dream for watershed restoration that is grounded in concrete experience. AI questions move the group forward toward invention rather than backward in dissecting problems.

QUESTION: How can you adopt an AI ethic in your personal and professional experience? Do some of your relationships fall in the category where you can only see what is wrong rather than what works well? How could you alter your frame for thinking about those relationships or experiences to one that focuses on the positive things that work well?

APPLICATION: Take an appreciative frame to your most challenging relationships for a couple of days. Shift your thinking from tolerating to appreciating. You may be surprised by the results.

Innovating as Collaborative Praxis

This section will explore how AI can be implemented as a part of our collaborative praxis. The section concludes with a review of the well-known method of brainstorming. This tool may be included as a part of AI, or it can be a stand-alone method for generating solutions.

Appreciative Inquiry as Methodology

Earlier we mentioned the 4-D process of AI.[15] The AI *methodology* is a specific cycle that can move groups toward idea generation and planning. In this section, we expand the discussion of discovery, dreaming, designing, and destiny to decrease ambiguity about the stages of AI and to help you visualize how a collaborative group might utilize the process. After discussing the stages of the process, we will consider the challenges of adopting a strict AI methodology before offering an example of an AI process that loosely followed the methodology. AI can be useful even if not strictly applied in community decision making.

Discovery. The discovery phase of AI is about crafting positive questions that can get to the strengths of the group or community—*the best of what is.*[16] Always rooted in the positive core elements of the collaboration, the discovery phase is an in-depth data-collection moment for the collaboration to uncover strengths and ideas already working. The discovery phase frames the future in a positive context—in contrast to a deficit reduction conceptualization that is an issue with the problem/solution format. This phase seeds participants' excitement about what is to come as members of the collaboration begin to share stories and craft a future that is rooted in previous successes. The discovery phase is the jumping off point for the entire AI process; it is imperative that everyone participating is actively listening to each other and that data are recorded as accurately as possible. One of the most powerful communicative practices associated with the discovery phase is the appreciative interview. Appreciative interviews could be used in strict fidelity with the AI methodology, or they could be a practice adopted by any collaboration that is interested in generating solutions rooted in each other's experience.

The appreciative interview is based on the idea that our questions will evoke the positives that take place within the domain of the collaboration, leading to positive actions. This is why creating questions that have a positive bias are so important. Depending on the size of the collaboration, stakeholders can interview one another or choose to engage constituents from their respective communities. Some guidelines for producing appropriate appreciative questions include: invite participants to use storytelling and narratives; phrase in rapport talk, not report talk; allow ambiguity; value what is; help people locate experiences worth valuing; convey unconditional positive regard; evoke essential values, aspirations, and inspirations.[17] The questions should help the participants tell a narrative story. These questions also give the interviewer the ability to probe the narrative and the respondent to go further and connect their past experiences with the future topics and vision of the collaboration. Soon after completing appreciative interviews, stakeholders will need to make sense of what they heard and the data they collected; the interviews launch the next phase of the process, dreaming.

> **APPLICATION:** As a group, take a "problem" that you see in your community or university community—for example, you may think your university lacks diversity. Think of ways to rephrase the problem so that you can generate ideas for what *is* working rather than what is *not* working regarding the problem. Write as many positive-oriented questions as possible. Now construct an interview questionnaire that you can take to other people in the community that will elicit positive stories and examples about what is already working toward strengthening campus diversity.

Dream. When we teach public speaking in the basic communication course, one of the speaking patterns we discuss is Monroe's Motivated Sequence. One of the reasons it has been found to be such a successful pattern for speaking is that it adds a "vision" step where the orator asks the audience to envision the future. The dreaming part of the AI process uses a similar idea to get the group members to start thinking forward based on the stories and narratives told in the appreciative interview. As with Monroe's sequence, when we start to see ourselves doing something in the future, we find that we start naturally moving in that direction.

In the dreaming phase, we are asked to talk about *what might be* in terms of what can be done in the organization and the world.[18] While we are dreaming, the goal is to take the positive parts of the collaborative core discussed in the discovery phase and start bringing those aspects forward when talking about the future. The dreaming phase is both practically grounded and a generative process of building on the skills and strengths of each other moving forward.[19] The two main goals in this part of the AI process are to: (1) get people talking in the larger group, retelling some of their stories from appreciative interviews, and (2) to allow everyone in the group to start processing the common themes of each other's stories. By accomplishing these two goals, the stakeholders are sharing their own skills and experiences while also anchoring them in the topics and joint vision of the collaboration. This creates an energy and collective identity that points toward the future and what can be done.

Experts recommend that whenever possible dreaming should start soon after the discovery phase.[20] At this time, stories are fresh in people's minds, and stakeholders are less likely to forget or edit those stories. As part of the methodology, dreaming is formally facilitated with all of the relevant stakeholders, sometimes in the forum of what is called an AI Summit.[21] Individual stories should be retold to the larger group to build bonds between the collaboration members. Creativity helps stakeholders explore the collective dreams of the group.[22] Groups may choose to draw aspiration trees that grow toward topics and future visions, or they may draw a river of discovery that places emerging themes along a river that terminates at the sea of accomplishment, such as the river drawn in the case that opens this chapter. These creative exercises stimulate people's thought processes in different and important ways. When the dreaming is done, the larger dream narrative is composed for the group (AI avoids using the word "report" to encourage sharing rich data in a narrative format). Common themes and ideas expressed by everyone during the dream dialogue are made more explicit. The result of dreaming is that ideas and stories about the future of the collaboration are all based on the history of stakeholders' previous successes. Collaboration members will find "there is no question as to whether the new vision is achievable; the participants have already demonstrated their desire, willingness, and ability to make it possible.[23]

Figure 12.1   Drawing change

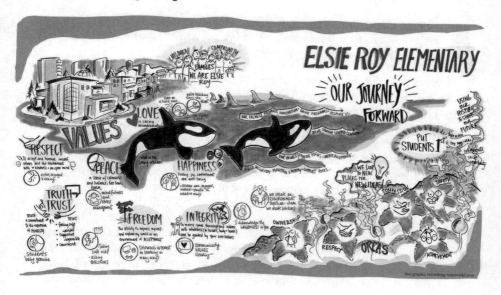

> **APPLICATION:** After collecting stories from the interview phase of your project, begin dreaming together. What themes do these stories elicit? What dreams for your community/university as a whole can you imagine based on the stories you heard? Depict these visually to your group.

Design.   The main process in the design phase is the writing of *provocative propositions*. These propositions (written in the present tense) guide the group to consider *what should be*.[24] The purpose of this crafting process is to keep the best practices at the forefront as stakeholders seek to deliver what they envision. Provocative propositions (a) represent the best examples from the appreciative interviews, (b) are determined by what made that the best (i.e., the skills/people/values surrounding the example), (c) take examples and envision what might be in bold terms, and finally (d) are written describing a future as if it is already happening.[25] The core of the proposition is rooted in what has worked in the past and the positive ideals of the future, creating the bridge between discovery and dreaming. For example, if your campus is working on strengthening diversity, you might have a proposition that says, "Every student on our campus builds strong mentor relationships with students with whom they share common experiences." This statement could have easily been elicited from appreciative interviews based on stories of mentor relationships happening among some students but perhaps not all students. The stories of the best of what is are combined with a vision for the future and described in provocative propositions.

APPLICATION: Write provocative propositions that weave together the best practices from your appreciative interviews with the dreams your group has for strengthening diversity on campus.

Destiny.   The final phase of the AI methodology, destiny, calls for formalizing the momentum gained in the first three phases of the cycle.[26] This phase is different for every group and is about mobilizing and supporting the outcomes of the design phase. For most, this is the build-out and infrastructure part of the process. At this point, stakeholders have the positive strengths of each individual, collected into a positive core of the collaboration (discovery). They have directed those strengths toward a collective dream and have created present-tense provocative propositions that boldly state what they can do, should do, and will do. To achieve destiny (or what some call the delivery or doing phase)[27] stakeholders take each one of the propositions and ask the group, "What is required to be doing this right now?" Participants begin detailing the microlists that make the propositions possible. This time-consuming part of the process builds a road map of ideas to achieve the shared vision the entire group created.

APPLICATION: Take one or two of your provocative statements and articulate a plan to operationalize (put into operation) your vision for diversity at your university.

Our final spotlight scholar is prolific AI author and consultant, Diana Whitney. She reflects on her journey with the method, its generative principles, and the implications it has for interorganizational collaboration.

Scholar Spotlight

Lessons from an AI Expert
Diana Whitney

For the past forty years, the fields of organization development and leadership have been my fields of experimentation, service, and cocreation. Since reading Peter Berger and Thomas Luckmann's provocative treatise *The Social Construction of Reality*[28] in the early 1970s I have sought to understand and work from a social constructionist stance. Writings in systems theory,[29] family therapy,[30] and religion[31] helped to dislodge my thinking from scientific materialism—the search for "one right way" and move it toward inclusive, cocreative practices. Over the years, I have applied social constructionist, communication theory to personal, group, and organizational level challenges such as leadership development, team building, organization-wide culture transformation and the design of numerous international organizations including the United Religions Initiative.

My purpose in writing this essay is to share some of what I have learned along the way. First and foremost, recognizing that clients, leaders, and people throughout an organization always have stories about what is happening and why, I have learned that no matter what the story, "The answer is always communication!" For example, one executive client shared a story of great frustration. Repeatedly he asked his leadership team to cut costs, repeatedly they agreed, and repeatedly nothing changed. No matter how serious the story was, nothing changed until we began talking to people in the manufacturing plants and heard their stories. Yes, they knew of leadership's desire to cut costs and surprisingly, they were willing to do so, but they could not comply because they had no information about how much anything—equipment, materials, or staff—cost. Once a dialogue about the costs of doing business was opened up and financial information became accessible, ideas for cutting costs easily emerged and were carried out. In this case, changing the story from, "people won't cut costs" to "collaborative dialogue about costs and inquiry into how to save money" made a difference in both employee satisfaction and financial results.

As this example illustrates a second lesson is, "There are always multiple versions of the same story." To be effective, that is to achieve personal and/or organizational goals, one needs to seek out and hear multiple stories until the "polyphonic whole" story is revealed. Working organizationally this means seeking out the ideas, opinions, and stories from all levels and all functions of the organization and its relevant stakeholders. This can be done in a number of ways: one on one interviews conducted by consultant/researchers; appreciative interviews among organization members; small group dialogues within departments or across department lines; or whole system processes such as an appreciative inquiry summit. Whatever the process used, the intent is not to reach agreement.

(continued)

It is to strengthen relationships among people involved, to ensure that people have an opportunity to tell their story and feel heard, and to make the polyphonic whole story apparent to people involved. This means showing and accepting agreements and differences of opinion and wondering together how to go forward, together.

A third, and perhaps most powerful lesson is, "Don't talk about me without me." As I write this essay, we are in the midst of a global transformation. Around the world, in all sorts of organizations—communities, businesses, governments, health care, and education—people are demanding to be heard. The move away from paternalistic, hierarchical, bureaucratic structures toward collaborative, participatory networks is well underway. The old paradigm of some of the people, leaders, professionals, parents and/or educators making decisions and designing life for all of the people has outlived its vitality. New paradigm organizations are bold experiments in full inclusion, high diversity engagement, participation, and collaboration. This means that no one can rightfully speak for another as if they know what is best for the other without engaging with the other in dialogue and cocreation. In this age of collaboration, everyone is the expert of our own experiences, hopes, and dreams. We are all coauthors of our own realities, relationships, and results. In my book with Amanda Trosten-Bloom, *The Power of Appreciative Inquiry: A Practical Guide to Positive Change*[32] we write about how to engage all the stakeholders in a process of organizational change. In *Appreciative Leadership: Focus on What Works to Drive Winning Performance and Build a Thriving Organization*[33] I write about ways that leadership can include "all the people whose future it is."

Consider this small and yet meaningful example. I was invited by the director to work with a small-town family medicine clinic whose staff was expressing frustration over a number of issues related to their facilities. When we discussed who would be involved in the series of meetings our list included all stakeholders: all medical and administrative staff, patients, and to everyone's surprise janitorial and maintenance staff. Everyone was invited and they made arrangements to cover for each other so everyone could attend at least one of the four scheduled meetings. Much was accomplished including a decision to implement a new schedule and the design of new clinic administrative procedures. What made everyone the happiest, however, was the plan for two clinic wide Saturday workdays to paint the clinic and plant flowers in the front yard. The maintenance staff did not have sufficient time or people so it was decided that everyone who wanted to help would pitch in. It became a sign of change, everyone signed up and helped paint away the old frustrations! All stakeholders—patients, staff, and leadership—had a voice and a hand in creating the changes. And, as a result, they all felt proud to be part of the renewed clinic.

A fourth lesson is, "The more positive and life affirming the topic of conversation and inquiry, the more positive and life affirming are the relationships and results that occur." Topics of conversation can sink people and organizations. They can create downward spirals of energy, frustration, and dissatisfaction or they can create upward spirals of courage, hope, and inspired action. In the case of the family medicine clinic, conversations, attitudes and relationships were spiraling downward before the series of Appreciative Inquiry meetings. People were regularly complaining about their working conditions, and their attitudes were influencing patients. It was becoming increasingly hard to maintain younger medical staff who wanted to work hard but on a different schedule. Complaints bred complaints and lead to a dysfunctional organizational culture where the way to be accepted was to complain. Changing the conversation changes the organization. The four meetings held for members of the clinic were designed to follow the Appreciative Inquiry 4-D process: Discovery of what works well; Dreaming of what is possible; Designing what is wanted; and Doing what is wanted to realize the dreams. By changing the conversations among organizational stakeholders from "what's wrong around here" to "what works well and what we want more of" we changed the organization's culture, performance, and results.

It is important to remember that by analyzing problems, where they happen, what causes them, and what they in turn cause, we become wise in problems. By asking questions such as what works well around here, why does it work so well, how can we do more of this, what else do we want to work as well, etc., we learn and become wise in how to succeed. Don't waste your time or energy on complaints, problems, or conversations about why something can't be done. Whatever your wildest dreams, find people who do them well. Study their patterns: what, where, why, when, and with whom they do what they do. In the process, you will learn how to realize your wildest dreams. This applies to people, relationships, groups, and organizations.

In summary, the main ideas of this essay are:

1. all work and life accomplishments get cocreated though human communication;

2. whatever the situation, there are always multiple stories about it, and to understand a situation we must seek out and hear as many different stories as it takes to get a sense of the whole;

3. the best people to tell their stories are the people whose stories they are. Sincere, collaboration and cocreation is an invitation to include all the people whose future it is;

4. what we talk about and are curious about matters.

Appreciative, life-affirming conversations bring out the best of people, lead to high performance, and foster organizational excellence.

Considerations of Appreciative Inquiry

AI as a methodology calls for a very specific commitment to positive language regarding change. As such, collaborative stakeholders must consider how this approach might work based on a number of contingencies, which include: the level of skilled facilitation at their disposal; the history of stakeholder partner relationships; and the conflict that may already exist among participants. As with all communicative processes, we do not offer a panacea or prescription for working toward solutions. Appreciative Inquiry is just one technique for generating actionable ideas, and it is sometimes critiqued for its emphasis on the positive. For example, an AI project conducted across the city of Cupertino (California) focused on "cultural richness" but was critiqued for brushing over deep problems of racial prejudice and discrimination that existed in the city.[34] In another case study, AI practitioners encountered what they refer to as a "shadow"—when organizational members, who did not feel they could speak freely, rejected focusing on "strengths."[35] Rather than dismiss the process outright, these skilled consultants drew upon the theoretical assumptions of AI to address the concerns of the organizational members. They asked affirming questions (such as, "When do you feel the freest to offer opposing opinions?") to craft a process that would feel authentic to those involved.[36] At first glance, it might appear that the AI process was hijacked with concerns and problems, but the authors remind us that positivity is just one of five principles of AI that can be used to move groups toward innovation.

Another consideration regarding adapting the AI methodology is the need to tailor the inquiry to the interorganizational context. AI as an approach has been very successful as an organizational development tool. For example, employees at British Airways used AI to build a vision for the organization out of their best customer service experiences.[37] It also has a successful history in interorganizational contexts. For example, a partnership among Pennsylvania community hospitals and medical centers effectively implemented AI to spark cultural change within the hospitals and local industry.[38] However, in interorganizational collaboration, organizations are likely to have disparate experiences in the domain they are trying to affect. It may be hard to identify what works if the collaborative members have not ever explored what they can do together. Appreciative questions will thus need to be designed to fit the interorganizational collaboration context. The most powerful parts of AI—its principles and assumptions—can be applied in interorganizational collaboration, but it may look different than the process described above as it plays out, as in the text box case below.

The case shared by Paul Harris (see text box) tells the story of a collaborative community effort that *adopted* an appreciative ethic in its approach to community visioning, and *adapted* the AI methodology to fit its needs. Mr. Harris, a developer and city councilor in Red Deer, Canada, narrates the story of The Red Deer Culture Vision, which engaged AI processes to accomplish city planning with multiple stakeholders.

The Red Deer process demonstrates how effective AI can be in moving toward creative and innovative ideas for a community. Paul's story illustrates that AI processes are successful in creating a strategic plan; it also illustrates how the process positively affected and inspired the community, built trust, and fed other tangible plans. The Red Deer facilitators utilized the principles and methods of AI as they best fit their community needs.

The Red Deer Culture Vision

In 2007 the City of Red Deer put out a request for proposal (RFP) to update their Culture Master Plan that was first undertaken in 2000. I had been the chair of the committee that wrote that original plan and participated in the many community discussions that formed the early direction of cultural development. Our proposal was based on Appreciative Inquiry—to allow citizens to tell their stories of deep cultural experience and community identity. It is an approach radically different from the first plan. It invites broad community conversation. Appreciative practice led us to an understanding that the questions we asked needed to be based on the community's values and identity. Our inquiry invited people to share their life experiences about what arts and culture had meant to them and how it had touched their lives in inspirational and positive ways.

In conjunction with the staff from Cultural Service, we first established a small working group. We were careful not to set the committee up as an authority but rather as a guide for the process of inquiry.

Early in the process we renamed the work resulting from the inquiries "Community Culture Vision" from "Culture Master Plan," both to reflect the significant nature and ownership of the document and also to put it into context as a guiding document for future work (and not within a slave-master relationship). Culture is emergent. We wanted the document itself to begin to set the tone as a guide to an emergent community process, not a ready-set solution that becomes inaccessible and all-knowing. We wanted the words we used to create the future that the community might invite. This was one of the early choices that the committee made that made a difference in the way that the community would work in the future and how they thought about the present. It is paramount that the community itself feels ownership and pride in the final rendering.

Imagine this process as iterative in nature, perhaps as a spiral beginning from the center, bringing new people as we proceeded along the journey. We worked to help select a group of representatives of the community to form our working group. Our goal as facilitators was to begin the journey together with a small circle of people, help them experience the process of Appreciative Inquiry, and then expand the circle to include more and more of the community. We wanted to move toward a gathering that invited the whole community.

It was important that the working group not only understood AI from an academic sense but that they also experienced it in action. We used a series of questions that invited them to participate in an appreciative and positive way. The first question was about their life's "high point experience." The group became fully engaged with one another. The next questions were about cultural experiences. We wanted to tease out stories from their lives about when arts and culture had a profound influence on them to help us understand how culture enhanced their lives. We were quite interested in learning where, how, and when these experiences became memorable, so that we might be able to think about how Red Deer could evolve in a way that offers more of these life-giving cultural experiences.

The session with the working group was eye opening. So powerful was the experience that some of the participants went home to interview their friends and family so they could share the experience of deep exploration of the life-giving stories. This is the start of the discovery process. It deeply connected the

(continued)

group, and they understood one another's hearts and minds much better. They formed real bonds and began to understand one another's perspectives and life experiences in a much more substantial way. The beautiful thing about working with a small group to start is that they developed relationships that were needed to support the whole community through the engagement process.

Once the group felt like they were comfortable with the appreciative interview process, we worked together to invite the whole community to take the next step in the discovery phase. We held a community summit for envisioning the future of arts and culture in Red Deer, which attracted about 35 enthusiastic and engaged people, and made for a wonderful day of inquiry.

Our team believes in dialogue—that every conversation changes the future in some way. Or as they say in Appreciative Inquiry, "we move in the direction of that into which we inquire." In our experience, the dream phase of the process cannot be separated from the discovery, design, or delivery phases. As we shared our experiences of the past, we began to dream about the future and indeed set it on a different course.

We gathered rich and aspirational stories and ideas from the people that day, but we recognized that more would be better. The working group met and decided to continue with interviewing people in the community one-on-one. We translated our interview questions into Spanish as well. With the work group and others that joined the conversation, we conducted another 200 interviews in the community. The stories and insights we gathered were remarkable and added richness and depth to the picture that was starting to emerge in the conversations.

After we felt like we had gathered sufficient material to form some early conclusions, we combed through it looking for themes underlying the stories. As facilitators, we discussed what we were experiencing, and we believed we saw four common values and five themes emerging in the stories. We presented these to the working group and discussed the relationships between them. We looked for meaning and understanding that came from all of the shared stories. Together we found a place that we feel strongly represents and honors the many stories that we've heard and shared. We next found an opportunity where over the course of a day we shared this material with the community. They were invited to come down to a local theatre, make comments and additions on what they saw, and add new color and texture. It was quite a success, and the community felt like they had been heard and had participated.

As facilitators we began the hard part of synthesizing all of the material into a final document that could be used by the city administration and the community to guide them over the next number of years. The Community Culture Vision 2008 was written and presented to city council. In the end, it became the first of four touchstone documents that guide the city in its planning.

—Paul Harris, March 2016

QUESTION: Consider the ways the case of Red Deer follows the AI methodology. In what ways does Paul's experience differ from the 4-D process? In what ways does it follow the AI sequence? What were early outcomes of the discovery phase? What core principles of AI are visible in Paul's approach to community visioning?

Whether stakeholders adopt an ethic of appreciation or commit fully to the AI methodology, there is value in the act of asking appreciative questions. We believe that an appreciative ethic is always appropriate as a way of thinking about and listening with others, but we also believe there are times when relationships among stakeholders require validation of the existence of problems *as stakeholders see them*. Renaming a problem, (i.e., discrimination) to an affirmative aspiration (i.e., cultural richness) too soon risks alienating stakeholders who need their perspectives validated. Thus, adopting the AI methodology must be done with care. We advocate for collaborative groups, especially those grounded in conflict, to begin with dialogue, listening, and validation (dialogue orientation). As collaborators become skilled at AI practices, or a have access to an experienced AI facilitator, they will find the *AI methodology* is rooted in a dialogic, narrative approach that is compatible with validating deep-seated hurts.[39] Experience with the AI methodology will develop a praxis of knowing when and how to shift from a venting/listening/validating stage to an appreciative reframing stage. Until that skill has been developed, we believe the spirit of AI is more important than following the exact method.

Brainstorming Solutions

We now shift our focus from the AI world to brainstorming—one of the most familiar techniques groups use to generate solutions. Brainstorming is a feature of many informal and formal group-visioning processes. Whether used in an AI process or as a stand-alone method, brainstorming is part of the vocabulary that composes a praxis of collaborative solution-generation. The idea of brainstorming is common, and most of us have practiced it in one form or another. It is actually accompanied by an ethos that facilitates its success. Several characteristics of brainstorming are well-documented, including the need for a creative and open environment, the necessity of matching the brainstorming process with the group's needs, and the practice of avoiding the premature critique of ideas.[40] We introduce these features of brainstorming and ponder more recent research on dissent and debate as perhaps counterintuitive, but arguably helpful, in some brainstorming situations.

A Creative Environment. As a faculty member of the Communication Studies department at The University of Portland, Renee annually participated in a strategic planning day for the department. The first thing faculty members did was to "get out of Dodge," so to speak. They met on a day when no one had any other commitments; they wore casual clothes and gathered in a comfortable, homey space off-campus, replete with culinary treats. Brainstorming requires preparation—and more so if a collaborative group has experienced prolonged conflict. One way to foster a creative mind-set is to remove stakeholders from their usual meeting spaces and get into a physical space that will help participants think out of the box. If you look up brainstorming on youtube.com, you will find hundreds of vivid examples of meetings. You will note noisy, energetic spaces. People might be standing, or laying on the floor; the meetings do not look like typical business meetings. You will note the use of color through props such as markers and sticky notes. Mentioned in the case that opens this chapter, it has also become a trend in business to hire graphic artists or to have participants create visual presentations of the outcomes of the brainstorming session. Sometimes the graphics are displayed on a banner of paper that covers the entire length of the room. You might hear music during different times of the brainstorming activity as a way of escalating the energy in the room. You may have people move around and brainstorm at different tables with different partners. Many facilitators hand out candy and sometimes hand-held brainteasers are positioned on the tables to cultivate the creativity needed to think outside of the box. The point is that creative brainstorming requires attention to the setting and environment to stimulate thinking.

   Match the Process with the Group Need.   Matching processes to group needs is another good rule to follow. How many people will be participating in the brainstorming activity? What type of space do you have? Will the brainstorming take place synchronously, or will it happen throughout the day? Is conflict or transparency an issue with the group? These are a few of the considerations in matching processes to group needs. We teach three brainstorming techniques; for all of them, a good guide is to keep the brainstorming contributions visible to all who are participating.[41]

   First, brainstorming on flip charts or a whiteboard is a useful and familiar technique.[42] Deborah Mackin recommends participants take turns contributing ideas about the topic, visibly record ideas, hold comments and criticism, "keep the tempo moving with an anything goes attitude," allow one idea per turn, permit others to pass, [and] take turns until all have said pass.[43] She also recommends expanding ideas by asking four questions:

   1. How might a characteristic of something be changed or modified?
   2. How could something be bigger or larger?
   3. How could something be smaller?
   4. How could something be used in place of something else?[44]

We have also used digital applications in large brainstorming sessions. Participants inputted their ideas electronically to a running stream of comments projected on a large video screen. The contributions energized the room as participants read their own words reproduced on a jumbo screen. Digital formats are excellent when engaging large groups of stakeholders and can be a good way to integrate the technology we already have at our fingertips such as smart phones.

   Another twist on brainstorming is *brainwriting,* which occurs on paper or digital formats. Brainwriting is an effective tool to use when stakeholders may be reticent to share their ideas.[45] For example, a group experiencing conflict may be hesitant to participate in brainstorming. Brainwriting allows stakeholders to write their contributions on a matrix of twenty-one squares with seven rows and three columns. Each stakeholder writes three ideas in the squares and places their paper in the center of the table. Each person then draws a new paper from the pool and adds three more ideas—either new or an expansion of the ideas already written on the form. When the forms are full, members read the ideas aloud, crossing out duplicate ideas on the forms. According to Mackin, ten minutes of brainwriting will generate seventy-five to one hundred ideas.[46]

A third form of brainstorming, the affinity diagram, is useful for organizing ideas as they are generated.[47] It is also effective to use with large groups of people. For example, an affinity diagram could be made from sticky notes on a long wall in a public space that invites the community or other stakeholders to participate. Each idea is written on a separate piece of paper or post-it note and grouped with like ideas on a wall or table. Affinity diagramming facilitates quick organization of many ideas and moves participants toward consensus as they discuss the patterns that emerge in their brainstorming.[48] Affinity diagramming is also useful when you want brainstorming to take place asynchronously, perhaps over the course of a day or afternoon.

APPLICATION: Use a singular prompt such as, "How do we increase diversity on campus?" Divide into three groups and try these different techniques simultaneously. How did they work? How many ideas were generated? What are some of the benefits and consequences of each brainstorming technique?

To Critique or Not.   Finally, a fundamental rule to brainstorming is rooted in the early theories of advertising executive, Alex Osborn: avoid critiquing ideas too early in the process so as not to stifle creativity.[49] This rule endures today and remains a central part of the process for organizations in the business of innovating.[50] It makes sense that a premature critique of ideas runs the risk of quieting participants who will be less likely to contribute if they anticipate they will encounter judgment. The act of premature critiquing not only can change the energy in the room from positive to negative but it can also limit potentially good ideas by stifling the silly. Silly ideas actually play a positive role in creative brainstorming.[51] They can be a great tension reliever when passions and preferences surface during the process. If stakeholders feel stuck, a silly idea can propel them forward. They also can spark ideas in stakeholders whose contributions would have never been prompted if not for that silly idea. Accordingly, an important part of the brainstorming process is to express all ideas publicly because they have the potential to "prime" subsequent ideas."[52]

However, more recent research has questioned the efficacy of the "no critique rule" and has found that more ideas are actually produced when groups are given the permission to debate contributions openly.[53] Before we dismiss the "no critique" rule, let's consider the context of the argument and the context of interorganizational collaboration. The recent findings regarding the benefits of allowing debate in the brainstorming process are predicated on the assumption that creativity is equivalent to quantity, not quality, of ideas.[54] This finding has also been tested in experimental studies using zero-history groups—those participating in the studies have no social or historical relationship of any relevance to the context in which they are brainstorming. This is a very different situation than the one stakeholders in interorganizational collaboration experience. Studies in this area have also clarified that conflict or debate as it is related to the group's *task* may be effective in eliciting productivity—provided that criticism is not directed at people.[55] In other words, conflict that revolves around ideas may be useful, but conflict embedded in historical relationships would not be. Therefore, whether a group decides to implement the no-critique rule hinges on the level of trust and patterns of relationships experienced by the stakeholders at the time of the brainstorming.

From Solutions to Action

So what happens after idea generation? How do ideas get turned into action? The answer lies in the communication skills of collaborative praxis already developed. As stakeholders come up with ideas, they will eventually have to decide on how to proceed. Those ideas will be measured against the group values ("objective criteria" from chapter 9) and may invoke a new decision-making process. If the solutions that collaborative groups are considering already honor their shared values and interests, it may not be necessary to use consensus-decision making, as the solutions already respect the group's identity and priorities. In this case, the group may trust a small subcommittee or vote on the solutions that will be implemented. Groups at this stage can divide and conquer the tasks that need to be implemented. Members are likely to feel confident that the group's values will be fostered by individual stakeholders. However, if the solution generation phase prompts a questioning of group priorities, the iterative process of collaboration calls for the group to engage in consensus decision-making processes to decide on what strategies and tactics can and should be implemented. Thus, groups will draw on their collaborative skills developed throughout the stages of collaboration to move ideas toward action.

CONCLUSION

This chapter concludes our discussion of the communication orientations that comprise a language of collaborative praxis. We believe that the language and methodology of appreciative inquiry complements the cornerstones of the collaborative ethic—ethical communication, diversity, shared power, and principled leadership. It is a promising methodology for moving groups toward creative ideas. Yet, the AI methodology is also very developed and requires a shifting in language and thinking that may or may not be compatible within a particular collaboration context, especially one mired in long-term conflict or one that does not have access to skilled facilitation. Therefore, AI as a methodology is offered as a choice that stakeholders can adopt and/or adapt as it helps move them toward actionable ideas.

Brainstorming is traditionally associated with idea generation and can be a useful communicative tool for crafting and igniting the mental space toward creativity. A group that has spent a prolonged period of time determining who they are and what their primary focus is—immersed in dialogue, debate, conflict, contestation, and consensus decision making—will need to thoughtfully consider the communication needed to stimulate creativity. These two perspectives offer mechanisms for moving groups toward actualizing their hopes and visions. In the last part of this text we peek in on six bona fide collaborations and consider the links their practice has with the concepts presented in the book. Part IV gives the reader an opportunity to consider applications of the ideas and lessons presented in the first three parts of the book.

CHAPTER TAKE-AWAYS

- Understand why solution generation *follows* the foundational communication orientations of collaborative praxis
- Recognize appreciative inquiry as an ethic for thinking and communicating with others
- Identify the possibilities and challenges of adopting an AI methodology for interorganizational collaboration
- Articulate various methods for stimulating brainstorming

ENDNOTES

[1] Gerald Phillips and Julia T. Wood, eds., *Emergent Issues in Human Decision Making* (Carbondale: Southern Illinois University Press, 1984).
[2] Suresh Srivastva and David L. Cooperrider, *Appreciative Management and Leadership: The Power of Positive Thought and Action in Organization* (Crown Custom Publishing, 1999).
[3] David L. Cooperrider et al., *The Appreciative Inquiry Handbook: For Leaders of Change*, 2nd ed. (Brunswick, OH; San Francisco, CA: Berrett-Koehler Publishers, 2008).
[1] Ibid., p. 5.
[5] Ibid., p. 360.
[6] Ibid.
[7] David L. Cooperrider and Diana Whitney, *Appreciative Inquiry: A Positive Revolution in Change* (San Francisco, CA: Berrett-Koehler Publishers, 2005), p. 7.
[8] Online Etymology Dictionary, "Toleration," http://www.etymonline.com/index.php?term=toleration&allowed_in_frame=0

[9] Cooperrider et al., *The Appreciative Inquiry Handbook.*

[10] Kenneth J. Gergen, *Realities and Relationships: Soundings in Social Construction*, Rev. ed. (Cambridge, MA: Harvard University Press, 1997); Cooperrider et al., *The Appreciative Inquiry Handbook.*

[11] Cooperrider et al., *The Appreciative Inquiry Handbook.*

[12] Ibid., p. 9.

[13] Ibid.

[14] Sue Annis Hammond, *The Thin Book of Appreciative Inquiry*, 2nd ed. (Plano, TX: Thin Book Publishing Company, 1998). 14-15.

[15] Cooperrider et al., *The Appreciative Inquiry Handbook.*

[16] Ibid.

[17] Ibid., p. 88.

[18] Ibid.

[19] Ibid.

[20] Diana Whitney and Amanda Trosten-Bloom, *The Power of Appreciative Inquiry: A Practical Guide to Positive Change*, 2nd ed. (San Francisco: Berrett-Koehler Publishers, 2010).

[21] James D. Ludema et al., *The Appreciative Inquiry Summit: A Practitioner's Guide for Leading Large-Group Change* (San Francisco, CA: Berrett-Koehler Publishers, 2003).

[22] Cooperrider et al., *The Appreciative Inquiry Handbook.*

[23] Ibid., p. 116.

[24] Srivastva and Cooperrider, *Appreciative Management and Leadership.*

[25] Hammond, *The Thin Book of Appreciative Inquiry.*

[26] Cooperrider et al., *The Appreciative Inquiry Handbook.*

[27] Stephen Fineman, "On Being Positive: Concerns and Counterpoints," *Academy of Management Review* 31, no. 2 (April 1, 2006): 270–91, doi:10.5465/AMR.2006.20208680.

[28] Peter L. Berger and Thomas Luckmann, *The Social Construction of Reality: A Treatise in the Sociology of Knowledge* (New York: Anchor, 1967).

[29] W. Ross Ashby, *An Introduction to Cybernetics* (Martino Fine Books, 2015); Norbert Wiener, *Cybernetics; Or, Control and Communication in the Animal and the Machine* (M.I.T. Press, 1961); Ludwig von Bertalanffy, *General System Theory: Foundations, Development, Applications* (Penguin, 1973).

[30] Paul Watzlawick, Janet Beavin Bavelas, and Don D. Jackson, *Pragmatics of Human Communication: A Study of Interactional Patterns, Pathologies and Paradoxes* (New York: W.W. Norton & Company, 2011); Paul Watzlawick, *How Real Is Real?* (New York: Vintage, 1977); Paul Watzlawick, *The Language of Change: Elements of Therapeutic Communication* (New York: W. W. Norton & Company, 1993).

[31] John A. T. Robinson, *Honest to God* (Philadelphia, PA: Westminster John Knox Press, 1963).

[32] Whitney and Trosten-Bloom, *The Power of Appreciative Inquiry.*

[33] Diana Whitney, Amanda Trosten-Bloom, and Kae Rader, *Appreciative Leadership: Focus on What Works to Drive Winning Performance and Build a Thriving Organization* (New York: McGraw-Hill Education, 2010).

[34] Shawn J. Spano, *Public Dialogue and Participatory Democracy: The Cupertino Community Project* (Cresskill, NJ: Hampton Press, 2001).

[35] Stephen P. Fitzgerald, Christine Oliver, and Joan C. Hoxsey, "Appreciative Inquiry as a Shadow Process," *Journal of Management Inquiry* 19, no. 3 (September 1, 2010): 220–33, doi:10.1177/1056492609349349.

[36] Ibid., p. 230.

[37] Whitney, Trosten-Bloom, and Rader, *Appreciative Leadership.*

[38] Cooperrider et al., *The Appreciative Inquiry Handbook.*

[39] For more information, resources, and access to skilled AI professionals go to http://positivechange.org

[40] Deborah Harrington Mackin, *The Team Building Tool Kit: Tips, Tactics, and Rules for Effective Workplace Teams* (AMACOM Div American Mgmt Assn, 1994).

[41] David Perkins, *King Arthur's Round Table: How Collaborative Conversations Create Smart Organizations* (New York: Wiley, 2002).

[42] Mackin, *The Team Building Tool Kit*.

[43] Ibid., p. 96.

[44] Ibid., p. 97.

[45] Ibid.

[46] Ibid.

[47] Ibid.

[48] Ibid.

[49] Alex Osborn, *Your Creative Power: How to Use Imagination* (Dell Publishing, 1961).

[50] Charlan J. Nemeth et al., "The Liberating Role of Conflict in Group Creativity: A Study in Two Countries," *European Journal of Social Psychology* 34, no. 4 (July 1, 2004): 365–74, doi:10.1002/ejsp.210; Andrew Hargadon and Robert I. Sutton, "Technology Brokering and Innovation in a Product Development Firm," *Administrative Science Quarterly* 42, no. 4 (1997): 716–49, doi:10.2307/2393655.

[51] Josh Linkner, "The 10 Commandments of Brainstorming—Forbes," *Forbes*, April 20, 2010, http://www.forbes.com/2010/04/20/brainstorming-ideation-ideas-leadership-managing-innovation.html.

[52] Karen Leggett Dugosh et al., "Cognitive Stimulation in Brainstorming," *Journal of Personality and Social Psychology* 79, no. 5 (2000): 722–35, doi:10.1037/0022-3514.79.5.722.

[53] Nemeth et al., "The Liberating Role of Conflict in Group Creativity."

[54] Ibid.

[55] Karen A. Jehn and Elizabeth A. Mannix, "The Dynamic Nature of Conflict: A Longitudinal Study of Intragroup Conflict and Group Performance," *Academy of Management Journal* 44, no. 2 (April 1, 2001): 238–51, doi:10.2307/3069453.

PART IV
Wicked Problems
Revisited
Applied Collaboration

Part IV brings interorganizational collaboration to life through six short case studies written by practitioners about the wicked problems their collaborations are actively trying to solve. Their experiences illuminate the challenges and opportunities that arise in collaborative problem solving. The cases are loosely presented in the order of the book's three major parts. Several themes emerge from all the cases in part IV.

Demonstrating concepts from part I, Katherine Cooper introduces us to Community Reach in chapter 13; the collaboration is a cross-sector partnership aimed at improving educational outcomes. She introduces readers to the process and hardships of moving from talk to action on a topic (as does chapter 18). The role of systemic change emerges in this case study and the next. In chapter 14, Catherine Craig and Niñon Lewis highlight the complexity of interorganizational collaboration and the stakeholders involved in community health issues at the Pueblo Triple Aim Corporation. The case highlights the role of measurement and evaluation, as does the case that follows.

The next few chapters loosely parallel concepts in part II of the book. Chapter 15 is a case about racial disproportionality in our welfare and justice systems. Susan Lebold walks us through how one community is working to collaboratively address social injustice and marginalized voices. This case also brings to life shared leadership, missing voices, and participation. Carrie Staton highlights power and parity in chapter 16 that addresses environmental issues around community development in West Virginia. Staton describes the important contributions made by individual stakeholders based on their interests and expertise and discusses the role of systemic change.

295

The remaining chapters are exemplars of collaborative praxis in action (part III). In chapter 17, Michael Kramer, Carrisa Hoelscher, Eric Anthony Day, Christopher Nguyen, and Olivia Cooper unpack the collaborative constraints of a substance abuse task force, while also showcasing the very real issues that emerge with conflicting interests and how those interests affect consensus decision-making. This case and the next also highlight attainable goals. The final chapter uses specific facilitation processes and practices during the Bike-Walk Summits in Rockland. Lori Britt and Leanna Smithberger examine how collective identity is created around community development of alternative transportation planning. The case also addresses marginalized voices and measurement and evaluation. Part IV concludes with an invitation to the reader to join in solving wicked problems through interorganizational collaboration.

13

Educational and Economic Partnership
Community Reach

Katherine R. Cooper

LEARNING OBJECTIVES

▶ Identify the types of organizations/sectors and stakeholders represented in a community collaboration and understand how these affiliations shape stakeholder perspectives.

▶ Understand the communicative challenges inherent in community-level collaboration.

▶ Think critically about how one might identify and involve stakeholders in community collaboration.

BACKGROUND

The setting for this case study is "Community Reach," a pseudonym for a collective impact project consisting of cross-sector partners and convened for the purpose of improving educational outcomes. The case presents Community Reach in its early stages: collaborators have identified a particular goal for the partnership and are starting to coordinate their activities, but stakeholders are unfamiliar with each other and are uncertain as to how to participate in the collaboration.

The case introduces three stakeholders: Claire, the executive director of a nonprofit, Ben, the mayor of a small town, and Mark, a school superintendent. Each is introduced in terms of their prior and current involvement in Community Reach[1] along with a brief depiction of their reactions to the broader educational and economic concerns that prompted the collaboration.

297

INTRODUCTION

Another school year had started, and Claire was already feeling behind schedule. She was midway through another 60-hour work week at her nonprofit job, and she still had to drive two hours from her previous appointment to attend tonight's "Community Reach" meeting. Despite having been involved with Community Reach since its inception, Claire was becoming discouraged about her involvement in the partnership. Once again, she had come to hear more about how her organization could get involved in Community Reach's efforts to improve educational outcomes in the region. At the very least, Claire had hoped to see some representatives from the local schools in attendance. However, tonight was more of the same—only a couple of educators had come to represent the community. Claire was disappointed, though she acknowledged that there weren't many incentives for educators to come: "I can see how they would say, 'Another thing, another meeting . . . and then nothing happens. It's more of that talk.'" Claire was starting to feel the same way herself.

No educators had come from Ben's town either, but he understood—it was a long drive to make in the middle of the week. Instead, Ben was pleased to see members of the local chambers of commerce and area business leaders. As mayor of a small town, Ben was primarily interested in bringing new business to his community. "It's part of my job to do economic development," Ben said, "and Community Reach is part of it." Community Reach's goals were educational in nature—the primary goal of the collaboration was to encourage more residents to continue their education or vocational training past high school—but Ben understood that a better-educated population would result in a better-prepared workforce. "We have to make sure that kids or young adults—or even people who are my age—get trained so they can have a successful job," Ben said. The region was hit hard when farms and factories disappeared, and Ben didn't want to see any more jobs disappear from his town.

Ben and Claire nodded to each other as they walked out after the meeting, but they didn't stop to talk. Claire had missed a couple of the recent meetings that had conflicted with her work, and she relied on colleagues from other nonprofits to tell her what she missed—if they themselves were able to come to the Community Reach meeting. Ben recalled Claire's name but hadn't really ever talked to her. When he attended meetings, he usually stayed afterwards to talk with some of the area's business leaders to catch up on news from around the region. Community Reach represented 10 different counties. Although they shared a common educational goal, Ben thought that there were too many people pushing their own agendas at the meeting—he couldn't get to know everyone.

COMMUNITY REACH

Community Reach is a collective impact initiative, a form of collaboration that relies upon "the commitment of a group of important actors from different sectors to a common agenda for solving a specific social problem."[2] Collective impact projects are increasingly common in response to educational concerns, as in the case of Community Reach.

Like other collective impact projects, Community Reach had a specific educational goal—increasing the number of area residents with a postsecondary degree or credential—and it relied upon cross-sector partners. Because disparities in education start early in life and often involve contextual factors, Community Reach had sought to involve partners from education, nonprofits, business, government, and philanthropy.

My experience of working in the nonprofit sector had led to an interest in the process of collaboration, which was good in theory but difficult to practice. After leaving the nonprofit sector, I continued to see these challenges manifest in the organizations I worked with as a researcher—except that nonprofits often talked about "collective impact" as a new approach to collaboration. After I reached out to various collective impact initiatives, Community Reach invited me on-site to conduct some preliminary research to explore how stakeholders participated in this form of collaboration.

At the time that I met Ben and Claire, the partnership was starting to engage in more strategic activities. The director of Community Reach was interested in exploring how stakeholders characterized their involvement in Community Reach and to what extent they were familiar with other partners. To that end, we invited stakeholders from Community Reach's partner organizations to participate in surveys and interviews to share their experience thus far, and how they expected to participate in Community Reach in the future. We heard from more than 100 stakeholders, including educators, parents, and representatives from business, government, and nonprofits.

The inclusion of diverse stakeholders would ideally provide a more comprehensive understanding of the problem, but I found that this also created challenges for Community Reach. First, new partners were always joining the collaboration. Soon after launching, Community Reach had approximately 100 organizational partners. Although Community Reach had been hosting regular meetings, it was possible to be involved on a regular basis—like Ben and Claire—and not know others in the partnership. Second, the presence of different organizations suggested that stakeholders tended to think differently about the problem. Some stakeholders, like Claire, were primarily concerned about education. Others, like Ben, knew that education was a concern in the region but saw this as primarily linked to a lack of job opportunities.

STAKEHOLDER PARTICIPATION IN COMMUNITY REACH

Ben told me he was pleased with his involvement in Community Reach. He admitted that he personally hadn't done much to participate in Community Reach outside of attending meetings, and sometimes he got confused as to the specifics of the goal. But, ultimately, Ben had come around to the idea of collaboration.

"I had no idea what Community Reach was when I got elected," said Ben. "I just wanted to try to get a factory or something to my town. I didn't care about any of the neighboring towns." Ben, like others in Community Reach, acknowledged that the community had lost family farms, factory jobs, and opportunities for unskilled laborers. Upon being elected mayor, Ben immediately set out to improve his own community's economic outlook, but he ultimately concluded that his town needed to be part of a team.

Ben found that Community Reach introduced him to others who were concerned about job creation as a means of helping individuals seeking employment out of high school and keeping families with school-age children in the area. However, Ben admitted that parents and educators in his community were almost certainly unaware of the Community Reach's educational efforts.

That was what concerned Claire. Like Ben, she had noticed that educators tended to be absent from the meetings; unlike Ben, she was bothered by their absence. "It says a lot when you can't bring community schools to the table," said Claire. Claire's nonprofit work spanned Community Reach's region and put her in regular contact with families that often needed extra help. She worried that if schools weren't involved, local families would be left out. When asked why schools didn't come, Claire said, "I have no idea. I keep thinking, is Community Reach talking to them?"

Claire herself had been involved with Community Reach since the beginning. But now, having been involved for a couple of years, she was frustrated. She felt that there was little for her to do beyond attend meetings, and she doubted whether Community Reach could be successful if local schools and families weren't involved. Claire had seen different schools and nonprofits become interested in Community Reach, only to step away from the partnership when they found out that it was a long-term commitment without financial resources available to partners. She knew from experience how overextended and under-resourced nonprofits and schools could be, but how would Community Reach succeed without them?

Although Claire worried about educators being left out, some of the educators I spoke with didn't mind. While Claire and Ben were attending the Community Reach meeting, Mark, a superintendent, was attending to matters in his own school district. Although I had met with Claire in person, and Ben had driven more than half an hour to meet me at Community Reach's office, Mark couldn't make the 45-minute trip at the start of the school year. Instead, we spoke by phone, and Mark told me that he didn't necessarily see a need to get involved in Community Reach.

Specifically, Mark felt that Community Reach's emphasis on job creation and retention took priority over the needs of local students. He knew that Community Reach was working to create local jobs in the hopes of retaining the local workforce, but those efforts did not necessarily fit with Mark's goals for his students. "Those jobs just don't exist in our community," he said. "Even though I would like to retain those folks, I still want to see them be prepared to have those opportunities in other communities." Mark suggested that Community Reach had instead targeted the groups that they wanted to participate, with schools being further down on the list.

However, Mark admitted that he hadn't made much of an effort to get involved. He had decided that his role as superintendent meant he should be aware of Community Reach, but overall it was a better use of his time to work within his own district. "I don't want them to think I'm apathetic to those issues," Mark said of Community Reach, adding that he hoped he didn't offend anyone by his lack of participation. "I just don't want to spend time on something that is taking me away from something else that may have a bigger impact in my district."

LOOKING FORWARD

The large number of stakeholders made it difficult to communicate across the partnership, and the different stakeholder perspectives on economic and educational interests sometimes made it seem like stakeholders were having different conversations altogether. But as Community Reach moved from the planning phase—and its many meetings—to coordinating activities, the leaders made an effort to listen to stakeholder concerns.

Systems change—the goal of collective impact—typically involves some planning before shared activities to improve education get underway. For example, StriveTogether—a national network of collective impact initiatives—describes its early stages as "exploring" and "emerging" before moving on to the "sustaining" phase.[3] Community Reach expressed an interest in hearing how stakeholders had been involved in these early stages of collective impact. As it turned out, stakeholders were also thinking critically about their involvement thus far and how they could participate in the future as Community Reach worked towards its goals.

Ben mentioned that he was hearing regularly from Community Reach, but he also described the importance of having someone in his community who could report on the activities of Community Reach. One of Ben's colleagues from the county consistently attended meetings and reported details back to Ben. "He does a nice job of keeping us informed about what Community Reach is doing," Ben said. Although Ben was always going to be primarily interested in the region's economic growth, he added that they were getting more guidance in uniting the partnership's educational and economic goals—for example, they instituted a manufacturer's certification at the local high school.

Claire took a different approach. She had been frustrated about the lack of involvement from other partners in Community Reach and uncertain as to what she could contribute to the collaboration beyond attending meetings. But Claire's desire to involve other partners ultimately suggested a new way for her to participate: rather than rely solely on Community Reach to reach out to other partners, Claire decided to play this role herself.

In one conversation, she mentioned several people who hadn't been invited to get involved in Community Reach activities. But she later acknowledged that she met with some local educators in her own work and could reach out to them rather than relying on Community Reach's leadership to make all these connections on their own. Claire also realized that it was difficult for some people to get to meetings, and so she also suggested that Community Reach leaders come to her community. In an effort to learn more about the connections between education and the region's economic growth, Claire invited local business leaders to attend.

As Community Reach initiated more activities to improve education, there was still work to do to convince skeptics. Mark supported Claire's idea of getting Community Reach leaders out to each community, as well as having a local liaison to Community Reach as Ben's community had done. "Someone from our own community or someone from a neighboring school could help me make that connection better," Mark admitted. Although he was still uncertain about the benefits for his community, he was open to hearing more about Community Reach's ongoing efforts.

"It's getting better," Claire said. "I feel like they are trying to reach out more and do a better job of communicating with people." However, Claire realized—as did the Community Reach leadership—that community collaboration to improve education is a long-term endeavor requiring a significant commitment from partners.

DISCUSSION QUESTIONS

1. How would you identify which stakeholders need to be involved for Community Reach to meet its goals of improving educational outcomes?
2. How might organizational affiliation influence the ways that individuals participate in collaboration?
3. What are some of the challenges associated with organizing a collaboration of this size? What could be done to address those challenges?
4. What role does the presence or absence of interdependence among stakeholders play in this collaboration?
5. How could stakeholders relationships be improved?

AUTHOR INFORMATION

Kate Cooper is a research associate in the School of Communication at Northwestern University, where she also serves as the Associate Director of the Network for Nonprofit and Social Impact. Her research interests include nonprofit and cross-sector collaboration in response to social problems as well as stakeholder participation in collaborative or collective impact models. Kate's research has appeared in *Management Communication Quarterly* and *Communication Yearbook*; her work also includes the development of the bona fide network perspective to explore collaborative networks convened around complex social problems. Kate holds an MA and PhD from the University of Illinois at Urbana-Champaign and a BA from Wheaton College.

ENDNOTES

[1] Community Reach and stakeholder names are pseudonyms.
[2] John Kania and Mark Kramer, "Collective Impact," *Stanford Social Innovation Review*, Winter 2011, p. 36.
[3] See StriveTogether's theory of action, http://www.strivetogether.org/sites/default/files/images/StriveTogether%20Theory%20of%20Action_0.pdf

14

Institute for Healthcare Improvement's Triple Aim Initiative

Catherine M. Craig & Niñon Lewis

LEARNING OBJECTIVES

▶ Explore collaboration membership and governance structures of a health-focused coalition.

▶ Understand catalytic moments in stakeholder engagement that create a sense of urgency and interdependence among sectors or groups.

▶ Recognize the interdependent needs of different sectors related to health.

▶ Identify innovative results of a collaboration.

INDUSTRY TERMS

Managed Medicare Organization
An organization that combines the functions of a health insurance plan, delivery of care, and administration to manage the delivery and cost of care for a particular population.

Care Coordinator
A member of the health care team whose role is to partner with the patient and to ensure provision of all needed services.

Behavioral Health
The Substance Abuse and Mental Health Services Administration (SAMHSA) defines behavioral health as a state of mental/emotional being and/or choices and actions that affect wellness. Substance abuse and misuse are one set of behavioral health problems. Others include (but are not limited to) serious psychological distress, suicide, and mental illness.

Nonemergent Needs
A mental health need that does not require immediate intervention.

Population Health
The health outcomes of a group of individuals, including the distribution of such outcomes within the group.

Motivational Interviewing
Motivational interviewing is a technique in which you become a helper in the change process and express acceptance of your client.

BACKGROUND

Pueblo Triple Aim Corporation (PTAC), founded in 2012 to make Pueblo County the healthiest in Colorado, serves as a governing organization to coordinate all Triple Aim efforts in Pueblo County. This interview is with Matt Guy, PTAC Managing Director.[1] He recently served as Executive Director of the Southeastern Colorado Area Health Education Center (SECAHEC). The interviewers are Catherine Craig and Niñon Lewis, two leaders from the Institute for Healthcare Improvement's (IHI) Triple Aim initiative (simultaneously pursuing improved population health, individual's experience of care, and per capita cost of care).

WHAT ARE PTAC'S MARCHING ORDERS?

In 2012, a steering committee of several partner organizations launched PTAC as an independent nonprofit organization charged with overseeing collective work to improve community health. This was the culmination of two years of strategic discussions and community meetings. Together, the community decided that we needed one organization whose sole interest was improving Pueblo County's health.

WHAT BROUGHT STAKEHOLDERS TO THE TABLE?

In 2010, changes converged at the federal, state, and local levels. The Affordable Care Act was coming, and a new IRS regulation required nonprofit hospitals to assess community health needs and plan to address them. Colorado's public health authorization was renewed, bringing community players together to draft and carry out the plan. Kaiser Permanente grew from a managed care Medicare organization to work as a deliverer and payer of care in the region, with clinics, pharmacy services, and hospitals. These circumstances set the stage for collaboration, and a diverse group came together to do something comprehensive—rather than the useful, but isolated projects that we collaborated on in the past with no real movement on health outcomes. We had movers, shakers, and doers: everyone from community health workers to hospital CEOs.

A critical moment came in October 2010, when a senior leader from IHI visited Pueblo to present the Triple Aim as an organizing framework for our efforts. Having someone from outside the community come in and tell us frankly that we needed to work together to take it to the next level was a catalyst; we reflected on stand-alone projects and realized the only way to achieve community health was to look at all aspects that play into health, together as leaders from all sectors.

We had "ah-ha" moments at that meeting. As we discussed worrisome local health statistics, including the rates of obesity and illness, unnecessary emergency room (ER) use, and teenage pregnancy; we realized some important things. One was that even with 25 years of concerted effort around teen pregnancy, we had not made a dent. These poor health outcomes have had systemic impacts on our community. Businesses didn't want to move here because health care costs were too high. Kids weren't getting to school because of health issues, either their own or those of parents or grandparents. We saw how health, education, and poverty were interwoven, and we realized it was time to stop working in silos. We figured that if together we could positively impact two or three community health challenges, the effects would ripple across the community, and education and economic development would also improve.

WHAT IS YOUR COLLABORATION STRUCTURE AND HOW WAS IT CREATED?

Many stakeholders take part, including: the county department of health, health care organizations, community clinics, mental health and substance abuse providers, local foundations, chambers of commerce, state-wide entities and local government, including schools. Our governance structure comprises a board, steering committee and Portfolio Advisory Groups (committees of community organizations). This collaboration structure emerged organically. Pueblo is a relatively small place (approximately 160,000 people), and everyone involved in improving the community knew each other before we cobbled together this structure. We built on existing committees and identified needed roles—creating the board and PTAC to fill them.

The board comprises CEO-level representatives of nine member organizations: five health care and four community organizations. This group of leaders enacts bylaws, vets metrics, and formalizes the strategic plan. I meet with each board member every quarter to support their involvement and ensure they see the alignment between their and PTAC's priorities.

Our steering committee, an advisory council of community organizations, includes people from community members to high-level management, all serving the community in health-related ways. This committee ensures projects and measures are right for the community and provides expertise and support. It was created at the transformative meeting in October 2010.

Portfolio Advisory Groups oversee specific focus areas: obesity, teen and unintended pregnancy, smoking. Members are movers and shakers, including direct service providers and mid-level management. They bring programs to the community and provide expertise and problem solving to PTAC, ensuring the work is accomplished iteratively, and measures are appropriate. We built upon existing groups around our focus areas, refining their focus without taking away from their work. One example is the food action council, which promotes healthy eating and includes the public health department, hospitals, state university nutrition educators, school districts, and nutrition businesses. Food action council leadership participates in PTAC's obesity portfolio group, emphasizing food systems to combat obesity.

PTAC allocates resources, is the voice of the collaborative work to improve the health of Pueblo County, and influences and convenes partners around that common goal. PTAC has three staff members: I am the managing director, working alongside a community data manager and community engagement director.

HOW DO THESE GROUPS WORK TOGETHER TO IMPROVE THE HEALTH OF PUEBLO COUNTY?

Our project portfolio focuses on decreasing unhealthy behaviors: obesity, teen and unintended pregnancy, smoking, and a new effort to decrease unnecessary ER visits and avoidable hospital readmissions. We selected these four areas based on data, available resources, and most importantly, the community's desire to take on these problems.

There are many contributing causes to unhealthy behaviors, as well as multiple potential solutions. The fire department leads the effort to decrease unnecessary 911 calls and ER visits. Diverse partners collaborate to coordinate care for people who call 911 frequently, including a social service agency, Medicaid Accountable Care Organization, hospitals, community health and behavioral health centers, and PTAC. Together, we are identifying the goals and needs, locating resources for five of these individuals, connecting each person to a tailored set of resources to improve their health, diminishing their perceived need to call 911 in nonemergency situations. From this effort, we identify ideas for solutions to work with other individuals in this group.

HOW DO YOU ENSURE GROUPS WORK TOGETHER EFFECTIVELY?

To ensure our coalition is as effective as possible, we perform a stakeholder analysis to identify partners that may need specific support and those that could become leaders. We use a tool that helps visualize the strength of relationships among our stakeholders; we will complete and share the analysis with our steering committee twice a year. We think about how to add value to our stakeholders: something has to keep them coming to the table, and we have done a good job maintaining strong relationships for years. We use another analytical tool to project our impact on health outcomes by reducing quality of life challenges such as violent crime and poverty, which galvanizes our stakeholders to continue working collaboratively. At the organization level, we keep track of PTAC's board and steering committee engagement.

In 2012, the steering committee was curious about how we could take the temperature of how our group was melding. I happened to attend a conference and saw a friend I knew through other work. Yvonne Keller-Guenther is an organizational psychologist and developed a tool to measure collaboration, with specific emphasis on trust built within the group. We worked together to tailor questions for Pueblo's stakeholders. We gave the survey to the steering committee. The first result was a good one: everyone completed the survey! There was a lot of interest in supporting each other's organizational missions and a desire to interrelate better as a group. So we began setting aside time in our meetings to discuss supporting each other.

People continued the conversation outside the meetings, and some organizations brainstormed new partnership methods. Leaders of the community health center and hospital met and discussed challenges posed by inappropriate use of emergency rooms (people visiting the ER with minor complaints instead of seeing a primary care physician). They developed a strategy to help patients connect to primary care. The community health clinic began placing a care coordinator at the hospital. The coordinator meets patients with minor health needs, partners with hospital discharge coordinators to arrange the patient's hospital discharge, and schedules a clinic appointment. This arrangement connected over 20 patients to the community health center per month and eased pressure on the ER. The behavioral health clinic does the same thing now, placing a behavioral health care coordinator at the hospital to connect patients with nonemergency needs to community-based mental health care.

HOW HAVE YOU SUSTAINED THE COLLABORATION OVER THE PAST FIVE YEARS?

Our governance structure was designed collaboratively and builds on community assets (positive aspects and strengths). Among our partners are: community members, including those who work on infrastructure such as parks and bicycle lanes, librarians, and employees at corner stores and barbershops. Future targets include those not yet involved in PTAC. As I mentioned before, PTAC is a three-member team. My role is to align leadership, meet with partner organizations and each board member every quarter, and keep the focus on the strategic direction. Our community data manager collects, manages, and analyzes data from partner groups and external sources. The community engagement director's job is to know who does what and where; she meets with community groups, shares our work at community meetings, and engages people living in the community. This is behind-the-scenes hard work to keep the collaboration going and to make the time our stakeholders spend in collaboration the most fruitful it can be.

Beyond that, you have to become good at understanding the landscape and figuring out which potential partners to meet with and when to forego engaging a partner. We begin with the willing partners and let others know "we'll get you involved when you're ready." Take the Fire Department (FD), for example: they currently lead the work of reducing unnecessary 911 calls, but 3 years ago when we approached them about partnering, they stated they were more interested in fire prevention. Time and data made the difference. When we reviewed with them the time the FD spent transporting people to the emergency room, they decided to work with us. You can reach every level of partner this way: every time I meet with a board member I ask, "How can I help you?"

WHAT ARE YOUR KEY LEARNINGS?

We have a lot to be proud of. Tangibly, as of August 2015 we saw a drop in teen pregnancy by 40 percent in six years. That has been astonishing; we reached 20 percent beyond our goal!

It pays to be deliberate and thoughtful about outreach and partnership. Now, I am seen as "All Things Health" in Pueblo, and our partners call on us for data analysis and support in interacting with their partners, and they share their data with us. We engaged community leaders and made health a community issue. Funders are looking at new ways of paying for health care, and there are statewide efforts through the Colorado Coalition for the Medically Underserved to foster collaboration among 28 local health coalitions in Colorado. People are seeing the value and necessity of collaborating to improve population health by working across sectors in a community-wide push.

WHAT DO YOU KNOW NOW THAT YOU WISH YOU KNEW AT THE BEGINNING?

I wish we understood patience better. I definitely have more patience now than I did at the beginning. I understand that it takes lots of time to develop the depth of relationship among partners required to get the work done. And meeting with people and groups to talk together and explain the Triple Aim work in everyday language takes patience.

In March 2011, we and our partners were ready to host a big community meeting to share information with community members and to learn their priorities. We reached out to our stakeholders to choose a date for the meeting. Leaders of two local hospitals had such busy calendars that the first time they were both free was in November—seven months later! So, we waited, and we held the meeting in November. Of course, that meant that we needed to work hard to keep momentum and energy among all our partners. In the meantime, we met with our partners to learn more about their work and to ensure our collective aims were aligned. In these one-on-one meetings, we discussed the November meeting as a step in a 30–50 year process, and we sold the November meeting date as allowing us to accomplish plenty of work ahead of time and be ready for what followed.

The ongoing work of fostering a coalition requires patience. I explain to potential partners: this is how you are important to this work; this is how it relates to the strategy and priorities of your organization. I talk to them on their terms about what is important to them: it's motivational interviewing (see industry terms), in a way, and it helps me know their challenges. The biggest challenge we had in getting a group to the table (and staying at the table) was the hospitals. I needed to be clear that this coalition was not a "bash-the-hospitals" project. I highlighted how our work would impact them financially and enhance their preparation for the Affordable Care Act.

Another area that requires patience is achieving our goals. It can take 18 months to make a one percent improvement on a population health metric. For example, it took us five years to see our results in teen pregnancy. You have to celebrate small wins, no matter how small, to keep the momentum going.[2]

DISCUSSION QUESTIONS

1. How did the collaboration structure stakeholder involvement and leadership?
2. How did they determine and recruit appropriate stakeholders?
3. What catalytic moments created urgency for collaboration?
4. What role did trust play and how was it supported? What else did Matt say he needed to succeed?
5. What role do measurable outputs and outcomes play in this collaboration?
6. What examples of innovation result from this collaboration? How has the larger community changed?

AUTHOR INFORMATION

Catherine M. Craig (MPA, MSW) has more than 15 years of experience in collaborative systems change and bridging research and practice. Since 2009, she has served as faculty in the IHI Triple Aim initiatives and is currently the lead faculty for the Better Health and Lower Costs for Patients with Complex Needs Collaborative. She provides technical assistance to various Triple Aim in regional initiatives and the 100Million Healthier Lives' SCALE communities. She was a founding director of Community Solutions, a national nonprofit where she served as the director of healthy communities.

Niñon Lewis (MS) is an Executive Director at the Institute for Healthcare Improvement (IHI). She currently leads IHI's Triple Aim for Populations Focus Area, which encompasses innovation, content, and programming in the areas of the Triple Aim, population health, population management, primary care, and community-wide improvement efforts. Over her time at IHI, her work has focused on leading large-scale initiatives on population health and the Triple Aim, including the IHI Triple Aim Improvement Community and the Scotland Early Years Collaborative.

ENDNOTES

[1] Matt Guy, PTAC Discussion, interview by Catherine Craig and Niñon Lewis, October 2015.
[2] John W. Whittington et al., "Pursuing the Triple Aim: The First 7 Years," *Milbank Quarterly* 93, no. 2 (June 1, 2015): 263–300, doi:10.1111/1468-0009.12122.

15

Racial Disproportionality in Child Welfare and Juvenile Justice
Why Are So Many Black Children in Foster Care or Locked Up?

Susan Lebold

LEARNING OBJECTIVES

- Understand the importance of crafting a contingent collaborative process that strengthens the ability of stakeholders to work together.
- Understand the importance of identifying missing voices and incorporating those voices into the collaborative process, while also effectively addressing the diverse needs of all stakeholders.
- Identify tools and structures that maintain or increase the level of stakeholder participation, engagement, and productivity over the course of a long-term community collaboration.

INDUSTRY TERMS

Child Welfare (CW)
A network of courts and public and private agencies that promote the well-being and safety of children and strengthen families. Services are court ordered and include foster care, health services, parenting supports, and case management.

Disparity
Differential likelihood of a child from one racial or ethnic subgroup entering or exiting the CW or JJ system compared to a young person of another background.

Disproportionate Minority Contact (DMC)

Overrepresentation or underrepresentation of a subgroup of youth at different decision points in the CW or JJ process, relative to their proportion in the general population; a rate of contact with the CW or JJ system among juveniles of a specific minority group that differs significantly from the rate of contact for whites or other minority groups.

Juvenile Justice (JJ)

The area of the law reserved for children, usually between 10 and 18, whose behavior generally would be criminal if committed as an adult. The emphasis of the juvenile justice system is rehabilitation. Juveniles placed in detention must be provided educational and other supportive services.

NATIONAL CONTEXT

Racial disproportionality in child welfare and juvenile justice is well established.[1] Because minority children are detained or removed from their homes at much greater rates than white children, the government requires states to report the level of racial disproportionality in their child welfare systems and efforts to address the problem.[2] The federal government also requires states to report and address disproportionality within juvenile justice systems.[3]

STATE CONTEXT

States trying to meet the federal mandates struggle with overburdened bureaucracies, overworked staff, and insufficient funding. Those making the most progress tend to take a collaborative approach, which can be a new experience for communities, requiring individuals and institutions to put aside long-standing tensions and mistrust.

In a Midwestern state, a study of the child welfare system had revealed deep racial disparities. African American children were more likely to have abuse or neglect investigations initiated and were more likely to be placed in foster care, despite the fact that investigations substantiated fewer cases of abuse or neglect compared to white families. Once removed, African American children were more than twice as likely to "age out" of the foster care system without being adopted or returned to their families.

Facing these realities, Midwest leaders formed the state Race Equity Coalition (REC) and hired Marc Springs to guide its work. Marc runs a consulting firm with expertise in data collection and analysis and works with communities and organizations on public policy issues. The Coalition included the courts, state legislators, educators, health professionals, philanthropic leaders, law enforcement, and advocacy groups. The Coalition was formed to examine the scope and causes of disproportionate outcomes in the state's child welfare and juvenile justice systems and to propose solutions.

COMMUNITY ACTION

Early in the state process, the REC provided three years of funding to Smith County as a local demonstration site. While the state coalition focused on state level changes, the demonstration site worked locally. Ample evidence supported the choice of Smith County. The county seat was known as one of the most dangerous small cities in America, with unusually high per capita murder and violent crime rates. In addition, data consistently revealed African American children experiencing the child welfare or juvenile justice systems at rates disproportionately higher than state averages. For example, minority children were three and a half times more likely to be arrested, two times more likely to be prosecuted, and almost twice as likely to be sent to detention.

Armed with this knowledge, Marc approached Judge Marsha Evans, who had deep roots in the county and a thirty-year track record of working in child welfare and juvenile justice. He asked her to lead a coalition of local stakeholders through a data-driven decision-making process with the goal of understanding and addressing the root causes of the county's racial disparities. She eagerly accepted the role. Judge Evans assembled a four-person planning team to work with her as the project unfolded. Her first recruit was Marc because she understood that the nature of this particular project required an "outsider." As she saw it, his firm had no stake in the outcome when it came to collecting or analyzing data. Also, Marc would be able to provide continuity and linkages between the state and local projects. Finally, the judge hoped that Marc's independence might help neutralize the tensions and mistrust likely to emerge during the race-related discussions that lay ahead. The other planning team members were local leaders the judge knew well, with proven track records of successful collaborations.

The planning team recruited a locally-based steering committee to direct the overall work. Stakeholders invited to participate included not only representatives of the Department of Human Services, courts, mental health and social service providers but also police, prosecutors, detention supervisors, faith and advocacy groups, and schools. The goal was to invite representatives of any population group that impacted or were impacted by the child welfare or juvenile justice systems. Once the project got underway, anywhere from twenty to thirty participants regularly attended the discussions.

FIRST CRITICAL MOMENT—SETTING THE RIGHT TONE

Marc recognized that conversations involving race can be highly emotional; he wanted to address up front the potential contentiousness of future discussions. Given the diversity of professions, power differentials, personal experiences, and ideologies of the participants, Marc determined that some "prework" was necessary to ensure a productive process.

A two-day race sensitivity training was planned, and all stakeholder representatives were encouraged to attend. Planners were thrilled when forty-six people showed up, representing a significant cross section of the steering committee. A test of the steering committee's ability to navigate difficult waters arose several months after this training. Prior meetings had discussed the data collected regarding the racial disparities, where they were occurring in the systems, and potential causes. The discussion that day was intended to prioritize possible solutions.

At one point, a white chief of police who had been silent during the long discussion, said, "I'm concerned that all this focus on data will keep us from doing our jobs. When we're in the community, we don't have time to think about data. We have to react. If black kids are doing the crimes, then that's who we're going to arrest. We don't need data to tell us that the poor areas of town have the highest crime rates. Officers need to follow their instincts about where the trouble is likely to occur, and that doesn't mean we're racist." The chief went on to say that more black children were in foster care because, "culturally speaking," black parents were more likely to abuse their children when disciplining them. Another white police officer agreed and added, "The reason more black children are arrested is because the parents in poor neighborhoods don't care enough to make them go to school and help them stay out of trouble."

Silence pervaded the room as those present struggled with how to respond. Marc remained quiet, waiting. Jackie, a social worker, spoke up. "Let's not forget that we can't always trust our instincts when we're interpreting information or making choices." She then described a parent she assumed was a drug dealer and neglectful because her daughter wore mismatched socks to school; there was no bed in their apartment; and the curtains were closed during the day, suggesting nefarious activity. Jackie explained that, upon investigation, the family's circumstances had everything to do with being poor and nothing to do with neglect or drugs. "We can't just jump to conclusions and leave poverty, unemployment and other socioeconomic factors out of the equation," she said. "Social workers and police may think they act reasonably, but it can still lead to bad results for families."

The atmosphere in the room was tense but respectful as different people offered thoughts about where reasonable discretion ends and racism begins. Marc let the discussion continue without interruption but was prepared to jump in if the discussion gave way to personal attacks. Once everyone had said what they needed to say, he acknowledged the different concerns that had been raised and pointed out that "everyone has a different lens." He tied the different comments together by recognizing the complex lives of struggling families and emphasizing the importance of considering different perspectives when making decisions.

Core values adopted during the initial training included maintaining respect and appreciation for the experience and perspective of others. Several people present that day had participated in the training and were able to model a professional demeanor and openness to learning throughout the tense discussion. Marc was pleased to see a "spillover" effect emerge, which positively influenced the behavior of participants who had not attended the training. The meeting was able to continue with the planned agenda.

SECOND CRITICAL MOMENT—GETTING THE WORK DONE

To maintain the engagement of the steering committee volunteers and to address the problem of people drifting in and out of meetings, the planning team adopted several strategies. First, to guide the overall project, Marc used a process model developed by the Office of Juvenile Justice and Delinquency Prevention (OJJDP).[4] This model involves five steps: (1) data collection and identification; (2) assessment; (3) intervention; (4) evaluation; and, (5) monitoring and reporting out. Each meeting first reviewed where the group was in the process before moving forward with that day's agenda.

Second, the planning team wanted to involve committee members directly in the project while also dividing the workload between meetings. They proposed the formation of four workgroups, which were approved by the committee. These were: (1) data and assessment; (2) policy; (3) training; and, (4) funding. This organization of the work proved useful, and the groups were very productive between steering committee meetings.

Third, Marc made sure all attendees introduced themselves at each meeting and summarized previous accomplishments before addressing that day's agenda. In the second year, Marc noticed that members of the Latino community were no longer regularly represented, and he urged Judge Evans to personally phone key leaders she knew. She did so, and they did begin participating regularly again.

Fourth, Marc noticed in the second year that new stakeholders were attending meetings but had not been part of the early discussions. To educate these stakeholders on the nature and scope of the overall project, Marc developed an orientation packet that provided a brief history, the connection to the statewide effort, and goals and accomplishments. This eliminated the need to spend valuable meeting time bringing new people up to speed, and it enabled the new members to jump right into the discussions.

THIRD CRITICAL MOMENT—FOSTERING INTERDEPENDENCE

At the beginning of the third year Marc had to admit there was a flaw in the process that needed to be fixed. Up to that point there had been virtually no involvement by those most impacted by the work—children and parents. Marc knew that input from these stakeholders was essential to the integrity of the steering committee process. Marc raised the issue, and the committee immediately agreed with his assessment of the problem. "It needs to be real." "Families will listen to other families, and youth will listen to other youth." "Nothing about us without us." These were just some of the comments made in recognition of the need to get the parents and youth more directly involved. The big question was how to accomplish this.

The steering committee included judges, prosecutors, police, school principals, and agency supervisors—the very people involved in bringing youth or parents into the system. Given that many of the families lived in poverty, were unemployed, had limited education, or suffered from addictions or mental illnesses, participating on the committee was potentially very intimidating for them. As one person put it, "We need to be very careful. We don't want to alienate people right at the beginning because they can't follow the conversation. The families need to be and feel that they are the most important people in the room."

The committee wrestled with how to engage the families. After much discussion, a two-day orientation retreat was planned. Marc knew this would slow the project, but he also knew that familiarizing these new stakeholders with the research, data, and overall context of the work was more important than maintaining the timeline. Marc recognized that breaking down barriers and fostering mutual understanding was critically important—both for those with the power and education and those with little or none.

Several months of planning were required to fully address the unique needs of this population. For example, many poor families have transportation difficulties, so accessibility to the venue was important. Many parents worked several jobs with unpredictable hours, so the event accommodated both the children's need to attend school and the parents' need to attend work. The uneven education levels required careful framing so that information could be understood by all without demeaning anyone.

The event planners made sure that a cross section of committee members participated in the two-day event and designed the agenda to foster relationship-building among retreat attendees. To welcome everyone, the first day included a shared meal with seats assigned in a way that intentionally mixed different stakeholders together. There were structured activities at each table to help dinner companions get acquainted. After dinner swimming and other recreational activities at the hotel provided additional opportunities to relax together. The second day had a more formal agenda and included both large-group and small-group sessions. These were designed to educate the new committee members about the work of the prior two years, while also encouraging their thoughts and questions. Mealtimes and breaks provided space to continue developing personal relationships and to build rapport and trust between participants.

Everyone deemed the event a success. At the next regular committee meeting, parents and youth fully participated as the work moved forward.

CONCLUSION

The collaboration has continued past the initial three years. Shared funding networks were created as a direct result of the committee's work and have opened up new opportunities for related projects. Marc has remained as consultant and facilitator. Judge Evans retired, but her replacement is leading the ongoing work. The steering committee is implementing its recommendations, and early results are promising as disproportionality rates begin to improve.

DISCUSSION QUESTIONS

1. What are the implications of stakeholders attending meetings sporadically or dropping out of the steering committee altogether? As the facilitator and member of the core planning team, what would you do to maintain a high level of commitment, passion, and momentum among the volunteers over the course of a long-term project such as this?
2. What do you see as the primary rationale for beginning the collaboration with race sensitivity training? Do you think the planners' concerns were warranted? What are other ways these concerns could have been addressed?
3. By waiting until the third year of the project to engage the parents and youth, the data gathering and research regarding the causes and effects of racial disproportionality had already occurred and had been thoroughly discussed. To what extent do you think that the voices of the parents and children were critical to those discussions? If you had been Marc, what might you have done differently to engage them earlier in the process?
4. What were the implications or advantages of identifying core values early the process? What other communication actions fostered constructive dialogue?
5. In what ways did Marc enact principled leadership? What communication structures and strategies led to success for the collaboration?

AUTHOR INFORMATION

Susan Lebold is a social worker and lawyer. She teaches social policy and community practice at the Wayne State University School of Social Work. As a private consultant, she worked with the Race Equity Coalition described in this case study, evaluating the state process and documenting the work of the local demonstration project. Susan's work culminated in her authoring a publication, *Addressing Racial Imbalances in Child Welfare and Juvenile Justice: A Comprehensive Guidebook for Local Communities,* to help states and communities develop collaborative strategies to reduce the overrepresentation of children of color in the child welfare and juvenile justice systems.

ENDNOTES

[1] Child Welfare Information Gateway, "Racial Disproportionality and Disparity in Child Welfare" (Washington, DC: U.S. Department of Health and Human Services, Children's

Bureau, 2016), childwelfare.gov/pubPDFs/racial_disproportionality.pdf; Development Services Group, Inc., "Disproportionate Minority Contact: Literature Review" (Washington, DC: Office of Juvenile Justice and Delinquency Prevention, 2014), http://www.ojjdp.gov/mpg/litreviews/Disproportionate_Minority_Contact.pdf

[2] Joan R. Rycraft and Alan J. Dettlaff, "Hurdling the Artificial Fence between Child Welfare and the Community: Engaging Community Partners to Address Disproportionality," *Journal of Community Practice* 17, no. 4 (November 19, 2009): 464–82, doi:10.1080/10705420903300025.

[3] Melodee Hanes, "Disproportionate Minority Contact," *In Focus*, November 2012, http://www.ojjdp.gov/pubs/239457.pdf

[4] Office of Juvenile Justice and Delinquency Prevention, *Disproportionate Minority Contact Technical Assistance Manual*, 4th ed. (Washington DC: U.S. Department of Justice, 2009), http://www.ojjdp.gov/compliance/dmc_ta_manual.pdf

16

Environmental Community Development in West Virginia
Country Roads Bring Us Together

Carrie Staton

LEARNING OBJECTIVES

▶ Identify how communities and service providers share decision making.

▶ Recognize the expertise of service providers and community members and their interdependent roles.

▶ Understand challenges faced by communities attempting brownfield redevelopment.

▶ Recognize power and parity in the West Virginia Redevelopment Collaborative.

INDUSTRY TERMS

Blighted
Neglected, abandoned, or dilapidated; refers to a site in need of cleanup and reuse.

Brownfield
A property on which expansion, redevelopment, or reuse may be complicated by the presence, or perceived presence, of contamination.

Brownfields Redevelopment Teams (BRTs)
Multi-disciplinary teams composed of agency, faculty, and private service providers who help communities address complex projects.

Redevelopment
Rebuilding, cleanup, or restoration of a blighted property or neighborhood.

Renewal
Rebuilding or remediation of a blighted site for a productive use.
Structured engagement
An approach to event facilitation in which participants are asked to complete activities designed to promote problem solving and interaction.

BACKGROUND

In West Virginia, many resources are available for communities working on redevelopment projects. Unfortunately, many communities are unaware of these resources or how to identify them. Often, service providers working in redevelopment are not aware of other resources available to assist in planning, assessment, and redevelopment. The West Virginia Redevelopment Collaborative implements an approach to redevelopment using Brownfields Redevelopment Teams composed of experts from the public, private, nonprofit, and academic sectors to help communities capture the maximum benefit from the adaptive reuse of strategically located properties. Through collaborative efforts, redevelopment projects receive new life, create momentum, and replace blighted community eyesores with vibrant hubs of activity and renewal.

NARRATIVE

Since 2005, the Northern West Virginia Brownfields Assistance Center (NBAC) at West Virginia University has worked with community stakeholders to promote economic development and environmental and public health protection through innovative redevelopment of brownfields. Brownfield redevelopment offers the opportunity to make significant change, turning once blighted properties into positive community assets. Complex issues that require communities to navigate resources, regulations, and research from the private and public sectors accompany these opportunities. Many communities are unaware of how to identify resources—much less how to navigate them effectively.

In our work across West Virginia, NBAC identified trends in the challenges communities face throughout the redevelopment process. Our communities faced two significant issues: capacity (i.e., ability to complete redevelopment projects) and uncertainty about the services available and the potential for success on a project. Small, rural communities were unable to identify the resources they needed to take on projects. Because of this, they were abandoning projects altogether or spending a lot of time trying to track down the right people to help them, leading to project delays, lost momentum, and depleted community support. Stakeholders became doubtful that projects were possible due to environmental liability, little visible progress, and fear of regulatory issues. Meanwhile, our partners were looking for ways to share their technical assistance more effectively, often having trouble gaining traction in the communities who most needed their assistance.

To help address these issues, NBAC created the West Virginia Redevelopment Collaborative (WVRC) in 2011. We had seen that federal, state, nonprofit, and academic organizations (known as service providers) were providing technical assistance and funding and were working with many of the same communities. It became apparent that service providers were missing opportunities to collaborate on projects. Recognizing this, the WVRC invited representatives from diverse agencies to work together on specific projects to help communities solve problems more efficiently. By working collaboratively with one another, we hoped to keep communities from rehashing the same questions repeatedly, to share information across programs, and to find solutions without having to restart each time a new agency came to the table.

At first, partners were reluctant to work on specific projects. They had concerns about providing support outside of the traditional requirements of their programs. Upon learning this, we invited 15 partner organizations to help us nail down not only the flow of the redevelopment process in West Virginia but also exactly what services were available to communities—and at what parts of the process those services made the most sense. For example, the Main Street program offers assistance with feasibility analyses for new businesses in historic downtowns. Is this more useful during the project assessment or during the reuse planning stage of a project? The WVRC looked to service providers to clarify the answers to these questions for communities.

In May of 2012, partners from all sectors met for *Redevelopment Wargames,* a single day event designed to encourage dialogue. To achieve this goal, the WVRC employed a strategy that would become integral to our approach: structured engagement.

Using a combination of event themes, creative activities, and theatrics, the WVRC creates dynamic, engaging events that encourage people to work together in new ways. For this event, the theme was *wargames*—how do we prepare for the redevelopment battlefield. A seasoned, well-respected facilitator set the mood early in the day, taking on the persona of a drill sergeant:

> "We are here to tackle some of the biggest challenges faced by West Virginia communities. This will require your full and undivided attention through a series of critical tactics. You are ordered to silence all cellular devices for the duration of this day. If your phone rings during these exercises, you must immediately drop and give me twenty!"

With that, the stage was set. Participants were eager to work hard and to have fun.

Over the course of the day, participants looked at hypothetical case studies and identified the services those projects required. The anonymity of these hypothetical situations allowed participants to feel more at ease offering advice for how to use their programs, without feeling pressured to commit to a project. Next, participants received a Battle Plan—an illustration of what the WVRC envisioned the redevelopment process to look like. Working in teams, service providers evaluated the process, made adjustments based on experience, and noted where services fit into the process. This gave us a solid, collaboratively defined picture of the process and a better idea of how communities could tap into redevelopment services. This more clearly defined process allows communities without strong backgrounds in redevelopment or those without professional staff to understand and navigate the process more easily.

Perhaps the most surprising and rewarding result of the day was the response from participants. These partners had already been working with the WVRC, but many of them stressed an inability to work on specific projects. During the event debrief, a surprising nugget of feedback emerged.

"This was a great day," one funder said, "but it would really be better if we could work on actual projects, provide real feedback to real communities." After years of difficult collaboration, and over a year of specific efforts to formalize collaboration, these partners had finally reached the "aha" moment we'd been waiting for. They were ready to interact in a new way to help communities on complex projects. Luckily, we had the framework ready for them to plug right in.

The core of the WVRC approach is the creation of multi-disciplinary teams of academic faculty, public agency, and private sector experts to help communities tackle the remediation and adaptive reuse of strategically located properties. To address complex issues of community development, the WVRC has developed a network of partners, bringing public, private, nonprofit, and academic organizations to the table with community and project representatives to increase the likelihood of success. As WVRC Coordinator, I facilitate this approach, working with partners and communities to identify the skills and needs of all and to build effective teams to address locally identified redevelopment issues on specific projects.

On one of our first projects, we worked with a small county on an old machine repair shop that the community wanted to turn into a recreational complex. I worked with that community to determine what kinds of questions they had, what kind of expertise or assistance they needed, and how to get it. Some of those questions included:

- What environmental contamination is at the site?
- What kind of recreational opportunities are already available in the area? What's missing?
- How can we fund a public recreational facility when our local governments are facing significant budget cuts?

With this understanding of the issues in mind, we identified collaborators for their Brownfields Redevelopment Team (BRT). To answer environmental questions, I pulled someone from the state environmental protection agency. To explore recreational opportunities, we connected with a college recreational program to conduct a needs assessment. To look at creative funding options, we looked to someone familiar with capital campaigns and crowdfunding. When the WVRC first started, finding these partners meant developing new relationships, exploring our network to identify new resources. After almost four years of implementing this process, we've developed a strong network of partners and potential team members. By developing strong relationships, we have created a deep bench of experts we can tap when a community need arises.

Once assembled, BRTs work closely with each other and the communities, allowing for an interweaving of experience and expertise, building the effectiveness of the programs and the impact on the community. In the WVRC approach, the project representatives' knowledge of the project and community is recognized in the same way that academic or professional expertise is. Each perspective and background is given equal weight and consideration in the search for a collaborative solution to a community problem, as the role of the collaborators is not to solve problems *for* the community but *with* the community.

Individual members of the BRT work with a community on a project *concurrently*, allowing for dialogue that leads to solutions that might not otherwise be discovered. Partners are not asked to provide technical assistance that they do not already provide. Instead, they are asked to do it collaboratively, based on decisions reached within the BRT, and with the work of colleagues in mind. As experts from different backgrounds, including community experts, share their experience and perspective, new ideas emerge organically, leading to more efficient provisions of services.

For example, on the recreational complex, if the community were not working with a BRT, they might reach out to service providers individually. In that case, the environmental experts might not be aware of the recreational research or plans for reuse. By working collaboratively, the environmental experts were kept abreast of the results of the recreational survey along the way. This allowed them to develop plans for cleanup and site design based on community priorities, rather than completing their work in a vacuum. Once a need for soccer fields, a playground, and concessions was identified, the environmental experts could modify remediation plans and site designs to not only remove contamination but also to prepare the site for field and playground construction, leading to a more complete and feasible reuse plan. Throughout the process of the WVRC, the importance of collaboration and teamwork is stressed, as teams meet regularly to share the progress of each team member's work, such as the recreational survey, and discuss new challenges so that a solution can be reached through dialogue and shared experience.

On projects diverse in both property size and reuse plans, we are seeing that where "groups think of themselves not only as responsible for their own work, but as sharing in a responsibility for the whole enterprise, there is much greater chance of success for that enterprise."[1] Communities have reported high levels of satisfaction with the process, and many collaborators remain engaged with projects after the initial project period, with some taking on new projects within the communities. For example, after working on designs for riverfront recreation in a city on the Ohio River, a landscape architecture professor used the relationship that project created to identify design projects for other parks in the city, giving the city more affordable design work and providing students with additional real-world examples for their studies.

Before the WVRC, communities often abandoned major redevelopment projects, feeling daunted by multiple service providers and retelling their project story in pursuit of assistance. Service providers often landed in communities for brief periods of time, working through specific issues without the benefit of the broader context of community needs. Through structured collaboration, open dialogues, and interagency cooperation, redevelopment projects have received new life, created momentum and excitement, and replaced blighted community eyesores with vibrant hubs of activity and renewal.

DISCUSSION QUESTIONS

1. What are the challenges faced by communities attempting brownfield redevelopment projects for the first time?
2. How does the WVRC ensure that all stakeholders are heard throughout the redevelopment planning process?
3. What role did parity play in the WVRC, and how was it accomplished?
4. What power types were visible in the WVRC, and how were they relational?
5. Why is redevelopment vulnerable to failure outside of collaboration?

AUTHOR INFORMATION

Carrie Staton manages the WVRC, a collaborative approach to redevelopment of strategic properties. Carrie is a key architect in the development, evolution, and implementation of the WVRC approach, including developing tools and resources for communities, establishing relationships with service providers, and overseeing the implementation of WVRC projects.

ENDNOTE

[1] Mary Parker Follett, "Co-Ordination," in *Mary Parker Follett Prophet of Management*, ed. Pauline Graham (Washington: Beard Books, 2003), 183–99, p. 196.

17

Substance Abuse Task Force
Navigating Collaborative Constraints

Michael W. Kramer, Carrisa S. Hoelscher,
Eric Anthony Day, Christopher Nguyen, & Olivia D. Cooper

LEARNING OBJECTIVES

Students will be able to identify:

▶ Multiple interests driving the collaboration.

▶ Characteristics of different types of communication including informal, transparent, and strategic, used to facilitate a governmental interagency collaboration.

▶ Challenges and complexities of leading a collaborative environment and meeting deadlines.

▶ Benefits and consequences of enacting specific communication and decision-making processes.

Keith could hardly believe what just happened. While balancing the need for collaboration with the need to make progress, the Safety Commission met their deadline. Keith reflected on their progress. Because his state experienced widespread substance abuse issues, a federal agency selected them for funding to create an interagency commission to craft a strategic plan to address the concerns. When his agency head, Stephanie, designated him to manage the commission, Keith had concerns about their ability to facilitate collaboration among government and nonprofit agency heads and to meet their deadline for receiving additional funding for the implementation of the plan.

Keith's first task was convincing agency heads of the need for the Safety Commission. To do that, he created "the perfect storm" metaphor to describe the problem. At the beginning of meetings, he described the situation this way:

> Our state is facing the perfect storm. We are in the top five for deaths related to legal and illegal substance abuse. We now face a new threat to public health and safety. As aging baby boomers face additional health issues, there is potential for increased problems caused by the accidental mixing of perfectly legal prescription medications. These problems cannot be addressed by any single agency. It will take prevention, enforcement, and treatment efforts by public and nonprofit agencies to address these problems. If we don't do something now, the combination of legal and illegal substance abuse will create a rising tide of deaths in our state, resulting from the perfect storm.

This message resonated with agency heads, but persuading them that the commission would accomplish something constructive was more challenging. To convince them that the collaboration could make a significant difference, Keith emphasized that all commission members would be agency heads with the power to make changes in their organizations. The fact that his agency head was involved helped convince others to join. Predictably, they elected Stephanie as the commission chair at their first meeting.

Next, Keith needed a structure in place that would be collaborative and that would enable them to meet the deadline for additional funding. The federal agency already conducted a needs assessment and created a list of possible recommendations as a starting point for their strategic plan. Since it was long, Keith needed to divide and delegate. Accordingly, he set up a two-tiered collaborative structure. He created seven subcommittees to work on administration, communications, prevention and education, law enforcement, the judicial system, program management, and treatment. Each group had a leader who selected representatives from appropriate agencies. These subcommittees would consider only recommendations within their expertise and make recommendations to the commission, which would craft the final plan. Keith wanted the assessment report to jump-start each subcommittee to avoid starting from scratch, but he also did not want the report to constrain their creativity. Before turning subcommittee meetings over to their leaders, he began each one by retelling the perfect storm metaphor and adding:

> This federal assessment report identified what we do well and what needs improvement. The report includes 75 starting recommendations, but you are not bound by them. You can delete recommendations you think are inappropriate, add ones you think are missing, or combine them any way you like. You will report your rankings of the recommendations to the Safety Commission, which will prioritize them into our strategic plan.

Attending subcommittee meetings provided a lesson in leadership for Keith. He selected subcommittee leaders based on recommendations and did not know how they might lead a collaborative meeting. Most groups had organized, assertive leaders who ran meetings efficiently using an agenda and also facilitated open discussion. After Keith's opening remarks, they took charge. Their agenda usually began with "Let's introduce ourselves," followed by "Let's look at each recommendation individually," and then, "What other ideas should we consider?" Keith rarely added opinions or clarifications.

In other groups, designated leaders lacked needed skills. One particular subcommittee had no agenda. People often talked over each other without listening, even occasionally becoming hostile. At a particularly chaotic moment, the leader commented to someone next to him, "I used to be in charge of this meeting." This subcommittee held two meetings, while most only needed one. Still, Keith remained in the background, only intervening to return them to their task. At their second meeting, they agreed on recommendations, including a few new ones.

Most subcommittees stuck largely to the assessment recommendations and made few changes. When Keith talked to committee members informally, they said they felt like they had the freedom to do what they wanted even though few changes were made. Being given the chance to collaborate on the strategic plan was more critical to them than whether they actually made significant changes.

Keith thought it was important that commission members felt like they were making tangible progress, so he emphasized "picking the low-hanging fruit," small or large steps that could be accomplished easily. To help accomplish this, he created a four-category system for "ranking" recommendations by ease of implementation: 1) recommendations already accomplished or in progress; 2) recommendations that one agency could accomplish independently; 3) recommendations requiring interagency collaboration; and 4) recommendations requiring changes in state law to be reserved for future efforts. This system allowed the communication subcommittee to begin working on a new statewide media campaign immediately. Other agency heads began working together on a statewide database for tracking offenders, since doing so did not require changes in state law.

Keith also learned it was important to make progress outside of meetings. The commission simply could not complete all of its work in quarterly meetings, and meeting more often seemed impossible. Consequently, he frequently talked to commission members outside of meetings. Because they were one-on-one, these informal conversations did not violate the state's open-meeting laws. (To avoid inappropriate alliances, some public entities, such as school boards, forbid members from meeting outside of public meetings to discuss business). Keith viewed these conversations as important in several respects. Pragmatically, Keith was able to gather more information on specific issues and to get feedback on progress already made. This led to tangible progress in a timely fashion by building consensus without sacrificing collaboration. It helped build commitment by showing that his agency was serious about this interagency commission. He recalled people asking, "Is this for real, or is this just a waste of my time?" when agencies first got word of the commission. Keith also felt these conversations increased the collaborative process given that some quieter members were much more comfortable voicing their opinions in private. These conversations enhanced participation, allowing the commission to better leverage its collective expertise.

This informal process sometimes meant there was little open discussion at meetings because Keith presented ideas everyone already agreed with informally. Keith heard a few complaints from individuals who felt there should be more open communication or at least that they should be told what was happening behind the scenes so that they did not feel like they were rubber stamping predetermined outcomes. Keith cringed when he heard this perception. He felt this informal process allowed for collaboration and efficient meetings.

Since Stephanie ran meetings as the chair, Keith served a secondary role at commission meetings. He always emailed the latest version of the strategic plan to commission members prior to meetings. During meetings, he projected the document onto a screen to show the recommendation under discussion and made wording changes when they were suggested. This process allowed everyone to see changes and easily make decisions. Even if he disagreed with some changes, Keith usually did not say anything. Similarly, Stephanie rarely tried to persuade members to her perspective because she felt it was more important to have participation and submit a plan on time than to have a perfect document. The combined efforts of Stephanie and Keith helped facilitate the collaboration in a timely manner.

Although the process generally worked well, there were some awkward moments. At first, subcommittees wanted to prioritize recommendations in order of importance. Keith reminded them that they only needed to designate recommendations as one of four categories for ease of implementation. This approach proved efficient since it avoided disagreements in subcommittees concerning which recommendations were most important. Then, to Keith's surprise, at the next Safety Commission meeting, Stephanie asked each subcommittee leader to give their subcommittee's top priorities, even though subcommittees had not set priorities. Keith thought about correcting this shift in the decision-making process but realized it was more efficient for the leaders to set priorities than for the subcommittees to waste time reaching agreement since the commission made the final recommendations anyway. He felt that sometimes it was important to balance making progress with having full participation.

At commission meetings, Keith observed that some individuals were more assertive than others. Surprisingly, this rarely created problems for the commission. One individual, Ken, definitely wanted things to go his way. Ken believed Testimonial Groups (in which offenders met victims), were an effective rehabilitation strategy that should be added to the strategic plan. The commission was instructed to include only "evidence-based, data-driven" programs in the plan. Although research clearly shows that Testimonial Groups are not effective long-term, no one searched for evidence or challenged Ken directly. When someone asked whether Testimonial Groups were the kind of evidence-based programs they were supposed to recommend, Stephanie smoothed over the issue by saying, "Although it's important that we adopt evidence-based programs, we don't want to stop using programs we know work." Keith wondered what the difference was between "evidence-based programs" and "programs we know work," but since the commissioners seemed comfortable with the ambiguity of Stephanie's statement, he did not question his boss.

In today's meeting, the commission needed to finalize the strategic plan. There were 65 recommendations after some were dropped, accomplished, or combined, as well as new ones added, like Testimonial Groups. When the meeting began, Stephanie explained:

> I hope we can go through this plan and approve it section by section. We do not want to get lost down a rabbit hole by doing a lot of line-by-line editing. We simply do not have time for that, unless you want to have additional meetings. I'm willing to do that if you think we should, but I'm not sure that's necessary.

The group accepted Stephanie's plan, and Keith noticed she went section by section rather quickly. Unless members had carefully read the document beforehand, they were unlikely to notice anything they disagreed with, and so sections were generally approved quickly. Occasionally, someone took issue with something in the plan. The ensuing discussions rarely went very long. If there was quick agreement with a suggestion, Keith modified the document on-screen. If the conversation seemed to be moving toward an extended discussion, Stephanie reminded the group that they were "getting lost in a rabbit hole" and "it might mean scheduling another meeting, although that's okay with me." These comments usually ended discussion quickly. Keith would have preferred something less heavy-handed, but everyone kept telling him informally that they felt like they had the opportunity to collaborate and voice disagreement.

Between Stephanie's efforts to maintain progress and Keith's on-screen editing, the commission adopted a final strategic plan during the meeting. Reflecting on the collaboration, Keith wondered if they had correctly balanced creating a collaborative environment and meeting the deadline. He hoped that what he learned from facilitating the development of the strategic plan would help when they received funding for the implementation phase.

Kramer, Hoelscher, Day, Nguyen, & Cooper   **331**

DISCUSSION QUESTIONS

1. How did the structure of the commission influence collaborating and meeting the strategic plan deadline?
2. What are the conflicting interests that the leaders must consider during the collaborative process?
3. What facilitative leadership practices were present or lacking in this collaboration?
4. What advantages did Keith's informal meetings have for the collaboration? What were the disadvantages?
5. How did Keith and Stephanie create transparency and use strategic ambiguity in the process? What were the benefits and consequences of their communication choices?
6. What type of consensus process was enacted to accomplish decision making? What were the strengths and weaknesses of their process?

AUTHOR INFORMATION

   Dr. Michael Kramer (PhD Texas) is a professor in the Department of Communication and **Dr. Eric Day** (PhD Texas A&M University) professor, **Christopher Nguyen** PhD candidate, and **Olivia Cooper** recent PhD graduate are in the industrial-organizational psychology program in the Department of Psychology at the University of Oklahoma. **Carrisa Hoelscher** (PhD Oklahoma) is an assistant professor in the Department of Communication at Missouri State University. This research team from the University of Oklahoma conducted observations of meetings and interviews of participants involved in a statewide, interagency task force during 2012–2014. The hypothetical case presented in this chapter is loosely based on this research. This research was supported by funding from the US National Safety Council awarded to Eric Day and Michael Kramer.

18

Collaboration among Bike/Walk Advocates
Facilitating Process or Empowering Action?

Lori L. Britt & Leanna Smithberger

LEARNING OBJECTIVES

▶ Recognize collaboration and stakeholder understandings of collaboration as emergent.

▶ Understand how collective identity develops and how it enables and constrains collaboration.

▶ Explore how facilitation can empower collaborative thinking and action by encouraging deliberation.

▶ Identify specific facilitation processes and practices.

▶ Recognize the potential influence of a marginalized perspective.

SUPPORTING BIKING AND WALKING IN ROCKTOWN

Located in a valley with rolling terrain, Rocktown enjoys a vibrant outdoor culture, which includes biking. In 2012 an area advocacy group, the Rocktown Bike Coalition (RBC), received a grant to host a community meeting to learn about opportunities for US Department of Transportation bike and pedestrian funding through the year 2020. This meeting spurred attendees to see the value of gathering area biking and walking advocates to encourage ongoing local collaboration.

A planning group made up of representatives of the RBC, city and county government planning departments, university transportation and recreation departments, and representatives from a district planning commission in the valley became known as the Bike Walk Committee (BWC).

The committee developed goals for a 2013 Bike-Walk Summit that merged the independent efforts the stakeholders were already making. The goals were to spread awareness of advocacy efforts and successes; to offer an opportunity for collaborative thinking on how the university, city and county bike and pedestrian plans could be coordinated; and to encourage continued citizen involvement in finding creative ways to fund, plan, and promote engagement in biking and walking. For the 2013 Summit, the BWC planned to overview the current status of infrastructure, programs, events, grants, and city and county projects. However, they sought outside help on how to facilitate collaborative thinking and planning.

Ron, as chairman of the BWC, used his connections as a faculty member at the university to reach out to Lori Britt, head of a university group specializing in designing and facilitating public processes. Lori agreed to lead a team, including her student, Leanna, to facilitate planning sessions of the summit. She began meeting regularly with the committee to coordinate the facilitation with the summit theme and structure. The BWC's goals for the facilitated portions were to have participants develop action steps that could be carried out in the next year and to encourage participants to take initiative and be involved in advancing these goals.

2013: FACILITATING AN "OPEN SPACE"

The 2013 summit kicked off with addresses from the university president and a state senator, as well as a presentation of area successes with regards to biking and walking events, infrastructure, and grants. At the coffee break one participant shared, "I thought I was involved, but I had no idea how much work is happening all across the community." Another participant noted, "Highlighting the successes of the year is powerful. Many people don't realize how much has been done."

Following this, the keynote speaker from a national cycling advocacy organization offered a look into other communities that have gained distinction as being bicycle friendly. He shared his organization's framework that suggests work on five fronts (5E): Evaluation and planning, Engineering and political connections, Enforcement and safety, Encouragement, and Education. Next, Lori asked participants to brainstorm what they needed to do to claim their community was the most responsive in the state and to write their ideas on sticky notes. While the participants enjoyed lunch, the facilitation team prepared for the afternoon action planning session by sorting almost one hundred multi-colored sticky notes using the speaker's 5E framework as a guide. The facilitators were so focused on this task, they were surprised to notice that the crowd had thinned significantly as many government, law enforcement, and city and university officials took their leave.

Using a model resembling Open Space Technology—a model that encourages self-organization, finding others with similar interests to engage in collaboration, and ownership of the process by participants—the facilitators assigned the five themes to individual tables, and participants were encouraged to join and move between small groups. Each table was provided all of the related input from the pre-lunch session and a set of worksheets to conduct a force-field analysis of factors that might add momentum to efforts or serve to constrain efforts in each of the five key areas as a way to consider short- and long-term steps that might be taken. As discussions began, many of the small groups stared at the force-field analysis sheets in confusion. "I don't really understand this," said Ian, a member of the RBC, as he held the 8 ½ by 11 paper in his hand, "but let's move on."

The facilitators reminded participants to move if they felt inclined and clarified the materials, but they largely remained observers. "For these action steps to leave this room we need champions who will lead the way," said Lori, referring to the goals displayed around the room as part of the large group debrief. "If you feel passionately about one of these actions, write your name next to it and champion that project." A few individuals heeded this call, but they were the "usual suspects," in many cases members of the BWC given that they comprised over half of the remaining group.

DEBRIEFING AND ADJUSTING: FALLING SHORT OF COLLABORATIVE ACTION

The planning team was hopeful as they reflected on the 2013 Summit and began to envision the 2014 event. "I've sent a link to a Google doc that has all of the plans and encourages people to sign up to help get things done" said Ian. "And the link is on the home pages of many of the area biking organizations." The group was still anticipating that others beyond those in the BWC would step forward to continue efforts to bring about the type of support, infrastructure, and engagement they envisioned for the area.

By late spring the Google doc remained virtually unchanged. Although there was more coordination among the city, county, and university regarding their formal bike and pedestrian plans since the 2013 summit, each of these organizations was already represented on the BWC. "People liked being a part of generating ideas and brainstorming, but we also may have tried to do too much. We essentially made a long to-do list, and new folks did not step up," noted Mark as he looked over the final report.

The committee agreed the next summit would need to encourage more targeted collaborative efforts. "If our goal is to encourage collaboration with particular organizations, we should narrow the theme to appeal to those organizations and then invite them," suggested Ian. The group recognized that one way to gain decision-maker support was to make the case for the economic benefits of visitors drawn to the area for bike-walk tourism. The narrowed economic focus offered a chance to invite other organizations to collaborate in shaping the summit and help dispel the notion that the planning committee was the main vehicle for post-summit action.

By summer, several area tourism representatives attended a BWC meeting, and the group had contacted the area economic development office to consider how to assess the impacts bike-walk tourism brought to the area.

2014: FACILITATING NEED-BASED ACTION GROUPS

The 2014 Summit was the second time the BWC worked with the facilitation team to plan the interactive planning sessions of the Summit. Lori attended most planning meetings, blurring the line between process consultant and committee member. This encouraged committee members to weigh in on how the facilitated portions of the Summit could support ongoing collaboration. Recognizing some of the participant burnout and diminished participation after lunch in 2013, the group opted to integrate facilitated activities throughout the day.

Guided by the spirit of Appreciative Inquiry, participants were first asked to write, "what they love" about the region's biking and walking opportunities as if they were sending a postcard to an out-of-state friend. After reflecting on the strengths, Lori flipped the question. "Now, what would you hope that friend wouldn't find out about our community before coming to visit?" One participant used humor to foster a collective regional identity by making light of the smell that settles in the town on rainy days due to the proximity of several poultry factories. "I don't want tourists to know that it smells like dog food every time it rains!" The announcement, met with chuckles and knowing glances, igniting a sense of community pride in Rocktown, flaws and all. The statements that followed were shared enthusiastically and optimistically, even when participants were mentioning problems like the lack of a central website or the lack of continuous mixed-use trail through the region.

After the official speakers and presentations, a brief session before lunch involved questioning participants: "what do we need in order to present the 'total package' to tourists." The conversations took place in four groups, with 10-12 participants in each group. In Leanna's group, the conversation started by addressing a need identified in 2013, the need for a regional map. Pete, a first-time attendee at the Summit and the only participant from the southern town of Stockton, had another concern. "I think first we need to decide what counts as 'the region,'" Pete began. "I know Stockton isn't right in the center of things, but I thought it was part of the region. But then I come here and no one is talking about our interests—the interests of the towns farther south."

After a brief discussion about who counted as stakeholders in the region and how to better include Stockton in the regional efforts, participants focused on identifying gaps and thinking systemically about the region from a tourist vantage point. Mary, a resident at the nearby Cove Mountain resort, was concerned about the lack of connection between tourist destinations. "So many people visit the resort or they're locals who would like to use the trails there," she said, "but we're not sending them to any of the breweries, wineries, or downtown areas. I just think that would increase tourism in the region, if we could link all those areas and have them mapped out clearly." Mark pointed out the potential of this idea, saying, "Maybe if we put them on the map, raise an interest, we can use that to show the economic value to the city council and county board of supervisors and get funding to build safe trails connecting those areas."

Using the ideas generated from these conversations, the facilitators categorized the input into broad need areas. After lunch, they encouraged participants to self-select into small groups based on these needs. Groups were asked to choose and focus on a program or project and to develop basic SMART goals—specific, measurable/monitorable, attainable/assignable, relevant, time-bound—for the project using worksheets provided. This framework helped groups avoid the generalized ideas that had failed to spur action the year before. Amanda and Stephanie, representatives of city government and municipal planning, joined Ian as part of the group working on developing a central bike and pedestrian tourism website. "We've talked about this for a long time now, and no one has time or the resources to build a website," Amanda began. "We need to hire someone. We need a full-time bike-ped person to do this kind of thing." Leanna, noticing the group was stuck, suggested that they focus on getting a full-time bike-pedestrian coordinator rather than developing a website. Although discouraged by past failures, Ian suggested the possibility of finding grants for a one-year position to get the website up and going, and Stephanie backed this idea. This shift in goals led to the development of specific components, including who would work on grant applications and a realistic timeline that acknowledged the long-term nature of the goal.

CELEBRATING THE EMERGENCE OF COLLABORATIVE AGENCY AND ACTION

Just one month after the summit, the BWC met to talk about the feedback from the event. Ron excitedly began, "Two of the action teams have already begun working. If these teams are going to keep their efforts going, they need to know they have somewhere they can turn to. Maybe that should be the role of this group?" Ron's comments drove home the need for continued ways to coordinate ongoing action, a supporting rather than starring role BWC members gladly assumed.

The 2014 Summit spurred the kind of collaboration the committee had hoped for. "The structure allowed people to take ownership," said Mark. "I think the theme and speaker on economic development helped to pull people in and get them engaged." "I liked the direction we were given. We had to focus on developing *an* idea. With brainstorming, it is easier for people to get on rabbit trails, but we had to focus," Ian mentioned. Amanda reflected on the opportunities and tools offered to participants to engage them in planning. "We knew each other better," she said of the BWC and the facilitation team. "We were able to think together and work backward from what we wanted to end up with and consider how we could work participants through a series of steps that resulted in real, actionable plans for the year."

As the year continued, the planning committee shared updates from the action teams, welcomed several new members, and new organizations played active roles in bringing some of the plans that had been dreamed of for many years to life. More time was spent at meetings discussing ongoing efforts rather than planning for the next summit. After all, the summit itself was meant to inspire collaborative action all year long, not just on a single day.

DISCUSSION QUESTIONS

1. How does the BWC as a community coalition define collaboration? How does their sense of collaboration emerge over time?
2. How does the identity of the BWC planning group emerge and how does this identity both enable and constrain collaboration?
3. What does this case highlight about the role of facilitators in helping shape collaboration?
4. What influence did Pete's interest, as someone from a part of the community that seemed marginalized in the discussions, have on the collaboration?
5. What other interest influenced latter conceptions of what the collaboration was trying to accomplish?
6. What processes from the solutions chapter are visible in this case? How were they consistent or different from what we have learned in that chapter? And how would you determine their effectiveness in this process? In other words, if you were to design the facilitation process, what would you replicate or do differently?

AUTHOR INFORMATION

Lori L. Britt (PhD) teaches organizational communication courses and directs the Institute for Constructive Advocacy and Dialogue, which serves as a resource to help organizations and communities structure productive talk. She offers courses that train students to become facilitators; community projects such as the one featured here become a training ground for students to consider how to discern an organization's needs and to structure processes to meet those needs.

Leanna Smithberger is a graduate student studying communication and advocacy. She has worked with the Institute for Constructive Advocacy and Dialogue for three years assisting in the design, implementation, and facilitation of communication processes in the community. Her research has focused primarily on dialogue, deliberation, and citizen efficacy.

Epilogue
Going Forward

We opened this text by developing the need for interorganizational collaboration amidst wicked problems. We acknowledged that changing organizational forms and changes in the values, attitudes, and skills of a new generation of workers provide the momentum needed to attend to collaboration. Collaboration is complex for a number of reasons, including the nature of the problems that stakeholders address, the composition of collaboration, and the saliency of stakeholder identities. We argued that groups should consider the ethics of their decisions, diversity, power, and principles of leadership. And we provided a language—communication oriented toward dialogue, interests, conflict, consensus, and solutions—that we posit constitutes collaborative praxis.

Although much more could be said about interorganizational collaboration, our original intent was to articulate a collaborative ethic and to suggest a language of collaborative praxis from what we have observed and learned. In chapter 1, we started out with several small vignettes about the wicked problems that many of our communities struggle with on a regular basis. We have argued throughout the pages of the book that collaboration is best suited to address these globally interconnected problems. We need leaders willing to engage in the complexity, ethic, and language of collaboration in order to solve—in a principled way—the pressing issues of our time that no one organization or sector alone can solve. Each of the authors of the case studies in part IV is that type of leader.

So what now? Going forward you will have to decide what you understand to be the moral obligation of situations you encounter. We hope the book inspires you to follow the example of the practitioners and join the effort. Armed with *phronesis* you have the ability to make the best choices regarding how you will communicate as you endeavor to diminish wicked problems.

Index

segmentIndex

349